PRAISE FOR THE BESTSELLING NOVELS OF

LAURA KINSALE...

THE DREAM HUNTER

In the deserts of the Middle East, a fearless adventurer meets his match in the daring young woman who conquers his heart...

"With this book, one's awe for Laura Kinsale only increases."

— *RENDEZVOUS*

"Romantic sparks fly in this richly detailed historical romance."

— *BOOKLIST*

"A deeply emotional, heartrending love story . . . a tormented hero and engaging heroine, dark pasts and midnight fears, eloquent prose and page-turning pacing . . . a masterpiece of romantic fiction."

— *ROMANTIC TIMES*

"Another winner from a writer who always provides a triumphant novel."

— *AFFAIRE DE COEUR*

FOR MY LADY'S HEART

A mysterious princess and a legendary knight risk their lives for the love that burns between them...

"Stunning."

— *RENDEZVOUS*

Berkley Books by Laura Kinsale

FOR MY LADY'S HEART

THE DREAM HUNTER

MY SWEET FOLLY

My Sweet Folly

Laura Kinsale

BERKLEY BOOKS, NEW YORK

MY SWEET FOLLY

A Berkley Book / published by arrangement with
Hedgehog, Inc.

PRINTING HISTORY
Berkley edition / March 1997

Book design by Casey Hampton.

The Putnam Berkley World Wide Web site address is
http://www.berkley.com/berkley

ISBN: 1-56865-276-3

BERKLEY®
Berkley Books are published by The Berkley Publishing Group,
200 Madison Avenue, New York, New York 10016.
BERKLEY and the "B" design
are trademarks belonging to Berkley Publishing Corporation.

PRINTED IN THE UNITED STATES OF AMERICA

My Sweet Folly

Prologue

Cambourne House, Calcutta
15 October, 1800

My dear Cousin Charles,

I disturb your peace at my father's behest. He wishes me to investigate the progress of a lawsuit concerning the proper location of a hedgerow. Knowing and caring nothing of this hedgerow except that it languishes, properly or improperly, in Shropshire, I beg you will do me the favor of not replying to this inquiry.

Your servant,
Lt. Robert Cambourne
1 Bttn. 10th Regt.
Bengal Infantry

P.S. However, if by chance you should happen to send me a copy of Malory's *Le Morte D'Arthur*, I should be forever in your debt, as my own has been appropriated by a mongoose. You may apply to the East India Company offices in Leadenhall Street to cover the expense.

Bridgend House,
Toot-above-the-Batch
Herefordshire
20 April, 1801

My Dear Lieutenant Cambourne,

As my husband, Mr. Charles Hamilton, suffers from a severe attack of greenfly to his roses, it falls to me to acknowledge your inquiry. He tells me that you are a third cousin of his, so I am afraid, sir, that in the name of familial duty we cannot in conscience comply with your request to ignore you. You may inform your father that the hedgerow is still in Shropshire, and shows every intention of remaining there as long as the lawyers have a breath left to make out their bills.

From your petition concerning the Malory, I deduce that you are an admirer of King Arthur and his Round Table? I delight in encouraging these notions of chivalry among the gentlemen, in hopes that someday some particularly astute knight errant will at last discover that under my paisley shawl and mobcap I am actually a royal princess in disguise. With this ambition in mind, and it being a slow day in Toot-above-the-Batch, quite flat after the elopement of the cook's piglet with the blacksmith's goose (they were missing overnight and found disporting themselves in a most disgraceful manner under the bridge, I am sorry to say, and so the piglet's reputation is in shambles), I took it upon myself to pursue the matter of your Malory. I walked to Tetham to see if I might discover a copy. I am most pleased, gallant knight, to present to you a fine edition, well-bound, as you will see. Never mind Leadenhall Street, you are to consider it a birthday present—I feel quite sure you must have a birthday. I send it with great satisfaction in the notion that it will travel from Tetham to Toot to some dark Indian jungle, perhaps transported upon elephants, or balanced on the head of a Native. I must warn you to keep your armor well-polished in such conditions, as humidity will be the worst thing for it.

Your cousin-in-law,
Folie Hamilton

Ft. William, Calcutta
17 September, 1801

My dear Cousin Folie,

What a pretty name you have! The Malory arrived (in a sepoy's pack, rather than upon an elephant, but I assure you that he was an excessively fierce and exotic-looking fellow in a turban). Thank you. I did not actually expect you to trouble yourself. My feelings are a little difficult to convey, I find. I am not a hand at letters. Thank you. I am keeping my armor brightly polished.

Your Knight,
Robert Cambourne

Ft. William, Calcutta
19 September, 1801

My dear Cousin Folie,

A Brahmin mystic and magician has informed me that your birthday is the 20th of March. I even have some unreasonable confidence that this will reach you in time. I thought it was rather pretty, like your name. The pearl is from the China Sea; it came in a pirate ship. I hope that I may have the pleasure of continuing to write to you.

Your Knight,
Robert Cambourne

Bridgend House,
Toot-above-the-Batch
Herefordshire
20 March, 1802

Dear Knight,

I think your Brahmin must be a powerful conjurer, for your present arrived precisely upon my birthday. I am twenty today, and I have never been past Tetham in my life, but now I have a pearl that has come all the way round the world to me, as your letters do. How I shall treasure them both! This morning I have put on my best blue dimity dress, pinned the bodice with your pearl stick and pranced all about the village, ruthlessly lording it over Miss Morpeth, who considers herself cosmopolitan because she has been twice to Shrewsbury. Even your cousin Melinda, who frowns upon me as only an eight-year-old can frown upon her stepmother, has admitted that I am a passable sight today, while our gardener has handsomely pronounced me "done to a cow's thumb." I must tell you, sweet knight, that Mr. Hamilton calls me a sad flirt, and says that gentlemen who send me pearl stickpins had better guard their hearts or they will find themselves helplessly caught in my toils. You are therefore requested and required to avoid falling in love with me, my dear Lieutenant Cambourne, and under those terms you may send me all the letters and pearls that you like. Indeed I do hope you will write to me again, and tell me about what you see from your window, or your tent, or wherever you may be. Tell me the color of the sky, and the feel of the air, and the sounds you hear, for I should like to know it all. Tell me what you did this morning. Did anyone make you angry? Did anything make you laugh? I so wonder what your life is like in that place, sweet knight.

Your cousin,
Folie

P.S. However weirdly exotic you may be, I'm quite sure you have nothing to match Mrs. Nettle's new hat.

Ft. William, Calcutta
25 October, 1802

Dear Folie,

My dear girl! I could never fall in love by letter. Though I have no doubt you are a notorious breaker of hearts, not to mention a princess in disguise, and if I were a few miles closer to Toot-above-the-Batch I would be in great danger. From the safe distance of another continent, I will admit to a modest desire to see how your pearl becomes you, even to know the color of your hair and eyes, but this is mere curiosity, I assure you. I have been reading the Malory since early this morning. You have guessed a disgraceful secret of mine. I believe I was born many centuries after my proper time; when I see the far mountains on our horizon, I confess to a burning desire to desert John Company, ride off to the bannered castles hidden there and live the life of a knight errant. This is a private confidence, my pretty princess, to be kept between us, if you will. Perhaps you are aware that my father is a director of the East India Company and a paymaster general of Bengal. He and my superior officers are fond of accounts. Regrettably I am not. In truth I am hard put to it to keep count of my dragon-slayings. However, you ask of India and my life here. The air smells of dust and charcoal smoke this morning, perhaps a bit spicy, the cookstalls turning out *dosas* and *samosas*. I have read your letter three times, and smiled each time. I drink tea, it is called *chai* here, with a great deal of milk and sugar. When I pause and think of what to describe to make this real to you, I realize suddenly how noisy it is. The air beyond the cantonment is full of cries and squabbles and the lowing of cattle and the shouts of the sepoys laughing. I am presently in my office, with a reasonable breeze from the windows. The view is not inspiring—I can see nothing but an empty parade ground and the compound wall, which is of mud. Apart from knightly heroics and poor arithmetic, I occupy myself with an investigation of the local religion. This is a very interesting topic to me, princess, but perhaps it will not seem so to you. I will just give you a brief account of the *guuruu* with whom I have established a friendship—he is a Hindu spiritual teacher, an ancient gentleman with a wild white beard and hair to his waist. As an adept of the discipline of *yoga,* Srí Ramanu is able to stand on one hand or twist his limbs into knots that I really feel must rival Mrs. Nettle's hat for oddness. He spends days at a time with his feet in the air and his head buried in sand, but I must admit that this seems to have given him an uncommonly amiable disposition; he is a great friend of all living things, exceedingly wise, and if you are not careful you will find yourself declared guardian of a flea which he has removed from his person but declined to dispatch out of benevolent principles. He tells me that all is Fated, and it is useless to struggle. There are times when I feel inclined to agree with him, and others when his philosophy only seems an excuse to lie down and give oneself up to die. This is a country where death is always close, so perhaps—

Forgive me, princess, I find myself rambling. I have no sense of direction at all, in letters or in life. Hand me a map and I will look it over, squint and puzzle on it, turn it upside down, and soon have myself lost beyond recall. What an exemplary knight errant!

Your servant,
Robert Cambourne

Bridgend House,
Toot above-the-Batch
Herefordshire
1 March, 1803

Sweet Knight,

I should think a tendency to lose your way would be the best possible talent for a knight errant. How else are you to find adventures and bespelled ladies like myself? I assure you that we are not planted alongside the road; you must wander about dark forests and climb unscalable cliffs which no one would ever climb if they were not lost. As a knight of the errant persuasion, surely you must be meant to put yourself in the hands of Fate, as your *guuruu* tells you, not to lie down and die but to discover where Fate will lead you.

You see, I am quite the philosopher myself, am I not? It comes of spending so many mornings at the Ladies' Church Committee, where one must develop resignation as a veritable creed. Perhaps I shall carry a bucket of sand along tomorrow and bury my head in it.

Which reminds me that I shall begin to feel guilty if I do not set you straight upon a certain point. While I am indeed a princess, gallant knight, I fear I am not precisely pretty. Mr. Hamilton once mentioned I am quite passable when I smile, so of course I married him immediately. Our engagement was a great shock to Toot, as the late Mrs. Hamilton was known to be the greatest beauty in three counties, and Mr. Hamilton naturally dotes upon her memory. His daughter Melinda bids fair to surpass her mother, so I find it convenient to smile often and avoid mirrors.

I hope this news is not a severe disappointment to you. If you wish to withdraw from the lists as my knight, you must feel perfectly free to do so. I am afraid I do like to flirt a little, a pastime which Mr. Hamilton seems to find amusing in me, when he takes time from his roses to notice. He is very good to me, very generous and obliging, but I find that it is sometimes a little difficult to converse with him after we have exhausted the black leaf spot and beetles. Mrs. Nettle says that is because he is an older gentleman, but I believe it is rather that he misses the late Mrs. Hamilton very much. Sometimes in the morning, I see the surprise in his face when he opens his eyes and discovers that I am not her. Then I feel sad for him, and wish I were a little prettier, or at least a better stepmother to Melinda.

But how melancholy I am! You will want to toss me out of my tower window for tedium. Please write me more of India and your *guuruu*. And of yourself. How old you are, do you wear spectacles, any little thing will interest me, I assure you! Please do write to me whenever you like, do not wait upon my answers; the intervals are so very long between. Somehow I think of you as a special friend. I say a little prayer for you every night, sweet Robert, in your dusty land so far away.

Folie

Camp, near Delhi
25 September, 1803

My dear Folie,

I must take strong exception to this notion that you are not pretty. It is impossible that you are not; there is such life and spirit in your letters that I know you would light up any darkness. Perhaps your face is not in the mode that is presently most admired in England, but these things are simply fleeting fashions. For instance, the Indian idea of beauty is quite far from the English, and in China a woman is not lovely unless her feet are bound up in a deformity that seems horrible to me. A woman's beauty is in her soul. As to me, no, I do not wear spectacles. I am twenty-six, six feet two inches, and weigh thirteen or fourteen stone. (We are always bickering over weights and measures in India; everyone has his own opinion as to what a stone and a quart and a bushel should be, so to be perfectly clear, as my colonel would advise me, I will render that more exactly as 190 lbs., and hope that I have multiplied and rounded correctly.) Lately I have been out of the cantonments more than usual, the army having given up on my soldiering abilities, for which I can hardly blame them after I thrice lost the way back to Delhi from Lahore with my patrol. (The wife of a Pathan robber very kindly led us into Ambala.) On account of my father, they cannot quite cashier me, but I have been assigned to the much-despised political side, which seems to consist of a lot of talk and roaming in bazaars, which suits me well enough. My father has warned me never to darken his door again. I suppose that suits me also. I believe that soon I will have collected enough knowledge of the local cults to write a book. Perhaps I shall send you the drafts. No, no, I am joking, I would not subject you to that, pretty princess. I should not write to you at all.

Well, I believe I should close now.

Your Knight,
Robert

P.S. Enclosed is a prize from my wanderings, a shawl of Kashmir. For your birthday.

Bridgend House,
Toot-above-the-Batch
Herefordshire
1 February, 1804

Sweet Robert,

What admirable taste you have, sir! The blue is heavenly, and the wool as soft as a baby's cheek—so soft that after wearing it on my shoulders all morning, I decided to spread it over my pillow. I promptly fell asleep upon it in midday and missed the Ladies' Committee meeting! Surely there is some spell upon this shawl. It has a little smoky scent of something pleasant about it—perhaps a magic perfume, for I dreamed of India with an intensity that was almost frightening. I dreamed of walking through bright alleyways of cloth, of many colors and sounds like wind chimes and bells. The wind blew silky material about me, and there were Indians and *guuruus* with strange twisted bodies daubed in white clay, not benevolent men like your Sir Ramana, but wicked somehow. I tried to find you—I knew that you were there, but you were not to be seen, and then I became afraid;

I looked among many passageways and tangled things, always sure you would be down the next. But I never found you; I woke before I could. Dreams are very silly and powerful, are they not? How I should have recognized you in any case I do not know, but in my dreaming mind it seemed utterly certain that I would. You, sir, are not very forthcoming with your description of yourself! Outrageously terse and uninformative, in fact, reporting only enough to rouse more curiosity. Yet still I could feel you there in my sleep, as one can feel rain on the air. I only had to find you to make you real.

While you are wandering in true bazaars, we of the Ladies' Committee are constructing our own modest version. We hope to sell many pincushions and have embroidered handkerchiefs in every letter of the alphabet. Afterward, there will be a charitable assembly with dancing, the proceeds to benefit the Steeple Fund. I cannot hope to match anything as lovely as your shawl, but as I was in authority over P-to-T of the alphabet, when I came to the Rs I took it upon myself to add a C to a half-dozen handkerchiefs, enclosed. Also I enclose a miniature of *myself*. This was painted several years ago, upon my engagement, but Mr. Hamilton misplaced it shortly afterward. I have just this morning discovered it in an empty tobacco jar. If my face must repose in jars, I prefer it to be in some more intriguing vessel, so I send it to you to place in a convenient spice bottle.

Your princess,
Folie

Bridgend House, Herefordshire
2 February, 1804

Oh, the postmaster is so vexing as to have actually sent my package away on the afternoon mail for once, so I cannot retrieve it. I must beg your pardon, I am ashamed of myself.

I was a little put out when I found the miniature, and wrote in such a style as I should not have. It was very childish of me to send it away in my annoyance. If you please, will you return it when next you write?

Folie, red-faced

Delhi Garrison
15 July, 1804

My dear Folly,

For that is how I think of you, you know. Not as the French spelling, Folie, although that is lovely, but for what it means in English. My Folly and my Fate. I am afraid that I cannot return your miniature. It does not seem that Cousin Charles' tobacco jar will miss it, and I cherish it very much. You look just as I imagined, pretty and happy. Such smiling eyes—I could gaze into them forever. How strange, that from your first letter I have felt such a vivid connection to you. I think it is possible to say that there has not been one day since that I have not thought of you at least once, and some in which I could seem to think of nothing else. Your dream of India haunts me; you do not know how clearly I know the place you saw in it. Perhaps we *are* bespelled, my princess, how else could I wish so strongly that you had found me in your sleep? Sweet Folly, I can't express to you what a profound change I've been experiencing since our correspondence began. Life looks better somehow. When I think about you, which is unbelievably often, I feel—well, it's rather hard to describe. It's just—*good!* Sometimes I wish I could just reach through the ether, through space and time, and pull you to me, feel you against me, look into your smiling eyes. In one sudden and blinding moment, I would crush this cage, make you *feel* my flesh and blood hands on you, my mouth against yours. I would cradle your face in my hands, place my lips very close to your ear, and breathe my thoughts and my feelings into you. And if I had the power, I would burn my image so indelibly into your mind and heart that you could never, *ever* forget me. And love, I just might be able to do it sometime, I've been working on it.

Robert

Bridgend House, Herefordshire
2 February, 1805

I have thought a long time about your letter. I have hidden it; it frightened me, and yet I could not destroy it.

I well know what I ought to do. I should not answer it. We should not write again.

Red Fort
Shajahanabad, Delhi
22 June, 1805

My dear Folly,

Please. Please do not say I must not write to you. I promise to say no more to frighten you; you have my sworn word. I shall write nothing that you may not read aloud in your parlor.

The weather has begun to be hot again. I have left the army garrison and moved here to a palace known as the Red Fort, an imposing edifice on a high rock overlooking the sacred river Jumna. The fort is quite beautiful, being a palace really, the seat of the Mughal emperor Shah Alam. It is full of open air arcades, long galleries of scalloped arches made entirely of white marble. There is a fountain shaped like an open lotus, its border inlaid with gold and silver. Thousands and thousands of red and yellow flowers in pots. (What is your favorite flower?) Persian carpets piled thick on top of one another, but no furniture, only cushions, except in my chamber there is a broken English chair, impossible to sit upon, but presented to me with such pride that I could hardly refuse it. I have my own elephant now. I like her; she has a tiny, merry eye; huge slow ears, a feminine taste for adornment, and an unpronounceable Hindustani name. If you would like to suggest one in English, I shall christen her immediately. In the meantime I just call her sweetheart. Although she can *salaam* and trumpet quite satisfactorily, her most pronounced talent is for finding her way home—it was her habit of meandering back there at any time she pleased that caused her to be such a bargain on the pachyderm market. But personally, I find it very reassuring to know I will always be home before dark.

What else can I write about? Doubtless the monsoon rains will be heavy again this season. I am so afraid that you will not reply. I never wished to frighten you, my dear.

Your Cousin,
Robert

Bridgend House, Herefordshire
17 November, 1805

Dear Robert,

Here I am, writing. Now we see what force circumspection plays in my character! None whatsoever. You are to name your homing elephant after me, of course. It would be much better if you had a ship to name after me, but we must make do as we can. I have thought and thought—how painful and knotty the world becomes, at the same time it is turned topsy-turvy and beautiful because you are in it. I wake each morning and my first thought is of you. I walk along the river Wye and see our white-faced cattle standing knee-deep and a salmon flash beneath the pool, and wish to tell you of it. I wonder at dinner if you prefer almond cheesecakes or apple tarts. How shall I say you must not write; how shall I look every day at my ink and pen and paper, feel my heart fill, and do nothing?

I do not know how. I come to no conclusion. I am perhaps a little dishonest in my life; I pretend to love my stepdaughter, I pretend to love my husband—and it is not quite that I do *not* love them, but that they really do not love me, and so I cannot seem to hit upon what will please them. Actually I do not seem to see them very often; Melinda is at her academy for young ladies, being polished to a high sheen; and Mr. Hamilton is a crusading amateur florist and hybridizer. He is creating a new rose. He spends a great deal of time in travel on account of this endeavor, and the rest of it in his hothouse. We feel that a blue ribbon is infallibly in our future, as long as I do not make the mistake again of using the wrong buds for the dinner table as I did last year. I am very much ashamed of this; it was a cruel blow to Mr. Hamilton's cutting schedule. I knew better, truly! Very stupid of me; I admit that I did not listen closely, or forgot; I hardly know. But it is a difficult thing for Mr. Hamilton to forgive, and I am still in disgrace. So I go about in the happy illusion that at least I must please *you,* sweet knight, you being at such a distance that I could hardly manage not to do so! It is a great comfort to me, you cannot know how deep and real my feelings for you run, my dear friend.

I had never imagined anything of this sort would happen to me. It is harder than I had ever fancied.

Your Folly

P.S. My favorite flower is the yellow rose. I am not fastidious as to the subspecies. Fortunately for the future safety of his buds, Charles now specializes in a pink variety of the Ayrshire rose, which is a seedling hybrid from our Rosa arvensis.

Red Fort
Shajahanabad, Delhi
12 April, 1806

My sweet Folly,

If you were mine . . .

Searching for parlor chat—the weather has become hot again. The monsoon is still months away. My work is interesting; politics and religion. I have been learning to make scale drawings of the architecture, and collecting recipes and superstitions from the *guuruus*. Certainly I shall have a book out of this eventually. I ride out every day, but my homing elephant dependably returns me to our abode by sunset.

If you were mine, sweet Folly, I should not leave you, not for a moment, not for any rose or any riches.

Robert

Bridgend House, Herefordshire
9 May, 1806

Dear Cousin Robert,

My husband, your cousin Charles Hamilton, died suddenly of a seizure on the 6th of May. He was visiting with friends in Surry; I am told that his passing was brief and painless.

Mrs. Charles Hamilton

Bridgend House, Herefordshire
17 May, 1807

Dear Robert,

I have received no letter from you for a long time; perhaps it was lost. Life is much as usual here. You will know of course that your father was named Melinda's guardian in Mr. Hamilton's will—at first I was concerned that communication to India would make this very awkward, but Mssrs. Hawkridge and James seem to have all necessary authority to act in his place. Mr. Hamilton left both myself and his daughter comfortably off, although Melinda's marriage portion is by no means as well-endowed as one could hope. She is, however, growing so beautiful that I have no doubt of her future. She returned from the young ladies' academy to live at home after her father's death, and I am pleased that we have become better friends lately.

I watched the cattle drinking in the river this morning and thought of you, sweet knight. I hope you will write again soon. If you do not, I feel that perhaps I shall do something wild and absurd, such as traveling out to Delhi to view this homing elephant for myself.

Your Folly

Red Fort
Shajahanabad, Delhi
10 October, 1807

My dear sweet Folly,

I am sorry. You received no letter because I have not written. I am married. All along, I have been married. Folie—I am sorry. You must not think of coming here.

Robert

ONE

HEREFORDSHIRE
1812

"HE IS A disgrace!" Mrs. Couch said. "A disgrace to the country, I say!"

Folie, her mind having drifted to the wind-whipped apple blossoms outside the window, thought for an instant that her caller was referring to the disreputable object at which Mrs. Couch was staring in indignation. Folie sought vainly for an appropriate reply—certainly Master George Couch was a disgrace, but to agree with his vehement mother on this point seemed a trifle hazardous. Mrs. Couch was no feeble dame.

George, uncowed by his mother's fury, turned to Folie and said confidingly, "Yes, ma'am, and his water is purple!"

"George!" Mrs. Couch gasped, turning an interesting shade of that color herself. "You must not—*Oh!*"

Folie realized that the topic was rather to do with mad old King George than His Majesty's untidy namesake regaling himself on lemon cakes in her parlor. "That is not drawing room talk, you know, George," she said, with a sidelong glance at the boy. "We shall all swoon."

"Oh, I say! I should like that!" George asserted.

"Yes, and Mama would adore it, so pray do not encourage her!" Melinda said, tossing her bright honey curls back.

"I thought Mrs. Hamilton would like to know," George said. "She's interested in that sort of—"

"George!" Mrs. Couch snapped.

Folie smiled. "You may tell me later, George, out behind the dustbins."

"Mama!" Melinda said, in much the same warning tone that Mrs. Couch had used with her son.

Folie merely replied with a superior smirk. For a full ten seconds Melinda, having matured to a beautiful and demure maiden of eighteen, managed to maintain a disapproving expression. Then her perfectly straight Grecian nose twitched, and she dropped her eyes to her lap. Several faint tremors disturbed her otherwise modest bosom.

Fortunately Mrs. Couch, their primary hope for entree into Society for Melinda's debut season, did not appear to notice this fall from grace. "It was the Prince Regent to whom I referred, George," Mrs. Couch said firmly, and then lowered her voice to a heroic whisper. "If he should go mad like his father, I know not what we shall do!"

"The first thing," Folie mused, "if they do lock him up, would be to make sure our Ladies' Committee gets supervision of the church bazaar. He owns such a number of extravagant objects, I vow we could rebuild the steeple this very year on a single estate sale."

Melinda properly ignored such disrespect toward the Prince Regent. "The papers say it is merely that he fell and sprained his ankle," she said. "He has taken to his bed to recover."

Mrs. Couch began to argue that this certainly proved the regent's mind to be weak, since any sane man of his enormous bulk must know that he could not accomplish a Highland Fling with any degree of safety. Folie watched the postman wander from door to door of the village's main street, his collar blown up against his neck and his scarf tails whipping in the spring wind. She did not expect him to cross to her door. When he did, her eyebrows lifted.

She stood up. "Now where is that Sally with more hot water for the tea? Do pardon me while I find her!"

Closing the drawing room door on Melinda's look of inquiry, she ran down the stairs in time to find the housemaid bidding the postman good day. There were two letters in Sally's hand, a thin one and a fat packet.

The cook, just coming up from the kitchen, gave Folie a dry look. "You make good speed on the stairs, ma'am, for a lady of your age."

Folie stuck out her tongue. "*Just* because I am thirty today! And refused to have a great number of cakes and a party, so that you have no opportunity to tell me that I eat too many sweets for my mature widow's digestion!"

"Perhaps there is a special birthday greeting, ma'am!" Sally said, proffering the post shyly.

"Perhaps it is! From our solicitors!" Folie gave the packet a mock grimace. "Always so attentive, dear Mssrs. Hawkridge and James."

She looked down at the address on the letter. For an instant she held the paper between her two hands, frowning at it. Then her face grew still. She slipped the letter into her pocket, grasped the banister, and ran up the stairs. She paused at the landing and whispered, "Pray, Sally—tell Mrs. Couch that I've taken a blinding headache and must lie down!"

Four years and three months it had been since she had seen that particular handwriting, that blue seal, the unmistakable *Mrs. Charles Hamilton,* the distinctive curl of the F in *My dear Folly.* She sat at her desk overlooking the red tulips and peeking green leaves in the back garden, smoothing open the paper.

My dear Folly.

She stared at her own name for a moment. For some reason, she hardly knew what, tears blurred the letters. She sniffed and blinked, looking up at the tulips. "Really, ma'am," she murmured reprovingly to herself.

It was nostalgia. It took her back so vividly. Four years

ago, she had been just out of mourning for Charles. Good kind steady Charles, gone much too early at sixty-one. For five years before that, a married woman, she had smiled whenever she'd seen this handwriting in the post; smiled and grown as breathless as if she were falling from a high cliff, and run up the stairs to this desk just as she had today.

My dear Folly,

I have left you languishing on your lilypad for a criminal length of time, princess. Can you forgive me? A dragon distracted me, just a small one, nothing to worry about, but I pursued him into an uncommonly sultry desert (you know how India is) and seem to have lost my way there. To be candid, I recall very little of it—I have no sense of direction, which is a great trial for a knight errant—but in the end I seem to discover myself in England. I think there was a magic door or a key or something of that sort involved. At any rate, I am at Solinger and you and Miss Melinda are commanded to repair here directly. On the instant. I am her guardian, you know, since my father's death. So I may command these things. And I do.

Your Knight,
Robert Cambourne

Folie shook her head. She read it again, and laughed angrily, giddily, to herself. "You must be mad!" she whispered.

An investigation of the fat packet and its contents showed that the travel plans and expenses had all been arranged by the efficient and attentive Mssrs. Hawkridge and James.

The bedroom door opened. "Whatever is it?" As Folie turned, Melinda slipped in, her pretty face clouded with worry. "What is the news?"

Folie stood up from the chair. "Your guardian wishes to see you."

"Oh." Melinda's expression relaxed. "Well, that is not

so bad! Sally and Cook said that from the look upon your face, it was something very shocking."

"It is shocking," Folie said dryly. "Considering that he has not lifted a finger on your behalf in years!"

"Lieutenant Cambourne? Well, he has been in India, has he not?" Melinda's lashes swept upward. "Surely he does not expect us to travel out there!"

"No, only as far as Buckinghamshire, I'm afraid. He is at Solinger Abbey."

"Solinger! Oh, I shall like to see that place! It must be very grand."

"As grand as all the gems in India can make it, I have no doubt. But happily for our self-respect, we need not concern ourselves with vulgar calculating designs on the Cambourne fortune. He is married."

"I shall pay him no mind, then." Melinda gave a pert grin. "Besides, as a calculating hussy, I insist upon having all the sport of hunting down my own rich bachelor—perhaps a few years younger!"

"Why, today of all days, is this household so haunted by allusions to decrepitude and old age?" Folie exclaimed. "The poor gentleman is but four years older than I. But never mind, if he is too dilapidated for your taste, you shall simper prettily at him anyway. We might move to his house in town for the season if—"

"Of course! Of *course!* Oh, Mama, you are wicked!"

"If the notion should happen to occur to him," Folie finished gravely.

"That will be no problem. You can wrap him about your little finger," Melinda said.

"I quite doubt that. He has not written since—" Folie paused. "Shortly after your papa died, God bless him. But we shall do our best to squeeze Lieutenant Cambourne for our own nefarious purposes. You are to leave for Buckinghamshire tomorrow."

"Tomorrow! As soon as that?"

Folie waved a limp hand at the packet. "Hawkridge and James," she said helplessly. "You know how they are."

Melinda made an unladylike snort. "I know for a certainty that you can wrap *them* about your finger. Why should we hurry so?''

''I see no reason to delay. Your spring wardrobe is quite ready.''

''But the packing—''

''Why, have you never stayed up all night to pack for a mad flight from your evil creditors? It is most diverting.'' She walked past Melinda, sliding a finger under her stepdaughter's chin. ''Seize your gowns and what's left of your jewels, my child, and you shall be off to skin fresh pigeons!''

''Such a shady character you are, Mama,'' Melinda said fondly.

''I know,'' Folie said from beyond the door. ''I really believe I should have been born a highwayman.''

She finished packing for her stepdaughter at 4 A.M., long after a somnolent Melinda had fallen asleep in a chair and been coaxed off to bed. Folie decided it was best simply to stay awake until seven, when the post chaise was scheduled to arrive at their door. She made herself a cup of tea in the kitchen and sat alone at the table, reading the letter again.

Her sweet knight. From half a world away, he had come to her through his letters, whimsical and intriguing, shy and flirtatious, a unicorn stranded in the solid beef of the Indian Army.

She sipped her tea and toyed with the corner of the paper. It had been a woman's dream, of course. All an impossible fancy.

She had not been able to remain angry at him. In the days after his last letter, she had hated him; hated herself for what she had allowed to happen to her. But that had faded, slowly faded, with time and an eternity of heartache. How could she blame him for deceit, for drawing her into loving him, when she had slipped and skidded so easily down that slope herself? She could hardly remember the unhappy girl she must have been, to develop such a passion for a man who was no more than ink upon paper.

It was best, the way he had done it. She did not doubt that. Folie knew herself; she had longed to write him, to maintain a connection, to remain friends. And yet at the same time she had known how impossible it must be—that she could not keep her heart out of it.

So she had not written. Only thought of him every day of the past four years, until he was a habit, a smile and a gentle stroke of the blue cashmere shawl when she rose, a little prayer for him each night.

Only a few months after his last letter, Mssrs. Hawkridge and James had informed her that the father had passed away, and Lieutenant Robert Cambourne, being next named in the will, was now her stepdaughter's guardian. But nothing had changed, no letter had come to her from him, and Folie had ceased watching for the post.

At least, she had ceased hoping. She had thought that she would watch for the rest of her life.

But now . . .

Now he asked her to come to him. Commanded it. By his letter, she thought his character must be much the same, but she was not so sure of her own. In the years after Charles' death, her heart had toughened in some places and grown softer in others. She and Melinda had become friends, and friendship had grown into a deep love.

Melinda was her priority now. Folie could remember the silent, frozen battles from her stepdaughter's childhood, but she could no longer feel them. Somewhere along the way the two women had thawed to one another—there was nothing in Folie's life more important than that Melinda should make an excellent marriage, a happy marriage. And Folie would settle somewhere close by, but not too close by, perfectly comfortable on Charles' modest pension, and there would be children to spoil and perhaps if she was fortunate some entertaining females to gossip with, and . . .

And she was commanded to meet him. To go to his home, to see his wife. A wave of despair washed over her. She did not want to meet him. She wanted him to stay forever as he had been in her memory, a perfect knight. *Her* knight, hers alone.

Her throat closed too quickly as she swallowed another sip of tea. She wrinkled her nose. With a deep unsteady breath, she folded the letter, slipped it into her apron, and stood up to wash her cup.

"Mama, this is perfectly absurd!" Melinda exclaimed, standing between her trunk and valise on the front stoop. An early morning fog obscured most of the village street. "I will not go alone!"

"Sally will do as a companion for the journey. The letters say you will be there before dark," Folie said, bending down to check the leather buckle on the valise. "I really do not feel well enough to travel, and once you've arrived, Mrs. Cambourne will be a proper chaperon."

"If you don't feel well, then all the more reason I should remain here with you!" Melinda turned to Sally, pulling back the stylish gray hood of her cloak. "You must go for Dr. Martin directly."

"No, no!" Folie said. "It's not as bad as that. Just a touch of the headache."

Melinda looked at her suspiciously. "Certainly your eyes are quite puffy and dull," she said. "You look as if you've been weeping all night."

"Thank you so much," Folie said. "I feel as if I have been packing all night!"

"Well, *I* did not insist upon it! This is entirely silly. It's no wonder you feel unwell, staying up till all hours. I simply do not see why there is this great rush—"

"There, that will be the postchaise," Folie said, straightening up at the sound of hooves and a creaking jingle that carried through the fog.

Down the street, a handsome carriage materialized, the horses moving at a slow walk while the postboy, mounted on the leader, peered about at the houses. There were even two footmen up behind, a most luxurious touch. Folie lifted her hand and called out to them.

"I am not going," Melinda announced. "I will not go without you, Mama."

The vehicle came to a halt before Bridgend House. Next

door, a parlor window opened and the two Misses Nunney leaned out like a pair of capped and gray-headed puppets.

"Of course you are going," Folie said under her breath. She motioned to the baggage as the two footmen leaped down. "This is all."

One of them came up the steps and bowed to her. "Mrs. Hamilton?"

"Yes," Folie said, looking up at the burly young man. In spite of his polished bow, there was an air of toughness about him, as if he could turn his hand to dock work as well as a lady's luggage. "Come, Sally, where is the small basket, the one I packed for inside the cab?"

"Here, ma'am." The maid picked up the basket.

"Put it in, then." Folie turned to the footman, who had made no move to begin loading. She waved her hand toward the trunk. "No doubt that one should be put up first," she said helpfully.

"I beg your pardon, ma'am," he said, "I'm to inquire if one of these cases is yours?"

"No, I am afraid not. I am not well enough to travel."

"Mama!"

Folie gave her stepdaughter a pointed glare. "Do not make a scene, Melinda. Half the village is watching. Sally, *do* put that basket in the chaise!"

"Beg pardon, ma'am." The footman produced a letter from his pocket. Folie tried to hide the little twist of her heart as she saw the familiar lettering. She slipped the note into her apron pocket.

The footman made another bow. "Mr. Cambourne sent instructions that you must read directly his letter that I put into your hands."

"Indeed!" Folie stood straight. "I do not believe I am under any obligation to him to do so."

"Yes, ma'am," the footman said. "Then I am not to do any loading, by Mr. Cambourne's instructions."

"I beg your pardon?" Folie exclaimed.

"Whatever has got into you, Mama?" Melinda hissed, waving cheerfully at the Misses Nunney. "Only read the gentleman's note. Perhaps it is a change of plan!"

Folie stepped back into the house, pulled the door closed and tore open the seal on his folded letter, scowling.

My dear,

You are digging in your heels, I see, if you are reading this. My sweet Folly, I know this is difficult for you. You need not forgive me, or even speak to me if you like, but muster your courage. You are no coward, of that I am certain. But if you do not come now, I shall not waste time about retrieving you in person.

Robert

She closed her eyes and leaned against the wall with a small sound of misery. ''Oh, do not make me come. Do not make me come.''

All the shame of that moment when she had read his last letter washed over her again, the shattering realization of her foolishness, her loneliness, of her secret treason. She had never had a right to love him, never a claim to any truth from him, and yet the humiliation had burned as deep as if he had courted her like a rightful suitor. She had done it to herself, had never asked or wished to ask if he were free; had forgotten that she was not; had fallen insensibly, irrationally in love with an unthinkable dream.

She looked down at his note again. ''Don't make me,'' she whispered. ''Oh, Robert, don't.''

But she knew as she spoke that she would go. He had chosen the words that compelled her. If she did not face him now, her own contempt would haunt her all her life.

When Folie woke from a weary, bumpy drowse against a folded cloak, their post chaise was rolling along beside a red brick wall that seemed to go on endlessly in the twilight. Before her, the rumps of the horses jogged rhythmically as the team splashed through puddles. A rain shower had mercifully avoided them, though Folie could still see it moving off across the far hills, blue-gray vapor cut by the golden rays of the late sun.

Melinda, her cheeks flushed pink from the wind, glanced at Folie over the maid who sat between them. "Almost there!" she said cheerfully. "The boy says this wall belongs to Solinger Abbey. It goes all the way about the estate."

The postboy, mounted upon the bay wheeler, rose in time to the horse's trot. Bare trees hung out over the brick, scraping over the carriage roof, scattering droplets against the glass. Though neat hedgerows and pasture bordered the lane on the open side, there appeared to be an extensive forest inside the wall. Black staghorn branches, leafless and dark with rain, seemed to reach blindly for the rainbow-hued clouds drifting past above.

"Most forbidding," Folie murmured. "I like it."

"Perhaps you will write a novel," Melinda said, and lowered her voice portentously. " 'The ancient dreadful oaks beckoned her to her doom . . .' "

"Of course," Folie said. "They always do." The chaise was slowing, approaching a perfectly mundane gatehouse of neat brick. A porter grinned, already stepping outside as the postboy hailed him.

"The Misses Hamilton arrive!" the postboy called.

The porter waved in friendly acknowledgment and unlocked the wrought-iron gate. The team swung around, sidestepping into the opening, blowing a little from their work. The chaise wheeled in place, then jerked forward and swept through as the horses resumed their trot.

Both Folie and Melinda leaned forward, looking for the house. There was nothing to be seen but the aged trees, a tangle of uncut brush swarming beneath their low branches. Ruts in the drive had been newly patched with gravel, so the ride was tolerably smooth, dipping and curving through the forest.

The house burst into view with a suddenness that made them all gasp like light-headed debutantes. Red brick glowed in the sunset, a Tudor fantasy of towers and twisting chimneys, the round turrets crowned by oriental domes and delicate spires of lead. It seemed to grow as they neared, revealing wings and windows, gabled fronts carved with the heraldic outlines of medieval creatures. The chaise bumped across a low bridge and moat.

"Oh, Mama, you *must* write a novel now," Melinda said, laughing.

"Very tempting, I admit!" Folie hid her tight fists beneath the cloak folded on her lap. It was just what he would like, this house. This whole estate, a quaint romance. One expected a knight to come thundering down one of the wooded rides at any moment, his banner flying and his armor glinting in the last misted rays of sun.

It would not be out of character, she thought wryly, for Robert Cambourne to arrange just such a fanciful greeting. It would not be beyond him to assume the guise of a medieval warrior himself; he would delight in it, adding some unexpected touch to make a joke of it all.

But their chaise was met by no such mythical figure. A bewigged footman opened the door as the vehicle rolled to a halt. Folie and Melinda crept out, surreptitiously stretching arms and legs and backs abused by a long day of travel. Sally scrambled to collect the scarves and combs they had managed to scatter about the vehicle.

Folie looked up at the leaded glass windows. A thousand diamond lights winked back at her from pointed lancet arches, reflections of the red sun. The air smelled of boxwood hedges and rain.

"Madam," the butler said, waiting beside the low steps. He was dressed in a suit of black velvet and white stockings, a square-jawed young man with his long sandy hair in a queue, barely old enough to have charge of such a large house, Folie thought.

They followed him under the heavy vault of the doorway. Just inside the entry, it was too dim to see much beyond some dark paneling. Folie's heart was in her throat. At any moment they would meet him, or even worse his wife, and no matter how she tried to compose herself, the anxiety had her in its sick clutches.

"Mrs. Hamilton." A masculine voice startled her so that she spun about. He stood in a side doorway into the buttery, a tall man who kept his eyes down deferentially. For an instant she had thought it would be Robert, but she saw that this must be the actual butler—he kept his hands behind his back and made no move of welcome or greeting, only a small deferential bow.

Besides, he did not look at all like Robert. She had never known what he would look like, but certainly not this. In the dim light this man's hair was black, his expression utterly forbidding—he never looked at her but seemed to be watching for something, his attention moving restlessly to the doors and corridor.

''Lander will take you up,'' he said. ''Dinner at eight.''

''Eight,'' Folie repeated, rather cross at this cursory hospitality. ''May we make our salutations to Mr. and Mrs. Cambourne before that?''

He turned his head a fraction to the side as he glanced toward her, as if she were a light that was too bright. ''I beg your pardon. I am Robert Cambourne.'' Then, for just an instant, he gave her a clear gray-eyed look, a gaze outlined in black lashes. It was like being caught in the direct stare of a wolf.

Folie gazed back at him. If he knew her, if he even recognized her name, there was no hint in his perfect features. Like some Renaissance prince, he was sinister and flawless, but his face held nothing of civilized humanity. High cheekbones, straight nose, skin sunburnt to darkness; a bleak mouth and black brows. And his eyes—light and violent, like a caged beast's.

His glance lowered again, finding nowhere to rest. ''Mrs. Hamilton.'' He made his faint, stiff bow. ''Miss Hamilton. Welcome to Solinger Abbey.''

Folie stood rooted to the floor. *You are not!* she wanted to exclaim. *You are not Robert. That cannot be true!*

Melinda put her hand on Folie's arm. ''We are honored to meet you, sir,'' she said, making a sketch of a curtsy. Her fingers squeezed. ''Let us go up, Mama.''

Propelled by her stepdaughter's hand, Folie turned blindly and followed the servant down the corridor and up the stone stairs. She did not see anything that she passed. Her whole body felt numb.

She found herself in a pleasant yellow bedroom, but she could not seem to make herself move beyond the middle of it. Melinda came up behind her.

"Do try not to look so horrified, Mama!" she said gently. "I'm sure you must have hurt his feelings."

Folie looked at her. "I don't believe that is him."

Melinda's mouth curved unhappily. "I'm so sorry if you're disappointed. But perhaps when you get to know him a little better—"

"I do know him!" Folie turned away and sat down on the bed. She shook her head, laughing without humor. "I thought I did. I would have thought—" She made a little shrug. "He might have been more—pleased to see us."

"Perhaps he is a little shy."

"I never thought he would look like that! He is so . . ." She shook her head.

"Devilish?" Melinda suggested wryly.

"Decidedly satanic!" Folie exclaimed. She spoke in jest, but a shiver seized her.

"I thought him quite handsome. Rather beautiful, really. For a gentleman."

Folie shook her head again. "He cannot be Robert Cambourne," she exclaimed. "My God, his eyes. I believe he is mad!"

"Mama, you are working yourself into a state. This is not like you." Melinda gave her a hopeful look. "But perhaps you are just rehearsing for your novel?"

Folie realized that she was well on the way to frightening her stepdaughter. With an effort, she summoned some steadiness. "Oh, there—you've found me out!" she said with forced cheerfulness. "Where have they put you, next door?"

"Round the corner," Melinda said. "The bedrooms are quite lovely, and every one we passed is different. Mine is all in red and yellow chinoiserie. I think they've just been fitted out not long ago."

"Oh, that *is* a bad portent," Folie said balefully. "Prepared for our arrival! We had best make a thorough inventory of the secret doors."

Two

ROBERT STOOD IN the small room off the passage. It was empty and dark, the haunt of long-vanished butlers—one place without the torrid furnishings and carvings that consumed the rest of the house.

He put his palm against the stone. It felt cold and blessedly smooth. He did not think he could bear one more phoenix or griffin or Chinese dragon, to see or to touch them. They worked their way into his demented dreams, and sometimes out of the corner of his eye he thought he caught them moving, but when he looked, they were only perfect decoration on perfect tracery, beautifully executed, carved by a master in wood. Feverish stuff: wyverns with necks that coiled like snakes; bodiless wings and claws; strange smiling faces and arabesques growing like rank foliage on every mantle and alcove and ceiling and staircase.

Amid that madness, she had come. He felt a spinning relief, to be certain that she was real after all.

He touched the miniature in his inner pocket. The painter had not caught the truth of her; she was less handsome and far more alive in reality. A face of glowing simplicity—not pretty, no, nothing like her extraordinary stepdaughter; in fact when she had turned and frowned at him, she was endearingly plain, with ordinary brown hair and features he had already forgotten, except for such expressive eyes that looked at him and right through him.

She terrified him. It had seemed imperative that he bring her here, safe within his protection, and yet he was afraid she could see through him. He was afraid he could not protect her. He was afraid there was no danger at all, and yet he walked through each day in a state of spring-wired tension, primed to defend himself, as if hands might rise out of the floors or the walls and pull him down and strangle him.

He must discipline himself to go outside again, because the sun would not kill him, the open space would not annihilate him.

It would not. It would not.

He closed his eyes and leaned his fists and his face against the cold stone wall.

In her shock, Folie had noticed little of the interior of Solinger Abbey on her way up the stairs, but on the way down she could hardly disregard it. Though the house itself was old, it appeared to have been entirely refitted, with no regard to cost.

The decoration was extraordinary. Everywhere were outlandish carvings painted in a delicate white. Some scaly beast even wound about the banister, so finely rendered that every shadow revealed an exquisite detail. No hands had marred the carving or worn off the paint—it was as immaculate as if it had been created only yesterday.

"This is gorgeous," Melinda said, and dropped her voice to a whisper. "It must have cost a fortune!"

"Lord only knows how they dust it!" Folie said, daring to reach up and touch a delicate wooden bell that hung from a carved falcon's jesses. The hunting bird had been caught in its moment of bounding upward from its perch; its curved beak was slightly open, as if it panted for the sky.

"A nabob," Melinda said wisely. "He can afford someone to go about blowing on them all day."

Folie made a face at the dusty black mark on her glove.

"Well, they had better put their lungs to work. This is positively squalid."

Melinda poked her fan at Folie's waist and whispered, "Do be civil to him, Mama! Only think what a debut I might have!"

"Of course," Folie said with a hurt look. "I should be civil to the devil himself for your debut. What sort of mother do you think I am?"

"And please don't use warm language."

"Let us hope he is easier to please than you!"

Melinda merely answered with her saucy grin. Folie thought it an expression that would win more male hearts than any number of lavish debut parties, but there would be no telling that to an eighteen-year-old. And there was still the problem of bringing her into the proximity of suitable male hearts, so all in all, Folie was determined to gird her loins and charm the satanic Lieutenant Cambourne down off his mound of bloody skulls.

He awaited them in the drawing room, dressed with old-fashioned formality: knee breeches and an unadorned tail coat of black silk. That appeared to exhaust his fund of conventional behavior. He barely looked at them, except for a swift, potent glance when Folie opened the door. There was something faintly startled in it, as if he had forgotten they were coming. Without delaying for small talk or an announcement from a servant, he merely made a taut bow and indicated the dining room doors.

Folie and Melinda exchanged a fleeting glance. Folie could read her stepdaughter's thoughts. An odd volume, this Lieutenant Cambourne. She started to precede them into the dining room, supposing Mrs. Cambourne must be awaiting her guests there, but to Folie's surprise, he suddenly walked forward and offered her his arm.

Folie felt that she must jump out of her skin, but she managed to place her fingers lightly on his sleeve. The dining room was empty as they entered. "Mrs. Cambourne is not to join us?" she asked breathlessly.

It was something of a relief to hear her own voice. She had not been certain she could force it out of herself.

''Mrs. Cambourne died over a year ago,'' he said to the air in front of him.

All Folie could hear was her own heart and the swish of her skirt against his leg. She walked with him in a blank daze. She had heard nothing of his wife's death. It seemed impossible, as impossible as the fact that she walked with her hand touching his arm.

''I'm sorry,'' she said, and had no idea if it had emerged as a whisper or as a steady sentence.

He lifted his eyebrow as he looked down at her, rather as if he were inspecting something that did not quite impress him. His height accentuated the air of aloof inquiry; he was quite tall, elegantly proportioned.

He gave a brief nod, saying nothing. His black hair, a little sun-burnished, a little too long, curled over his neckcloth in a disorderly way. He brushed it back from his ear with open fingers.

''Our rooms are wonderfully comfortable,'' she said, vexed to feel her heartbeat tremble in her voice.

''I'm pleased to hear it,'' he said, without a trace of pleasure. ''My father had the place fitted out sight unseen by correspondence from Calcutta. No one has lived here since.''

''I see!'' Folie murmured, trying to appear perfectly nonchalant about the four huge white dragons that adorned the corners of the dining room ceiling, their barbed tails hanging down to coil about the wainscoting.

Melinda followed them into the dining room. She gave a faint gasp. ''It is—marvelous! I've never seen anything quite like.''

''They tell me the carpenter was mad,'' Lieutenant Cambourne said dryly, holding Folie's chair at the middle of the long table. ''I'm quite certain he went mad in the process, at any rate.''

''But you have something so unique here—'' Melinda took the chair across from Folie, seated by the same young butler who had greeted them. ''It must surely captivate all your party guests.''

He left that hopeful gambit untouched, turning to nod at Lander, who began to pour wine.

"Yes," Melinda said gaily, looking up at the looming dragons. "We should give them all names, and make the guests conjecture."

Lieutenant Cambourne did not veto this notion, although he did not approve it either. He looked briefly at Folie and then down at his wine glass. It was his skin, darkened in a lifetime of tropical sun, that made his eyes seem so light and strange, she thought. And his black lashes, as extravagantly long and thick as a woman's, under black eyebrows that were straight and severe and entirely masculine.

"I'll take that one," Melinda said, lifting her hand toward one corner of the room. "I shall christen him . . . mmmmm . . . Xerxes! That sounds grand. Now you, Mama."

As the butler spooned clear soup into her bowl, Folie tilted her head to address the eagle-eyed dragon to her right. "Boswell?" she inquired politely.

Melinda laughed. "Of course!" She looked toward their host. "Now you must name one, Lieutenant."

For a moment he seemed as if he did not understand her. Then he said, "I'm no longer an officer, Miss Hamilton. I left the army several years ago."

"Oh, we are to call you Mr. Cambourne, then?"

Once again he did not answer. Folie had never seen a man who appeared bewildered by a query on his own name. He frowned at the clear soup as Lander served Melinda—such a deep frown, so lost in himself, that Folie suddenly spoke to reach him.

"Robert?" she said softly. And then instantly her heart began to beat in her ears, drumming a retreat from such impertinent forwardness, such a betrayal of . . . of the person he did not seem to be.

He gave a brief nod, watching Lander move to serve him from the soup tureen. "That will do. Call me Robert."

Melinda glanced at Folie, looking a little nonplused. It was an informality, not quite proper, but Folie gave a slight shrug of permission. They were cousins, and he was Melinda's guardian, after all. Though Folie wasn't certain he was even paying attention to them; he was still concentrated on Lander and the soup.

Melinda said brightly, "That is very kind of you, sir, if you don't feel it's too bold." She put on what Folie recognized as her best party smile. "Well, now we have named two of these beasts and my guardian. What will you call your dragon, sir?"

He seemed to draw his gaze away from his cover with a visible effort. He looked at Melinda. "I'm not—fond of the dragons," he said. He paused, and then a savage life came into his voice. "Frankly, I loathe them," he said, his mouth curving.

Melinda's sunny expression turned to mortification. "I'm sorry, I didn't perceive—I beg your pardon!" she said in a small voice.

Her stepdaughter looked so crushed that Folie was hard put to contain a tart remark on his manners. But she merely gave Melinda an encouraging smile, took a sip of soup, and asked, "When did you arrive in England, sir?"

He looked at her quickly, still with that hostile set to his mouth. As his eyes focused on her, light and fierce, she had the sensation that she had decoyed a wild animal away from its intended prey.

"A month ago," he said. "Or two. I'm not certain."

"Not long, then," she said politely. "Did you come direct from the east?"

"The east?" He was looking at her so intensely that he did not seem to grasp the question.

"From India."

"Yes," he said, and scowled. "Why?"

Folie lost her patience. "I am merely attempting to make a little conversation, sir. If you prefer I shall cease and desist, and Miss Hamilton likewise, and you may eat your meal in silence."

Melinda's blue eyes grew large at this rebellion against the guardian and host whose goodwill could prove so vital a support to them. But if Robert Cambourne had any emotion or reaction, he reserved it to himself. "I came from

India, yes,'' he said, his tone easing a slight degree.

Folie took this to mean that he was not entirely averse to discourse. Perhaps he was merely eccentric. He seemed so removed from the charming knight of her letters that she could only think of him as another person entirely.

''Do you plan to remain here, or return?'' she asked.

''Remain here,'' he said immediately.

Encouraged by that ready answer, she said, ''Have you collected enough material for your book on the Indian mysticism?''

He tilted his head. After a slow sip of his wine, he said, ''I had forgotten that I'd told you of that.''

Folie looked quickly down, mortified to have brought up a reminder of their correspondence. Of course he had forgotten; no doubt he had forgot the whole of what he had written. She vehemently hoped it was so.

She studied him under her lashes as she toyed with her soup. He had never truly described himself to her, and yet as she looked at him now, she knew that she had held a picture of him in her mind and heart; a bright image of a man who laughed easily, perhaps light-haired, with gentle brown eyes. He loved legends and tales of magic and adventure; puns and wit; dragons and firebirds were alive for him. Between the lines, she had read that he was not very happy to be a soldier, that he felt misplaced, that his powerful father thought him hopelessly frivolous and a severe disappointment to the family.

None of those things seemed to fit the man before her; none even seemed possible. In true life his strongly angular cheekbones and gray eyes gave him a baleful look, and if his mouth ever managed a smile, it would be the grin of a predator. She could not imagine him laughing. He was too haughtily tall to be her Robert; he was dark where he should be fair; he was taut and broad-shouldered where her Robert should be easy, perhaps even a little slouched from so much reading. Folie was woman enough to have hoped he would be handsome, but in a . . . a more friendly way. Not this brutal sort of male purity, for Melinda was right—he was in his own bizarre manner as gorgeous as some maddened night prowler in the Indian jungles.

She could not see him as her own dear Robert. It was simply impossible. There was no connection at all.

With a sense of relief, she ceased to try. He was a stranger, Melinda's guardian, an eccentric gentleman she had never met or known before. The thought brought a lift of her spirits; she could bear with him that way. She had a goal, Melinda's debut, and he could add a great deal to the success of it if he would.

She took a sip of soup. "If you are to be established here now, Mr. Cambourne, we hope that you will honor us with a visit during Miss Hamilton's coming out," she said, firing her first serious shot in the campaign. "We plan to go up to London by the first of April—though I have had some difficulty in locating a suitable town house."

He shook his head. "You must stay here."

"Here?" Melinda echoed faintly.

"Oh, you will be thinking of expenses," Folie said, "but I have put by quite a nest egg just for this purpose." That was true, although after paying for Melinda's wardrobe, the egg was hardly large enough to let a shabby house in Kensington.

"Expense is not a consideration," he said flatly. "I desire you to remain here."

"But—" Melinda began.

"Pray do not be pert, Melinda," Folie said sternly.

Melinda gave her a look, a wry combination of surprise and distress. She was not accustomed to being pulled up short; in fact more usually it was she who chided Folie's transgressions against propriety. But she bent her head in obedient silence, soft light blonde curls falling over her shoulders, the picture of a chastened girl.

Folie made no comment on this convenient transformation, though she could think of several. But they were in league now, with the same aim in view.

"Certainly we will be delighted to visit here for as long as you wish," Folie said to him, "but you will agree that Miss Hamilton must be in London well in time to be launched properly. I have already seen to her introduction at Court; she is invited to attend the Drawing Room on the twelfth of April.''

''That is out of the question,'' he said, looking down at the table before him as Lander removed his untouched soup.

''I beg your pardon, Mr. Cambourne, but it is—''

''You are to call me Robert,'' he said abruptly.

Folie took a silent breath. ''Perhaps you are not aware, Robert,'' she said evenly, ''that your ward will turn nineteen in June. It is perfectly appropriate for her to be introduced into London society this spring. Indeed, it is quite vital.''

He looked at Folie with a cool lift of his black eyebrows. ''Why?''

Melinda made a faint sound, but then pressed her lips together tightly, looking to Folie with anxious eyes.

''She must have a wider circle of acquaintance, of course,'' Folie said.

''Oh, fancy!'' he said sarcastically. ''Is she not happy with the available gossip now?''

The mocking sting in his voice startled Folie. She simply looked back at him blankly.

After an instant's stare at one another, he dropped his eyes and said in a distracted tone, ''I did not mean that as it sounded.''

Folie said carefully, ''An abundance of gossip is not our desire. London society is.''

''But why?'' he asked in a more reasonable manner, lifting his hand to beckon Lander.

''It appears that I must be unpardonably blunt,'' Folie said. ''We are on a hunt for eligible bachelors.''

He paused in mid-gesture. His fingers curled. His eyebrow lifted again, a cool disapproval. ''Indeed!''

''I'm sorry to have to mention it so forwardly, but yes—'indeed!' ''

He sat still and straight. ''You wish to marry again?'' he asked frostily.

Folie opened her mouth to retort, and closed it. She thought she heard Melinda make another faint noise, but when Folie looked at her, her head was bent demurely over her plate.

"I'm sure that my intentions are none of your affair, sir," Folie said stiffly. "It was my stepdaughter's prospects to which I referred!"

He transferred his wintry gaze to Melinda. "I see."

"Then you will understand why a season in the city is required at this time."

"I'm afraid that I do not."

"Perhaps things are done differently in India—I have no doubt they are, but here a girl's coming out and her first London season are essential, in particular for a girl like Miss Hamilton, whose—presence and breeding—recommend her more than her fortune. I need not scruple to mention this to you, as you are her guardian."

"I am aware of Miss Hamilton's circumstances," he said slowly. "But if it is money that makes London a necessity, then I can see no difficulty. I shall settle forty thousand on her myself. Will that suffice?"

Melinda's head lifted, her blue eyes growing wide.

"Forty!" Both of them stared at him in astonishment. "I beg your pardon!" Folie murmured.

"I think it will," he said, calmly answering himself. "Things may be done differently here than in India, but not that differently."

Melinda watched in a bewildered silence as Lander placed a dish of vegetables beside her. She did not even move to serve herself. The high color in her cheeks made her extremely lovely, the candlelight gleaming on her yellow hair and bright skin. Folie saw their host observe her stepdaughter for a long moment, his attention fixed upon her as if he could not tear it away.

A novel thought dawned upon Folie. Surely he could not, would not . . . would he want Melinda for himself? Her dower was modest, her connections the same as his.

Why—but that she was beautiful; and young and gay and everything he was not?

He turned, catching Folie staring at him. "I wish for you and Miss Hamilton to reside here. Permanently."

By now he could hardly surprise her any more. She tilted her head. "I beg your pardon, sir. Are you quite serious?"

"Yes," he said.

"This is certainly sudden."

He merely made a faint shrug. "I believe it is for the best."

"And are we to have any preference in the matter?"

"You would not like it?"

"I have not had time to consider it."

"You said that your rooms are pleasant." He gave her plate a glance. "I'll change the chef if you like. You've hardly touched your food."

Folie belatedly took a bite of the trout that had been set before her. "I beg your pardon. I have been—so disconcerted."

He did not answer that. For a few minutes, they all ate in silence. Folie noticed that he took very little food himself. Melinda kept her face properly turned down to her plate, but Folie could see the hot pink emotion still burning in her stepdaughter's cheeks, the fierce arguments stopped on Melinda's tongue.

"Are you not apprehensive to live alone?" he asked at length, while the fish was removed. "Two young ladies?"

"I daresay you mean it very kindly," Folie said, a little mollified by being considered a young lady along with Melinda. "Perhaps things are done differently in India, but here it is quite acceptable."

One corner of his mouth tilted up in a wry grimace. "It's perfectly true that things are done differently in India. They burn their widows, for one thing."

"How unprincipled of them!" she said lightly.

"It is in regrettable taste." He smiled slightly at her, which gave a strange new lightness to his arctic eyes. "My dear Folly. How fortunate that things are done differently here."

Three

"I WILL NOT endure it!" Melinda exclaimed, flinging her shawl across the bed in Folie's room. Her stepdaughter had said nothing all the way out of the dining room and up the stairs, past the dragons and wyverns and carved beasties of all descriptions. It was no surprise when Melinda pursued Folie into her bedchamber.

"I will *not* be cheated of my season, not after we have scrimped and saved and—"

"Not even for forty thousand pounds?" Folie interjected, lighting another candle. It cast a pretty glow on the creamy gathers and folds of the bed canopy.

"What good will forty thousand pounds do me, if I must live upon it as a spinster all my life?" Melinda sat down hard upon the dressing table bench, bouncing the stray curl that she had pulled artfully down on her cheek. "Besides, I don't believe a word of *that!* You are perfectly right, Mama, the man is mad!"

Folie smiled. "He does seem . . . eccentric."

"*How* am I to meet any eligible gentlemen if I am stuck away here?" Melinda wailed.

"Well, he cannot keep us prisoners, darling. And he could certainly help us—help you—if only he can be brought to see that his ideas are not quite right."

"I wish you all the luck in the world at that. He appears to be tenacious! And I shall be nineteen, Mama. *Nineteen!* This is my only chance; I'll be twenty next year!"

"Come!" Folie smiled. "Perhaps other girls find themselves on the shelf at twenty, but your looks are not likely to wither so soon. If you do not meet a suitable gentleman this season, then the next is soon enough, you may believe me." At a scratch on the door, she opened it halfway. Their maid stood waiting in the dark passage, squeezing a candle nervously. "Go to bed, Sally," Folie said. "You must be very tired! We shall take care of ourselves."

"Thank you, ma'am," Sally whispered with a curtsy. "I aired your bedclothes; the sheets are quite dry."

"Excellent. Are you frightened to sleep alone?"

"No, ma'am, they gave me a bed with a housemaid, just up the attic." Sally's mobcap dipped, a pale shape in the dimness as she looked back and forth. "But I don't like walkin' about with these awful creatures, ma'am, that I will say!"

"You'll soon grow accustomed," Folie said. "They are only carved wood, and quite exquisite, really. Go on now."

"Yes, ma'am. Thank you, ma'am!" Sally curtsied again and vanished in the shadows of the hallway.

Folie closed the door and turned, leaning back against it, looking at Melinda. "And I will just give you a hint, my dearest, that an overabundance of anxiety on the matter of a husband is likelier to drive the gentlemen off than anything. They can scent that sort of desperation from a mile away."

A faint familiar pout appeared on Melinda's lip, an echo of the mulish thirteen-year-old. For an instant, Folie felt her old helplessness, the dismay of being a parent when she had never really had a parent herself, of feeling as young and sensitive and inexperienced as the girl in her charge. At any moment, Melinda might fling at her the old bitter incrimination, "You're not my *mother!*"

"Of course," she said to Melinda, "a mile is not such a very great circumference. We've only to dig a rather large moat about you, cover it over with branches, and let the bachelors view you from a safe distance. Then as they come charging in your direction, they will drop through, become hopelessly trapped, and you may take your pick at leisure.''

She could see the threatening lower lip quiver. Melinda looked down at her hands in her lap.

''They may be a bit muddy, of course,'' Folie said blandly, ''and naturally they will create a great deal of unpleasant racket with their shrieks, but once we have them securely tied, then Sally can turn the laundry tub over them, and you shall have an excellent opportunity to examine your prospects.''

Melinda refused to go so far as a giggle, but she wrinkled her nose, making a face. ''Mama, you are quite silly.''

''Lack of sleep,'' Folie said, pulling pins from her hair. ''It has stupefied my brain.''

''I suppose that is a hint.''

''Well, if you will sit here at the age of eighteen and bemoan your years of spinsterhood, my dear, you must expect people to nod off.''

''Thank you very much!'' Melinda stood up. ''I shall go and cry myself to sleep in my lonely bed!''

''Don't forget to rub ashes in your hair,'' Folie said pleasantly.

''I vow I shall sleep on sharp nails. *Then* you will be sorry!'' Melinda stopped, her hand on the doorknob. She opened it part way and peeked through into the passage. ''It is certainly dark.'' After a moment's hesitation, she murmured, ''Mama . . .''

Folie picked up her candle. ''I'll walk you back to your room.''

In her own way, Folie thought, she was as green and fussy as Melinda. She closed the door on her stepdaughter's room and stood holding her light, gazing unhappily at a Chinese vase in a wall nook. Her light cast overwrought shadows on the peculiar tracery, making leaves and feathers tremble as if they were alive.

It was her own inner vision that had created the Robert Cambourne she had expected, was it not? The Robert that her heart insisted upon. From paper and daydreams she had conjured him—a girl's invention, really—the perfect gentleman, witty and loving and handsome, someone she could depend upon, someone who cherished her, who thought just as she did and offered just what she needed. A fantasy man.

It was hard to admit that. It was hardest of all to discover that he did not exist, that he had never existed. Easier almost to believe that this Robert Cambourne was an impostor.

Never real, her own sweet Robert. Never real at all.

A lump of something tender and bruised seemed to swell in her throat. He had been real to her. She felt as if he had died; the ache of grief was the same, the anxiety to change it, to wake up and find that it was not true.

She stood in the passage, unafraid of the shadows and grotesque carvings. They seemed insignificant to her, interesting but artificial. She was caught in a different twilight, an uncomfortable place in her mind where truths did not quite conform.

His letters were real; she could walk now to her room and touch the beribboned bundle. *He* was real; he had sat at the dinner table, certainly no dream or illusion. But the man at the table and the man who had written—they were not the same. How could they possibly be the same? Or was it simply that she could not overcome her own illusions? Expecting another face, an honest smile; admitting to herself now that hope and excitement had driven her here as much as any resignation to the inevitable.

She was not even quite convinced that Mrs. Cambourne was dead. Folie had heard nothing of it from the lawyers, seen nothing in the papers, though she had never failed to read the news of births and deaths and marriages in India. Perhaps he had left her there. Perhaps she was spending the season in town. He had lied to Folie before.

Not lied. No. Not precisely lied.

Robert, her Robert—he was not here. That was all she knew for certain.

Somewhere far off in the house, she could hear a man's voice. It began as a murmur, like an angry muttered undertone. Folie stood still. As she listened, it rose in volume, but she could not make out any words.

Their host, certainly. Scolding a servant, perhaps. The sound ceased suddenly.

Well, if he had poor service, it was hardly any surprise, considering the youth and lack of polish in his staff. Certainly the house showed no sign of a woman's touch. In spite of the recent redecoration, a close inspection showed any number of rather slovenly practices. Folie had noticed fly specks on her dressing table mirror, and the whole place needed a good airing.

She had no experience in managing a house of this size, but she was quite sure she could make some significant improvements within a day or two. She wondered if he had any care for his surroundings. Gentlemen were liable to be rather odd about housekeeping. Charles had seemed to care nothing for neatness and order save in his greenhouse—for a long time, Folie had thought that he paid no mind to any household matter, but when they had changed maids and he had found an unmended sheet on his bed, he'd not been tardy about taking Folie to task on the matter. Then suddenly he had begun to notice and comment acidly upon every detail for a month, after which his interest had subsided with the same precipitous transience.

She wondered what Mrs. Cambourne had been like. Beautiful, no doubt. An excellent hostess, sweet and good: Folie knew all about these late wives. Perhaps that was what had changed her Robert into this saturnine madman, grief for his lost love.

Who *were* these exemplary women; how did they manage to be lovely and competent and kind and true? Why did they never cut the wrong rosebuds or fall in love with fantasy men in letters? Married fantasy men at that!

"Well." She made a face at a carved griffin. "At least I am alive."

The griffin seemed to grin back fiercely, ugly and ardent, as if it would break free of the frozen wood and strike upward to the sky.

• • •

"So your little love is here," Phillippa said in her sweet, insolent voice. "Are you happy now?"

"Leave me alone." Robert did not pause as he walked toward the bizarre banister and stairs.

She followed him as she always did. "She's very plain, poor thing! Quite mousy."

He halted with his hand on the banister, closing his eyes. "I am going to bed."

"I'm sure she would be delighted to join you. I doubt she has had many offers."

"Not so many as you, I dare swear," he said through his teeth.

"Your insane jealousy!" Phillippa said, with bitter delight.

Robert laughed and shook his head. He started up the stairs.

"You beef-witted fool," she cried. "To choose that homely little nobody over me!"

"A thousand times," he murmured under his breath.

"What did you say?" she demanded.

"Nothing."

"Tell me what you said!"

"I said," he snapped aloud, "that however lovely you may appear to your legion of admirers, you are Medusa to me."

"I hate you," she cried. "I *hate* you!"

Robert's hand left the banister as he pounded up the stairs. Her voice followed him, an echo in his head, though he slammed the door of his bedchamber on it. And she was there too, the portrait his father had commissioned in Bombay—it hung from the picture rail, leaning out against the wires as if she leaned to cleave to him, reaching out and screaming in his brain, "I hate you! Why don't you love me, why don't you come to me, I hate you, I hate you!"

He stared at her. The artist had caught her in a moment of quiet tenderness, her hand upon her little Chinese dog, her delicate smile, the hair he had once thought was like filtered sunlight upon the great tree trunks of the Indian forests, shadow brown and mystery.

"Don't you think I'm beautiful?" she asked in her little-girl voice.

He hated it, he hated that high-pitched plea. "Good God," he said, yanking open his cravat. He could not bear to have anyone near him now, not even a manservant to undress him.

"You loved me once," she said fiercely.

"What of it?" he said. "I learned my mistake soon enough."

"I never loved you. I don't know why I didn't listen when they told me how paltry you are. I must have been mad!"

"No doubt." He pulled off his coat and sat down, kicking off his shoes. He was mad himself, utterly demented. It was all he could do to take off his clothes, crawl into the bed, and squeeze his eyes closed while his brain turned over and over in his head.

He felt Phillippa glide on top of him, a heaviness pressing down on his body. Malevolence filled the air he breathed.

"Love me, love me," she whispered urgently. She was going to kill him, suffocate him. He tried to sit up, but her weight opposed him, pushed him back, a force in the center of his chest.

"Get off!" he roared, heaving her away, sending the bedclothes flying.

He stumbled from the bed and grabbed a chair. He yanked it to the window and sat down, gripping the arms, staring through the open curtains to the misted landscape outside. But he knew she was there. He could see her reflection in the glass. It grew clearer, so clear that he could not tell if she was in the room, leaning over his shoulder, or glaring at him from outside the window. He could hear his own breathing, harsh as a child trying not to weep.

"Love me," she moaned, fingers at his throat. "Touch me! Oh, why can't you love me?"

"I can't!" he shouted, flinging himself from the chair. Blindly he seized the wardrobe, feeling for the handle, yanking open the doors. His coats brushed his face, solid and real as he pushed among them, tearing them down with him as he pressed his body in. He pulled the doors closed against her, sinking down to the floor, his shoulders cramped in the small space, his face pressed into a mass of woolen coats on his knees.

She could not reach him there, in a place barely large enough to hold his own body. Jammed awkwardly against the hard wooden walls of his prison and his safety, he could find refuge from his madness.

For a diversion on their third long day at Solinger, Folie and Melinda stood on a footbridge looking down into the water. The stream formed the boundary between the ancient forest and the rolling lawns, emerging clear from some unseen spring among the trees. Late afternoon sparkled on the surface, sliding and rippling across green moss. Folie tossed an oak leaf, dried from last autumn, and watched it spin away over the stones.

''Will you speak to him tonight?'' Melinda asked, as if she had not asked the same thing five times already over the course of the day.

''Certainly I shall speak to him, if I have the opportunity,'' Folie answered.

''Surely he will come down to dinner tonight.''

Folie gave a helpless shrug and tossed another leaf, then brushed a faint smudge from her fawn gloves.

''Mama, it has been three days! We have not set eyes upon the man in three *days!*''

''What would you have me do, Melinda? Hunt him down all over his own house?''

''Perhaps he is ill,'' Melinda said. ''He might need help. Perhaps he is dying in his bedchamber!'' She gave a little gasp, and then added, not without a tinge of hope, ''Perhaps he is dead already!''

''Piffle,'' Folie said. ''I'm sure the servants would have taken note when they changed the sheets.''

"I suppose so." Melinda's lower lip turned sadly downward. She raised her head, looking into the distance along the boundary of the forest. "Perhaps you might—" She paused. "Look."

Folie looked up. At first she saw nothing against the white sheen the sun threw on the water, but then as she followed Melinda's gaze, she noticed a shadow moving slowly along the bank beneath the trees. "A deer," she murmured.

"No . . ." Melinda had the better eyesight. "No, it is a man."

Folie squinted. But the stream's silver glare misted the detail of the woods. "I can't see him."

Melinda shook her head. "He's gone now." She frowned slightly. "Do you suppose it was him?"

"I couldn't tell anything."

"I believe he was there all along," Melinda said uneasily. "I only noticed him when he moved."

"Fishing, no doubt." Folie smiled. "Now wouldn't that be a typical gentleman for you, fishing for days while his houseguests languish?"

"Let us go in, Mama." Melinda pushed away from the wall. "I wish to dash a note to Miss Vernon."

Folie glanced at her. "If you like."

Melinda swept her skirt up around her ankles. "I'll race you to the door!" she cried gaily. Her bright hair bobbed beneath her pink and white straw hat as she began to run.

"Unfair! Head start!" Folie picked up her hem and pelted after.

Melinda's idea of "dashing a note" was to spend three hours crossing and recrossing the pages of her letters to her droves of schoolroom friends. She sat at a desk in the drawing room, framed by a carved pagoda infested with chinamen and peacocks. While she bent her head in silent concentration over her voluminous correspondence, Folie toyed with a cup of tea.

Folie had no one to whom she cared to write. Somehow

she could not summon the desire to pen a note to the Misses Nunney. What was there to say, after all? "Our rooms are quite pleasant. The house is outlandish, the host a madman, and we see no one but ourselves at breakfast, tea, and dinner. Give my regards to Pussy. (And pray keep her out of my vegetable garden!)"

There had been a time when she had thought of nothing but the letters she would write. Folie gazed out the tall window. The lawn and shrubbery gleamed green, faintly distorted by the glass panes, as cheerful and English as the room she sat in was dim and mysterious with its pagodas and silent Chinamen.

She smiled wistfully, remembering the days she had spent composing her letters to India in her mind, when such simple tasks as mending and polishing the plate had been infused with a new glamour as she thought of how she might describe them to him. *This is how I do it, first the whiting with the soft leather—we always use the same piece, as it gets better with time—the coating rubbed in hard and let to dry all dull and gray, and then with linen cloths I wipe it off, and polish round and round, so that a hundred silvery colors begin to gleam through.* She had always imagined him looking over her shoulder with great attentiveness as she executed these banal offices—as if he would be interested in such dull things! She had never actually written of those everyday occurrences, of course—but she had narrated her whole day to him in her mind. It had been a way of keeping him with her, walking beside her, a real presence in her world.

She shook her head a little. How she had delighted in discovering some episode that she could actually write about, something that would please and entertain him. Those she had cherished and cultivated, polishing them to as fine a sheen as the silver plate before she ever set pen to paper.

Near the wall of glass-fronted bookcases, a delicate desk ornamented in red chinoiserie awaited the unknown lady of the house. Folie stood up and wandered past the tightly bound new volumes. She paused by the desk, stroking her finger over the glossy, enameled surface. She lifted the stopper on the inkpot and found it full.

Drawing up a chair, she opened the top and took out a pen. The paper was heavy and rich, impressed with a crest and the name of the house. She mended the pen with a silver knife and paused.

Sweet knight, she wrote.

And stared at it. But then she thought, of course I am not going to post this to him. Not to the Robert Cambourne in this house.

To the Robert in her mind she could write what she pleased. She ached to do so. Yearned to write to him, to read his letters again. She had long ago learned not to permit that feeling any room in her heart, or she would lie awake at night and weep for hours.

But it had a foothold now. She had allowed herself to dream of those days when he had been real and hers. She frowned hard at the crest on the paper.

Perhaps a pretend letter would put it to rest again. Just a mock letter, a little fantasy of her own.

I confess I am somewhat intimidated by the dignity of your stationary, she wrote beneath the embossed crest. *To be quite candid, I am intimidated by you! I do not believe this dark fiendish gentleman who claims your name can possibly be the Robert Cambourne who purchased an elephant for its homing instinct. So I shall simply put him out of my mind and write to my own true Robert, my dearest Robert—oh my friend, you cannot know how I have missed you and missed you. I know that you were right to cease writing to me; how foolish we were, and yet I never found it in my heart to regret. Not truly. I have always cherished you as my own somehow. It is as if I took a wrong turn somewhere, some random day when I might have walked on the left side of the street and run into you, but instead I turned right, or dallied too long over breakfast, or stayed to hem a skirt. And so I missed you forever.*

How am I to convince this stranger, this sham Robert, that he must let us go to London directly, and finance our sojourn there at that?

I must say that this empty mansion seems a prodigious waste of money that might be put to excellent use in firing off Melinda in style. No doubt a servant or two would hardly be missed if we should take them with us, and the cost of the candles alone must pay for that town house in Hans Crescent. I should be so pleased to see her suitably engaged—there is nothing more in life I wish for. Perhaps I seem quite the pushing Mama, but this is so very anxious a time—her whole life's happiness depends upon her choice now. How well I know that! I do not think I was very wise in these matters; perhaps I have not told you how it came about that I married Mr. Hamilton. I cannot say that I was forced by any wicked stepmother, although it is true that I had no mama to advise me, or perhaps I might have waited a little longer. My mother died before I had any memory of her, and my father when I was seven, and so I was brought up as a young lady by a pair of rather jolly uncles and a good strict governess; I loved them very dearly but they were so old and life in Toot seemed so flat, and no one ever dreamed of a London season—or perhaps they were just too kind to mention that without beauty or funds or a noble lineage I could hardly expect to take there. And in truth I should not claim that some unfortunate fate led my feet wrong and caused me to miss you, sweet knight, for no young gentlemen ever do come to Toot to be run into, whether one walks on the left or the right or parades down the very middle of the only street in town. So I was nearly seventeen and very anxious that I would become an old maid like the Misses Nunney, when Mr. Hamilton happened to mention that I was quite passable when I smiled—and there you have it.

I am determined that Melinda shall not make the same—I will not be so harsh as to call it a mistake—but that she shall not suffer a day's qualm over her choice. She simply must have a London season.

A deep booming sound made Folie look up. She and Melinda glanced at one another.

"Oh . . . it was only that a door slammed," Melinda said, as a faint wash of air ruffled their papers.

Before Folie could answer, angry shouts echoed from the

great hall. The words were indistinct, impossible to comprehend amid the sounds of a rough scuffle. Melinda jumped to her feet. ''Whatever could it—''

''Wait!'' Folie cried, lifting the desk cover and tossing her letter inside as Melinda ran out the door. ''Melinda, you come back!''

She caught up with her stepdaughter at the foot of the stairs. Melinda stopped with her hand on the carved head of the creature that coiled its way down the banister. She was staring at the ruckus in the staircase hall, where the butler and a strapping footman were bodily ejecting what appeared to be a bundle of rags with arms and legs.

For just an instant, the intruder's face was visible, unshaven and wild, a long strand of white hair hanging between his eyes. He glared toward the stairs and screamed, a garbled pleading that sent chill fingernails down Folie's spine. He screeched again, and this time she heard a name in the sound; she heard *''Robert!''* in his drawn-out howl, or she thought she did. The men were shoving his face against the door frame; he clawed for a hold and lost it as they pushed him out. The butler hauled on the big door. It boomed shut again, closing out the sounds of the commotion, leaving only dying reverberations in the hall.

''It was him!'' Melinda whispered. ''Mama—that man in the woods!''

''A poacher, perhaps,'' Folie said bravely. ''The men will deal with it. Let us go up to our rooms. It's almost time to change for dinner.''

''A poacher?'' Melinda's fingers were white as she pinched one hand inside the other. ''Breaking into the house?''

Folie mounted the stairs, taking her arm. ''Come, what will you wear tonight? The apple green?'' Clothing could always be depended upon to divert Melinda's attention.

It worked. Melinda gave the door a dubious glance and turned with a shaky sigh. ''What difference can it make what I wear?'' she asked fretfully. ''There is no one to see me.''

''Thank you so much! I am someone!''

"Well, but you are my mother."

Folie gathered her skirt as she paused at the landing. "Humpf!" she said, and bounced ahead with a great show of indignation, hiding a little burst of pleasure at being so unequivocally installed in that category.

FOUR

ROBERT PACED HIS room with a ferocious drive, pressing his fists to the walls when he met them as if he could shove through them and escape. The sound of the beggar's howl would not leave his brain.

"You're dead," he muttered. "Damn you. God damn you, don't come back!"

Phillippa's harrying was horrible enough—he could not endure more. If his father had returned from hell to pursue him, Robert thought he must kill himself. But there was no release there either. Perhaps being alive was all that kept the precarious barrier between, kept them from consuming him now, dragging him down into their black, strangling inferno.

And there was Folie to hold him here—his Folly—he heard her voice, too. Soft and bright and unafraid; he wanted her so much that he froze, body and soul, when he saw her. All he heard coming from his mouth were biting replies to her common courtesy. He knew she was puzzled. She must think him utterly demented.

He laughed at the ceiling. Of course he was demented—dead people haunted him, confusion followed him, he could not go out into the open day. But he did not want her to know. He had reclaimed his reason once; his mind had slowly cleared on the passage from India, mired in tropical doldrums, a leisurely drift around Africa that had taken ten months. It was there that he had begun to remember. To realize that Phillippa was dead. She was truly dead; only a demon that haunted him and not a living nightmare at his side. And as he grasped that, he began to recall other things, to recollect his roving in the bazaars and his haphazard inquiries, his notes and diaries. Small things—ashore in Zanzibar, some flutter of silk, some particular way the lamplight fell on a stranger's turban would bring to him the memory of a Delhi shoe-stall, drinking *chai* in the back. He thought that was the night he had gone mad.

The more lucid his mind became on the ship, the more he could recall of his derangement. There had been visits from *guuruus,* some that Robert recognized and some that he didn't. Phillippa had been there—but Phillippa was dead. She had murdered his dog; someone whose face he could not see had held Folie's letters over a fire and threatened to kill her.

He leaned his head into his hands. Even at his most rational, he was not certain what had been real and what delusion. It was all dream-like, horrific. He did not even know how he had gotten out of Delhi to the coast.

On the ship he had been safe and sober. He thought he had escaped to England, to sanity—but at Solinger, Phillippa and distraction had found him again.

No doubt demons preferred the overland route, he thought blackly.

And now his father. He was certain it had been his father's voice. He reached abruptly for the bell rope and rang it.

After several long minutes, he rang it again. This time he got an answer, a breathless footman, his coat pocket half torn away. "Beg pardon, sir!" he said. "We just had to give old Sparkett the heave; he'd somehow got himself all the way inside the front hall! Mr. Lander's on his way up directly to speak to you."

"Sparkett?" Robert asked warily.

"He's harmless, sir," the pink-cheeked servant confided. "Has spells, you know."

"You know him?"

"Oh, aye, he's been on the village charity since me mother was a girl. Mad as a March hare, she always says, and feeds him the odd potato pie. We don't like to handle him rough, sir, but in his bad spells there's not much else can be done."

"You are certain it was him?" Robert asked sharply.

The young man gave a shrug and slight laugh. "Oh, aye, sir, I'd never mistake old Sparkett! Known him my life long."

Relief and mortification surged inside Robert, bleeding into an unreasoning anger. He held it checked, turning away to the window. "He must be kept off the grounds. He'll frighten the ladies."

"Aye, sir!" the footman agreed vigorously. At a scratch on the door, he added, "That'll be Mr. Lander."

Robert scowled. "Let him in," he said coldly.

He turned back as the butler was dismissing his subordinate with a jerk of the chin. The door closed.

"You're to see to the security of the place!" Robert took a quick step toward Lander, and the butler almost imperceptibly drew himself up and back.

"I beg your pardon for this incident, Mr. Cambourne!" he said tightly. "It will not happen again, you have my word."

"My God, this Sparkett devil was inside the door!" Robert stood still, willing the anger into coolness, into control.

Lander watched him; they faced one another like vigilant mongrels.

"Do you understand the danger?" Robert demanded. "No one is to come into the grounds, no one is to come through the gates. No one!"

Lander's jaw was stiff. "Perhaps if you would give me a fixed idea of the nature of this danger, sir."

Robert glared at him. He turned suddenly away. "It is not a fixed danger," he exclaimed. "You must watch for it from any quarter!"

"But you expect someone to attempt the grounds, Mr. Cambourne?"

"I am not—" He swung back again. "I don't know." Lander gave him a steady look, a look that filled Robert with shame and fury. "Just do the job I employed you to do," he exclaimed in a low voice. "Watch!"

"Yes, sir," Lander said.

Robert wanted to warn Folie to take care, even here under his protection. But he could no more explain to her what to fear than he could to his servants. He should not have brought her here at all; he saw that now. What use was his protection? He himself was the danger. Lunatic—he had thought for a while he was sane, that in England all was well, that he could bring her near—then just as she had arrived, he had fallen again into this abyss.

He should send her away. If there was a real menace, he had only brought her to the center of it. He must tell her to go. Already he had avoided her for days, avoided food and drunk only water to clear his brain. He was safe when he did not eat or drink; safe, but slowly killing himself. He walked into the library with his blood pounding in his head, dizzy with tension.

It was empty. He stood at the door, looking at the two writing desks, both abandoned with the pens and ink left unheeded to dry. A bolt of fear seized him, but he managed to think his way through it, remember that he had heard the two ladies go up the stairs, heard Folie's voice through his father's ringing in his ears.

He stood in the silent library, thinking of her voice. It was lower and lazier than he had expected, soft even when she was annoyed. In her letters she had seemed breathless sometimes, excitable and happy. She was so much more a quiet gentlewoman in life—he wondered if she had changed, or if it was a misinterpretation he had made, seeing more than was real.

On one of the writing desks, letters were stacked neatly, waiting to be folded. He did not read them, but he could see Miss Melinda's signature on the top sheet. The other desk held only a stack of blank stationary, a pen and an inkwell. But a white curve of paper dangled out from under the lid.

There was writing on the sheet. He looked down at his cuffs, at his hands, feeling oddly embarrassed.

Of course he should not read it. She never wrote him anymore; he had told her not to write, and she had not. A wave of intense longing swept over him, a physical ache to be back in Calcutta on the hot verandah, the fan swinging with its slow squeak above him, her letter held between his palms as if it were a small bird.

Just to see her handwriting again—the way the words slid up to the right even though she ruled her paper like a careful schoolgirl, the faint double period after each sentence—he only wished to see it.

He lifted the lid of the desk. The paper swept to the floor, and he stooped to pick it up.

Sweet knight.

He made a faint sound as he straightened, a hungry laugh. He could not even look at the page again; he was afraid the words would be different. Folding it carefully, he slipped it inside his coat. Like a pi-dog that had snatched a morsel from the bazaar, he left the library quickly, retreating to safety with his prize.

''There, that should do nicely.'' Folie held her own garnets against the shimmering cream of Melinda's overdress as it lay on the bed. ''I'll call Sally.''

''No, I don't want Sally,'' Melinda said, fussing with her combs on the dressing table. ''You help me dress, Mama.''

''Well, I mislaid something downstairs, I'll just go and—''

''No,'' Melinda said anxiously. ''Please don't go down there.''

''My dear, you heard the maid say that it was only a poor madman from the village. He is spending the night in the jail by now.''

''Please, Mama!'' Melinda turned a flushed face toward Folie. ''I don't feel well.''

''Oh, come . . .''

''No, truly.'' Melinda stood up. ''Does my forehead feel warm? And that tea had no taste. Truly, Mama, I'm not funning.''

Folie touched her stepdaughter's face. ''Well . . .''

''I don't feel hungry at all,'' Melinda said. ''I have such a headache.''

''Perhaps you are a trifle warm,'' Folie admitted. ''I'm sure it's nothing, but it cannot hurt you to lie down for a bit. I'll go down and see the cook about a tisane.''

''Cannot Sally do that?'' Melinda said, pushing the dress aside and folding herself down across the pillows with a tragic air. ''May I have a cold compress? Would you hold it for me, Mama?'' Her voice grew faint as she closed her eyes. ''I want you to do it.''

Hours later, Folie sat bolt upright in her bed. That letter! She scrambled out from under the bedclothes, searching for the bedstool with her bare toe.

How could she have forgotten it . . . even in the commotion about the housebreaker; left it there for any servant to find! But Melinda had been in such a strange temper, alternately petulant and loving, as if she were indeed coming on with a fever. Still, she had never seemed to grow hot or damp, and had even eaten much of the broth and toast Sally had brought for their dinner.

Folie found her candlestick and lit it hurriedly. Likely enough no one had been into the library after they had left it; most of the housekeeping, such as it was, seemed to be completed by noon each day. The floorboards were chilly beneath her slippers. She closed the door behind her and made her way along the passage and down the stairs, sliding her fingertips along the scaly creature that coiled in and out of the banister. At the foot of the stairs, she gave the beast's nose a friendly flick with her middle finger and tiptoed across the cold marble hall, shielding her candle.

The door stood partially open. Folie touched it gently, pushing it inward with her shoulder. The veiled glare of her own candle prevented her from discerning the faint glow inside until she was standing in the wide open doorway.

She started, expecting to see someone there. But a quick glance around the library showed no one, only a guttering candle on the desk where she had been writing that afternoon.

Folie bit her lip. It had been found, then. Quick heat came to her face as she hurried to the table. A sealed letter lay on it . . . directed to her in that familiar hand.

If she had stumbled upon him there in person, she could not have been more agitated. For a few moments she stared at it—he had read it; he had answered her—she did not know whether she was embarrassed or terrified.

She set down her candle and picked up the letter. The wax was cool but still slightly soft, the impression of the Cambourne coat of arms blurring under her finger. She broke the seal.

Folly, I am here. Perhaps it seems otherwise. I am lost, my dear sweet Folly, well and truly lost, and I cannot seem to find my way back this time.

Robert

Folie put her fingertips over her mouth, holding the note gently. She sat down slowly at the desk, frowning at the words.

It had not been long since he had written it. As she touched the letter, a sensation came back to her vividly—she felt as she had felt in that dream of India so long ago . . . as if he were just out of sight; as if she could reach out and touch him if only she knew how. If only she knew where; and yet she followed and followed the echo of an image and never quite saw him, put out her hands and met only blowing silk and silence.

''Robert,'' she whispered.

There was no answer. Motionless figures stared back at her from the deep shadows of the room, enigmatic blank eyes. She tucked the letter inside her robe, pulling it closer about her.

That is not him, she thought vehemently. *That man in this house is not him at all. It cannot be him.*

It was a strange thought; she knew it even as it came to her so strongly. This was undeniably his handwriting. He was clearly the master of this house, which had been a well-known Cambourne property for decades. And yet the suspicion had dogged her from the first instant—now that she gave it free rein in her mind, a rush of wild speculations followed one upon the other.

Robert Cambourne was wealthy. A veritable nabob. It had been something of a legend among Charles' kin, one of those things mentioned as an aside, a murmur of awe, of pride and just a trace of jealousy—the vast Indian fortune and political influence that the Cambourne branch of the family had amassed in two centuries of service to the East India Company. The Cambournes sent their sons and daughters home to England to be educated and married, but their adult lives were spent in foreign opulence, a leisurely swim through cascades of precious jewels, marvelous banquets, and marbled palace halls—at least, that was the impression in the Hamilton branch. Only through her letters from Robert had Folie caught a different glimpse, though she had never mentioned it to any of the Hamilton kin.

But Robert Cambourne was rich. Very rich, that much she did know. Mssrs. Hawkridge and James made no bones about it. And if he was rich, then there might be Unsavory Elements who wished to steal from him. Extort money from him. Even kidnap him.

She frowned blindly at the glossy scarlet surface of the desk. It was a ridiculous notion. She had no reason to entertain any such idea.

I am lost. I am here. Perhaps it seems otherwise.

She opened the letter again and bent over it, looking closely. It was certainly his handwriting, or an extraordinarily accurate imitation of it.

But it was not the writing that convinced her. As she held it up near her face to examine it, she breathed a memory, a scent so faint that it seemed to vanish even as she drew it in; the scent of her sky-blue shawl and his letters.

She knew it instantly and unequivocally. She pressed the paper to her face and breathed deeply.

He had written this. Handwriting, diction, greeting—all that could be imitated—but not the imperceptible incense that brought a lightning re-creation of those days when she had eagerly broken open his letters and thought of him from moment to moment.

Folie laid the paper down again, smoothing it open. A part of her tried to remain reasonable and sober, arguing that it was all a nonsensical flight of imagination; a part of her wanted to flee this place immediately, as frightened as Melinda by its strangeness and shadows—but as Folie spread her fingers across the letter, she felt a deeper welling of fear.

If this was him . . . the real Robert, her Robert . . . she was in another sort of danger altogether.

A moment of near panic seized her heart. Somehow until this moment, this letter, this scent, he had not seemed quite real; she had not ascertained her jeopardy.

Oh, God save her. If it was truly Robert—she would fall in love with him again. How could she not?

She made a soft whimper of dismay. It seemed unlikely . . . the man in this house was hardly attractive to her, but four years ago she had learned a lesson that she would never forget. Love was not for her. Better a practical marriage, safe and quiet, as hers had been, than the foolish flight and terrible fall from those airy heights. She should not have written that letter to him, even in fancy. She must not allow any such thing to happen again.

With a quick move, she tore the reply in half, and half again, crumpling the pieces in her hand. She must not stay here, not another day.

Robert received the message in his dressing room, delivered by a silent Lander with his breakfast tray. He had been doing nothing, simply sitting in a chair staring at the rows of books and bound journals that lined the small dark room, holding his neckcloth dangling in his hand.

Doing nothing. Thinking nothing. When he saw the tray, smelled the fragrance of warm bread and tea, his mouth watered painfully. The note lying beside the silver cover made his heart squeeze hot blood into his brain. But he merely nodded dismissal to Lander.

The butler bowed, remaining in place. "It is from Mrs. Hamilton," he said. "She requests the favor of an immediate reply, sir."

"All right," Robert said, snapping up the note. "All right, then."

He tore it open. He was afraid his hand was shaking visibly from hunger and suspense—and then he had to stand up and carry it to the window to read it in the dim little room.

Dear Mr. Cambourne,

It is my understanding that we are here at your request, that you are our host. We will expect to see you at dinner. If you cannot come, I shall conclude that our presence here is inconvenient at this time. Therefore, we shall depart this morning. Please inform me of your decision before 10 A.M. *If I do not have an answer from you by that time, then Miss Melinda Hamilton and I extend our thanks and our farewells by this note.*

Mrs. Charles Hamilton

Robert looked up at the butler. "They are not to leave the grounds."

Lander made a slight bow of his head. "I do not quite understand you, sir."

"What time is it?"

"It is half past nine, sir."

Robert gazed at him. He had hired Lander for his military stance, for his air of pugnacity. He had hired him, frankly, for protection. And now he did not trust the man, though he could not tell why. He wished that he had held the note and examined it in private, to see if the seal had been tampered with, while at the same time his crazy suspicions mortified him.

"Take the tray," he said. "I am not hungry."

"Yes, sir," Lander said. He gathered up the breakfast and carried it through the door, closing it behind him with one hand.

Robert waited a few moments, and then pulled down books from the shelf. Late in the night, he'd stolen five bottles from his own cellars. He wiped the dust from a brown vessel marked Devonshire cider and pried out the cork. He drank straight from the bottle, tasting the waxy edge, downing the warm sweet gingery liquid with inelegant greed.

After a few deep draughts, he would have sat down and consumed the cider more slowly, but he did not have time if he was to prevent her leaving before ten o'clock. He upended the bottle, finishing off the drink. He hadn't drunk cider since he was a schoolboy at Eton; it was hardly common in India, but he thought it ought to be mild and somewhat nourishing. It would keep him alive, at any rate.

He replaced the books quickly, hiding the bottles behind a set of his Indian diaries. For a moment, he paused with his hand resting on the spines. He remembered Phillippa laughing at him. But he narrowed his eyes and stared hard at the diaries, at their green calfskin edged in gold. Imagination. Imagination. He must control it. God, he hated her.

He counted the numbers he had inked on the backs of the twelve volumes, one-two-three-five-four-seven . . . the clock chimed the quarter hour. Robert hastily rearranged the books, glanced around for where he had laid number six—there on his father's lead-lined chest of drawers. He stuffed it into the space and went to the door.

She swept into the room wearing her cloak, facing him with an assumed belligerence. She would not reveal that she was quaking in her boots. It was not as easy as she had determined it would be. The moment she saw him, her stride broke. He stood before the tall windows, too much silhouetted for his expression to be clear, his posture an unyielding stiffness, hands locked behind his back like an officer staring down his troops.

Folie stopped for just an instant, consciously preventing herself from making an apologetic curtsy, as if she were late to an appointment with the headmistress. She made a brief nod. "Good morning, Mr. Cambourne." Then she walked to the window and looked out on the gray drizzle, her fingers resting lightly on the sill.

"You must not leave," he said.

Folie turned to him, her eyebrows lifted. He did not look at her, but remained in profile, his gaze fixed on some unknown point in the middle of the room. She could see him more clearly now—his straight solid jaw and high-bridged nose, his hair making black curls against the crisp starch of his neckcloth.

"Why ever not?" she heard herself say boldly. "I do not feel that I know you. I am uncomfortable here. Melinda is unhappy and anxious."

His gaze flickered, as if he were searching for something in the room that he could not find. He frowned.

"I do not understand why you wish for us to stay," she said.

He moved away. "I wish it."

"Do you indeed?" She made a light disbelieving laugh. "I beg your pardon; this is quite confusing to me. I am not a woman of the world, perhaps I know little of society manners, but I have never been so comprehensively ignored by a host!"

He looked up at her suddenly. "Have you been ignored?"

Folie met his eyes. They were gray and stern, not so fiercely strange as they had seemed before.

"Well," she said, slightly taken aback. "We never see you."

"That does not mean that I have not thought of you every minute," he said.

Folie drew in her breath. She tried to remember the clever lines she had prepared as she had lain in her bed staring up at the darkness. But all she could feel was her nerves; all she could think to say was, "What did you mean? In that note?"

His eyebrow lifted. "Note?"

"You wrote me a note, did you not?" She gestured toward the writing desk. "And left it there."

He looked down at her disapprovingly, as if she were an unruly servant. "I suppose that I did."

"What did you mean? To say that you are lost?"

There was a long pause. He gave a cold smile. "No doubt I had taken too much wine. Kindly erase it from your memory."

She bit her lip and turned to the window.

"What shall I do to convince you?" he asked.

She turned back. "Convince me of what?"

"That I wish you and Miss Melinda to stay." He gave a faint shrug. "I will come to dinner, if it pleases you."

"That would be most kind!" Folie said.

They stood in silence.

"Shall I—" He seemed to come to an impasse with his sentence, and then said suddenly, with a gesture toward the door, "Shall I show you the garden?"

"It is raining," she murmured.

"Then the picture gallery."

Folie moved restlessly away from the window. "I have seen the picture gallery."

"What a difficult princess you are!"

"Well, I do not mean to be difficult—" Folie said quickly. She stopped. "*I* am difficult?" She gave a huff. "That must make *you* impossible!"

He gave a bare nod, as if to accede to the verdict. "I believe ladies always find gentlemen impossible, do they not?"

"No doubt," Folie said coolly.

"That is what my sisters tell me."

"Oh yes. You have sisters." She recalled that he did, although it seemed as if he must have sprung from no family at all, have walked one day fully grown from some cold mountain cavern.

"Two," he said. "Lady Ryman lives in London. Mrs. Coke is in Bombay, but I believe she is intending to return here with her children this year. The boy is six; he'll enter Eton, I suppose." He paused a moment, and then said, "I am glad that Frances will come."

"You are close to her?"

"Close?" His brow lifted again, as if the question were an impertinence. "No, I cannot say so. I am not close to either of my sisters, in truth."

Folie tilted her head. "But you are glad she will come to England?"

"With her children." He shrugged. "I think it a good thing, that their mother comes home with them. It is difficult for a child of six to travel so far and begin school alone."

"So I should suppose!" Folie exclaimed. "Surely that is not common practice?"

"In some families," he said briefly.

"Poor things!"

"It is India. The boys must attend school, the girls must learn their English manners. If the wife prefers to remain with her husband, then the children must come alone, or with friends or some relative. Or as I did, with a hired bear-leader."

"Cannot they go to school in India?"

He smiled dryly. "No, they cannot."

"You are quite right, it is a great good that your sister comes." Folie looked at the writing desk. "I did not even know my mother. And yet I missed her every day of my life."

"Yes," he said.

"I should like to be the best of mothers to Melinda. But it is so difficult sometimes."

"You are an excellent mother."

Folie lifted her head. "I should not suppose you had enough evidence to judge."

"One reveals a great deal of one's character in letters." One corner of his mouth turned up crookedly. "You do, at any rate."

She felt herself becoming flustered. It seemed as if the conversation had somehow reeled off into topics she had never meant to discuss with him. "I have spoiled her dreadfully. But she is very good, and hardly needs to be curbed."

"And she must have an exemplary husband. You are determined."

"Yes, certainly. We are not aiming over-high, titles and that sort of nonsense; though I vow she is beautiful enough to deserve a duke. A gentleman of good substance and breeding will suffice, in high health and not too old, and I should hope that she will find someone who can—" Folie came to an abrupt halt. "Feel some moderate degree of affection for her," she finished tonelessly.

A long silence fell between them. He picked up a pen from the desk and began to stroke it lightly, his sun-darkened hand moving up and down the quills. "You do not hold love to be a requirement in marriage?"

"No," Folie said briefly. "I am quite old-fashioned on that point; I have not encouraged her to be romantic."

He rolled the quill between his thumb and fingers, looking down at it. "I must agree," he said. "I married for love. It was a transcendent disaster."

Folie's heart beat harder. "I am sorry to hear that," she said crisply. "But this is hardly to the point. To be quite frank, Mr. Cambourne—"

"Robert," he said.

"Robert, then," she repeated with a faint impatience. "To be quite frank, it is time that Miss Melinda and I departed for London."

"No," he said, "it is not time."

Folie arched her brows. "I beg your pardon."

"I am Miss Melinda's guardian. I have barely become acquainted with her character."

"Indeed? A little more time in her company might have made you more efficient in this laudable aim. I fear that we are unable to oblige you further. What you know of her now must suffice."

"You said that if I came to dinner, you would stay."

"I said that we would not leave today. Tomorrow, however, we must depart."

"No."

His voice did not rise, but the quill in his hand rotated rapidly, then bent in two with a soft snap between his fingers. She looked from his hand up to his face.

He was frowning. His eyes met hers for a moment, a look like a silver-eyed sentinel, wary and hostile, his mouth set hard.

"You cannot prevent us!" Folie said sharply.

"I will stop your income if you leave the house."

Folie stared at him. She shook her head slightly.

Nothing in his expression changed. He did not smile or pass it off as a poor jest.

"You cannot," she said faintly.

"Certainly I can," he said.

She shook her head again, trying to find her breath. She turned away, looking about as if she could find some answer in the corners of the room. "But why?"

"I wish you and Miss Melinda to remain here. You will not go to London."

"But *why?*" she exclaimed.

He did not answer. When Folie turned back to him, he would not look at her, but by the sullen curl of his mouth she saw that he would not be moved.

"I wish to leave!" she said. "I cannot remain here!"

He turned his back to her, facing the window.

"*Robert!*" she cried.

He shook his head slowly, never looking away from the window.

Folie sucked in her breath, poised between astonishment and angry tears. She hurried from the room, afraid that she would humiliate herself, pulling the door hard after her.

FIVE

"SIR HOWARD DINGLEY calls, sir."

Lander's calm voice made Robert turn sharply from the window. He could hardly tear his mind from what he had just done.

"Sir Howard?" he asked vaguely.

"Yes, sir. Shall I send him away again?"

"Who is he?"

"Sir Howard Dingley of Dingley Court," Lander said, with the calm air of a teacher explaining a fact to a dull student. "He is the squire and justice of the peace. He has called three times." Lander cleared his throat and added apologetically, "The father of seven promising daughters."

Robert suddenly recalled the times he had sent Lander back to refuse this neighbor entry, claiming indisposition. God knew he had been indisposed; not fit for any civilized society, and the local squire, no doubt some fox-chasing red-cheeked country gentleman, was the last sort of company Robert wished to endure.

"Show him in directly!" Robert said.

"Sir?" Lander's flicker of surprise alone was almost worth it.

He gave his butler a wolfish smile, one carnivore to another. "Show Sir Howard into the drawing room immediately."

"Yes, sir." The butler did not hesitate further. A moment later, a lean gentleman came striding into the room, shoving his hat and stick at Lander with something of a defiant air. Straight shoulders and leathered skin gave him the air of a hundred Company officers Robert had known. He wore his hair in a queue, unpowdered, as if to worry over his early strands of gray was too much nonsense.

"Sir Howard," Robert said, walking forward to offer his hand. "I apologize for my inability to welcome you before now."

Sir Howard brushed his chin down with his free hand as he gripped Robert's. He stared a moment into Robert's eyes, and said, "Ha! Indisposed! A wily trout, more like! You don't mind my plain speaking—it's my wife made me come a-begging. Daughters! See to it that you never have one, that's my advice!"

"Come to dinner tonight," Robert said.

Sir Howard's brows rose in astonishment. "Dinner?"

"Yes. Do me the honor."

"Eh? Well, I—" High color burned under the tan in Sir Howard's cheeks. "Certainly! If you wish!" He gave Robert a wary look.

"I would be pleased. And my guests, Mrs. Hamilton and my ward, Miss Hamilton—they will be more than delighted to have company, I assure you."

Sir Howard made a slight, stiff bow. "Aye, ladies. Of course. You have ladies here."

"Yes." They stood awkwardly. "Mrs. Hamilton and my ward." Robert reached for the bell pull. "You'll take some Madeira, Sir Howard?"

His guest seemed to relax somewhat at the offer. "That I will." He sat in the chair Robert indicated. "I'm obliged to you, sir. Obliged to you. What do you think of this weather, eh? A wet spring, but not the worst I've seen, by far!"

Robert nodded, as if he had the slightest notion what the

weather had been or was, and put his mind as well as he could to polite conversation.

Folie did not look forward to dinner. She had deliberately avoided Melinda, no easy task, by setting her and Sally to a complete inspection of every stitch of the London wardrobe. Since anything to do with her debut was heaven to Melinda, and sewing a known antidote to Folie, this sufficed to keep her stepdaughter from making uncomfortable inquiries into their plans for the future. Unfortunately, it rather encouraged the notion that they would be leaving for London directly, but Folie could not help that.

She sat at the window of her cheerful yellow bedroom, clenching the spine of an unread book in her lap. It seemed impossible that they really might not go to London. More incredibly, that for all practical purposes they could actually be prisoners here. An overwrought fancy, and yet however she turned it over in her mind, she could find no other way to describe it to herself.

That man; that dark and rigid stranger—he had all the control that he claimed over their lives. All of Charles' will; both her own jointure and Melinda's portion went under his hand. He could not leave them penniless, no, the will did not allow that, but he could decide where they must live and how much they might have to spend each quarter. Until now Folie had consulted upon all these matters herself with Mssrs. Hawkridge and James, and more—contriving her own affairs under their benign eyes, keeping a conservative profile in the funds, saving and planning, saving and planning. Once, when she had requested that their stock in a banking venture be sold at a modest profit, while the shares were still on the rise, Mr. James had even complimented her on her prudent management.

And Robert Cambourne said he would take it away if they left this house. But why? Why, why, and why?

Robert, she thought fiercely. *You are not Robert. You cannot be the man I loved; he would never be so wantonly cruel.*

At least there was no fear that she would fall madly in

love with him again. All the love she had felt in her dreams transformed like alchemy into a narrow-eyed hatred for this stiff, ungenerous, closemouthed, willful person. Without an inquiry, without a reason, he dictated their fate. She could not comprehend him. There had been a moment, an instant or two, when she had felt . . .

But no—that was mere imagination. Just the sort of absurdity that had led her into disaster with him before, believing that she could ever see or know what lay beyond the part of him that he allowed her to see.

Still her feelings moved like quicksilver, turning toward him and away. She thought of the note; she thought of that faint way that he smiled at her. So fleeting—and somehow, somehow, so fascinating.

Oh, she was fascinated. Like a bird frozen before a serpent, she thought ferociously. She leaned her elbow on the windowsill, her forehead in her hand. She was too old for this, for love, for hate, for nonsense. She should never have come here alone. She should have brought Mrs. Couch, at least for company, if not for wise advice.

Too old for love, too young to be a mother—when there was a knock at the door she sighed in dread, certain it would be Melinda.

It was not. A chambermaid curtsied, offering a note and vanishing.

Sir Howard Dingley and Lady Dingley will honor us with their presence at dinner tonight. I hope this will please you.

Robert

"How delightful!" Folie murmured dryly to herself. "Let us go to London; *that* will please me!"

But at least it gave her something to distract Melinda. She rose, opening her dressing case to take out the pearls that her own mother had left her, the ones that Melinda loved to be allowed to wear.

• • •

As they entered the drawing room, Melinda was chatting of how they must find a brighter ribbon for her pink chip-straw bonnet, something the color of a daisy's center. Folie nodded and smiled. Melinda looked as well as she ever had, her skin and eyes as lustrous as the pearls at her throat, every move of her gloved hands, each turn of her head a simple grace. Folie felt a rush of love and despair. She could not let her stepdaughter be cheated of the life that was so rightfully hers. Folie must find some way. This was merely another obstacle, a final hurdle to be cleared.

He awaited them as he had the first night, standing alone beside the fireplace, his hands locked behind his back. The black of formal attire gave him a beautiful erect elegance, yet his eyes—ice gray, dark-lashed—seemed to regard them with the cold calm interest of a jungle hunter. Melinda's girlish voice faded suddenly to silence.

''Sir,'' she said hesitantly, dropping a curtsy. ''Good evening.''

''Good evening, Miss Melinda,'' he said in a cordial voice.

When he looked up at Folie, she made a brief sketch of a bow, lowering her eyes.

''Good evening, madam.'' He came forward and offered his hand to her with a brisk move.

She took it, keeping her gaze averted, not even glancing at him as he brought her hand near his mouth. He did not kiss her glove, but his fingers curled lightly over hers a moment. He pressed a yellow rosebud into her palm before he lowered her hand and released it.

Melinda made a faint sound, the ghost of an astonished giggle. Folie hardly knew what to do; she only looked down at the rose and turned away. She was glad of Lander's appearance at the drawing room door to announce the arrival of the dinner guests.

Sir Howard brought a welcome ease as he strode into the room. Folie liked him instantly. He reminded her of Charles, a rangy man; gruff and imperfectly tailored, as if he thought that he ought to fit into his coat whether it was a jot too loose across the chest or not. Still, he was quite markedly good-looking. She did not think him very far past forty, in spite of the gray in his straight brown hair. She gave him an affectionate, pert smile as she curtsied, and was rewarded with a laugh and wink from direct green eyes, as if they had known one another all their lives. There was no Lady Dingley at his side.

"Sends her deepest regrets," Sir Howard said cheerfully. "Don't get out much, you know. Fancies herself stricken by the headache."

Folie and Melinda expressed polite sympathy, but Sir Howard waved it off. "Nothing a bit of fresh air could not cure, I tell her. But she pays me no mind."

"Naturally not, if you are so brutal," Folie said. "Ladies must have a very strong dose of fellow feeling before they can recover the headache."

"Brutal!" he said. "Ha!"

Folie shook her head. "I often wonder that gentlemen can be so slow to learn these simple facts."

"And you, missy, are entirely too full of sauce for a chit of your age, I see that at a glance."

Folie dropped a curtsy. "Why, thank you, sir! You are quite charming for a barbarian!"

Robert stood by the fireplace, watching Folie's face, caught between a vague angry disgust at this flirtation and the laughter that had come into her eyes the moment she responded to Sir Howard's bow. It was like a strong touch on a place he had locked in his heart, the way he had locked her miniature in a velvet strong-box. "I hope your daughters are well, Sir Howard?" he asked coolly.

"Too well!" his guest said. "Would that *they* would all take to their beds with the headache!"

Folie laughed. "How many children have you, sir?"

"Seven girls!" Sir Howard exclaimed. "Can you believe it?"

Folie thought it was no wonder Lady Dingley had developed the headache. She glanced inadvertently toward Robert. Their eyes met. A roguish, stifled smile changed his whole aspect so suddenly that Folie felt as if a spike of sweet lightning had struck her throat.

"What fun!" Miss Melinda said. "I should love to have so many sisters!"

"Take any number you please off my hands," Sir Howard said carelessly. "We have plenty to spare."

Folie turned in surprise when Lander entered to announce dinner. It was far too early for any normal civility. Robert stepped toward Folie, but Sir Howard had already tucked her hand into his arm with a jocund announcement that he knew Mr. Cambourne would not begrudge him the honor of taking Mrs. Hamilton in. Folie accepted his escort with relief. Deliberately, she laid the rosebud on a side table as she passed through the door.

Robert looked at it. He lifted his eyes and found Miss Melinda regarding him with interest. He offered her his arm and took her in.

With the ladies seated, Sir Howard took a leather chair at the foot of the table and cast a glance about the dining room. He shook his head at the dragons. "Damned feverish mind it took, to carve this stuff! Don't think I could live with it more than a day, myself."

Melinda sat with her hands in her lap, looking uneasy. Folie said archly, "We do not dare mention the decoration here, Sir Howard. Our host dislikes it. Although I must say I find myself growing rather fond of Xerxes and Boswell." She nodded toward the dragons.

"Mama," Melinda warned in a soft voice.

Folie lifted her chin and took a sip of wine. She felt a light flush coloring her cheeks, as if she had already drunk much more than a swallow of the claret Lander had just poured.

Sir Howard cleared his throat, looking down the long table at his host. "Well then. Do you hunt, sir?"

"No, I have hunted very little," Robert said.

"Pity, pity . . . I keep a pack of hounds—five pups this morning—thought you might like to take a look at 'em tomorrow."

Robert felt an instant misgiving at the thought of leaving the house. "How big is your pack?" he asked, turning the subject.

"No more than twenty couple. Quality over quantity, eh, Mrs. Hamilton? Do you like dogs?"

"Yes, certainly," Folie said. "But I haven't brought myself to have another since our last."

"Brandy," Melinda said stoutly, "was the *best* dog in the world."

"Indeed?" Sir Howard grinned. "It can't be so. My Maggie was the best by far. Why, she could bring home a stray lamb from the next county, save a drowning child, and then fetch a fellow's slippers before she was dry! Tell me what your Brandy could do to match that!"

Folie and Melinda laughed and exchanged glances. "Oh, Brandy was not that sort of dog at all." Folie gave a smile and a shrug. "He would merely put his paw upon one's knee and look up as if to say, 'I have something to tell you that will please you very much.' " She traced the silver engraving on her spoon with a fingertip, smiling wistfully. "Everyone loved him."

A vision visited Robert, one of the strong bright ones, of salt-and-pepper fur, brown eyes; a scruffy, panting, mischievous face. "Yes," he said in a stifled voice. His guests all looked toward him. He hardly realized he had spoken until the expectant pause invited him to say more.

"I had a dog," he said uneasily.

"Our house is always full of 'em," Sir Howard said. "I could not trust the man or woman who don't like dogs."

Folie was looking at Robert. He had a horrible moment in which he felt a sickness in his chest, a burn behind his eyes and nose. He stared straight ahead, breathing slowly. *Do not think, do not think of that; don't think, don't think, do not think of it.*

"And have you filled your stable?" Sir Howard was saying. "There's a pair of grays up for sale at Camden . . . known 'em for three years, very nice-going creatures—you might like to think of them for a phaeton if you have the need."

"Thank you." With an act of ferocious will, Robert put his mind on Sir Howard's words. "I will be sure to look into it."

''Miss Hamilton, this reminds me that I am charged with discovering your age!'' Sir Howard thumped his hand on the table. ''I am not to go home without the information.''

''I am nineteen in June, sir,'' Melinda said modestly.

''Very good, very good!'' Sir Howard said, helping himself from the mutton. ''My second girl is nineteen. I've just bought a little chestnut hack for her to take to town. All my girls ride like demons, I'll say that for 'em.'' He looked to Robert. ''Does Miss Hamilton have any sort of seat?''

Robert stared at him a moment, his mind so distracted that he felt as if he had to translate the question from a foreign language. ''I don't know,'' he said, his mouth twisting in a wry smile. ''I have not inquired.''

''Your daughters go to town this season, Sir Howard?'' Melinda asked, leaning forward. The light of eagerness gave her beauty a striking glow. Robert glanced at Folie and saw her dismay.

''Ha! They do if their mother can recover the headache. I'll be jiggered if I'll take 'em on my own, though she's threatened to task me with it!''

''Perhaps we will see you there!'' Melinda said.

''Do you go too, then?'' Sir Howard looked toward Folie with an interest Robert found all too transparent.

Folie opened her mouth as if she would answer, fixed her gaze on the base of the silver candlestick before her, then gave Sir Howard a look that seemed to Robert full of entreaty.

''No,'' Robert said coldly. ''They do not go to town. Mrs. Hamilton and Miss Melinda will be living here.''

Melinda's radiance froze. She turned a white face to Folie. ''Mama . . .''

''We will discuss it later,'' Folie said, lifting her hand as if to brush away an uninteresting subject.

Melinda sat up very straight in her chair. ''We are not to go to town?''

''Later, my dear,'' Folie said, but there was an uneasy note in her voice—Robert saw the girl fasten on it, saw how the blood mounted dangerously in her face.

''Tell me now,'' Melinda said. As her back stiffened, her

voice took on a piercing note that was all too familiar. "Are we to go or not?"

"Melinda—" Folie's voice faded.

"We are not!" Melinda's eyes grew wide and wild as Folie hesitated. "We are not to go!"

"Now, my love—"

"I do not believe it!" Melinda gasped. She pushed her chair back from the table. "I cannot—you have let him convince you, haven't you?"

"We will discuss it later," Folie said firmly.

"Discuss what? Discuss that we are not to go?"

Folie tilted her head meaningfully toward Sir Howard. But Melinda seemed oblivious.

"Ohhh, I knew it!" her stepdaughter hissed. "You have let him ruin everything! And I know why! For that forty thousand pounds!"

"Melinda!" Folie said sharply, her voice trembling.

"I don't care! I don't care what everyone thinks! It is not fair! It is monstrous! I hate you—"

"It is my decision," Robert said, keeping his voice cold and steady. "Not your mother's."

Melinda turned on him with a look in her eyes that he knew too well, that touched a well of dread deep inside him. "*You!*" she cried. "Why should you have anything to say to it? Where have you been? Away off in India, living in a palace! You don't care what happens to me! You don't care for anyone but yourself—" She stood up, flinging her hand wide. Her fingers hit her wineglass. It shattered like an explosion as it struck the candelabra, spilling a wave of red across the cloth, glass fragments flying in all directions.

Robert found himself on his feet. He felt a sting on his hand, but his body seemed to slow down, immovable. His hands froze in fists.

"*There!*" the girl cried, "There! I don't care! See what you've made me do! Oh, I hate you all!" Her shrill voice broke into a sob.

"Melinda!" Folie pleaded. "Sit down!"

"I won't!" Melinda held the back of the chair and

banged it against the floor. ''I hate you, I hate you!'' She glared at Robert with a furious venom, filling the room with wooden thumps. ''I don't want your horrid money! I hate you, I hate you, I hate you all! Oh, I want to die!'' she wailed. ''I'm going to—''

''*That* will do, miss!''

It was Sir Howard's deep voice, filling the room like a resonant bell, startling everyone silent.

Melinda looked at him, holding the chair poised. Then she gave a choked sob. The mask of rage seemed to collapse and turn to a child's tragic plea. ''Oh,'' she whimpered. ''Oh. But we aren't to go.''

''Curtsy to your mother and Mr. Cambourne and beg their pardon,'' Sir Howard commanded in a tone that brooked no disobedience. ''And sit down.''

Melinda blinked rapidly, her mouth in a pinched bow. Then suddenly the pinch relaxed into a helpless tremor. She bowed her head, weeping, but more calmly.

''Make your apologies,'' Sir Howard said.

''Yes, sir.'' Melinda bit her lower lip. She started to move toward Robert. He felt struck into stone. He could barely breathe and hardly see her; it took all of his focus simply to contain the flinch when she came close enough to touch him. Through Phillippa's silent clamor in his head he heard Melinda make her apology as if she were speaking through a thick blanket.

He said nothing in reply. Speech was beyond him.

She moved away, curtsied to her mother. As she tried to beg pardon, falling into a deep curtsy, her voice caught on uncontrollable sobs. Folie shook her head mutely and drew Melinda to her feet, pulling her into a deep hug.

''I'm sorry, I'm so sorry, Mama,'' Melinda moaned. ''I didn't mean it.''

''Never mind,'' Folie murmured, stroking her hair. ''Never mind. It will be all right. I promise. It will be all right, darling.'' Over her stepdaughter's head, she looked at Robert. Her eyes glistened with tears, but there was pure rancor in them for him.

He stood numbly. Some distant part of his reason told

him to speak, to say she might go, that he did not mean to keep her incarcerated here with him. But he saw that she would go and not return, go out where he could not reach her, to London, to life, to sanity. He could not bear it; he could not even bear a girl's tantrum. He felt as if he might shatter into a thousand shards of bleeding glass.

"I must go," he said beneath his breath, and walked blindly past her to the door.

Folie did not think he had even seen them as he left, or felt the bloody cut on his hand. She drew a deep, shaky breath. With a soft push, she set her stepdaughter away from her. "Sir Howard—"

"Do not say it!" he exclaimed roughly, shoving to his feet. He shook his head at Melinda. "Good God. I daresay you are hardly old enough to leave the schoolroom, miss, far less disport yourself in London, if this is how you intend to go on!"

"Oh no, oh no," Melinda said in meek rush. "I beg your pardon, Sir Howard! Truly! I am abominable."

"That you are! If you was my girl, you would go to bed on bread and water!"

Folie started to protest, but Melinda shook her head vigorously. "No, Mama—I—I should. I could not eat, not now. Please—if you would just go up with me . . ."

For the first time, Folie realized that Lander had come into the room. He stood attentively by the side door, his face expressionless.

"Take the child up while the table is set to rights," Sir Howard said.

"I don't know if Mr. Cambourne will return—" Folie began, but he cut her off with a significant look. Folie was too flustered to keep her mind straight; she kept seeing Robert Cambourne's white frozen countenance in the face of Melinda's histrionics, and the blood that dripped unacknowledged from his hand.

"Yes, of course," she said in a confused voice. "You'll accept my excuses, Sir Howard."

Melinda gave a curtsy, bidding Sir Howard a humble

good night and begging his pardon again and again. He nodded impatiently, apparently unmoved by her pretty, tear-stained face. As Folie passed him, following Melinda from the dining room, he leaned toward her and touched her arm.

"You will come back down," he murmured. "I wish to speak to you."

Folie nodded blindly.

"Good. I shall await you in the drawing room."

"My dear." Sir Howard closed the drawing room door as Folie entered. She had left Melinda in Sally's tender care, swearing upon her heart that it would all be fixed tomorrow. "I have no right to advise you," Sir Howard said, "but I cannot deny I am deeply concerned at what I saw here tonight."

She drew an unsteady breath. He reminded her so much of Charles that she could hardly recall that she had only met him an hour ago. "I should be glad of advice. I am in desperate need of it."

"What is the situation, my dear?" he asked warmly.

"He is my trustee and Miss Melinda's guardian," she said. "He insists that we live here, and is adamant that Melinda will not go to London, though we have planned a season for her for years. As you saw. I know not why."

Sir Howard frowned. "He strikes me as a strange fellow. Refused all my calls until this very afternoon, when he up and invites us to dinner. Ha!" He shook his head. "I wish I knew more of him. How long have you been here?"

"A week, no more."

"You had made his acquaintance before you came?"

Folie pressed her hands together. "No. Not in person. We have had . . . some correspondence."

"You will forgive my impertinence—he makes no reasonable explanation of why you must stay here? That the chit is too untamed? That lack of funds requires it?"

"Neither is the case, I do assure you! Our funds have been perfectly adequate to our needs for the past five years, and I have already put back enough for a modest season.

And Miss Melinda . . .'' Folie made a helpless shrug. ''I have not seen her have the hysterics since she was a child. She is most well-behaved and gentle-mannered, though I do not ask you to believe me after such a scene.''

He waved his hand. ''Oh, I am accustomed to girls. They are easy broke to bridle, but the meekest will buck if you put a sufficient burr under her saddle. And I daresay that to deny a chit her day in London qualifies as such. Though if I were you I would not let it pass unpunished, or she will be spoilt in a trice.''

Folie lowered her head in deference, though she had no intention of castigating Melinda further.

''You tell me you had made plans for town already?''

''Oh, yes—we were to go up on the first of March, but I was not quite satisfied with the house we had obtained. I understood from a neighbor more experienced than I that it is in an inferior street. I confess, I had entertained a little hope that Mr. Cambourne might lend us the use of his town house, but . . .'' She trailed off.

''Ah!'' He gave her a smile. ''I see now why you are here.''

''He is Miss Melinda's guardian,'' she said, with a faint defensive lift of her palm.

''You need not blush! Dear God, when I think of how I have beseeched the man for the favor of a mere morning call! It sickens me. But it is the way of the world, my dear. I do not fault you for doing whatever you can for Miss Melinda.''

''Well, it has been a complete disaster. I should have predicted!''

''Predicted? How could you predict such strange conduct? I do not like you staying here without an older companion.''

''Yes, I have thought the same,'' she said unhappily. ''I was under the misconception that his wife was still living, and would be here. But—he is Melinda's guardian, and I am a widow of respectable age myself, you know.''

''A respectable widow!'' he exclaimed with a grin. ''What talk. As if you are not barely beyond the schoolroom yourself. A respectable widow. Ha!'' He shook his head. ''No, I tell you, Mrs. Hamilton, I do not like you being here alone with him. I believe he may be a little unsteady.''

''Oh! I am so frightened that is the case! I fear he is mad.''

''Mad?'' Sir Howard drew back his chin in surprise. ''Well . . .''

''Oh, I should not have said that,'' Folie said quickly. ''It is nonsensical.''

He rubbed his jaw. ''No . . . no . . . I understand what you mean. There is something about him that disturbs . . .''

Folie turned away guiltily, fixing her attention on a tabletop. The yellow rosebud lay there. He had remembered. Her own Robert.

She turned back, lifting her chin. ''I must go back up and see to Melinda. I should like to call upon Lady Dingley tomorrow, if she is well enough.''

''I hope you will, my dear. I assure you that she will be well enough to receive *you!''* His tone said that she would be well enough or be the sorrier for it, which made Folie smile a little. ''Now I shall bid you goodnight. It would seem that our host does not intend to reappear. Will you be quite all right?''

''Oh yes,'' Folie said, picking up her candle. ''I'll have Lander light me upstairs.''

Sir Howard made a bow over her hand and gave her a wink. ''I am charmed to meet you, Mrs. Hamilton. And in such intriguing circumstances!''

Folie smiled and made a little curtsy. ''It is my pleasure, sir.''

He turned smartly and left her. Folie stood looking at the door after it closed behind him, feeling slightly giddy at the attention, her cheeks burning. She was not used to the compliments of gentlemen, that was all.

Six

"I ORDERED THE carriage nigh a half hour ago," Folie said in surprise, as she and Melinda stood in the front hall, dressed in hat and gloves for their call on Lady Dingley.

The footman bowed and said unhappily, "I was told, ma'am, that they are charged in the stable not to bring the carriage to you."

"Not to bring it?"

"Aye, madam. I do fully beg your pardon, ma'am."

"We are not to use the carriage?"

"No, madam."

Folie drew in a sharp breath. "Indeed! Then you will give me the direction to Dingley Court. We shall walk."

He looked uneasy. "Ma'am. I'm sure I don't know, ma'am. Perhaps the gatekeeper may tell you."

"Come, Melinda," Folie said, and swept out the door.

The morning was foggy and chill, and neither of them had worn pattens to keep their shoes free of the dew, but Melinda did not utter a word of protest. Both of them walked quickly. Folie felt as if each step was a jab at Robert Cambourne's throat. She barely saw the nodding branches, and did not even stop to look after the rabbit that darted across the drive.

She was breathing rapidly by the time the gatehouse

came into view. The wrought-iron gates were closed, a pair of dragons united at the peak. Folie strode to the green door of the gatehouse and rapped hard with the knocker.

A servant answered, one of the burly sort that Robert Cambourne seemed to favor. He pulled his short forelock and gave his apologies as the footman had done; he was not to open the gate for them.

"What?" Folie frowned at him. "This cannot be true!"

The gatekeeper stood with his head bowed, silent.

"We are not held in hostage here!" she cried. "I will not believe this for a moment!"

"The master's orders, ma'am," the gatekeeper said, crushing his hat in his hands. "There was nothing about hostage said, only that I was not to open the gate for you. I'm sorry, ma'am."

Folie felt a wave of panic. She had not, until this moment, really allowed the truth of the situation to reach her. And Melinda was standing silent, her face pale, the cheerful yellow ribbon on her bonnet drooping in the damp. Her mouth made an anxious bow, trembling a little at the corners. She stared in wide-eyed question at Folie.

Folie looked back at her stepdaughter. Her heartbeat doubled with anger and mortification. She felt her jaw lock. She turned without a word and began to walk with strong strides back toward the house, her mind boiling with the words she had for him. No, she would not even *speak* to him; they would pack their things and quit this place if they had to climb the wall in their slippers to do it.

Robert had known it the moment she left the house. He stood by the window of his dressing room, watching her walk with her stepdaughter down the drive. She went away with a soldier's stride, as if there were fifes and drums playing; as if she meant to put miles behind her before the march was over.

His hands pressed hard on the windowsill. A shout clenched in his throat. If he moved one inch of his body, if he even took a breath, he would begin to howl with despair. The room and house would fly apart around him and he would rip anything within his reach to bloody shreds. Even her.

Especially her.

She was leaving him, and he could not go after her. He felt like a trapped animal, faced with the choice of dying in the snare or escaping by chewing off his leg.

This was Phillippa's doing. Long ago he had retreated into a bunker to evade her, closed down the hatches, bolted the doors, for fear that he would lose his reason, lose himself completely. And that was something he had known he must guard against with all the strength he could muster. He had lost his career for it. He had lost his future and forfeited his friends.

And now Folly. Folly, Folly, Folly.

He watched her figure vanish among the dark trees at a curve in the drive.

Why should you have her? Phillippa's voice said. *Why should you have her when you wouldn't have me?*

''Quiet,'' he muttered. ''Be quiet.''

She wouldn't take you anyway. She's going, leaving as fast as she can. Even a plain little mouse like that won't have you.

Robert made a low noise in his throat, staring at the empty grounds.

What is wrong with you? she whispered. *You paltry bore, always on about your hideous natives and your ugly dog; Good God, it's no wonder I couldn't bear it.*

''Shut up,'' he said savagely.

I can't bear it, I can't bear it! Her scream rose like a wraith's cry in his ears. It echoed in the halls. He could see her fingers clenched thin; red and white against the pale muslin gown she wore. Red and white marks on his cheek in the looking glass.

He held himself stiff. That maddened her; the colder he made himself, the more hysterical she became. The arch of her screams rose; she danced furiously, stamping her slippers like a child. *You never think of me! You never think of me! I hate you! Why can't you think of me?*

Long ago he had tried to reach out to her, to tell her that

he thought of her, that he loved her. He had lived his life trying to foresee what she would want, trying to give it to her before she asked, a daily scramble to anticipate her mood—money, dresses, compliments, parties; he had begged for funds from his father; he would have stolen the jewels from the sultan's turban—anything to stop her from weeping until she could not find breath. But it had not been enough.

Never enough. There was never enough for her. He could not make her happy. He could not stop her from hating him for it. He froze himself, congealed to ice, retreating to whatever safety he could make in his mind. He let her shriek and cry and smash what was in her reach; he managed to lose himself in the bazaars and his notes, and often enough even lose his patrol, too. So his father had disavowed him and John Company had removed him from any responsible office, which only drove her fury at his failures to a new height.

But he had not cared, not by then. By then he had Folly. His Folly, the simple voice of reason and friendship. He had clung to her letters like a man drowning, loved her so that sometimes he slept at his desk with them beneath his hand, as if somehow he shared a physical bed with her that way. With his cheek pressed against the hard wood he dreamed hot ecstatic dreams of her body. From the *guuruus* he had learned an eroticism that consumed his mind with all the ways he could love her and please her. When Phillippa demanded why he never touched her, he looked through her and saw Folly, kissed Folly, lost himself inside her soft welcome.

Her! Phillippa hissed. *That common little tramp, homely as a goosegirl. And married, too! I dare swear she's the village trollop, carrying on with any man who'll give her a second glance.*

Robert's lip curled. "Oh, Phillippa," he murmured. "And you must know how that is."

The instant he allowed the thought to become words he regretted rising to her bait. She swelled with zealous eager wrath. *That was your fault!* she cried. *If you had loved me;*

if you were a better man. I could not live without love. Why should I be lonely, why? You left me alone. You loved me once and then you left me alone. It's your fault, you selfish little man. Go after your strumpet. Leave me, leave me; I can have any man I want.

He stood in a marbled ballroom in the stifling heat, leaning on a column while she danced with Harrington and Storey and Mayer, the easy vivacious beauty she had once been with Robert. Still was, with anyone else, anyone but him. He stood there when she vanished; he did not move or look to see what officer was missing. He counted one hour before he left.

Don't touch me! Her voice was like a spitting cat's when he opened the front door to her at three in the morning, having sent the servants to bed. *Don't touch me; I hate it, I hate it when you touch me.*

Robert found himself at the foot of the stairs. The carved beasts of Solinger regarded him silently.

Slowly, he became aware that his butler was standing near the front door. They looked at one another. Lander made his bow that somehow always seemed to carry a faint air of disdain.

''Call the carriage,'' Robert said.

''Yes, sir.'' Lander turned immediately, leaving him alone in the hall.

Robert gripped the head of the carved brute that coiled around the banister. Already he could feel his heartbeat rising. The very thought of going out there, of the huge sky above him and the wide lawns, brought a sweat to his palms and his chest. It was the worst of it all, this panic fear of the open. It stripped him of any claim to manhood; he was barely even human in its grip. When Lander returned to tell him that the carriage waited, Robert could only stand like some imprisoned maniac, held by invisible bars that seemed to press until they crushed his breath inside him.

''I do not need it,'' he managed to say. ''I do not need it after all.''

Lander no longer even looked surprised at such peculiarities. He bowed and walked back to the front door. Robert did not wait for him to open it; he turned and mounted the stairs in a desperate hunt for a place of safety, a place he knew he could not find.

Folie was walking so fast that she could hear nothing but her heart and her own breath between her teeth. Her feet flung her sodden hem; it trailed and tugged at her ankles. She yanked it free every third step, clenching her skirt in her fists.

The carriage was almost upon her before she even knew it was there. With a clatter of harness and wheels, the horses loomed suddenly in the drive, a pair of blood-red bays, their black hooves and legs splattered with mud. Folie took a hasty step to the side, panting with exertion, and stared up as the vehicle creaked to a stop.

The door opened. Folie's shoulders drew straight and stiff with hostility. She expected Robert Cambourne—but it was Lander who stepped lightly down from the carriage.

''Here is your conveyance, ma'am,'' he said. He did not look directly at her, but held the door with blank courtesy. ''I will accompany you to Dingley Court.''

There was no explanation, no excuse for the delay. The horses stood nodding. Their bits chimed. Folie tried to govern the uneven clouds of her breath.

After a long moment, she looked around for Melinda and nodded. The two of them climbed into the carriage, aided by Lander. They were hardly fit to be seen in public, damp and bedraggled, but Folie had no intention of turning this opening aside.

They sat facing the front, while Lander climbed up beside the driver. Folie said nothing to Melinda; she did not think she could speak without her voice shaking. The carriage lurched forward, moving slowly, too ponderous for a pair—it should have had four horses put to. But Folie was glad for any number. She heard Lander speak to the gatekeeper, the muffled words and the gatekeeper's uncertain reply. From the corner of her eye, she saw Melinda's hands squeeze tightly together, and realized that her own were clamped so hard that they hurt.

At the clang of the gate latch, both of them exhaled as if they had been holding their breath. Folie tucked a stray lock behind her ear as the carriage rolled through. She smiled bravely at Melinda. ''What a pack of servants he keeps!'' she said brightly. ''I daresay it was all some stupid blunder from the start.''

''Yes, I daresay,'' Melinda said. She leaned over, looking down at her wet shoes. ''I shall be chagrined to call on Lady Dingley in such a state.''

''Do you wish to return and change?'' Folie asked.

''Oh, no!'' Melinda sat up straight. ''No, I think not.''

They had made one another as presentable as possible by the time they had reached Dingley Court. It was a house of the antique mongrel variety, anchored at one end by a tower with medieval slotted windows, and at the other by a matching addition that revealed its modernity in the fresh-cut stone and gleaming glass windows. In between, a sequence of additions appeared to mark a regular building impulse across the centuries, but somehow the whole had been appended in a pleasingly balanced manner. A swarm of young girls and dogs, all yelping equally with excitement, dropped their sticks and balls and came running down a lane of blossoming fruit trees to meet the carriage.

Folie felt a wry gratification at the girls' bedraggled presentation, as if it somehow made their own disarray less impossibly obvious. One of the children pulled open the door even before a footman could descend.

''The Hamiltons!'' she cried, her round face flushed with exercise and pleasure. ''Tell us it's so!''

Folie smiled in spite of herself. ''No, I am afraid I am the Princess Caroline, and this is my favorite lapdog.''

''Mama!'' Melinda protested calmly. ''Yes, we are the Hamiltons; I am Melinda, and this my dear mama.''

The girls stood back, laughing and smirking and pushing one another, as Lander held the door. Folie and Melinda stepped down to the graveled drive.

''Papa, they are arrived!'' one of the girls cried. Folie looked up from her muddy hem to see Sir Howard emerging from the door beside the great stained glass window that marked the hall.

''What luck you've come now!'' He strode to greet them. ''Lady Dingley is just set to try out the new pianoforte. Do you play, Mrs. Hamilton?''

''Indifferently, I assure you! But we shall be delighted to hear it.''

''I daresay Miss Melinda will perform for us,'' he said, with an engaging grin and a wink at her. ''Come in, come in, and welcome.''

In a motley procession, they entered the house, girls and dogs rushing ahead of them like a gay school of darting fish. Inside, a dim timber-framed passage led into a great hall, a surprise of flooding light across a huge trestle table. Sir Howard ushered them past the tall leaded windows, their simple panes adorned only with three rows of armorial bearings in stained glass, the dark chairs covered with worn red cushions. After the frenzied ornamentation at Solinger Abbey, the plain, shabby English style was a relief. Folie felt her anxiety begin to dissolve.

A toddler burst through the door at the end of the hall, crying and running headlong in her white pinafore into her father's legs. He swung her up and deposited her in the arms of a nursemaid who hurried past, barely pausing to curtsy. The child's screams rose to a crescendo, and then died away as the pair vanished up a flight of stairs.

Sir Howard opened the door. ''The Hamiltons to see you, my dear,'' he announced.

It was as if they walked from one century to another as they crossed the threshold from the Elizabethan hall to a pretty, apple-green room with delicate plaster ceilings picked out in white and cream. Tall damask drapes adorned the windows; a golden bird cage looked out upon the garden. A slim lady sat at the new pianoforte, picking at a note. She picked at it one more time without turning to them, and then slid off the bench.

She touched her raven hair, though it was tucked perfectly under her cap, and did not look at her husband. ''How do you do? Mrs. Hamilton? I am Isabelle Dingley.''

Folie introduced Melinda. They all sat down in elegant chairs while Sir Howard reached for the bell. His wife was one of those ladies whose regular features could not be faulted, but could not be called remarkable. She had a vague air about her, as if her mind were on some grave problem elsewhere.

"What charming girls you have," Folie said, hoping to draw her more to the present. "Full of fun!"

A slight, wry smile touched Lady Dingley's lips. "Oh, yes, full of fun."

"Where are Jane and Cynth?" Sir Howard demanded. "They must meet Miss Melinda."

"Riding," Lady Dingley said with a hopeless shrug. "I had hoped they might take an interest . . ." She waved uncertainly toward the instrument and then fell silent.

"I knew t'would be a waste of money," Sir Howard said. "But you must have the thing!"

"They ought to learn to play," Lady Dingley said faintly.

"Our girls?" Sir Howard snorted. "Who is to teach them, pray?"

"I was used to play." Lady Dingley looked out the window as she spoke.

"Yes, I remember." He gave a short nod. "Lovely it was, too. But you were a girl yourself then." He turned a warm smile on Folie and Melinda. "Perhaps Miss Melinda will play for us, and show 'em the way!"

"Oh, no," Melinda said modestly. "I only know what I was taught at school."

"At school! Well, then, you are far in the lead! Come, you must." He reached for her hand, so that she had no choice but to rise. She glanced uncertainly at Folie.

Folie gave a faint nod, seeing no alternative. Melinda played beautifully, as she did everything well, but this did not seem the best time to exhibit her talent. Sir Howard was adamant, however, and seated her at the instrument with a gallant flourish.

Melinda closed her eyes for a moment, and when she placed her fingers on the keyboard, Folie noticed that they were not quite steady. Several of the early notes of the Scarlatti sonata went awry, but then the sprightly tune started to carry itself. Folie thought it a wonder Melinda could play at all with her nerves strung so tight.

The notes filled the room, enlivening the little chaffinch in the cage. It fluttered from its perch to the bars and back again as Melinda's playing gained spirit. The prelude flowed into a bright arpeggio. Her head nodded softly in time to the animation of her fingers. Folie smiled; she loved to watch Melinda play. For herself, she could pick out a simple country dance or two that her governess had drummed into her, but had never had the patience or discipline to master the rilling keyboard cascades herself; her fingers stumbled over one another as if they were frantic farmboys all trying at once to throw water on a burning haystack.

Folie glanced at Sir Howard. His attention was entirely engaged on Melinda; his foot tapped slightly in time as he gazed at her. Lady Dingley was still staring out the window.

Folie's smile faded. There had been days of marriage that she had stared out of her own window, perhaps with the same unblinking aspect, as if looking at someplace or something far beyond the birdcage and the garden. Was it impossible to hope that Melinda would not know it too, that sense of living alone even in the midst of a household? Or worse, that she would take that furious ride to the heights of infatuation and suffer the same unhappy fall that Folie had endured?

There were times, looking back, that Folie wondered how she had lived through it. Hiding in the greenhouse, where Charles' roses had gone to a thorny tangle; sitting on the bench and weeping until she thought she had no more tears left. Weeping for a dream. How a dream could take such a hold on her spirit that she grieved for it as if for a real man, she had never fathomed. Even still, after all the shocks of disillusionment, it seemed as if Robert, her own loving Robert, was alive somewhere, such was the grip that mirage had upon her brain. But everything this Robert

Cambourne of Solinger had done was a jarring contradiction, a shattering of the delusion; a solid proof that she had misjudged and misinterpreted and fallen in love with a chimera of her own making. No sweet lover, but a petty selfish oddity, determined to imprison them and deprive Melinda, to have his own cold way at any cost to those under his care.

How Folie hated him! He had no heart, he had no character; he did not even have a sense of humor. If he had been anyone else, she would have been dismayed and bewildered enough, but that he was *Robert*—Robert who had written that he loved her . . . who had lured her to give her love to him, asked her not to forbid him to write to her, taken her in like the silly openhearted country miss she was! Never again would she succumb to false hopes and fantasies. She would live alone till the day she died to avoid it.

The tune came to an end as Folie was contemplating the many advantages of becoming a nun. A lusty applause broke the silence after the last note—Sir Howard clapping loudly, Lady Dingley patting her hands together. As Folie turned, she saw two girls of Melinda's age standing beside the door clapping as enthusiastically as their father.

"Come in, come in," Sir Howard said, motioning. "Mrs. Hamilton—Miss Jane Dingley and Miss Cynthia, my oldest pair."

As a maid left a tea urn, bundled their red cloaks over her arm, and vanished out the door, Miss Jane and Miss Cynthia came forward and dropped curtsies to Folie. They brought a scent of horse with them in the full navy blue skirts of their riding habits. Miss Jane, the eldest, returned Folie's smile with an engaging grin that might have been her father's own. Miss Cynthia glanced at her older sister and then gave a smile that was more subdued, but still sweet. "What a pretty tune!" she said, turning to Melinda as she rose from the instrument.

"Let these girls get acquainted among themselves!" Sir Howard said, drowning Melinda's thank you. "Off with you; there's a fire in the back hall."

''Oh, Papa, we cannot take her there—'' Miss Jane began to protest, but her father only shook his head.

''Your know your mother doesn't like you in all your dirt. Off, before you give us all the headache! Miss Melinda, you do not mind.''

''Not at all, I—'' Melinda began a polite assent as Miss Jane took her arm. Miss Cynthia fell in behind. The three of them went out the drawing room door, already employed in friendly questions before they disappeared.

''There!'' Sir Howard sat down. ''Mrs. Hamilton, will you do us the honor of pouring?''

Folie filled saucers of tea from the urn. Lady Dingley accepted hers with an indistinct murmur. Sir Howard took his cup in a strong, well-shaped hand, smiling up at her.

''How did you leave things at Solinger?'' he asked as Folie sat down with her tea. His tone was merely polite, but he looked at her keenly as he spoke.

Folie took a brief sip to clear her voice. ''Much as last night,'' she said uncomfortably. ''You must pardon our bedraggled appearance, Lady Dingley. There was some confusion about the carriage at first, and we set out to walk before we knew how far it would be.''

''Confusion?'' Sir Howard asked quickly.

Folie hesitated. He set down his cup and leaned forward in his chair.

''You need not scruple to be frank, ma'am,'' he said. ''Lady Dingley and I would stand as friends to you, if you will allow us. Not one word will leave this room; I sent the girls away with that thought.'' He turned to his wife. ''I'm sure you agree, my dear.''

''Yes, of course I agree,'' Lady Dingley said, stirring her cup.

''Well, I—'' Folie hesitated between embarrassment and the desperate desire to lay her troubles and fears on someone's shoulders.

''There was confusion about the carriage?'' Sir Howard prompted. ''I dare say it was hardly a morning to set out to walk five miles.''

''No,'' Folie said. She took another sip, stared down at

her cup a moment, and then said in a low voice, "The servants were informed we were forbidden to use the carriage, or even to leave the grounds." She looked up quickly. "But perhaps it was all a simple misunderstanding. Lander came at last with the carriage, and accompanied us. He is here now."

Sir Howard nodded. "So I saw."

A silence descended. The songbird made a small whistle and rustled in the cage.

"I think," Folie said slowly, with a sense of unreality as she spoke, "that we ought not to return to Solinger."

She found herself staring at Sir Howard, as if she had never seen him sitting there before that moment. She could hardly believe she had uttered such a thing, and yet she knew with a blinding certainty that she could not put Melinda and herself into the carriage and allow the gates of Solinger to close behind them again.

"I don't know what we shall do!" she exclaimed.

Sir Howard stood up. He nodded briefly, as if she had opened an important matter of business that he had expected. Lady Dingley put down her saucer and watched her husband with unblinking eyes, an expression of impartial expectation.

"Of course your things are still there; your clothing and so forth."

"Yes," Folie said. Her voice seemed to come out without any breath behind it.

"You must stay with us tonight." Sir Howard turned toward the fireplace and yanked the tasseled bell rope. "Lander can return for your things."

"Oh, no—we should not impose—that is beyond anything we can ask of you." She glanced at Lady Dingley. "I'm sure there is an inn—"

"Nonsense," Sir Howard said. "It is no imposition, my dear." He leaned out the door to speak to the servant who answered his ring.

"It is beyond kind of you, but surely, ma'am," Folie said to his wife, "you have not been feeling well. We had only wished to call briefly, not throw ourselves upon you! If we could be directed to an inn—''

''And how are you to pay for this inn?'' Sir Howard demanded, closing the door. ''You must pardon my plain speaking, but I doubt that you brought a full purse along on a morning call?''

That was entirely true; what money Folie had was still at Solinger, but before she could discover a reply amid the confusion and indecision in her mind, there was another scratch at the door. Lander entered and bowed.

''The ladies will not be returning to Solinger,'' Sir Howard announced. ''They desire that their things be packed and brought here.''

Lander looked toward Folie. His expression registered neither surprise nor dismay, only a quiet vigilance. She had never known quite what to make of him; too young to have charge of a large house, with more the aspect of some untamed gambling buck than a butler. With his long natural queue and muscular shoulders, he appeared perfectly capable of manhandling anyone who objected to his intentions.

''Ma'am?'' he asked.

''Yes,'' she said. ''I think we must . . . depart Solinger today.''

''As you wish, madam,'' he said calmly.

''I'll send one of our men and a maid back with you; they can bring the baggage here in our gig,'' Sir Howard said.

Lander made a brief bow, but kept his gaze fixed resolutely upon Folie. ''This is permissible, ma'am? I will be pleased to return with it myself if you prefer, or make any arrangement you wish for your accommodation.''

Folie felt herself blushing. ''You must be sure to—'' She stopped, and then glanced at Sir Howard. ''If you will forgive me for a moment?''

''Certainly!'' Sir Howard said on the instant. He offered his hand to his wife. ''Come, my dear, you should see to having the chambers made ready.''

"Indeed, yes." Lady Dingley rose, smiling, but seemed almost to sigh inaudibly at the same time.

"You are too kind," Folie said, "to take in a pair of strangers at no notice."

"Oh, it is you who favor us, Mrs. Hamilton. I am so pleased for the girls to make your daughter's acquaintance."

She did not linger to expand upon this statement, which surprised Folie, as Lady Dingley had not seemed to take to Melinda at all. But she had no time to contemplate that, for Lander stood awaiting her instructions.

"I do not quite know how Mr. Cambourne will receive this," she said hesitantly.

"Nor I, madam," Lander said.

"Perhaps I should write a note," she said.

He nodded slightly.

Folie looked about her, and sat down at the portable writing desk atop a table. She helped herself to the pen and paper inside—if she was to be so beholden to the Dingleys, what was a sheet of parchment?

Dear Mr. Cambourne, she wrote, and then found herself at a complete stand.

Dear Mr. Cambourne, your pigeons have flown. Dear Mr. Cambourne, I have had enough of your nonsense. Dear Mr. Cambourne, you are as mad as May-butter, so I fear we must take our leave . . .

She sighed. Here, away from the strange heated carvings and dark halls, it all seemed quite fatuous and unreal. And yet when she thought of entering the carriage again, she knew that she could not.

Seven

Dear Mr. Cambourne,

We must take our leave of you. Hereafter, it will be convenient to maintain our necessary correspondence through Mssrs. Hawkridge and James.

With respect,
Folie Hamilton

Lander was laughing, Robert thought, though the man's face was austere. God knew, he would have laughed at himself; such an impotent fool he must appear. Robert crushed the note and tossed it into the fireplace under Philippa's looming portrait. "Where are they?"

"Lady Dingley has invited Mrs. Hamilton and her stepdaughter to stay at Dingley Court."

"You took them there."

Lander did not reply.

"Damn your insolence," Robert muttered. He stared at the portrait. "I suppose . . ." He stopped, and then said with a bitter chuckle, "She is greatly relieved, doubtless. To escape my evil snare."

"She said no such thing, sir."

Robert gave him a satirical look. ''She was in love with me once. Can you imagine that?'' He lifted his face toward the ceiling. ''Oh, God. Are you poisoning me, Lander?'' He laughed, shaking his head. ''Come, tell me that you are, and this is not really madness.''

Alarm rose in him as he spoke, for the peril of saying such words. He turned quickly toward his butler. ''I jest, of course!'' Robert said. ''Indian humor.''

Lander's gravity changed to attention. ''Poison, sir?'' he asked, without shock or bewilderment. ''You hired me for your safekeeping, Mr. Cambourne. If you have some suspicion of poison, I hope you will speak plainly of it.''

Robert tightened his jaw. He focused fiercely on the gilded frame, avoided Phillippa's face looking gaily down on him. He did not trust Lander. He could not bring himself to trust the man.

''I beg your pardon, sir.'' The faintest trace of impatience touched Lander's words. ''How am I to provide the guard you desired if you will not confide in me?''

''Guard!'' Robert snapped. ''After I ordered you to prevent their leaving the grounds, you kindly provide a personal escort as they go!''

''Dismiss me for it if you will, sir,'' Lander said grimly. ''I will provide you with all the protections I am capable of rendering, as you engaged me to do, but I cannot participate in incarcerating ladies here against their will.''

''Fine words! And if you have put them into danger?''

''What danger?'' Lander's voice rose. ''Tell me what danger!''

The edge in his voice matched Robert's, hardly the tone of a servant to his master. Robert turned sharply, staring at him.

''Begging your pardon, sir.'' Lander lowered his eyes, but there was still a doggedness about the set of his shoulders.

''I suppose if I hire a thief-taker out of Bow Street for a butler, I should not be astonished at his cheek,'' Robert said.

''I beg your pardon, sir,'' Lander repeated.

"I do not know precisely what danger. I have told you all that I know."

Lander gave him a clear-eyed look. "If you will give me leave to speak."

Robert let go of a harsh breath and waved his hand. "Speak."

"If you suspect poison in the house, even the slightest chance—surely the ladies are not safe here."

Robert smiled sardonically. "And less so if it is not poison, eh? If I am only a—" His throat closed on the word *madman*. He did not say it, but it hung in the air.

Lander did not appear to hear the unspoken implication. In a quiet voice he said, "Those of the staff that I installed here I trust, but I cannot say with certainty that the others are beyond doubt. The cook and the charwomen are mine, though, and I see to it that I bring your meals myself." He frowned. "You eat and drink next to nothing. With respect, sir—you will kill your own self that way, poison or no." He paused, and then said, "If you have moments of—of confusion in your thoughts . . ." He did not meet Robert's eyes. " 'Haps it is from starving yourself, sir. Begging your pardon."

Aye, Robert thought, *and if 'tis you who taint my food, would you not want to convince me to eat what you bring?*

"What do you suggest?" he asked coolly.

"If you do not trust me, sir," Lander said, "and I see clear enough that you don't, then go into the village and eat there. Buy a loaf, eat at the cookshop. Go alone, at some odd time, so that neither I nor another can touch what you swallow."

"You do not understand," Robert said.

"No sir," Lander said. "I don't, for I don't take you for a fool. I'm sure you have thought of this."

"I cannot go out there." Robert turned away from him. "I cannot go out."

"But who do you fear? What is it?"

"Out *there*," he shouted. He could not turn around to face the butler's silence. He gripped the bedpost, staring at the game of chess that he played endlessly against himself on a bedroom table; black queen and white knights that never won and never lost.

"The outside?" Lander asked slowly. "You are afraid to go outside?"

His clear bewilderment touched Robert at the core. Suddenly, wildly, the shame rose up in him to such a pitch that he could not contain it. He felt himself move; he felt as if his whole body was afire and acting beyond his own will. He seized the chessboard; flung it down. Carved pieces flew across the floor. The black queen smashed against a foot of the bed, bursting into two fragments.

Her headless torso came to rest at his boot. Robert reached down and picked up the broken chess piece. He closed his fingers, crushing the black queen in his hand.

"I am not afraid," he said coldly and deliberately. He looked up at Lander. "Ready a horse."

Lander did not obey. "You intend to go after them?" he asked in a strange, half-angry tone.

"What is it to you?" Robert snarled. "Get me a mount!"

Lander hesitated, standing between Robert and the door, his jaw working as if he would speak.

Robert's hands shook. He felt the sudden red tide of passion receding, leaving him stranded, imprisoned under Philippa's portrait.

You won't go, her voice taunted. *Little man. You're too frightened to go.*

The chess pieces lay scattered across the floor. Robert ran his thumb across the sharp edge of the headless queen in his hand.

He moved, forcing Lander out of his path, striding furiously free into the void that awaited him.

After an awkwardly polite nuncheon with Lady Dingley and her oldest daughters, Sir Howard excused himself to estate business. A maid led Folie and Melinda up to the guest room. The chamber Lady Dingley had prepared for them held the musty, venerable scent of last having been used to accommodate some Royalist cavalier on the business of Charles the First. What weak sunlight that leaked through the leaded glass was soaked up by oak paneling that was shiny and almost black with age; Folie needed a candle just to brush out Melinda's hair. The centerpiece, a monster of a bed with fat, carved posts and faded red and gold damask hangings, appeared to have bowed down the very floorplanks beneath it with ancient dignity.

Without Sally and their own dressing boxes, it was impossible for Folie to set Melinda or herself completely to rights. ''Go and make yourself comfortable with the girls,'' Folie told her, tying her stepdaughter's bonnet in place as well as she might. ''I shall go back down to Lady Dingley in a few moments.''

Melinda flitted away, already buoyant with new friends, the strained smile of Solinger vanished from her expression. But Folie lingered in the guest chamber, nervously smoothing down the fresh linen cloth that the chambermaid had lain across a heavy chest. She wandered the room, looking up at a pair of portraits painted onto panels over the hearth, some bygone master and mistress of Dingley, their faces almost obscured by the film of age. Folie tilted her head, trying to see some likeness to Sir Howard in the gentleman with the pointed beard and wide ruff. She could see none: Sir Howard was too uncompromisingly robust and plain-speaking to have anything in common with his lace-embellished and pearl-bedecked ancestor. It was the lady of the pair who appeared to bear the most resemblance to the present daughters of the house—even beneath the dim gauze of centuries, her square, honest face and searching eyes seemed familiar, looking out with the same frank curiosity that had met Folie and Melinda at the carriage door.

Folie gave the portrait a little fidgety curtsy. ''We are much obliged to you for the hospitality,'' she murmured. Then she turned away, squeezing her hands together, her heart having a troublesome tendency to stick in her throat. ''Oh, you silly noodle—Folie, Folie—why did you ever let us leave Toot?''

Here they were, without money, without belongings, among strangers they had no claim upon—what if the servants returned with nothing? What if he would not give up their possessions, what if he kept her purse? He had threatened as much—why should she expect that servants could wrest from him what he meant to have? All of Melinda's wardrobe and enough of Folie's savings to crush any hopes of even a few weeks in London, left there in her room at Solinger.

She sat down in a massive rocking chair, pushing hard with her feet to move it to and fro. The floor creaked. The ebony wood was slick beneath her damp palms, but she needed the motion and the noise to soothe her. A few more minutes to calm herself, before she went down and faced Lady Dingley again, before she had to conceal her fears and agitations. She had eaten little of the bread and cheese and gingerbread served at nuncheon, and now as the time approached that news could arrive from Solinger, her stomach felt empty and ill with dread.

She stopped rocking, her body paralyzed, when she heard a scratch at the door. "Come," she said faintly.

A maid opened the door halfway. "Mr. Cambourne calls, ma'am," she said calmly. "He requests the honor of your attendance."

"What?" Folie sat up straight.

The maid dropped a curtsy. "Will you honor Mr. Cambourne?" she repeated mildly.

"Mr. Cambourne?" She could hardly squeak the name. "Mr. Cambourne from Solinger?"

The maid nodded, with a little lift of her brows, as if it was a delicious tidbit. "Yes, ma'am!"

Folie shook her head vigorously. "No, I—I am indisposed. I really cannot—" She began rocking powerfully. "If Lady Dingley will make my excuses," she said faintly over the squeak.

The maid looked doubtful. "M'lady said she was certain you would wish to speak to him."

"I cannot." Folie shook her head again. Really, she felt quite ill. "I must lie down."

"Yes, ma'am." The chambermaid withdrew with another curtsy. Folie heard the door latch click. She had a demented idea of locking it, but a quick search of the drawers and tabletops revealed no key.

She went to the window, leaning on the cushion that padded the deep stone seat. She looked out, hoping to see Sir Howard's horse, but all she saw was a stableboy walking a lean chestnut that steamed lightly in the chill. She recognized the mount from daily tours through the half-empty Solinger stables; she and Melinda had fed it lumps of sugar, one of their few diversions there.

She waited, her heart thumping, to see him leave the house in the wake of her refusal. She could not, would not speak to him—but she found that somehow she craved to see him one time . . . oh, one last time. Her throat ached with sudden longing, as if the days she had loved him in dreams had become reality again. As if, as if. It had always been "as if." As if he were hers, as if he were there, as if falling in love was a tangible joy that could last longer than the flash of a salmon in a summer stream, longer than the wisp of breath from the chestnut's muzzle; as if it could be more than this heart's toll of yearning which was all that it had ever truly been.

She bent her head, turning from the window. She must let it go, that dream. How long and hard she had tried to let it go—and in the end she was running away from him, hunted by this alien reality, this intruder on her fantasy, running and running and somehow longing not to go, somehow still hoping she would find that her dream was real.

The door handle turned. Folie whirled at the sound. Lady Dingley stood in the doorway.

"Ah, you are not in bed," she said calmly. "Perhaps it will not tax you too much to see Mr. Cambourne? I've brought him up, since you are not well enough to come down."

There was a faint triumph in her mildness, but Folie hardly noticed it. She caught a glimpse of Robert Cambourne in the passageway, standing stiff and tall behind Lady Dingley. In a rush of mortification, Folie turned away.

There was no escape. She heard him come in; heard the

door close. But she could not look up at him; she simply could not.

Silence stood between them. She took a step away from the window, turning her shoulder to him. The floorboards creaked; from the corner of her eye, she saw that he moved away from her, pointlessly, as if they were two magnets that repelled one another.

''I wished to apologize,'' he said in a low voice, though there was little hint of regret in his harsh tone. ''I should not have attempted to keep you at Solinger against your will.''

''No,'' she said to her dirty slippers. ''That was not well done of you.''

Having nothing to do with her hands, she took up one of the paper candle screws left on the bedside table and turned the scrap tighter and tighter, torquing it about itself until it began to tear in the middle.

''Will you stop Melinda's allowance?'' she asked abruptly, her voice as harsh as his.

''No.''

Folie took a deep breath. She laid the paper screw down and dared a glance at him, but he was not looking at her. With a tentative new courage, she studied him. If he felt any of the confusion or unease that Folie did, he showed nothing of it. He seemed remote, his black eyebrows lifted in that expression of elegant disdain—directed, as far as Folie could tell, at the fire irons. He stood very straight, like a man at a funeral. For an instant he looked up; his eyes grazed past her and settled resolutely on the washstand.

Strangely, she began to feel herself somehow in command of the moment. It was as if now that he was here, he had lost whatever force had brought him. He seemed caught in a cold trance, unable to look at her, wordless.

''Is that why you came after us?'' she asked, moving to the window. She sank down upon the cushioned seat. ''To apologize?''

As if her action released him, he moved again, this time crossing to the bed. Abruptly he sat down upon it. Folie felt as if they were engaged in some peculiar dance, each step of hers matched by one of his, but none taking them anywhere. Still he did not look at her, but seemed intensely engaged in a study of a brass ewer on the chest.

The faded light touched his face, lighting it with a particular softness. The set of his mouth and arch of his brows remained, and yet now what had been inflexible arrogance seemed almost wistful. Sitting on the bed, he did not appear so stiff; he looked down at his hands and shook his head.

She waited. After a long moment, he made an unhappy laugh. ''Folly.'' He shook his head again. ''My sweet Folly.''

She closed her eyes. All the vivid years of his letters and his love seemed to accumulate at the base of her throat, caught hard there. She had never heard them spoken, those words. It sounded so different, so strange, so harsh and rueful; nothing of what she had dreamed.

Suddenly, without any purpose to what she did, she rose and went to him. She sat down beside him on the bed. It felt like a clumsy move, a silly thing to do. But he shifted slightly to accommodate her, as if he had expected it. They sat side by side, not looking at one another. She looked down at his hands, saw the red cut, untended, from the smashed wineglass.

''Oh, well, then,'' Folie said, angrily. She sounded petulant, as if she had given in to some whim of Melinda's. She touched his hand. She barely skimmed the back of his palm, her fingertips tracing the rough line of the cut. ''Your poor hand,'' she whispered. ''I'm sorry.''

He shrugged. ''It's nothing.''

He turned his palm over and opened it. She looked down at the broken chess piece he held, a black queen with the head broken off. ''What is this?'' she murmured.

''Nothing,'' he said. He let it slip into her fingers.

Folie held the damaged piece, feeling the warmth in it. She could feel his body's warmth beside her. It was as close as she had ever been to him; she breathed the familiar scent of his letters, of him. She had no notion of what she was doing or what she wished to happen. But her heart was pounding.

Robert, Robert, she thought. It seemed her mind would revolve on nothing else.

He moved his hand from beneath hers. She thought he would stand up, but instead he brushed his fingers against her throat. Folie made a faint sound of protest, drawing back, but he slid his hand behind her neck, pulling her toward him. His other hand came up and cupped her cheek; he held her chin between strong fingers and kissed her.

She had never been kissed on the mouth before. He tasted of ginger—or she did; she hardly knew. Her hands pushed against his shoulders, but he had a purpose in his movements now; he held her, exploring her mouth, his breath warming her lips, his fingers pressing into her jaw.

She broke away, turning her face. ''I've never done this!'' she whispered in agitation.

''Done what?'' He ran his fingers gently over her cheek, across her mouth, his gaze following his touch.

She moistened her lips, lowering her chin. ''Kissed,'' she said stupidly. She made a sound like a frantic half-laugh. ''Not this way. I don't know how!''

''Yes, you do,'' he murmured urgently, leaning to draw her back, kissing her again. ''Yes, you do.''

He touched her lower lip with his tongue, teased it, and then tasted her whole mouth. *This is Robert,* she thought in wonder—*Robert kissing me, now, now, the first and last time.* She could feel the heat in him catch her, like a fire igniting from a hidden coal beneath the ashes. The air she breathed was Robert. Her body flamed with shame and yearning, but she did not move. She could not, she should not; she did not wish to do this.

Oh, but it was him, really him.

He leaned suddenly very close to her, bent down, his arm sliding under her knees. He scooped her up. In the loss of dominion over her own balance she clung to him, her arms about his shoulders as he lifted her. She sprawled back against the pillows, looking up at him wide-eyed. He leaned over her, on her; she felt his weight, all hesitation lost. And something in her answered, something hot awoke, a deep demented thrill that Charles had never stirred. Her breath came quickly; as Robert pressed her into the bed, her body arched upward, meeting his kiss, his heaviness on her.

He splayed his fingers into her hair, holding her trapped, kissing her jaw and her cheeks and her ear. She arched her head back, and then gave a whimpering gasp as his hand cupped her breast. ''Don't, don't,'' she whispered, but through her muslin gown he circled his thumb, pulled her nipple down against the edge of her stiff corseted petticoat. Folie's eyes opened wide with the sensation. She bit her lower lip, and he ran his tongue across her teeth, nudging and searching, sucking her lip free in a way that made their tongues meet wickedly.

''Folly,'' he said fiercely against her mouth. His hand left her breast, formed her waist under the muslin and corselet. ''Do you know how much I need you?'' He turned his head down, kissing her throat, gripping her skirt and drawing it upward.

All this, all this she had dreamed of in the deep nights lying awake and still at Charles' side, but in reality it was none of the fanciful tender delicacy she had imagined. It was deeper and wilder, as if he took over her very will, as if he knew every part of her, thrusting two fingers inside her and pressing upward into a place that sent white fire to her breasts and her throat. She reached blindly, clutching at his other hand, locking her fingers in his and lifting her arms above her head.

''Yes,'' he breathed into her ear. ''Yes, yes, yes.''

Folie shook her head. Through his clothes she could feel him aroused and ready to take her; the shape of him solid on her bared thigh. Suddenly he rose above her, leaning on his hands, and pressed his clothed body against hers as if he drove himself inside. He looked down at her, moving against her in hot rhythm, urging her over and over to arch upward. She made sounds like a puppy's dreaming moans, half-pleading, half-denying.

She had never in her life felt anything like this. She began to pant with extremity, her modesty, her reason, her whole body beyond her command. Each lift of her hips meeting his made her gasp. He pressed her down and down against the bed. Folie twisted under him, pushing up frantically.

"Folly." He met her, kissed her, urged her with his tempo. "Never leave me. Never leave me. Never leave me."

She gave a low cry, a frenzied shudder. Joy burst and bled through her under his body, washing her with fiery light. She clutched his shoulders, holding onto him as if a wave carried her out to sea and only he could save her.

She gulped for breath as she lay weak beneath him, trembling uncontrollably. She kept her eyes closed; for a long moment she could not open them, full of chagrin and delight, too near to tears. She felt him search out the pins in her hair. He pulled them free, gently fanning it out across the pillow.

She opened her eyes. He was looking down at her, his gray eyes deep and light.

"There," he said. "That's how it would be."

Then he lifted himself away. He stood up. Without speaking or looking back, he left Folie alone in the room.

After he was gone, she turned to her side and lay huddled on the edge of the bed, lost in time, listening to the faint sound of the pianoforte and girlish voices lifted in a merry duet. A dog was barking somewhere in the house. Each sound, each scent, seemed utterly crystalline; a new world.

She put her fingers over her mouth and drew in a deep breath. *Robert,* she thought, smiling against her hand. She shook her head in disbelief.

With a faint terror, she recognized this feeling. This tumult, this deep comfort, this giddy laughter welling up in her throat.

"Oh no," she moaned, rocking a little. "Please no."

But she felt as though her soul had found its home again. And as if she were falling free into a black cavern with no floor. Some lost part of her settled into place; at the same time a high wind tore her apart into a thousand helpless fragments.

Silent tears slid down her cheeks and onto her hand. Oh, she knew this dreadful feeling. She knew it all too well.

She was in love with him again.

Eight

My Dear Mrs. Hamilton,

Upon consideration, I give you my permission to take Miss Melinda to London for a visit of one month in the company of Lady Dingley and her daughters, as per the proposal conveyed to me by Sir Howard. My permission is contingent on several conditions: to wit, that the entire party reside in my house in Curzon Street, the hire of all servants to be under the auspices of Mr. Lander. This excludes the use of Dingley servants, unless approved by him. All outings and parties are to be attended under the escort of Mr. Lander, all transportation arranged by him. Neither Miss Melinda nor yourself are to leave the premises without a footman. I trust that you will have callers, however, no gentleman must be admitted into the house except by Mr. Lander. You are not to question or discuss his decisions on these points with anyone save myself. All household disbursements will be drawn on my accounts, so you need not concern yourself with expenses. A sum accompanies this letter—it is a gift from me to Miss Melinda in honor of her debut. Certain personal expenditures related to yourself will be covered as well. I hope that you will accept these conditions. None of them are negotiable.

Your Servant
Robert Cambourne

Folie handed the letter to Melinda, who stood waiting with her hands clenched together fretfully. Jane and Cynth pressed beside her, their arms about her waist, expressions of adolescent calamity on their faces. All three of them peered apprehensively down at the note.

Jane was the first to emit a joyous squeal. Within an instant, Folie was treated to the spectacle of three shrieking, laughing teens hugging one another and flinging their shawls and caps toward the ceiling with victorious abandon.

Lady Dingley looked away from the window, with her vague expression of having just strayed into a room she didn't quite recognize. Folie had already spoken to both parents before giving the news to the girls, with some trepidation, but to her surprise, neither Sir Howard nor his wife had taken exception to the rather insulting "conditions." Indeed, they had seemed quite gratified.

"It is most generous of Mr. Cambourne," Lady Dingley said. "You must write him your thanks immediately, Jane."

"Oh, yes—but after we call on Charlotte Pool, Mama! Curzon Street!" Jane exclaimed. "I vow I cannot *wait* to see the look upon her face when she hears!"

"Jane—" Lady Dingley said helplessly, but her eldest daughter was already leading an exodus from the room. Left alone with Folie, she gave a small shrug. "Well, I shall write to him, of course. He is very kind."

"Oh, indeed," Folie said, with a dry smile. "Extremely kind."

Sir Howard escorted them to town, presiding over a horseback cavalcade of his daughters while Folie, Lady Dingley, Melinda, and the youngest girls rode in the carriage, but he adamantly refused to install himself in a house with "a tribe of babbling females," for even one night. He betook himself to his club, promising to provide Folie and Melinda with suitable mounts by the next afternoon. Folie was less relieved to hear that than to have no responsibility for the small herd of ponies and horses he took away with him to the mews behind Cambourne House. Straw bedding was not foremost in her mind; linen bedding was.

Cambourne House was a mansion suited to a nabob, three times as large as its neighbors, with beautiful arched windows two stories high set across the drawing room facade and twelve bedrooms arranged on three upper floors. But the shouts and squeals of the Dingley girls echoed in gilded rooms that were almost empty of furnishings. Lander introduced her to the grim-faced housekeeper of his choosing, Mrs. Cap, who immediately began to complain of the poor condition that the previous tenants had left.

Lander might be an adequate butler, although Folie would sooner have cast him as a pugilist, but he was perfectly hopeless at providing for the Babbling Tribe. They had arrived at dusk after two days of maddeningly slow travel, hungry and cranky, to find an empty larder, no cook, six strapping footmen standing idle, and one harried charwoman hanging out sheets that were still soaking wet.

"I must find a cookshop directly," Folie said to Lander. "Melinda, you and the girls make sure that all the feather beds are turned over and shaken out. Sally, we shall need plenty of water. Mrs. Cap, see to it that the men get fires started in every room. The place is like a grave! I pray there is coal. The good Lord only knows what we shall sleep upon tonight." She gathered up her shawl and purse and started for the door.

"Madam," Lander said sharply. "You are not to go out alone."

Folie stopped. She had completely forgotten Robert's orders. In Toot, there had never been any reason to hesitate to go out alone at any hour. But this was London, of course.

"Well, come along then," she said, pulling her shawl about her. "Perhaps I can stuff a little common management into your head on the way."

He pursed his lips, but only bowed and followed her out into the darkening street. On the front step, Folie paused and took a deep breath. London smelled of horses, smoke, and a cold spring. There was still a bustle of traffic in some large thoroughfare nearby. To her delight, a lamplighter was just illuminating the street. She paused for a moment, watching the pools of light grow upon the pavement.

"How pretty it is!" she murmured.

"Yes, ma'am," Lander said at her shoulder.

Folie started, unused to having a servant at her heels for simple errands. "We must have milk," she said. "Where will we find it?"

"In the Shepherd's Market at this hour, I think, ma'am." He looked at her dubiously. "I am not certain a lady ought to be seen there so late in the day—"

"Perhaps she ought not," Folie said briskly, "but you have left me no choice in the matter. Food before footmen, Lander. Food before footmen! If I can but convince you of that single truth, I shall increase your administrative merit immeasurably."

"Yes, ma'am," he said meekly. "I have not been able to locate a suitable cook."

"Hmmm!" Folie replied. "But six footmen quite fell into your hands!"

"Yes, ma'am," he said.

The market was only a few steps below Curzon Street. Lander at least appeared to be well acquainted with the neighborhood, and led her there without delay. Folie felt instantly at home among the close streets and half-timbered buildings, as if she had wandered into market day at Toot—but tucked behind the elegant houses of Society and showing no signs of closing for dark. Light from fires in barrels and tubs gave the milkmaids and shop stalls an exotic air, and the accents of the people were so thick as to be almost a foreign language. The Punch and Judy booth was curtained, but there was a silent juggler spinning his multicolored balls in the flickering light, his painted eyes following Folie with an intent, unnerving smile.

She located a cookshop easily enough, by the smell of baked pudding. She placed an order that made the proprietor's eyebrows go up, but after a little negotiation and an appeal to his wife, who laughed at the story of Lander's six footmen and no cook until she could hardly breathe for sputtering, arrangements were made to have fifteen pork pies, a cold roast, an assortment of cheeses, ten loaves of bread with butter, five gallons of fresh milk, a kettle of vegetable soup, and a block of ice delivered within the hour.

''That shall do to break our fast in the morning, too,'' Folie said as they walked back into the narrow market alley. ''What a wonderful place London is, that one can get fresh milk at seven in the evening! And a block of ice! It's almost April!''

''Yes, ma'am,'' Lander said.

She was about to make a comment upon his vast range of conversation when she looked up at the juggler. The mummer had followed her and Lander, apparently considering them his best hope of any profit tonight. He pulled a paisley scarf from his sleeve, wadded it into his hand until nothing could be seen in his fist, then reached out toward Folie, opening his fingers.

She laughed in spite of herself at the bright peering eyes and black mask of a small ferret that stood up amid the unfolding scarf on his palm. Folie clapped. The mime cupped the ferret between his hands and set it upon her shoulder. She felt the creature nuzzle at her bonnet. The juggler's painted face smiled, weirdly expansive in the unsteady light. With a magician's flourish, he made a circle about his head and then held up four fingers.

She hesitated. ''Four crowns?''

The juggler nodded with enthusiasm. His ferret put one paw on her cheek, patting it gently.

''Well! I think Mr. Cambourne will buy us a pet,'' she said, giving Lander an arch look.

''As you wish, madam,'' the butler said.

Folie had meant the ferret as a diversion for the younger girls, to occupy them while she and Lander and Mrs. Cap got the house in some sort of order, but when she attempted to leave it with them in the back drawing room, it slipped from twelve-year-old Letty's hands and scampered up Folie's skirt. From then on, the little creature made it clear that Folie was its mistress. As long as she was in the room, the animal would play with the girls; but where Folie went, the ferret went, too.

There were a few moments of tearful protest, but to Folie's relief, Melinda and Cynth seemed to have taken upon themselves the responsibility for keeping the younger ones happy. Melinda appeared entranced by all the hectic chatter, proposing games and mediating arguments with the glad grace of a girl who had longed for sisters all her life. Miss Jane, proving as practical and forthright as her father, had already found out from the charwoman the name and direction of a seamstress from whom more bed linens might be obtained straightway, and sent a footman out for them. When the food arrived, she joined in laying out the table. In a system that Folie considered masterful, Miss Jane called in three at a time to the dining room, each pair of young ones escorted by an older girl who supervised the filling of their plates. By ten o'clock, everyone had eaten, including Folie. The rooms were warm and the new linens installed.

There were only five beds, but the Dingley girls, accustomed to sharing their rooms, had already haggled out their distribution. Even the littlest, who had wept tragically when she discovered her nurse was not there to tuck her in, finally found a cozy spot in bed between Melinda and Cynth and drifted off to sleep.

"What good girls you are," Folie said warmly to Miss Jane, as they stood in the dim passage after seeing the eight-to-twelve-year-old contingent put in bed. "I believe you could have installed yourselves quite handily, without a bit of help!"

Miss Jane grinned. "Oh, we often do for ourselves, Mrs. Hamilton. Perhaps we aren't as elegant as our mother could wish, but we sleep on clean sheets!"

"You are treasures. The gentlemen will want to snap you up in a trice," Folie said.

"Do you think so?" Her round face lit with pleasure. "We're none of us very beautiful, you know," she added humbly.

Folie felt a little twinge at the base of her throat. "Piffle,'' she said. ''A woman's beauty is in her soul.''

''Oh, yes, certainly.'' Miss Jane nodded, with a wry purse of her lips.

Folie smiled. ''A gentleman told me so.'' She lifted the ferret from her shoulder, wrinkling her nose at it. ''Of course, he had never laid eyes on me,'' she added cheerfully. ''But naturally I have held to it buckle and thong ever since!''

Jane laughed and dropped a curtsy. ''Then I shall, also! Good night, ma'am.''

Folie turned away, carrying the ferret with her to the formal drawing room. This chamber held most of the furniture left in the house; the light of a single candelabra glinted on gold frames and mirrors, the smooth curves of chairs and sofas. Lady Dingley looked up from a graceful mahogany secretary, the desk before her covered with sheets of stationery. If she noticed the furry animal perched on Folie's shoulder, she did not mention it.

''Mrs. Hamilton!'' she said, with more animation than Folie had ever seen her exhibit. ''I have been searching my memory. I believe you and I may call upon Lady de Marley and Mrs. Whitchurst. Not with the girls, of course, until they have been presented at court. But I went to school with Catherine de Marley, and she begs me to visit every time she writes, so we need not stand upon ceremony there. And I am thinking . . . I don't know . . . Lady Melbourne . . .'' She pursed her lips. ''I am afraid . . . Sir Howard might not quite like it, but . . .'' She looked hopefully at Folie, as if she might have the answer to a difficult conundrum.

''Lady Melbourne?'' Folie said.

''Yes, I—'' She lowered her eyes. ''She is my godmother.''

''Oh, my Lord!'' Folie put her hand over her breast, making no attempt to hide her awe. ''Lady Melbourne! Oh, my dear! What famous news!''

''Yes, it is an honor,'' Lady Dingley said honestly. ''I love her dearly; she is my mother's cousin, and we were used to be great friends when I was a girl, but Sir Howard does not like me to write to her."

"But—"

"She is a Whig, you know." Lady Dingley dropped her voice to a whisper, as if Sir Howard might be hiding behind the door.

"Oh," Folie said. "Sir Howard dislikes her politics so much?"

"He becomes livid on the subject. But!" Lady Dingley drew a deep breath. She clenched her fists. "Her daughter is Emily Cowper. One of the patronesses of Almacks."

"Ahhhh." Folie watched with intense interest as Lady Dingley's face took on a look of militant determination. Tickets to the exclusive assemblies at Almacks would be tickets into the highest society. It was something Folie had not even dreamed of for Melinda, having no acquaintance in such circles who might provide the precious vouchers.

"I shall call upon her," Lady Dingley announced. "She is my godmother."

"Certainly you must," Folie said firmly. "It would be the height of disrespect to come to town without seeing your godmother."

"Yes!" Lady Dingley exclaimed. "Precisely!" She sat up. "And any girl without a ticket to Almack's may as well turn about and go home."

"Put on her spinster's cap directly," Folie agreed with emphasis, hiding a smile. "Her case beyond hope!"

"Indeed, yes!" She looked at Folie excitedly. "You explain it all so well, Mrs. Hamilton—perhaps you will speak to Sir Howard."

"I!" Folie laughed. "No, no. It is not my place!"

"Oh, but I can never seem to make him understand anything." Lady Dingley stood up in agitation. "He is so—he does not listen."

Folie looked at her sympathetically. "I know a little of what that is like. But I am already too much in your husband's debt. I shan't impose more on him with requests that won't please him."

Lady Dingley sank down again with a look of despair.

"Oh, it is hopeless. He will never see." Her mouth quivered a little. "Whatever I say, he must have it be silly and unreasoned, just because it was I and not he who thought of it!"

A depressed silence descended on the room. Lady Dingley rustled her papers together listlessly.

"Perhaps . . ." Folie strolled along the row of exquisite arched windows, watching her own reflection pass in the panes. "Perhaps you need not decide what to do right away," she said casually. "La, things are so topsy-turvy here, I daresay you've not a moment to think of Lady Melbourne!"

"I can think of nothing but!"

"Sir Howard has said he must return to Dingley Court tomorrow, has he not?"

"Of course he will go. He can't abide female—" She stopped suddenly. Her body was still, but her eyes flickered and grew wide. She turned a look on Folie.

They began to smile at one another.

Folie found out from Mrs. Cap that she was to sleep alone in a fine, cold room, one of the two best bedchambers. Folie pushed open the door and put her candle down on a desk beside the window, glancing briefly up at the elegantly plastered ceiling. Her trunk, still packed, sat at the foot of a florid tent bed crowned by cupids and flower garlands and draped in rose chintz. There were no curtains. Why the former inhabitant had not taken the yards of tent fabric with her also, Folie could not guess, but the bed appeared comfortable enough, if excessively floral.

She held up the ferret, looking into its masked face. "And what am I to do with you, now that I am so foolish as to have you?" she asked.

The little animal took her chin between its paws, sniffing at her. Folie smiled at the tickle. The juggler had sold them a small cage for another half crown, but when she set the creature on the bed, it instantly ran up to the pillows, curled between them, and began grooming itself industriously.

"What shall I name you?" she mused. It appeared to

have no opinion on the matter, but finished its task and rolled itself into a ball with its tail over its nose, looking at her for a moment and then closing its eyes with a faint sigh.

"I'll call you Toot," she said. "I am a little homesick, you know, though it wouldn't do to admit it." She sat down at the desk, pulling her shawl close in the chill. The coal fire had been started, but seemed to have gone out before it really caught. Folie stared out the window. She could not really see what it overlooked, but she thought it must be the garden and the stables. All was quiet and dark.

That's how it would be.

She watched her reflection, thinking of his voice.

There had not been one communication between them since she had heard it; only that stiff letter that began, "Mrs. Hamilton."

"Never mind," she said to her pale image in the glass. "Never mind. Some things you are well out of, my dear."

She stood up briskly and opened the desk. She took all the rich stationery that was in it and crumpled the pages, stuffing them under the dead coals. With the tinderbox on the mantel, she set them alight, and when the fire was well started, she threw the quill pen on it, too.

A servant brought Robert his meal in the dining room. He presided alone at the head of the table, his face in his hands. The smell of food both seduced and nauseated him. He sat there in self-imposed torture, under the icy eyes of the carved dragons, refusing to retreat.

She had been gone for a week. A week. They would be in London by now. They must be. Every day he expected to hear from Lander.

Half-drunk on cider, he stared at the food on his plate, and then looked up. A maid stood at the sideboard to wait on him. She curtsied, watching him uneasily.

Robert gave a chuckle. He felt a black mirth at the apprehension in her face. "How do you do?" he asked. "Who the devil are you?"

She hesitated. "Kathy, sir." She bobbed again.

He took a small bite of the curried fruit. He looked down the table at the empty chairs. She had been there. He had touched her—God, her warm body beneath him, the scent of her on his hands. Somehow he had reached her, driven by demons; somehow in his crazy need he had kissed her and laid her out, and if he thought more of it, he would go wild.

"Gone, gone, gone," he muttered. He ate again, pushing his hair from his eyes like a proper madman.

He had let her go away. It was best. She wanted to go. Wanted to go, wanted to go.

Left you, Phillippa whispered.

"Of course," he exclaimed, lifting his wineglass in a mock toast and taking a deep drink. "Why should she not go? What am I to her?" He slammed the glass down. "A sham Robert. A fiendish gentleman. A stranger. She is in love with . . ." He smiled and looked around the table and nodded his head, as if to honor an imaginary guest. "Why, with *you,* sir! The other Robert Cambourne." He flicked his finger against the wineglass, making it ring. "Lucky fellow."

He and the wary maidservant stared at one another. Robert dropped his eyes. Bite by bite, he ate all of the fruit. What difference did it make? She was gone. He was lost.

"Phillippa. I am yours now, my dear." He laughed. "Yours alone."

He felt himself drifting. It began to rain hard. The monsoon.

Can I trust that devil Lander? he said to himself, again and again. Vaguely he recognized it as a fixation, something that had been running through his mind for days. *Can I trust him? I have no choice. Can I trust him? I have no choice.*

"I shall make a song out of it," he said out loud. "Shut the windows, Kathy. It is raining."

"It's not raining, sir," she said.

He looked at her. She was a maid like any other maid, brown hair tucked under a cap, a few freckles, perhaps a little plump about the waist.

"I hear it," he said. "Bring me more wine."

She curtsied, lifting the decanter from the sideboard. "The windows is all closed, sir."

"Kathy," he said reasonably. "It is time to kill me. I know it is raining. I can hear it. Don't let Phillippa have me."

"Sir, sir—" Her voice held a strange note. "You are all right?"

Robert looked at her as she bent over, filling his glass. Her hand was shaking visibly. He could not hear over the roar of rain in his ears, but he thought she was panting from the way her starched bodice trembled.

He laughed, toying with his fork. "Just—have mercy on me. There is poison in this food, Kathy. I know it. Just give me enough to kill me."

The bottle slipped from her hand. She gasped and caught it before it hit the table, but a splatter of wine spilled across the cloth. Instantly she began to sponge it with her towel, her motions jerky. "I'm sorry, sir. Pardon, sir, beg pardon."

Robert felt himself move. He trapped her hand, locking her wrist down on the table.

"Beg pardon!" Her voice cracked. "I didn't mean to, sir. I didn't mean to!"

She began to sob, standing with her hands pressed down on the towel. Robert gripped her wrist until he could feel the bones in it. The reverberation in his head was like thunder. Slowly, weeping, she sank to her knees.

"Oh, sir. I got a baby in me, sir," she mumbled. "I didn't know what to do. And he said he'd see me taken care of, and he give me a guinea, and said he'd kill me if I failed him, an' I didn't know what to do, sir, I swear I didn't know what to do—"

"Who?" Robert squeezed her arm until she whimpered.

"I didn't know him, sir!" She tried to pull free. "I swear. I only saw him the once. There was a crown every Sunday under the flowerpots by the drain."

"Not Lander?" Robert was leaning close to her; now he

could hear her panting desperately through the clamoring devils and the rushing monsoon.

"No, sir," she whimpered. "No, sir."

"The truth!" he hissed.

" 'Tis the truth, 'tis the truth."

He let go of her. She scrambled to her feet. Robert could not gather his wits enough to stop her as she ran from the room. For an infinity of time he stared at the red wine stain spreading across the cloth, his eyes fixed on it as if it were the gates of hell. His mind tumbled and howled.

He must move. He could not remain here. But he could not move. He looked at his hands locked on the table edge; it did not seem that they were his. As if his will influenced someone else's body, he saw his arms shove his chair back from the table. He stood up.

The house seemed to pass before his eyes. The drawing room, the staircase hall—he went through it shouting, *"Kathy!"*

But she did not respond. Other servants gathered around him, flustered and frightened faces.

"Where is Kathy?" he demanded. "Where is Kathy?"

"Who, sir?" a footman asked.

"The maid, the maid!" he shouted. "Kathy! Where is she, for the love of God?"

All he received were bewildered looks. He went through the house, down the back stairs to the kitchen, shaking off the hands of servants who tried to help or detain him, he did not know which or care. In the kitchen, he grabbed the cook by the neck-strap of her apron. "Where is she? I want Kathy!" The woman tried to curtsy, but Robert yanked her close. "The serving maid!"

"W-we have no Kathy, sir!" the cook babbled, her eyes wide with terror.

"She served my dinner!" Robert yelled. "Where did she go?"

"Foster took your dinner up," the cook stammered. "Foster . . . him just there, sir."

Robert turned to see a red-faced footman nodding vigorously.

''No,'' Robert said, letting go of the cook. ''There was a girl.''

''I give it directly into Foster's hands, sir,'' the cook said, wringing her apron. ''By Mr. Lander's instructions.''

Robert's head was aching. ''There was a girl!'' he shouted. ''I am not mad!''

They stared at him, silent. Robert could not seem to find enough air. He pushed past the servants and plunged up the stairs.

Nine

"I AM SO glad you came with me, Mrs. Hamilton," Lady Dingley whispered, as four tall and dignified footmen ushered them into the hall of Melbourne House.

Folie only nodded. She had resisted to the last, feeling it too forward of her to join Lady Dingley in such a personal call on an old and distinguished friend. She wished even more now that she had not come, for the rich livery and number of attendants made her feel impossibly dowdy in a dress made up from a pattern out of a three-year-old copy of *Ladies' Quarterly*.

"Lady Dingley and Mrs. Charles Hamilton," the footman intoned, bowing them through the drawing room door.

"My darling Belle!"

Even before Folie could locate their hostess behind a Chinese screen, Lady Melbourne's voice drew them like a sweet siren into the room. The source of this melodic utterance proved to be a dark-eyed lady, tall and very stout, holding out her hands to Lady Dingley as she rose from her chair.

"Oh, do not stand, dearest Godmother!" Lady Dingley cried, taking her hands and sinking into a deep curtsy. "Please do not trouble yourself."

Lady Melbourne chuckled. "I will not stand for long, I

assure you, or you would have to hold me up! But how shall I not take you in my arms after such an absence?'' She enveloped Lady Dingley's slight figure in a deep hug, patting her back with a feathered fan. ''Now! Do not weep! What will Emily think of you?''

''Indeed, I shan't!'' Lady Dingley stood back and helped her godmother into her chair. ''I am too happy! Lady Cowper!'' She curtsied to the smart young woman who sat across from her godmother. ''How do you do?''

For one of the fearsome patronesses of Almack's, Emily Cowper seemed absurdly youthful, a fawn-like creature with an impish rosebud mouth and masses of dun curls. She greeted Lady Dingley in a small, warm voice, and nodded toward Folie.

''Do present your companion to us,'' Lady Melbourne said.

''Godmother, Lady Cowper, this is Mrs. Hamilton.'' Lady Dingley gave a nervous laugh. ''We must thank her, for it was she who insisted to Sir Howard that he must allow us to call.''

''Then I do so!'' Lady Melbourne exclaimed. ''These ironclad Tories! What shall we do with them? Bless you, indeed, child, if you succeeded in turning his mind even ten degrees from its true north!''

Folie curtsied, feeling blood rise in her face at Lady Dingley's barefaced prevarication. She had not said a word to Sir Howard. ''Please, ma'am,'' she said quietly. ''I deserve no esteem on that score, I assure you.''

''Mrs. Hamilton's late husband was a cousin of the Cambournes,'' Lady Dingley said quickly, placing Folie in her small plot on the social landscape. ''We are staying at Cambourne House for the season.''

''Sit down, sit! Both of you—place a chair for Mrs. Hamilton,'' Lady Melbourne ordered the footman. ''She is connected to the Cambournes, you say?''

''Mr. Hamilton's mother was Sir James Cambourne's youngest sister,'' Lady Dingley said. ''Mr. Robert Cambourne is Miss Melinda Hamilton's guardian.''

''Robert?'' Lady Melbourne asked alertly. She patted her

cheek with the fan. ''That will not be Sir James' direct branch.'' She shot an inquiring glance at Folie. ''No . . . Robert Cambourne would be Lady Ryman's younger brother, I think. They are most of them out in Calcutta or some such.''

''Yes, ma'am,'' Folie said. ''Mr. Cambourne has only recently returned from India.''

''Direct him to call upon me, Mrs. Hamilton!'' Lady Melbourne said. ''The Company charter is up for renewal next session. I should like to hear his opinions on the matter of these conquests in—what, Sind, was it? Or Java?''

Folie pressed her lips together. ''I beg your pardon, ma'am. I doubt Mr. Cambourne will have opinions on it.''

''Not a political animal, is he?'' Lady Melbourne asked indulgently. ''Well, he must call, at any rate, and speak to me of elephants and cobras; you are to tell him so.''

''Certainly, ma'am. I will be happy to do so, but—'' She paused. ''He has not been quite well, and remains in Buckinghamshire.''

Lady Melbourne shook her head. ''Convey my best wishes for his full recovery. India! It has slain more good young men than any heathen place has a right to do. What is that upon your shoulder, Mrs. Hamilton?''

Folie's cheeks burned. ''It is a ferret, ma'am.'' She glanced at Lady Dingley, who had pledged that her godmother would relish the circumstance of a caller with a ferret. Toot was seldom still, but popped back and forth, peering out from beneath one side of Folie's bonnet and then the other.

''Yes, so I thought,'' Lady Melbourne said. ''I daresay it will not be parted from you.''

''It is loathe to leave my person, ma'am,'' Folie admitted.

''Will you allow it into Almack's, Emily?''

''I think not, Mama,'' Lady Cowper said with a smile.

''But you will find my darling Belle some vouchers?''

''With pleasure. How many will you require, my dear?''

''How kind of you!'' Lady Dingley exclaimed, as if it were the greatest surprise. ''Only Miss Jane and Cynthia will be out in society, you know. They will be in raptures!"

"Three, then . . . and Mrs. Hamilton?"

Folie had hardly dared hope; she had lectured Melinda fiercely on the wisdom of cherishing no unwarranted expectations. If she had beauty, then Miss Jane and Cynthia had tickets to Almack's; it was only just.

"You are too good," she said faintly. "My stepdaughter Melinda would be so happy to receive one."

"And you must be admitted too, of course," Lady Melbourne said. "You will both be made acquainted with the proper society there."

"Thank you, Lady Melbourne. I confess I know so few people in London that it is the greatest blessing I could imagine."

Behind them, the door opened. The footman announced, "Lord Byron."

"Ah!" Lady Melbourne's eyes grew mischievous; suddenly it was clear where her daughter had inherited the gypsy sparkle. "Now, Mrs. Hamilton, you shall be made acquainted with the *im*proper society!" she whispered.

A gentleman drifted into the room, moving so slowly that at first Folie thought him ill, for his pale complexion and weary air. But at the sight of Lady Melbourne, the derisive twist of his mouth transformed into a smile. He went forward without looking at anyone else, bowing deeply over her hand. "Madam! The day begins!"

Folie watched him curiously. She had no idea who he might be, but Lady Dingley showed considerable signs of agitation, glancing over at Folie and then down at her hands and up at Folie again. She seemed so flustered that for an instant Folie entertained the wild idea that there was some sort of secret connection between them.

"Our beloved poet," Lady Melbourne said, laughing. "I entreat you to allow me to present you to these ladies."

He glanced at Folie and Lady Dingley. "If you contract with me that they will not swoon," he said coolly.

"Make no such pacts, ma'am," Folie said, instantly on her mettle with this scornful stranger. "I have not yet had my morning fainting fit."

He lifted his eyebrows. He looked Folie over, taking in Toot on her shoulder and her unfashionable gown in an impudent appraisal. "Now *that* one you must present to me, certainly."

It was a condescending examination, but really, Folie felt that Robert Cambourne could have shown him the way when it came to an air of naturally aloof arrogance. A little too overdrawn, this poet.

"George, Lord Byron, my dears," Lady Melbourne said. "Pay him no mind; his Childe Harolde is all the kick this week, and it has made him insufferable."

He made a bow. As he straightened, he smiled at Folie—a sudden, startling charm. "Try me again next month. I shall endeavor to be humble by then."

"You undeserving boy, I have the honor of making you known to Lady Dingley, my goddaughter, and Mrs. Hamilton," Lady Melbourne said, with a graceful turn of her wrist.

"Very pleased," Lady Dingley said in a stifled voice, rising. "Really we must go, Godmother. Lady Cowper. Sir. Pray excuse us."

"Of course," Lady Melbourne said. She accepted Lady Dingley's kiss on the cheek. "Call on me again, Mrs. Hamilton. Any woman who can twist an unyielding Tory like Sir Howard about her finger must be esteemed here. And do bring your ferret. I prefer a little absurdity in my visitors."

"Do not whisper a word of it!" Lady Dingley exclaimed as the carriage rolled away from Melbourne House. "Have mercy on us! Lord Byron!"

"Who is he?" Folie asked.

"He is—" Lady Dingley dropped her voice, "—a voluptuary."

"A voluptuary?" Folie echoed.

"Yes, that is what Sir Howard says."

"Oh!" Folie cleared her throat. "I am not quite sure—what is a voluptuary?"

"Well, I am not perfectly certain myself, but I assure

you that he is a horrid poet and *not* a true gentleman. How rude and arrogant he was! I cannot comprehend why my godmother would receive him.''

''She prefers a little absurdity in her callers, as you know.''

''Did you dislike her?'' Lady Dingley asked anxiously. ''I know she is somewhat . . . quaint in her character.''

''Certainly not!'' Folie smiled. ''I liked her very much! I only hope I may be as engaging when I am equally seasoned in years.''

''She liked you also, or she would not have asked you back, you know.''

''I am honored. And Almack's!'' Folie stood Toot up and pretended to dance with his forepaws on her fingers. ''I'm so sorry you cannot be admitted, sir, but your lineage is disgraceful. And I believe you have a reputation as a voluptuary.''

The ferret did not seem to find this overly amusing, gnawing on Folie's glove instead of applying itself to a minuet. Neither did Lady Dingley appear to detect any humor; she put her hand on Folie's wrist and said, ''You must not say that word abroad, you know!''

''No, no,'' Folie said meekly. She was too grateful to embarrass anyone. ''I shall be very good! I am resolved!''

Lady Dingley gave her a dubious look. Folie returned Toot to his cage on the forward seat and gazed out at the street, watching the pedestrians. The Dingley's carriage was picking and lurching its way across a busy intersection. Having two of Lander's imposing footmen up behind to protect them from any highwaymen or French infantry to be found in Mayfair, they had earlier agreed to progress to Conduit Street after their calls, to seek out a milliner recommended by Lady de Marley. Lady Dingley thought that this was better done without the girls, at least on the initial visit.

After nearly a week in London, Folie was growing accustomed to the swarms of people out in the street at any hours, but she found it all endlessly fascinating to watch. So many strangers! In Toot-above-the-Batch a new face had been a cause for commotion—here she did not see a person she knew outside the house. But she had noticed that people seemed to come in types, with faces and forms that somehow resembled one another, though one might be the coal porter pouring his fuel into a hole in the sidewalk, and another might be the casually-dressed gentleman speaking to a maid on the corner. In profile and frame they both rather favored Sir Howard's type, leaning forward, intent in their concentration.

The carriage halted in the middle of the intersection, while the driver shouted at some blockage. Folie watched the coal porter straighten, rubbing his back. He looked toward the corner, and she saw that in full-face he hardly favored Sir Howard at all. But the other man . . . in the moment she had to study him, he glanced up from under his hat.

Folie blinked. She sucked in her breath silently. Instinctively she looked away, just as he jerked his hat down and turned. With her heart pounding, she glanced at Lady Dingley, but she was gazing calmly out the other window. She had not seen her husband.

Folie looked back. The woman was still on the corner where he had left her. She had a shawl pulled over her head; she glanced about her, and Folie received another strange shock. Not only was her face red with weeping, but Folie knew her. Before that realization quite dawned, though, the girl had begun to hurry away in the direction Sir Howard had gone. The carriage lurched forward, leaving the intersection behind.

It all happened so swiftly and silently that it hardly seemed real. Sir Howard was in Buckinghamshire; having seen to the horses and stabling he had departed London, with a great show of relief, the day after their arrival. She could almost think she had imagined seeing him. Another gentleman, perhaps, with that sort of passing resemblance she had just been pondering. There were so many people on the street.

And yet—the look upon his face when he had seen the Dingley carriage. Folie frowned down at Toot, who was earnestly attempting to pick the lock of his cage. That girl . . .

She had a country look, her skirt showing her boots and her shawl tied under her chin, unlike these smart London maids. But Folie was quite certain she was not from Toot, or even Tetham, which pretty well covered the possibilities, unless she was a serving girl from Solinger or Dingley Court. Neither was impossible—it was not the housemaid who had tended their chambers at Solinger, surely, but another girl had once or twice served them tea in the library there, though Folie had paid her face little mind, and there were so many maids and nurses and laundresses at Dingley Court that Folie had made no attempt to sort them out.

"There! Hookam's Library!" Lady Dingley exclaimed, touching Folie's hand. "You were asking where it was."

"Ah!" Folie said, leaning over to look out the window.

"Sir Howard has a membership there. I am sure you may use it if you like."

"Thank you," Folie said.

"I must say, I do not miss him at all." Lady Dingley pulled her cloak about herself and lifted her shoulders. "I thought I would. But we are having quite a jolly time on our own, I think!"

"Yes. Consorting with voluptuaries."

Lady Dingley giggled and slapped Folie's wrist with the ribbon of her reticule. "Don't you dare say a word!"

"Indeed not," Folie said. She sat back straight on the seat. "No. My lips are sealed."

Robert had chosen the only hotel he knew in London, a stuffy haunt of clergymen and scholars. It was little changed from his Etonian days, when his tutor and keeper had brought him into town for edifying visits to the museums and galleries. There would be no one to recognize Robert there; the audacious gentlemen in the service of John Company were hardly the sort to frequent Hubbard's Hotel in Clifford Street.

The beginning of the journey from Solinger had harrowed him, an act of will and domination over the demons in his head. He had not gone straight toward his destination; had taken no route at all, simply begun riding alone in any chance direction, losing himself among anonymous village inns and towns for a sennight, finally coming upon the Great North Road and turning toward London amid the coaches and wagons, loaded donkeys, and goosegirls with their flocks.

Yet now, as he finished a turtle soup, half a roast duck, a cutlet, a fresh salad, and a chocolate cream provided from the hotel kitchen, he began to believe that his mind was sufficiently clear to begin a rational inquiry into what was happening to him.

His diaries from India lay before him, twelve volumes of densely written notes and sketches. He was not a neat scribe. His own handwriting gave him a headache, and his vague notions of one day producing a book had always evaporated when he contemplated transcribing the scribble into something organized. It had always seemed more interesting to investigate the next temple or teacher; the next Sanskrit poem; to wonder at the ancient dreams and strange phenomena; to walk the multicolored borderland between purity and dirt that was India.

But he had no other place to begin. He knew the volumes contained something important.

What?

He sat back in his chair, staring into the candle flame. He could not trust his memories. Or his friends, such as they were.

During his farcical years in the political service, plots and intrigues had abounded. His colleagues had conspired with princes and spied upon everyone from illegal missionaries to Pegu ponies, but Robert had never paid serious attention to any of that. No one confided in him, or gave him any responsibility, which had suited him admirably. His job had never been defined, beyond a vague directive to "collect information on the engineering of the major buildings and temples in the locale." He had never even known which "locale" he was to scrutinize, so he had simply explored whatever ground took his fancy, kept his notes, and assumed that if someone wished to see them, they would ask. In truth, his reputation as a careless buffoon was not undeserved; he had no patience for sober and disciplined pursuits such as writing reports to his superiors. At least his wanderings had kept him out of the compound, and away from Phillippa.

At the thought of her, a curl of dread and loathing tightened in his belly. He listened to the silence in the room, waiting.

She did not speak. His chamber was a quiet one, at the back of the hotel. Through the shuttered windows, he heard only the sound of pigeons gurgling on the sill.

"Are you gone?" he sneered aloud.

A drop of hot wax slid down the side of his candle, puddling in the holder.

He made a growl and flipped open his first volume. The entries began so long ago that he hardly thought there could be anything of use there, but he was determined to examine every detail. With pen and paper ready to note whatever seemed pertinent, he began to read.

By half past midnight, he regretted ever having started. It was a humiliating experience. Amongst the observations on Indian culture and religion were the shards and fragments of his life, the whole anguished tale of his marriage, beginning with his first wild infatuation with the girl his father had brought out from England for him to marry, complete with such effusions as *O God she is the sweetest, loveliest creature in Heaven or Earth, I cannot comprehend a word she says for staring at her*. Would that he had paid more attention to her conversation. But he had been consumed with jealousy, filling whole pages with entries about how he would call out Captain More if the devil kept it up, or put a glove across Balfour's cheek for his impertinence.

Robert squeezed his eyes shut and groaned. What a greenhorn. He had barely turned twenty, but surely that was old enough to have more sense.

He could not even bring himself to read the page written the night before he had proposed. Robert had rebelled against his father all his life, but in that one fatal moment he had cooperated gladly. In spite of the unspoken understanding that the Duke of Alcester's daughter had traveled out to Calcutta not only to visit her doting godfather but to marry into the Cambourne fortune, he was frantically afraid that she would turn him down. Any eligible British female at all in India was feted and courted with high intensity, and Phillippa had been so beautiful and nobly bred, so truly charming, that the fervor rose to impossible heights. Everyone admired her, adored her, was her devoted slave for eternity. He saw now how it had gone to her head, how she had come to live for the worship and attention, but then he had known only that he must vie for her against the competition of men who seemed to be everything he was not.

But she had said yes.

YES!!!! he had written across the whole of a page.

He turned past that and skimmed a few more pages of high-minded ecstasy about her. Then there was a long interval, nearly a year represented by one blank space, and the serious entries on Hindu cults began.

Robert expelled a slow sigh and rubbed his eyes. He supposed there must have been some happiness, but he could not remember it now. She had not been cold; she would kiss him and tease him prettily until he grew so agitated that he could hardly think, but he was shy with her— afraid of her, frankly—afraid that he loved her so much that he would lose himself in it. At first he had been exhilarated by complying with her requests, hurrying to do whatever she bid, elated when he won her smile. But slowly he had begun to believe he should not allow himself to be consumed by this. It was alarming. *She* was alarming; an aristocratic English girl, exacting in her many feminine needs.

Ah, but then she would kiss him. He did remember that. As long as he responded ardently, as long as he told her, over and over, how beautiful she was, as long as he declared his devotion in fresh and glowing terms, she rewarded him with passionate caresses. And yet, after each avowal of his love, she would look up at him with a faint air of expectation, as if he had not said quite enough, or quite the right thing, and she was waiting.

It began to chill him, that pregnant look. Hidden in it was a threat and a misgiving—that some other man could love her better—that she had mistaken him.

Robert shook his head. He marked his place and rang the bell, summoning a sleepy bootboy to his door. He ordered coffee and fried potatoes, for a bit of a snack, then on consideration, added a request for toasted cheese, a minced pie, and an orange. He would have enjoyed rice and a good curried stew, in the mulligatawny style, but Hubbard's did not cater to East Indian tastes, and he had no intention of calling undue attention to himself. He felt safe ordering from the hotel's kitchen.

His early notes were simple enough; he could see nothing in them of particular interest—short passages on the great Hindu triad: Brahma the Creator, Vishnu the Preserver, Shiva the Destroyer, about as sophisticated as a schoolboy's essay. Anyone who scratched the surface of religion in India would discover this stuff. It was not until he had become acquainted with Srí Ramanu that he had begun to penetrate the Hindu philosophy and its views of life and suffering. But long before he had grasped anything of *karma* or *maya* or *moksa,* he had discovered a great deal about suffering.

He could almost feel pity for the bewildered boy he had been—pathetic fool, floundering in love and writing grave descriptions of Indian ritual. His first mention of Phillippa, after the blank space and religious reports, was the single line, *She is still afraid. God help me.*

For Phillippa, he had discovered after their wedding—in spite of her passionate kisses, her heated caress—Phillippa was afraid of childbirth. Or so she said. She would lie down with him; slowly her modesty lessened and she answered his desire with her own; she let him go farther and farther until he could touch her, kiss her anywhere. She would pant and arch and reach for him, pull up her own gown and draw his body against her until she died blissfully in his embrace, but he was never allowed the same release. Any attempt to enter her met instant stiffness and panic. She would roll away and weep, accusing him of being unfeeling.

She drove him mad with it. He could not speak of such things, he could not reason with her or threaten her. So he would silently retreat, leaving her asleep in her bed and walking out into the bazaars and alleyways to cool his blood.

He flicked past the pages, forcing himself to read each one. Here was his first meeting with Srí Ramanu, carefully recorded from one of those uneasy night walks. *Ramanu perceives in my soul a deep distress,* he had written earnestly. Robert rolled his eyes to the ceiling. At the sound of a knock, he gladly marked his place and closed the volume.

His food gave him an excuse to rise from his chair and leave the diary shut. But he had revived the memory now; he could not escape it. He thought of the night he had lost his head, driven by Phillippa's delicious body and blind lust. When he had felt the shudder of ecstasy come over her, he had not rolled away; he had not obeyed her hands pushing him off. He could not. The more she had fought him, the more despair and fury had made him fierce—he had thrust himself in, deaf to her cries, handled her as the soldiers handled their whores, without mercy.

He had gone to the bazaars that night with her hysterical weeping still ringing in his ears. Srí Ramanu had seemed to find him—certainly Robert had not been looking for the *guuruu.* He had been on the edge of tears himself, in no state to conduct rational investigations or interviews. But Srí Ramanu had only bid him rest and be still. Robert had knelt, while Ramanu sat with his legs crossed in the fashion of yogis. And after a long time, sitting there watching Srí Ramanu in silent contemplation, Robert had felt strangely lifted out of himself. It was as if the anger and doubt and emotions boiling in him had died down, burned away to ashes by the *guuruu*'s luminous gaze. He could feel tears running down his face, but he felt no grief or guilt, or even any very clear sense of himself at all; only a great stillness and radiance from everything about him.

How long ago and impossible it seemed now. Robert did not have to look in the diary to know what he had written after that night. *Srí Ramanu is an extraordinary man.*

Perhaps, Robert thought, as he ate fried potatoes and toast, he should have joined Ramanu's disciples after all. Let his hair grow long and don a loincloth and live in that celestial radiance for the rest of his life.

But he could no more believe in it then than he could now. He remembered the experience with an intense clarity, but he could never repeat it or even accept its ultimate reality, though Phillippa had accused him many times of aspiring to become a Hindu mystic. He did not deny it, or blame her for holding him back; he would have if it had been in his power. But he could not cut himself off from the world, from his earthly dreams and passions. Even when they tore his soul to shreds, he could not let them go.

And so he had studied instead, committing Srí Ramanu's teachings and rituals to paper, where the brilliance of that night became no more than scribbles of ink. He had followed rumors and stories, observing esoteric cults and tracking them down with a kind of yearning fixation, a hope he never even admitted to himself, that in one of them he would find the way back to that intangible sensation, that one transcendent night with Srí Ramanu. He watched wild dances and sat enveloped in smoke and incense, writing every detail.

Then he went home to Phillippa, who was fervently interested in his advancement and wanted to invite all the important officers and supervisors to balls and picnics. All the men he loathed. She would not let him into her bed again. But she would kiss him still, and beg prettily to be allowed to give a ball. She so wanted them to recognize his ability—he was being overlooked; he was too modest; in England it was expected that a gentleman would entertain on a scale appropriate to his station in life. Her adored papa the duke was so very disappointed in him.

Robert sipped his coffee with a saturnine smile. Oh, his

station in life. He opened the diary again, peeling the orange with his thumb. Twice he had gone to his father to borrow against his allowance for Phillippa's balls. Twice had been two times too many. She did not seem to realize that his real station in life was enslavement to the Company and his father, to accounts and the Cambourne repute; or understand how deeply he hated it all. He did not truly realize it himself until he had stood before his father the second time, and heard how he must learn to control his wife, for as charming as she was, she was a little too saucy, and beginning to make a spectacle of herself in the stiff upper echelons of Calcutta society.

Have put my foot down, the diary said, with a fool's optimism. *She seemed to take it quite well. Kissed me.* The sweet pleading and caresses had been difficult to resist, but he had only to think of facing his father again to defy them.

Missed dinner, did not hear the servant call me.

He had not seen the storm warnings for what they were at first. They were only minor entries scattered among his notes. *Delay this morning to pacify the laundress and cook. Phil forgot to distribute the wages I gave her yesterday.*

Spent the day pasting and recopying; Phil cut up the January brigade accounts to take a design off a pattern-doll. She did not realize what the paper was, for God's sake.

Robert chuckled darkly. From this time and distance, he could almost appreciate her artistry. But he had been too thick-witted to hear the message then . . . or perhaps he had heard it clearly enough, somewhere beneath his waking thoughts, but had no useful answer. So he had taken his notebook and closed the door on their bungalow and slipped away to his noisy incense scented refuge in the alleyways and temples. Slipped away from the knowledge of her budding affair with John Balfour; from the cool disgust of his brigadier general, who called him a useless idle blot on the Union Jack; from his father's verdict, which matched General St. Clair's; from the Duke of Alcester's letters demanding some alleviation of his daughter's wretched unhappiness. More clothes. More parties. More money. And why was there no child yet—was Robert impotent? He slipped away from it all to be alone.

He turned the page. And there, tucked firmly into the spine, a little dark around the edges from folding and refolding, was Folly's first letter to him.

Robert did not open it. He only traced his forefinger lightly across his name and direction, and turned another page.

TEN

FOLIE SAT VERY straight in her chair, sipping tea and exchanging polite greetings with Mr. Hawkridge. She was seated alone before the desk, having managed to convince Lander that she was quite safe from attack within the solicitors' chambers. She had sent him on with Lady Dingley and the girls for their first visit to the milliners.

''Specifically what are Mr. Cambourne's powers?'' Mr. Hawkridge murmured, repeating Folie's question. ''I should have to refer to the will, of course, but I believe the terms are not unusual. Trustee over a competent livelihood for the wife of lands and tenements, to take effect upon the death of the husband for the life of the wife. Both you and Miss Melinda are to be maintained in genteel circumstances.'' He smiled kindly, a large, jowly man in an old-fashioned bagwig. ''Cambourne House would seem to qualify there! Lander has already presented us with several bills for fitting out the rooms with furnishings, to be settled on Mr. Cambourne's personal account. Has a difficulty arisen?''

''No,'' Folie said. She moistened her lips. ''No, I cannot say so—''

He looked at her quizzically.

''There is no clause in the will that might grant some

independence—at least to myself?'' she asked in a rush.

He cleared his throat. ''Ah. If you should remarry, of course. Your husband then would assume the responsibility of administering your freehold jointure for your lifetime, after which the remainder would revert to Miss Melinda.''

''I see,'' Folie said. She paused, and then said, ''But if—if . . . ah . . . generally speaking, what occurs in the case of a trustee who is not . . . competent?''

Mr. Hawkridge shuffled papers with a thoughtful air. Then he said, ''Would you care for more tea? I wish you had allowed me to call upon you at Cambourne House, Mrs. Hamilton. I should have been honored to do so.''

''I preferred a little more—privacy,'' she said. ''No more tea, I thank you.'' She began to rise. ''It is of no consequence. I will not trouble you longer.''

''My dear madam, it is no trouble. Please stay a moment. I feel that you are not quite comfortable with Mr. Cambourne's authority?''

Folie lifted her eyebrows. ''Have you met Mr. Cambourne?'' she asked, sinking back into her chair.

''Alas, I regret to say that I have not met him in the flesh, no. I understand that you and Miss Melinda spent a week at Solinger Abbey. I trust that all went well?''

She smiled wryly. ''Mr. Hawkridge, I do not like to speak ill of people, but you may take my word, you would not wish to encounter Mr. Cambourne on Midsummer's Eve.''

He tilted his head. ''I fear I do not quite take your meaning.''

''Let me be blunt, then,'' Folie said briskly. ''He is queer as Dick's hatband, as we would say in Toot-above-the-Batch.''

''Indeed? A little eccentric?''

''Quite raving mad,'' Folie said cordially.

''Mrs. Hamilton, I note that you seem to be carrying a ferret upon your shoulder.''

''Yes, that is so.'' Folie raised her chin.

''I have not had reason, over the several years of our correspondence, to suppose you anything but a sober and well-informed young lady. However, when you arrive in my office, accompanied by said ferret, and tell me Mr. Cambourne is raving mad, I confess you render me a little uneasy."

"*My* mind is perfectly clear, Mr. Hawkridge. I am simply carrying a ferret on my shoulder. Mr. Cambourne, however, is in another category altogether. I suggest that you make his acquaintance and judge for yourself."

He smiled. "As it falls out, I shall have that happy occasion in a few minutes—he is expected at three."

"Here?" Folie exclaimed.

"Yes. I must say that my clients are uncommonly obliging today, to call upon me in my chambers!"

"I must go!" Folie said, standing up.

Mr. Hawkridge rose, coming around the desk to bow over her hand. Folie had promised to remain at the solicitors' office until Lander returned for her, but she could not stay now. Hurriedly she accepted the lawyer's parting compliments and went down the stairs. Fortunately she had not relinquished her cloak and muff when she had come in, as the muff was Toot's preferred refuge from the cold. She lifted the ferret off her shoulder and encouraged it into the furry nest as a servant opened the front door.

A cab stood at the curb. The passenger was just handing up his fare to the driver. He turned, his hat brim pulled down, his face lowered. But she recognized him instantly.

Folie went quickly down the steps, hoping against hope that he would walk right past her, seeing only her toes and hem. He stood aside at the foot of the stairs. She turned away from him onto the pavement.

"Mrs. Hamilton."

Folie increased her stride, pretending not to notice.

"Mrs. Hamilton!" His voice was commanding. Before she had gone two yards, he caught her elbow.

Folie stopped. She thought wildly of pretending not to know him, but it was too impossibly witless. She turned her head slightly, barely looking at him under her bonnet. In his tall black hat, pulled so low, and a dark cloak with many shoulder-capes, he looked positively wicked. She thought that if she were to scream, some passerby might come to her rescue on the strength of his evil air alone.

"Folly," he said, in a voice so at odds with his baneful appearance that she bit her lip. "It's Robert."

"Yes. I know." She stood with her eyes on the pavement.

He held her arm for a moment, and then released it. "Where is Lander?" His tone changed, hardened.

"He is with Lady Dingley and the girls, shopping."

He gave a soft curse. "You were not to go out without him."

"He did accompany me here," she said. "I sent him on with them." She could not quite meet his eyes. "If a guardian is a necessity, it seemed more reasonable that he should escort them about the streets. I did not feel that anything really dreadful could befall me in a solicitor's office."

"You are not, I perceive, *in* a solicitor's office," he said darkly.

She fiddled with the braid on her reticule. Pedestrians brushed past them as they stood on the curb. Her cheeks were burning.

"You are not to walk out alone," he said. "I will wait with you until they return."

"Oh, no," she protested. "Pray do not trouble yourself. You have an appointment with Mr. Hawkridge."

"You knew that?"

"Mr. Hawkridge mentioned it."

"I see," he said dryly. "Come inside."

Like a chastened child— or a recovered prisoner—she turned back and mounted the steps. He followed. Inside, the clerks and servants bowed and fawned, identifying him without a card. To Folie's infinite chagrin, Mr. Hawkridge came down the stairs himself.

"Come up, come up directly, Mr. Cambourne!" He bowed to Folie. "I see that you encountered Mrs. Hamilton—we were just having a most pleasant visit."

Robert Cambourne nodded briefly. "Sir." He glanced toward Folie. "I must take a few minutes here, madam—

I trust you will await me,'' he said. ''Is there a comfortable place she might sit, Mr. Hawkridge?''

''Certainly! If you will just come into Mr. James' room, Mrs. Hamilton—he is in the country for a few days. Can I persuade you to take tea?''

She kept her face down, but that only caused her to be looking at Robert's hands when he pulled off his gloves—his dark, strong hands that had been in her hair and on her throat and . . . she could hardly find her breath for the rush of blistering mortification. ''Thank you,'' she said, stifled. ''Yes. Tea. I believe I will.''

He did not take long with Mr. Hawkridge. Not nearly long enough. Folie had attempted to stow Toot and the muff underneath her chair, but the ferret took one of its notions and insisted upon exploring the office. Just as she caught him back from an investigation of the lowest row of legal volumes in Mr. James' bookcase, Toot made a slithering twist between her fingers and skimmed beneath the desk. A scratch at the door signaled her tea. Folie straightened quickly, hissing a dire warning under the furniture. She sat down, smoothing her skirts and composing herself for the benefit of the clerk who brought the tray. After he left, she dropped to her knees and dragged Toot bodily from where he was playing among the dustballs beneath the solicitor's desk. She stuffed the struggling ferret into the muff and wrapped her crocheted shawl about it. Toot poked his nose through the open knit like a tiger in a miniature zoo, but ceased his attempts at escape.

She had hardly steadied her hands enough to sugar her tea before she heard the door open behind her. Robert Cambourne stepped inside, closing it behind him. He made a formal bow.

''I'm glad we encountered one another here, Mrs. Hamilton,'' he said, with the air of a prepared opening. ''For reasons I shall not go into, I cannot call at Cambourne House, but I wished to . . .'' He paused. ''I have not been—perfectly myself. At Solinger—at Dingley Court, I behaved in an ungentlemanly—'' He cleared his throat. ''A reprehensible manner.''

Folie stirred her tea vigorously in the silence.

''Well,'' he said. ''Will you look at me, at least?''

Folie lifted her face resentfully. It was the most irksome thing, the way she was agitated by his physical presence, as if all her wits scattered to the four winds. He might be as handsome as Lucifer, as Melinda claimed, but that was not what perturbed her. She could not say what it was. Even before he had kissed her and touched her, she had felt completely at sea with him, constantly out of her depth. He did not appear quite so gaunt and diabolic as Folie remembered from Solinger. She stared at him with considerably more aplomb than she felt, her brows lifted in cool expectation.

''I was not myself,'' he repeated, resting his fingertips on the desk, tapping them slightly on the smooth wood. ''I would like . . . I wonder if it would be possible—for us to . . . begin afresh.''

''Afresh in what sense?'' she asked.

''I do not know.'' He glanced toward the window, looking out on the grim brick wall of the building across the way. ''Perhaps that we might—'' He gave a shrug. ''We were friends once.''

Folie stood up abruptly. She turned her back on him.

''Were we not, Folly?'' he asked.

She read the spines of legal tomes. *Proceedings of the 12th Circuit court, 1797–1800. An Introduction to the Principles of Morals and Legislation. Commentaries on the Laws of England,* by Blackstone.

''You have forgotten our letters,'' he said in a low voice.

It was the first time the letters had been openly mentioned between them. Folie felt a thickening in her throat.

''I have not,'' she said. ''But I do not believe it would be wise to place a great deal of confidence in that as a basis for any particular affinity between us at present. I was quite young when our—correspondence took place.'' She was astonished at how assured her voice sounded. ''We have matured. We are entirely different people now.''

He said nothing. She did not suppose he could argue.

"It has become clear to me that we never knew one another well, Mr. Cambourne," she added. "That was an illusion."

"Perhaps so," he said.

"We grow beyond the many foolish fancies of youth." She ventured a glance at him. "Maturity brings about a notable alteration in one's life and character."

"I begin to believe it can render someone unrecognizable."

Folie returned her gaze to the bookshelves. It was safer to look there. A newsboy's piercing cry touted headlines in the street below. Carriages growled along the stones. Somewhere in the distance, a donkey brayed in harsh complaint. The silence in Mr. James' chamber was profound.

"Will you take tea?" Folie asked.

Without waiting for an answer, she poured him a cup, set it on the desk, and left it there.

"Thank you," he said. He added four lumps of sugar and poured in a quantity of milk. Folie watched him. *I drink tea, it is called* chai *here, with a great deal of milk and sugar,* he had written. As if she could ever forget a single line.

Folie drew a breath. She sat down and picked up her teacup. "I am charged by Lady Melbourne to command you to call on her."

"Lady Melbourne?" he repeated, politely blank.

She had confounded him, at least. And changed the subject, too. "Yes, she wishes to hear your opinion on the recent conquests in Sind and the renewal of the Company charter."

"Sind?" He sounded more bewildered. "We have made no conquests in Sind."

"Well, then you had better set her straight on the matter. We would not wish for the Whigs to be misinformed."

"If they are that misinformed, it is no wonder they are out of power." He seemed willing, even relieved, to allow the talk to dwell on impartial topics. "Who is Lady Melbourne?"

"Very highborn, married into the Lambs. She has been

a great society hostess for decades. All the political gentlemen of the Whig party gather at her parties.'' Folie repeated Lady Dingley's summary. ''Amazing kind,'' she added on her own behalf. ''And acute. She knew precisely who you were, merely from your name.''

''Did she?''

''She said that you could not be in Sir James Cambourne's direct branch, and named your sister, Lady Ryman.''

He shrugged. ''Sir James was my uncle. I only met him once, when I came up to London as a schoolboy.'' His brow creased with a faint frown. ''I don't know why she should know so much of him.''

''Was he in the government? A Whig?''

''A Whig? My God, I should think not. He was a company director.'' His expression grew reflective. ''He took me to Westminster to watch the opening of the Hastings impeachment trial. There was a great affair. As good as a circus.''

''Oh? I don't think it was reported upon in the Toot Tattler.''

''It was long ago. While you were still busy with your ABCs.''

''And you saw it? Who was on trial?'' she asked curiously.

''Ah.'' He smiled at her. ''That I do know, for all my father said I never had a proper appreciation for Company history. Warren Hastings, my dear, first Governor-General of India. They waited until he retired and came home, and then dragged him before the Lords to pay for all his erstwhile sins. He is still alive, I believe, but he must be an old man now. I was twelve, perhaps, or thirteen.''

''What did you think?'' She leaned forward a little.

''Think?''

''Of Parliament? Was it interesting, or a terrific bore?''

''It was quite extraordinary that day. The place was crammed—it was in Westminster Hall. I barely understood a word at the time. All I remember is that poor old gentleman on trial—how mild and serious he was—sitting there while those fellows dripped withering scorn on his head. 'I impeach him in the name of the people of India!' " he intoned in a dramatic voice, lifting his arm like a public speaker. " 'I impeach the common enemy and oppressor of all!' " He lowered his hand and smiled. "Whig prosecutors."

"Was he an oppressor?"

"He didn't look one to me. Courteous little man. He did well enough by India, I think—and he never made any money out of it, like most of 'em. It's the money brings on the dogs, you know. They were after John Company in truth, convinced we were all pirates." He smiled ironically. "Which is true enough, in its way."

"Perhaps they were jealous, and wished a fair chance to be pirates themselves."

"You are shrewd. Of course they wanted to tear the heart out of the East India Company, open up trade—abolish her privileges and let their own friends have a go at the booty. Still do, no doubt. And my uncle in tears of rage. If we had met a Whig on the street, I believe he would have thrust his cane-sword through 'em then and there. I think I might have myself. They spoke beautiful rhetoric—Fox and Sheridan and Burke, I'll never forget them—but not a one knew a beggar's scrap of India or what they were saying of that poor devil Hastings."

"Oh, yes . . . oh! I remember now. Mr. Warren Hastings. Did he fight a duel?"

"Yes. Probably with a Whig."

Folie laughed. "I think Lady Melbourne will like you," she said.

"I had rather you liked me."

She lowered her face, taking a sip of cold tea.

"I have not often been able to talk to anyone this way," he said.

"What way?" she asked in surprise.

"This way. A conversation." He looked down at her through his long black lashes. "It is pleasant." The corner of his mouth lifted.

"I am happy that you think so. But it is not difficult, you know. One simply opens one's lips and speaks."

''Ah, but the words make all the difference. You do not bark orders or catalog my deficiencies.''

''Well, I do not have a talent for barking, and if I begin upon your deficiencies, there is always the risk that you will start in with mine.''

''Would I?'' He tilted his head. ''If only I could think of any.''

''Now you are absurd!'' she said.

He shrugged, smiling slightly. ''None at all come to mind.''

''I have all sorts of deficiencies.''

''No. If you had, I would have noticed.''

''In a moment you will have me listing them myself,'' she said tartly. ''Very crafty of you!''

He grinned. ''Ah, my sweet Folly.''

''Please do not do that!''

''What—do not call you aloud what I have called you every day in my heart these five years past?''

''Do not. Do not.'' She turned her face down, picking at the ends of her gloves.

''Folly.'' An intensity came into his voice. ''Will you not trust me? Can you not?''

She stood up. Without looking at him, she bent down to pull the muff from under the chair. She rose again, blowing air from her cheeks. ''On what do you propose that I base this trust?'' She looked him in the eyes. ''On your frankness and candor? On your stability and sound mind? On your gallant and civil behavior toward the ladies under your protection? Pray inform me, Mr. Cambourne, in what manner you have earned my trust?''

His face went bleak as she spoke, as dark and still as the water beneath a winter lake. Folie fumbled with the muff, uncoiling her shawl.

''Four years ago, upon receiving your last letter to me,'' she said, ''I discovered that I had been living in a fantasy. A daydream. A foolish, foolish, foolish dream. I do not reproach you for this. I have only myself to blame for what I allowed—that is, for my . . .'' She lost her voice. After a moment, she swallowed the squeak in her throat and said, tolerably evenly, ''For the emotional attachment that I allowed to occur in my own mind. It was utterly wrong of me.'' She looked away. ''And I paid for it. I paid, to what felt like the last drop of blood in my heart. That is enough. I will not pay more.'' She shook her head. ''No. I will not trust you, Mr. Cambourne. Not in the way that you imply. Never again, you or any other gentleman.''

Quickly she walked toward the door, still trying to disentangle the shawl. Toot poked his head out, struggling to escape, nipped her glove when she tried to push him back in, and then snagged his paws in the crochet. While she stood beside the door, fighting tears and trying to unravel the ferret from the wool, she heard the sound of familiar voices from below—Lander and Melinda returned for her at last. She had no hand free to open the door. ''Oh, you odious creature!'' she muttered furiously.

''What the devil is that?'' Robert asked in a peculiar voice.

''A ferret!'' she cried. ''Oh—here!'' She thrust the wriggling shawl and muff at him. ''Take it, give it away, it only cost a guinea. I must go. I must go.''

The thing bit him immediately. Robert yelped, juggling the ball of woolen wrap. He dropped it on the desk, cursing and sucking his finger. The muff tumbled about as if it had a life of its own, scattering the neat stacks of paper. He tried briefly to rescue them and then abandoned the desk to its destruction, walking out onto the stair landing in time to see the front door shut on Lander's back.

Robert stood looking at the closed door, gripping his bleeding cut between his fingers.

After a moment, he pulled a handkerchief from his pocket and wrapped it around the cut. He went back into Mr. James' office.

The muff and shawl had ceased their frantic motion. From inside a hopeless snarl of yarn, the ferret stared at him intensely. Robert bent down, retrieving the strewn papers and stacking them carefully on the desk. He checked his finger. When the bleeding seemed to have stopped, he pulled on his gloves, wincing at the sting. Gingerly, he picked up the ball of wool and fur. Without pausing to take his leave of Mr. Hawkridge, he went down the stairs and let himself out the door.

On the pavement, he stowed the muff and ferret under his arm and began to walk.

"Where is Toot?" Melinda asked, as Folie climbed into the carriage.

"I have given him away," Folie answered shortly.

"Oh."

"He was a considerable nuisance," Folie said. She squeezed into the place that Lady Dingley made for her and nodded at Lander to shut the door. "An embarrassment, frankly."

A chorus of disappointment and censure met her announcement.

"The little girls will be crushed," Lady Dingley said.

Folie said nothing. She could not and would not go back in there and retrieve Toot from Robert Cambourne. It was only a ferret, she thought fiercely. A silly little animal; a nuisance, a pest, a bother. She reached up and yanked the check string vigorously, signaling the driver to move on. The carriage jerked forward.

"Mama!" Melinda protested. "Lander has not yet got upon the box!"

The vehicle bounced, the familiar sensation of a servant springing onto the footman's rest. "There," Folie said. "He's up behind now."

"He might have been hurt."

"Lander?" Folie snorted. "I doubt a shipwreck on an iceberg could kill the man."

Melinda's mouth took on a mulish set. She did not reply, but turned to look out the window. Folie suffered the silent reproof, in no mood to cajole for a smile. She had not thought Melinda was so attached to the ferret.

"We have had great success!" Lady Dingley said, proffering a package hopefully. "Look at this pretty blonde lace, Mrs. Hamilton!"

Eleven

ROBERT HAD NO notion where he was. He had walked unseeing, passing among crowds of strangers, carried by the traffic across a river bridge, chagrin and a vehement shame striding with him. He could not have said if he was wandering in London or a Delhi market. He could not stop—if he paused, it seemed as if they might see through him, see inside to a whole futile lifetime spent in hiding.

He walked. But there was no Sri Ramanu, no alien temple to attract him, no place to go with his anger and humiliation. Only dusk falling on a field beyond the last house, aproned housewives arguing on a stoop, the road beneath his feet no longer paved.

He was hungry. The evening wind cut through his cloak. There was a blister on his heel from a pair of new boots.

"I don't suppose you are a homing ferret," he said to the muff.

There was no answer from the creature under his arm. Robert peered into the fur. He squeezed it a little, wondering if the thing had smothered itself. Nothing moved.

He poked his gloved finger inside.

"Christ!" He jerked back from the hard nip. It went right through the leather. Robert dropped the bundle and stood nursing his hand. ''No doubt you learned this technique from your mistress.''

A deep-throated horn heralded the approach of a stagecoach along the dirt road. Robert retrieved the muff, keeping his hands carefully clear of the openings, and stepped out of the way. After the coach had passed, he stood in the quiet village street. He had hardly been aware of leaving the city. He could see the chimneys and smoke behind him, and smell it too, like the breath of a great panting black dog crouched on the horizon.

A sign creaked on its hinges. ''The Highflyer'' was lettered in red beneath a painting of a carriage with absurdly tall, light wheels. The advertised inn was hardly so elegant as its namesake, with a lowering thatch roof that hung nearly to the ground and a stone threshold worn so deeply concave that water puddled in it. The bowed tilt of the half-timbered walls seemed almost to defy gravity.

But a warm light fell from the single window onto a tiny garden in bloom with yellow daffodils. Robert's head ached from lack of food. He pushed open the garden gate and ducked inside the door.

Inside, a portly woman looked up from her knitting. ''Good even', fine sir. What will ye?''

''Dinner?'' he asked.

''Aye, that she can.'' The woman stood up, setting her work aside. ''Cold pork pie, or a mulligatawny soup?''

''Mulligatawny?'' Robert echoed in pleased surprise.

''Aye, 'tis a curry dish, for me son Tucker,'' she said apologetically. ''It be main tasty, but full o' spice. That Tucker Moloney, he got such a relish for the peppery morsel off there in India! Maybe ye'd take to the pie better.''

''Keep the pie.'' He grinned. ''I'm an old Qui Hai myself.''

''Oh, you won't think I know them words, but I do! I do!'' The tip of her nose turned red when she laughed. ''A gentleman of Bengal, aye. My Tucker taught his old mother a good bit o' that talk. I could listen to him go on for hours, I could.''

''Tenth Regiment, Bengal Infantry,'' Robert said approvingly. "You are an excellent student. Where was your son?"

"Madras," she said promptly, and then added with a wink, "A Mull. But I'll have your soup up in a blink, sir—you look some weary and leer. Ale for you?"

Robert nodded. He settled in an age-blackened booth beside the fire, looking up at the cutlass hung below a native *havildar's* foraging cap. A cheerful shepherd dog nosed up to him, black and white tail wagging, and sat down with an ecstatic sigh under Robert's stroke.

"What pleasing manners," he murmured. "Not like some ferrets I might name."

The landlady's white cap bobbed up from the depths of a staircase. She carried a steaming bowl and a spoon. "Get away now, Skipper," she said, nudging the dog with a foot. "There's your pepper-water, sir. Take care with it."

Robert smiled a little. "So I shall." He took a bite, watching Skipper move obediently away and curl up on the hearth.

His hostess brought him ale and bread and sat down in her rocker. "You must tell me how ye likes it."

"Superb," Robert said. It was fairly spiced, as she had warned, full more of potatoes than of meat. But he was glad enough to taste curry again. He ate slowly, gazing at the dog.

Her knitting needles clacked. "Do ye miss the place, then?" she asked.

Robert glanced up at her. He shrugged. "Not really."

"Ye had such a sad far look just then," she said.

"I was thinking of the dog, I suppose." He took a deep swallow of ale. "I had a dog named Skip."

"Ah," she said, shaking her head sympathetically. "A good 'n?"

Something about the quiet room, the easy way she rocked, made him speak of Skip. "He was just a pariah dog—the yellow sort. Ugly."

"It don't matter how they look, do it?"

Robert took a hot bite of curry. His eyes ran. He shook his head.

"A mite spicy?" She gave a happy laugh.

He nodded, turning his face down so that she could not see him.

" 'Tis the way me son will have it."

Robert soaked his bread in the golden broth and ate.

"Not many of the gentlemen from town stops here," she said. "You come afoot?"

"Yes. Just walking." Robert pulled out a clean handkerchief and blew his nose. "Do you have a room for the night?"

"Surely," she said. "Very wise of you, sir. It's late. You won't want to walk back alone. We have the footpads now and again, so close to town. Bad times, it is." Her needles paused. She gave him a quizzical look. "And I believe you are low."

Robert wiped his eyes. "It is the curry."

"Oh, aye," she said, nodding.

"I do not know what has got into you this afternoon, Mama!" Melinda said, following Folie into her bedroom.

"I am having a fit of the dismals, if you please," Folie snapped, tossing her bonnet onto the dressing table. "Kindly go away and leave me to it."

"Did Mr. Hawkridge give you bad news?"

"Nothing that I did not know already. We are entirely at the mercy of Mr. Robert Cambourne."

"Oh, that," Melinda said dismissively.

"Well enough for you to say 'oh that'—you will have a rich husband to dote upon you the rest of your life!" Folie sat down and began to loosen her shoes.

"Well . . . perhaps."

"While I shall be a slave to that—that—*madman.*" Folie kicked a shoe across the room. "Oh!" She pressed her fists against her eyes.

"Mama—" Melinda said. "I wanted to talk to you."

"Not now. Please. Let me rest a bit."

"But—"

"No!" For the first time in her life as a mother, Folie let a note of impending tantrum leak into her own voice.

She shook her head behind her hands. "I cannot, Melinda."

"But Mama—"

"*Please* go away!"

Folie heard Melinda breathing sharply. After a moment, her stepdaughter's footsteps crossed the floor. The door opened and closed.

Folie dropped her hands.

She stared at the patterns on the India carpet, reds and blues and golds running together. With a speechless sound, she flung herself on the bed and curled her knees up against her chest.

"What do you know?" she whispered, clinging to a pillow. "What do you know? Silly girl, you won't have to live alone. You won't have to live on stupid dreams."

As night fell, the soft chatter of the knitting needles did not cease. There was a strange sheltered silence in the room, a hush between the fire and the rocking chair. Skipper stretched and slept.

Robert sipped his ale. "What are you making?" he asked at last.

"I don't know," she said. "Sometimes I just knits, and see what comes of it. Often enough, I pull it all apart again. But now and then, ah, my hands just seem to know what they want to do."

He smiled in the darkness. Skipper stood up and turned around, lying down again in the firelight.

"I love the best what I make that way," she said. " 'Just make a scarf,' me husband he'd say. 'Ye can turn out lovely stuff. Just make me a waistcoat, can't you? How hard can it be?' But even if I tried, it would come out ugly. And I took it apart. Don't know why. It was because my hands wanted to make something else."

He thought of Phillippa. *Can't you just put your mind to something useful? You've wits enough. How hard can it be?*

"Makes no sense, I know," the landlady said.

Robert stared into the flames. "Yes, it does," he said quietly.

"Do you think?" The rocking chair creaked a little faster. "I never met a man before who didn't laugh over it."

He was not laughing. He drank, watching her needles move with such smooth certainty. "I've never known what my hands wanted to do."

She smiled. "You must just let them move," she said.

"Ah. The secret."

She lifted yarn over her forefinger deftly. "They don't always do the handiest thing for me. Times I would have liked a soft little cap for me grandbaby, and I got a shawl fit for a fine lady. But afterward I seen that the wool weren't soft enough, and the ribbons I bought to weave in were too stiff for a baby. But the hands knew it, y'see, before I did." She chuckled. "So I give it to me daughter-in-law, and never said naught o' the cap at all. And she's a happy mother, full o' love. May be it's that shawl, for she was main pleased by it."

Robert made slow circles with his thumb on the tabletop. "I wrote letters once. That way. Didn't think. Just let my hands move."

"Did ye? And did it come out gainful in the end?"

He smiled wryly. "She fell in love with me. The lady that I wrote to."

His hostess rocked, her needles working evenly. "You're low tonight," she said. "Thinkin' of her?"

"She says we never knew one another. It was all a dream."

"Was it?"

"Of course." He drew a long breath. "Of course she is right. I was in India—married, unhappy. She was here, and the same."

"Oh?"

"We're both free now. But I didn't do well by her." He laughed harshly. "She says she has paid too much heart's blood. Won't pay more. Who could blame her?"

"Hmmm," the landlady said. "Hmmm."

"God knows why I'm telling you this," he said, rubbing his palm over his face.

"Happen He does," she murmured.

He shook his head. "What am I going to do?" he asked the dark. The despair in his own voice shocked him.

The landlady nodded in time with her rocking. "I conjecture ye'll walk a good deal."

Robert chuckled bitterly. "Yes."

"Walk here and there. Never get nowhere."

"You must have known me in another life."

She smiled. "Men, they drink or they walk. As if there was something comin' up behind 'em, and if they stopped they might look round an' see it."

"We have our reasons."

"Oh, aye. I reckon we all got reasons." She paused in her knitting. "Like your old dog, the ugly yeller one."

"My wife had him shot." Robert took a deep swallow of ale. "He tore her best petticoat off the line."

She nodded, as if she had already known it. "And this other lady, the one fell in love with your letters? She the sort kill an ugly dog over a petticoat?"

"No." He pushed the bundle of shawl and muff forward on the table. Gingerly he nudged the bundle. "She just handed me a damned ferret that bites me every time I touch it."

At the disturbance, the masked creature poked its head from its prison, upside down, and craned to look in all directions. Its tiny eyes glittered with malevolence and mischief.

His landlady opened her mouth and laughed soundlessly. She began to knit again. "Well, sir. I think ye'd better stop walkin'. I believe ye'd better turn around and fight for that one. You won't find diamonds worth so much."

Robert walked into his hotel rooms after noon the next day, carrying the ferret in a reliably locked cage. It was the third one he had bought—the thing had managed to escape all the others within moments. He set it down on a side table in the parlor and walked into the bedchamber to take off his hat and cloak. The animal began to run in frantic spinning circles, rattling the enclosure.

In the doorway, he came to a sharp halt. Across the bed,

neatly laid out, were a housemaid's apron and cap. They were both covered in blood, steeped from the top down, as if from a cut throat.

Robert stood frozen. Like a nightmare vision, he saw the girl Kathy's terrified face, memory rising up to gag him. He stepped backwards into the parlor, looking around. The door to the wardrobe stood ajar. He yanked it open.

The satchel where he had packed his journals was gone.

His journals. Folie's letters in them.

It took only a minute to bundle what little he had brought with him into his valise. The cap and apron he stuffed into a linen bag, not daring to leave it. He wrote a note advising that his horse was to be stabled until further notice, folded inside twice the amount he calculated for his bill, addressed it to the manager and sealed it with a hotel wafer. He left the packet on the secretary.

A vigorous clatter made him pause with his hand on the doorknob. The ferret was plucking energetically at the locked cage.

"Right," he muttered, and grabbed the trap as he went out the door.

Folie was dreaming of Toot. He rattled his cage, speaking to her in Robert Cambourne's voice, whispering her name urgently. Folie tried to open the cage, but her hands would not move.

"Folly!" The imperative whisper came again. "Wake up."

His paw brushed her cheek lightly. Folie whimpered, trying to move, her mind surfacing in and out of the dream.

She became aware of faint light, squinting her eyes against it, turning her face down into the pillow.

"Folly." Something touched her again.

She leaped in the bed, turning over. A scream came out as a throttled whimper. She scrambled up, flinging herself back from the intruder looming over her. He jerked his hand away from her shoulder as if she had burned him.

"It's all right," he whispered quickly. "It's me. It's only me."

Folie stared at him through the dim light of daybreak. She panted, clutching the pillow in her fists.

"Don't be afraid," he said, standing there in the half-light beside her bed, wrapped in his cloak like a black warlock.

"Oh, my God." Folie swallowed, closing her eyes. "Oh, good God."

"We must talk."

"You are mad! Utterly, utterly mad! What are you doing here?"

He stood straight, his brows lifted. "It is my house," he said, as if that explained everything.

"Oh yes, and so you prance in at dawn over the back windowsill!" she hissed. "Why can't you act this way in front of the solicitor? Why must you be *perfectly* reasonable after I have sworn to Mr. Hawkridge you are a lunatic, and then behave with me as if you have a screw loose?"

"It must be love," he said dryly.

"Oh, quite." She glared at him. "What do you want?" She pulled the covers up to her chin. "And do not suppose I am letting you near me this time!"

He gave her a look, a lift of his eyelashes that followed the shape of her body from her toes to her throat. Then he bowed. "As you wish, madam."

Folie drew in a deep breath. Her heart was still beating high in her throat. "What do you want here?"

"I have to talk to you."

"Talk to me? In my bedchamber at this hour?" She shook her head in disbelief. "I must suppose they do not practice the civil morning call in India."

"Hush," he said intensely. "Listen to me."

Something in his voice made her fall silent. He stood at the foot of her bed, holding himself very erect, as if he could impose himself on the room by his confident posture. She drew her knees up tight against her chest. "What is it?"

"I know you believe I am irrational. In fact . . . I admit—that I have been." He paused, looked down at her.

"Excellent," she said. "Perhaps you will put that in writing."

"Damn it!" He took a step around the bed, closer to her. "Listen to me."

She thought that she had better humor him. She lowered her face. "Yes. All right. I am listening."

"We are in danger."

"Danger!" Folie looked up.

"I know it is startling," he said. "But I fear your life may be at risk, and I am certain that mine is."

Folie watched him warily. She had heard of this—lunatics who began to believe that some evil stalked them. "Risk from what?"

"I don't know," he said seriously. "I am not sure."

"Then how do you know there is danger?" she asked in a careful voice.

He turned suddenly away. "They've been poisoning me," he said. "I discovered it at Solinger. The girl Kathy admitted it."

Folie felt a sinking sensation. He began to sound as if he were losing any grip on reality at all. "Why," she asked slowly, "would anyone poison you?"

"I don't know!" he exclaimed, turning back. "I was not even sure of it—but I have found . . ." He scowled. "Well, it is not something I wish to describe to you. I threw it in the Thames. But I believe they have murdered poor Kathy."

"Murdered! Who is Kathy?"

"A maid—a housemaid at Solinger. I only saw her the one time. After you had left. She served my dinner. And she admitted it. That is, as good as admitted it, that she was being forced to poison my food. And when I went downstairs to find her, they would not—they claimed there was no Kathy on the staff."

Though she tried to school it, something in Folie's expression must have conveyed her incredulity. He made a sound of disgust, flinging his hand.

"Of course you don't believe me," he snapped. "Why should you? I know it appears absurd. I would not be here,

I would not tell you at all, but they've taken my journals."

"I see."

"No, you don't." He leaned over her. "You don't know what I've found. You don't know what I've been through." His face was close; she could smell the cold smoke of night air that lingered on him and see the shadow of dark stubble on his cheek. "Folly—your letters, and copies of mine—I kept them in my journals. They have our letters."

"They?" She leaned back a little.

"I don't know who. I don't know. But they're trying to make me mad. If I had not gotten away from Solinger, I would have killed myself. And I'm afraid—I'm afraid that if they read those letters, if they discover what—" He stopped. With a sound in his throat, he moved away. His back to her, he said in a low voice, "If they realize what you have meant to me, they will use you somehow."

She put her fists to her cheeks. There was a tremor deep inside her. "Use me. Use me for what?"

"I don't know! Blackmail, silence—to drive me into a madhouse! I don't know!"

"Robert," she said, trying to sound very reasonable. "Robert. I do not think you ought to dwell upon this sort of thought."

"Listen to me!" He turned about. "I understand that you have no particular feelings for me now, but those letters—anyone who read them would think, would understand—"

He did not finish. He kept his eyes turned away from her. His hands worked. Suddenly he took hold of the bedpost and pressed his forehead against it, squeezing shut his eyes fiercely, as if against a vision. "For God's sake," he muttered, "listen to me. You don't know. You can't conceive. I would do anything to keep you safe. If I must shoot myself to please them, I will do it."

"Do not speak like this," she said sharply. "You must not speak like this."

He dropped his hands. When he looked at her, his face was wild and set, demonic. "Then you must listen to me, and do as I say."

"No, you must listen to me." Folie threw the covers off

and sat on the edge of the bed. "Do you suppose that it does not affect me to see you this way?" Her voice cracked. She creased her nightgown on her knees, gathering it in tight fingers. "Robert, do not do this to yourself. Please do not."

"It is not a delusion. Believe me. Believe me. Come away with me, and we'll find somewhere safe."

"Why do you do this?" she moaned, kneading her fingers. "Why do you say these things? Poison; some housemaid no one knows. Come away with you. As if I could. You frighten me."

"No." He shook his head. "No. Folly, I would never hurt you. I swear it on my life."

"You tried to keep us at Solinger! I don't know what is wrong; something is wrong with your mind."

"Not any longer. Please believe me." He knelt before her, cupping his hands over her knotted fingers. "I only want to keep you safe. Folly. You must come."

Folie looked down into his face. For a moment it was as if he was her real Robert, her own love, his gray eyes clear, his hands warm, gripping hers. And yet he said such things, such crazy things, so earnest.

"Robert . . ." she said helplessly. "I can't bear this."

"Let me take you away where I can protect you," he said. "I can't do it here. They'll be looking for us here. It's dangerous."

"I believe that you think that," she said desperately. "You think that."

"Damnation!" He flung himself away, rising. His cloak swirled around him in the increasing daylight. "You will never trust me again, will you?"

She said nothing. The tremor inside her had become a visible shake in her hands and shoulders.

"Well," he said, "I see now what they can do. Steal every shred of credit I ever had with anyone. No one will believe me, will they? If you won't, who will? No one will listen to a madman." He turned to her. "I can't stay longer. I don't want them to see me here."

Them. Folie twisted her fingers together. "Yes, Robert."

"Don't patronize me, damn it!"

She bent her head. "No."

"Be careful, Folly." His voice changed, became soft and urgent. "Please. If you ever loved me. Watch everything. Don't take a step outside the house without Lander. Promise me that, at least."

She nodded, still looking down at her hands.

She felt his hands on her hair, both palms sliding down the side of her face. For just an instant. Then he stepped back. Folie did not look up as he vanished; she did not know how he came or left. Her eyes were blurred. Cold drops fell on her fingers. He was so strange and alarming and insane, and she loved him so.

Robert thrust his hands into his pockets as the sun came up on a clear day, pouring pink and gold light across the facades of elegant townhouses. His breath made frost as he strode across the street. At a park gate, he bought bread and a mug of beer from a street vendor. It was one advantage of London, at least, he could always find food he was sure would be safe.

He stood in the open, breaking his fast with the laborers who gathered in the last wisps of early morning fog. It seemed bizarre now, how he had been afraid of stepping out under the unroofed sky. And yet, if he dwelled on the thought, he could feel the sensation growing on him, the sense that the crystalline blue arch would take him up, suck him upward into a spinning infinity, spinning and spinning until he flew apart. . . . His heart began to race, and the bread in his mouth seemed dry and impossible to chew.

He stood still, concentrating on the ground, on the green peek of bulbs at his feet. They were growing out of the ground, pushing up into the sky. The sky did not pull them up; they forced themselves into light and air. If he thought of the bulbs anchored in rich solid earth, his feet a firm base beside them, he could breathe again.

He shook his head slightly, like a dog shaking off water. From inside the park palings, he watched the far side of the street, waiting. Just as he had finished off the mug, Lander appeared at the corner.

Robert wiped his mouth and tossed the rest of his bread to the birds. The butler crossed and entered the park. Robert waited until he caught his servant's eye, and then with a faint gesture signaled him to follow.

As usual, Lander appeared to make nothing of the singular meeting. "Good morning, sir," he said, as Robert stopped beneath a budding tree.

They were out of range to be overheard. Robert nodded briefly. "I don't want you to be gone from the house long," he said. "I cannot say that I trust you utterly, but I have no choice."

The man betrayed no flicker of reaction. His eyes were so dark that they seemed black, but his hair was almost blond, tied back neatly. Robert thought he must be a seasoned gambler, from his square, inexpressive face.

"I have discovered that my fears at Solinger were well-founded," Robert said, plunging into it. "I was in the political service in India—something has followed me here, something pernicious. I have reason to believe that my—indisposition—at Solinger was the result of deliberate poison. I am convinced that it was an attempt to discredit my wits. It would appear that I am in possession of some knowledge—or someone thinks I am—something extremely valuable. I do not yet know what it may be, but it is consequential enough that they will kill for it."

The only change in Lander's expression was an increasing concentration on Robert's face. They were not quite of a height, but he did not have to look up by much.

"Perhaps you do not believe me," Robert said stiffly.

"I believe you, sir," Lander said without hesitation.

Robert lifted his brows. He had not expected to be taken seriously without considerable argument. "I am gratified."

"I can see that you are in possession of yourself now," he said. "I do not know how the poison reached you, for I did my best to watch. I beg your pardon; it was my failing."

The relief of being believed was astonishing. For a moment, Robert was at a loss for words. He shrugged, scowling. "Never mind. Did you know a girl named Kathy—a housemaid at Solinger?"

"Kathy, sir?" Lander shook his head a little. "No, sir."

"Brown hair, freckles, perhaps eighteen. She was increasing, she said. In trouble. They promised to take care of her if she did it."

Lander looked off thoughtfully. "That could be the gardener's girl," he said. "Mattie." He frowned. "Could you have mistaken her name?"

"Doubtless," Robert said ironically. "I was raving out of my mind at the time."

"I think—she might have been in distress. Now that I think of it, perhaps I saw her with red eyes. It's hard to know; I made nothing of it at the time."

"I think she is dead," Robert said.

Lander's eyes widened just a little. "Sir?"

Robert told him what he had found in his hotel room. The butler's jaw grew tight. "It was Solinger linen, sir?" he asked.

"I don't know." Robert cursed. "I didn't know you could tell."

"It would have SA woven into the waistband."

"I threw it in the river. Frankly, I didn't want to be accused of murder myself, if I was found with it."

"No, sir." Lander nodded. "Should I make discreet inquiries of Mattie in Buckinghamshire?"

"No. I want you here in London."

The butler said, "Then I shall remain, sir. But it is possible to inquire, I believe, without my leaving here."

"Make any inquiries you can, then—but keep them concealed, and do not leave here. I haven't told you all. My journals were stolen from my rooms."

Lander nodded alertly. "They want something you had written in them, sir?"

"God only knows. They are mostly full of rubbish." Robert gave a wry smile. "My wise observations on Hindu culture and religion, some descriptions of odd cults." He paused. A thought tugged at the back of his mind.

''No information from your political post, sir?''

The thought vanished as Robert laughed. ''My political post consisted of a few pillows and a broken chair. I was no Elphinstone parleying with the Afghans, I assure you.'' He shook his head. ''Unless it is some secret nefarious sect that has taken the trouble to follow me here, which I heartily doubt. One thing I have seen little of in England are gentlemen in turbans and loincloths, with beards to their knees.''

''Still, sir. Might it be a native reprisal for some accidental transgression? I understand that primitive peoples can be deeply moved by apparently minor acts.''

''Those I studied were no primitive people, Lander. Believe me. However peculiar their appearance, they live in the realms of highest consciousness. Light and kindness are their creed. Cutting a maid's throat? No—I think this is no Hindu plot against me. If I were still in India, I might suppose I had embroiled myself unknowingly in some conspiracy—we have bandit princes and *rajahs* by the dozens, all at John Company and one another's throats, but I can't conceive that such thing would follow me here, and I don't know what it would be in any case. I can recall nothing political, nothing at all. Sometimes I saw our people in the bazaars. I recognized them, but we never spoke.''

''Perhaps you saw someone who did not wish to be seen.''

Robert leaned his shoulder against the tree. ''Yes. That is possible.'' He cast a sidelong look at Lander. ''You have quite a mind for intrigue.''

The manservant shrugged slightly.

''What are you?'' Robert asked suddenly. ''You are no butler.''

Lander stood with his hands clasped behind his back, his eyes lowered.

''And no commoner, either,'' Robert said. ''You speak like a bloody aristocrat.''

''I beg your pardon, sir. I have not always been in household service, no.''

He volunteered nothing further, and Robert did not press

him. Likely as not, he would only get a pack of fabrications. He suspected that Lander was some nobleman's younger son who had disgraced himself—such fellows were thick on the ground in India, and in spite of the submissive "sirs" and "I beg your pardons," he had something of the same air of the highbred rowdy about him.

"Well, I believe you are a gentleman," Robert said, "whatever may have brought you to this point. And I ask you, on your honor as a gentleman, to keep your own counsel on what I mean to tell you. I would not speak of it, but I want you to understand why I must have you always on guard here. I have your word?"

"As it concerns nothing criminal, sir—you have my sworn word."

"Not criminal—not against the law, at least—unless it is against the law to write letters to a married lady."

"Of course I shall say nothing about such a matter, on my honor as a gentleman," Lander said.

Robert crossed his arms and looked at the ground. "Mrs. Hamilton and I exchanged letters for some time while I was in India." He lifted his face, squinting into the distance. "Anyone who read them would ascertain that I have—a great depth of feeling for her. I kept them in my journals. They have been taken also."

"I understand you, Mr. Cambourne," Lander said. "May I say that I am glad, sir, to have some clearer idea of the situation. At Solinger—I could not tell—I will admit that I was concerned and—puzzled."

"I was not myself there. I do not wish more to be said of it, ever."

"Is Mrs. Hamilton aware of the danger?"

"I tried to warn her." Robert gave a humorless smile. "I have succeeded only in convincing her for certain that I am fit for Bedlam."

"She was not alarmed?"

"Only by my presence, as far as I could discern." Robert pushed away from the tree trunk. "Go back to the house now. You've been absent long enough. They'll be stirring."

Lander bowed. ''Yes, sir. How shall I expect to hear from you?''

Robert shook his head. ''I can't say as yet. Be vigilant. Note any odd thing. If you receive a message marked 'Kali,' it will be from me.''

'' 'Kali,' sir?''

''The Hindu goddess of destruction.'' Robert paused. ''Speaking of which—I left that cursed ferret of hers on the back stoop.''

''Yes, sir,'' Lander said.

TWELVE

BY THEIR THIRD Wednesday night assembly, Folie had developed a positive aversion for Almack's. She hid it, of course. Never in her most ambitious dreams for Melinda had she supposed they would be mingling at this level of Society. She was eternally grateful to Lady Melbourne and Lady Cowper for the priceless voucher, and to Lady Dingley for her steadfast sponsorship. Upon entering the handsome assembly hall for the first time, Folie had felt she must burst with pride to see that Melinda was so much more beautiful than the other girls—perhaps it was a bad year, but the nobility seemed to have produced little better than a collection of snub noses, rabbity teeth, and thin hair in their female offspring. The crowd of young girls carried themselves gracefully, danced beautifully, sipped their orgeat with refinement, but in her white gown—last year's periodical pattern sewn up by Toot's best seamstress—Melinda outshone them all by simply standing in a corner.

Folie was not the only one who thought so. Things seemed to happen in a slow motion at Almack's; the dancing was stately, the conversations modulated and deliberate, the introductions careful. Folie and Melinda stood with Lady Dingley and her daughters along the wall. They were ignored at first, but then the languid notice began to come.

Old acquaintances of Lady Dingley found her out—matrons and weighty gentlemen, solemn sons who made desultory comments about the heat in the room and asked the Misses Dingley to dance.

But Folie saw how they glanced at Melinda even as they took Jane or Cynth out on their arms. And politeness allowed that, after a dance with Lady Dingley's progeny, the lesser members of the party might be recognized. By the second week, Melinda was dancing every set—an earl's fourth son, an Irish baronet, the brother of one of Wellington's ADCs—even a viscount. Mr. Brummel spoke with her briefly. He was known to have complimented her faultless complexion, enough to bring any debutante into fashion.

To Folie's astonishment, even she had her own share of admirers—seldom while Melinda danced was Folie left without a more mature gentleman's company or an invitation to play cards. Everything was going perfectly, a thousand times better than anyone could have hoped.

Folie hated it.

Somehow she had imagined that London society would have more brilliance. More wit. More . . . something.

She could not quite put her finger on it. Certainly the women were beautifully dressed; the men exquisite in knee breeches, chapeau-bras tucked under their arms. Lady Dingley was in raptures over the success of their reception. Folie had discussed the weather in London, the weather in Herefordshire, the weather in Buckinghamshire, the weather in France. Indeed, it was a most foggy spring. Or a dry spring, a wet one, an ordinary one, depending on the opinion of her confidant. It would no doubt rain this Sunday; she would be well advised to carry a rain umbrella. It would no doubt be quite pretty this Sunday; she would be advised to carry a sun parasol.

Society began to seem like a very large version of a meeting of the Ladies' Committee in Toot.

"Now, what causes you to smile so mysteriously, Mrs. Hamilton?" Colonel Cox asked, making his chair creak as he shifted his broad shoulders.

She sorted her hand at whist. "I was speculating if my head would fit into a bucket of sand."

He looked at her oddly, and then produced a hearty laugh; he was a widower with children, one of Folie's foremost devotees. "I vow, you are so droll. Is she not, Lady Walron?"

"Indeed!" Lady Walron said absently, laying down a card. "Do you follow suit, Mrs. Hamilton?"

Folie played her hand. Colonel Cox complimented her and vowed she would be his partner for the next rubber. He was quite a large, muscular man; he spoke with a gritty hush, as if to deprecate his considerable physical presence. He had lost three fingers at the battle of Talavera. He was pleasant and kind, but try as she might, Folie could not seem to think of much to say to him. He had a way of replying to each attempt at conversation by commending her wit or her wisdom—flattering, but hardly conducive to a dialogue. She had said, "Thank you," so often that she had finally resorted to a simple nod instead.

The music in the ballroom came to a conclusion. Supper time. Folie calculated that it was another two hours before they might leave.

"Ah, there is Miss Hamilton," she said, locating Melinda among the crowd of dispersing dancers. Her stepdaughter disengaged herself from the arm of a young man and went immediately to join Jane and Cynth as they came through the door, her discarded partner following with puppylike resolve. So far, Melinda did not seem to take a particular interest in any of her admirers. Perversely, she seemed more determined to matchmake for Folie than to concentrate on her own expectations.

"No, no, Mama," she said, as Folie and the colonel rose from the card table. "Don't stop your game."

It was Melinda who had first informed her stepmother that Folie also had serious marital prospects in London. Where this intelligence had sprung from, Folie did not know, but Melinda was already making her own circle of friends, young and old. At first, Folie had been inclined to call the idea nonsensical; she had neither money nor beauty nor youth to recommend her, but she had not counted upon the gentlemen of a certain age who had been bereaved of their wives and left with young children to raise. She had not thought anything of it until several of these gentlemen began to pay calls at Cambourne House. After a few assemblies, Folie could not deny that a genteel widow, barely out of her twenties but with the experience of bringing up a daughter and no encumbering children of her own, seemed to be an object of some moderate interest.

Colonel Cox was obviously attentive; he had called twice already and invited their party to the opera two nights hence. Most significantly, he never complimented Melinda, or mentioned her to Folie. Now he held out his arm to her. ''May I have the honor of taking you down to supper, ma'am?''

Under Melinda's merry look, Folie accepted. She could only hope that if Colonel Cox actually were to propose, she could stay awake long enough to notice.

But it was quite unjust and wrong of her, she thought as they sat through the tea and thin slices of bread and butter. Lady Dingley had made inquiries. Colonel Cox was a well-respected man, with a solid income and substantial property in Norfolk. He was gentle of manner and courteous. Folie began to think that she was possessed of some demon, that she could not bring herself even to take an interest in whether or not he would propose.

Certainly it would be a practical course, to marry again. Having no available suitors in Toot, she had been careful to avoid serious contemplation of such an unlikely circumstance, but there were numerous advantages—provided she chose wisely—and few reasons to regret a life lived alone on a moderate income. There had been moments—not often, but now and again, deep in the night, when she had looked ahead to the existence before her and grown so desolate that she had had to rise and take to the cordial like a gazetted old lady.

And yet here she was, in the midst of London, looking at an excellent hope of eschewing that dismal future—and all she could seem to think of was how soon she might with courtesy abandon his table.

What *do* you want, ma'am? she asked herself in exasperation. For she did want something. To travel, perhaps. To go . . . to go . . . somewhere. There seemed to be an intensity inside her that pressed for a voice, for motion, for talk of something besides weather and cards and people she had never met. Something that did not want to be careful and proper, and say only the right things.

"Perhaps I shall write a book," she said.

"A book!" Colonel Cox said. "What sort of book?"

"Far places. Perhaps there will be a lost princess in it."

"Oh. A novel." The colonel appeared dubious.

Folie supposed it would please him better if she wrote a collection of household hints. "The heroine will be excellent at mending sheets," she offered generously. "In fact, perhaps that is how she became lost; she was examining the linen for holes, when suddenly . . ." She paused, considering the alternatives.

"I am sure you are funning," he said indulgently.

"Of course," Folie said, and let the subject drop. She took a sip of tea.

There was a slight commotion near the entry. Heads turned idly. At the doorway, several gentlemen strolled in, dressed by the code demanded at Almack's, formal breeches and three-cornered hats, but carrying with them an air of cool rebellion.

"The night must be dull at the gaming hells," someone murmured nearby.

Folie was astonished to see Robert Cambourne walk in with the party. She set down her teacup with a slight clatter.

He did not notice her. The rakish gentlemen who accompanied him paused to pay compliments to several ladies; Folie watched as he was introduced. Oddly, she felt herself blushing, hoping not to be noticed, as if she had been caught out in some misdemeanor.

"I wonder who that fellow is," the Colonel said.

Folie turned her teacup, lowering her face.

"Been in the tropics, I dare say," Colonel Cox added. "They say it only rains at night there."

The room was not large enough that Folie could hope to go unnoticed for long. When she looked up again, Robert was just turning.

However he might have seemed at their latest meeting, or the ones before, he appeared far from demented now. She saw him recognize her, a pause in his survey of the room. Their eyes met.

All of Folie's indifference in the company had vanished the instant she had seen him. She had not heard a word from him since that extraordinary visit in her bedchamber. He seemed to have vanished, leaving her between worry and provocation; the only evidence that he had been there at all was Toot's new cage and indestructible lock.

He glanced at the colonel and then inclined his head to her, chilly courtesy. Folie took a deep a breath and nodded in return. He turned away.

"Do you know him?" Colonel Cox asked in surprise.

"Mr. Cambourne of Solinger Abbey," she said. "He is my stepdaughter's guardian."

"Oh?"

There was a note in the colonel's voice that made her look toward him. He was frowning a little.

"You do not approve?"

Colonel Cox made his chair squeak again, shifting uncomfortably. "It is not my place to approve! No doubt he is of excellent character. I cannot say I like the company he is in tonight."

"Who is it?"

"Deep players, my dear. But this is of no interest." He smiled. "Let me tell you what I heard today—the Duke of Cambridge wants us to believe that the Prince Regent's headaches are a sign of weakness in his brain! What do you make of that?"

Folie made nothing at all of it. She could barely keep herself from looking at Robert and the men with him as they made their progress toward the refreshment table, talking and greeting their acquaintance. He fit among them perfectly, with that casual satanic style of his, looking down upon the glittering crowd.

"I beg you to accept my excuses, colonel," she said, rising. "I must speak to Lady Dingley."

The colonel stood quickly, bowing. Folie left him, making her way to the door of the supper room. Her flight necessitated that she pass near where Robert stood with his party, but his back was turned. However, just as she gained the doorway, Lady Dingley met her coming in, Miss Jane and Cynth in tow.

"Ah! Mrs. Hamilton." She took Folie's arm. "I have just heard that Mr. Cambourne is here. Really the girls must express their obligation for his hospitality at Cambourne House." She patted Folie's hand. "If you will be so good as to present them to him." She lowered her voice. "I have left Melinda with Lord Christian—I did not insist that she come right away—an excellent partí, you know! But I must not leave them alone for long. You will understand."

Folie was not quite certain that she did, but Lady Dingley had already given her arm a squeeze and swept away, leaving the girls. Miss Jane's eyes danced. She opened her fan and leaned near Folie's ear.

"I believe Mr. Cambourne is in Viscount Morier's party," she murmured. "Mama would not dare introduce us, but *you* may be guilty of any excess!"

"Surely she does not wish you to meet this viscount?" Folie asked dubiously. "I understand he gambles immoderately!"

"He will be the Duke of Eaton."

"Ah," Folie said, with a little grimace.

"Yes," Jane said, nodding wisely. "Mama can be foolish, but I do not think it will do us any harm. Beyond appearing so absurd as to suppose Morier might be interested in such a pair of rustic milkmaids!"

Folie felt a surge of affection for pragmatic Jane. "Of course it will do you no harm! I only hope Lord Morier may fall madly in love with one of you on the instant, so that you can refuse him on account of his frivolous character and send him into a tragic decline."

''Oh, dear, must we refuse him only for that?'' Jane pouted. ''And I had so counted upon being a duchess!''

''Come along,'' Folie said. ''Let us put it behind us.''

She turned, taking Jane's arm. Robert and his companions seemed to have stationed themselves at a strategic point near the refreshment table, the better to make mocking comments about everyone who passed in and out, Folie supposed. Several ladies stood with them, smiling and flirting languidly with their fans. She moved within a few feet of the group, into his line of sight, and dropped a curtsy.

Robert lifted an eyebrow. ''Mrs. Hamilton,'' he said, turning to her with a short nod.

''Mr. Cambourne.'' She was aware that the gentlemen with him had fallen silent, watching. ''I hope you are well.''

''Perfectly well.''

''I pray you will permit me to present Sir Howard Dingley's daughters to you.''

He bowed, glancing at the girls. ''Please do me the honor.''

''Miss Jane Dingley.'' Jane made a curtsy and stood back. ''Miss Cynthia.'' Cynth bobbed and retreated. ''This is Mr. Cambourne.''

Both of the girls were as red in the cheeks as ripe apples. Cynth looked as if she might bolt at any moment, but Jane stood calmly, her moon-shaped face serene, her hands clasped. ''We must thank you, sir, for inviting us to stay at Cambourne House.''

''It is my pleasure.'' He smiled with a warmth that surprised Folie. ''I'm glad to see it full of girls and fun.''

''Girls and fun?'' echoed one of his companions. He lifted his quizzing glass, examining Folie and Jane. ''Do present me, Cambourne!''

Folie made a small curtsy as Robert introduced her to Lord Morier, a slightly built exquisite with heavy black brows over the eyes of a jaded hawk. She dutifully presented Miss Jane and Cynth. As expected, the heir to the dukedom barely glanced at them. He bowed to Folie. ''Ah! The notable Mrs. Hamilton! Did you bring your ferret?''

"No. I could not procure him a ticket," Folie replied shortly.

"My commiseration! I could hardly get one myself."

"Nay, my lord—you?" one of the ladies said ingratiatingly.

"My wicked character," his lordship said with a sad sigh, turning away to his friends.

"I vow he cannot match that ferret for an evil character," Robert murmured.

"There is nothing evil about Toot!" Folie objected.

He looked down at her. "A venal manner and a vicious disposition—clearly a member of the criminal classes. I am surprised you would associate with such riffraff, Mrs. Hamilton."

"Indeed!" she said. "And I am told that your companions are in the habit of gambling for large stakes."

"That is very much the case, ma'am."

"I might inquire what are *you* doing in such perilous company?"

"Why, gambling away Miss Melinda's inheritance, of course," he said. "And your jointure too. You have some objection?"

Folie wrinkled her nose at him. "You might at least engage to double our stake instead."

"As you wish." He bowed to her and the girls. "But I must not take up your time. Your gentleman friend is waiting for you at your table." Without waiting for her reply, he turned and spoke to the viscount, visibly excluding her from the group.

The brief encounter left Folie feeling flushed and vitalized, as if the whole dull company had come alive. She pursed her lips and conducted Jane and Cynth away with what composure she could muster. What a damnably irksome man. He must wake up every morning and decide to assume a wholly new character, the more unpredictable and inconsistent the better.

The only certain thing Folie could say was that he made something inside her come alive. Frustrated, puzzled, alarmed, enticed. Absurd. And utterly alive.

Colonel Cox stood up, moving to intercept her with a bow and a hope for that second rubber of whist. Glancing over her shoulder, she beheld a very beautiful lady touch Robert Cambourne's sleeve lightly with her fan.

So there. Let a female of that caliber tangle with him. He was quite out of Folie's class and always had been. She took the arm of her future, a thousand safe, practical, sheltered nights of whist. And wished violently that he had never put a pen to paper in India so many years ago, so that she might not have known the difference.

Robert handed in his card at Lady Melbourne's door. He had determined to make himself as conspicuous as possible. Play the fox to invisible hounds: he found no other way to proceed but to try to draw them into the open. He was done with living his life in hiding. He had called on every associate or connection he knew from India, few as they were in London. Nothing. Nothing but polite reminiscence and well-worn complaints about the Company, talk more inane than sinister.

He began to doubt himself. A cold fear was always with him, that he had been mad after all, imagined the bloody apron, imagined Kathy or Mattie or whatever her name might be. But he plunged ahead with his intention, moving into the world of the gaming hells, betting sums that would draw the attention of anyone—and did. He found himself welcome at the tables where Morier and his crowd laid fortunes on the green baize every night; invited into high society by the back door.

It should have been no surprise, of course, to see Folly at Almack's. When the viscount had announced that his dear mama insisted that he put in an appearance at the sedate assembly rooms, Robert had not thought of it. But there she was, seated with an attentive officer, no doubt a solid rock of trustworthiness, to judge by the size and substantial aspect of him.

Robert had intentionally kept a distance between himself and Cambourne House. If he drew any danger, he did not want to draw it there. He would not have wished to pay any particular attention to her in public for the same reason—but to stand by and watch her courted by some sensible and sound military man was more than he cared to support in any case. To have her take him to task over his disreputable companions made him burn.

He did not really expect Lady Melbourne to receive him without an introduction, but the porter returned and bowed him inside. Apparently the lady kept a lively salon, for the drawing room was full of company and several callers were just leaving as Robert was announced.

The statuesque Lady Melbourne received him with an absent wave toward an open chair, without ceasing to talk to an elderly man whose hand she held tightly. They seemed to be in the midst of some intense policy discussion. Robert watched with interest—he had never before encountered one of London's famed political hostesses.

He remained standing as he waited, looking idly about the room. Everyone seemed engaged in his or her own pursuits—conversation with the other callers, or even simply reading. He glanced down at a *Morning Post* that had been discarded on the side table. Columns of society gossip, marriages and deaths, letters, announcements of new novels—his eye stopped on the word *Hindustani*. Curious, Robert picked up the paper.

The distinguished Dr. Edward Varley, specialist in treatment of the headache, is favored by His Majesty the Prince Regent with a request for attendance. The translator of a number of significant reference works, Dr. Varley is an authority on the Arabic, Hindustani, and Egyptian medical science. We are informed that Dr. Varley has enjoyed considerable success in curing intractable headache in his patients, and comes to the Prince Regent with the high recommendation of several noblemen.

Robert looked up from the paper as a younger man joined in Lady Melbourne's talk, his voice rising audibly. There, too, the topic appeared to be the prince's health.

"Nay, he is beyond any sympathy!" the newcomer exclaimed. "I don't know how you can summon the least degree of feeling, ma'am."

"Well, when you are old and fat, my dear, perhaps you will have just a little more understanding of how lowering such things can be," Lady Melbourne said kindly.

"Perhaps so, ma'am, but when the *prince* has experience of famine, and knows for himself the pain of a meager belly and the weariness of hauling coals from sunup until midnight, then I shall pity him his headaches!"

"We shall not hold our breath until that happens," she replied briskly. "But I am more taken with the Duke of Cambridge's evil rumors. What can he be about, to spread this idea that his brother suffers from delusions like the old King? Cambridge is no radical, nor in line to be regent in the prince's place."

"Pure hatred," the older man said, while Robert's interest drifted. He had little interest in either royalty or democracy. He examined a tapestry of a medieval hunting scene while the man's voice droned on. "They have always been at one another's throats. And what do you make of Cumberland's sanity? After that incident with his valet."

"A strange pass." Lady Melbourne nodded wisely.

"Strange enough! Cumberland all cut up from being attacked in bed—so we are told! And the guilty valet then conveniently slices his own throat! What a pack of hounds, our princes."

"You cannot paint the poor regent in Cumberland's colors, though."

"Nay, he is a fat, stupid lapdog, not a hound. It will be no more than a hangnail keeps Prinnie to his bed, mark my words."

"Where there's smoke, there's fire," the rebellious young gentleman said ominously. "They say he starts screaming like a baby, crying that he will fly away if they take him outside."

The words caught Robert's attention. He stood looking at the snarling face of a woven boar.

"I cannot but pity the man," Lady Melbourne said, "if he has inherited his father's madness."

"But if it meant he could be removed from the regency!" the fire-eater said eagerly.

"Hush!" She shook her head, lowering her voice. "You are speaking nonsense."

"Nay, I only meant by an act of God." He sounded sour. "I can't drive the man mad merely to depose him, should I never so much approve the good Lord's sagacity if He happened to take a hand in the matter."

Robert stared at the tapestry, a strange idea crystallizing in his mind.

"Hmmpf." The white-haired gentleman grunted. "And who would replace him, I ask you? There's not a one of the princes worth a farthing."

The young man smirked. "Who could say? Perhaps—"

"None of your foolish reforming gabble here, sir!" Lady Melbourne said sharply. "I am a Whig, not an anarchist."

He bowed, smiling. "You know I only tease you, my lady!"

"Tease you may, but my drawing room is open; here is Mr. Cambourne of Calcutta, you see, all ears!" She turned to smile at Robert. "What a time I have, preventing these young men from casting themselves in jail with their fatuous talk! Go away now, Mr. Hunt. Enough of the Prince Regent. We shall have at the East India Company now! Mr. Cambourne."

Robert obeyed her beckoning hand, bowing over her plump, bejeweled fingers. The incredible notion that had just come upon him made his brain spin. The other gentlemen withdrew, but he could hardly concentrate on what she was saying.

". . . back from India?"

"I beg your pardon, ma'am?" he asked.

"Dear boy, I asked you how long you are returned from India?"

"Many months. Mrs. Charles Hamilton mentioned to me that you wished me to call."

"Yes. Shall we keep her or get rid of her?"

"Madam?"

"India! We seem to have collected an empire while we weren't looking. What is to be done about renewing the charter?"

"I suppose that depends upon what your interest is, ma'am. If it is riches for England, then get rid of her; she is an expensive mistress, dearly bought and costly to keep. If it is fortunes for a few, then keep her—now and again she smiles on a particular man."

"But perhaps it is expedient to parade her on our arm, loaded with jewels, to impress Napoleon and the rest of Europe, and keep her from Russia's embrace?"

He shrugged. "You are talking to the wrong man, my lady. I am neither a soldier nor a diplomat. This sort of question has never absorbed me."

"Ah. Mrs. Hamilton warned me that you were not political." She took a sip of a green liqueur. "But your observations are not empty, I think."

"I spent my time in study of the religion and philosophy of the place, mostly."

"I see. And what did you learn, besides the expense of conquest? Which is not an ill lesson to master, by the by. I think Napoleon may come to grief over it in the end."

Robert smiled. "My teachers would agree with you.

"Your teachers?"

"The religious men. The *guuruus* and saints. They have a way of making all the sound and fury of the world seem no more than wind blowing across a silent rock."

"As I grow older, I can begin to understand the wisdom of that," she said. Then she shook her head and lifted her hand, taking in the roomful of callers. "Though as you see, I am an old warhorse to the core, and the sound of the trumpets still stir me."

"That is your *karma,*" he said.

"And what might that mean?"

"It is the sum of all action, all that you have done in this life and all others. Your future fate and destiny determined by your past."

"Well, it is my character, at any rate." She tilted her

head, studying him with the piercing dark eye of an inquisitive raven. "But this is a delightful notion—can we never escape our folly, then?"

"I do not think we can," he said slowly.

"Perhaps it is wiser not to try."

"They would say . . ." He frowned, shaking his head. "Perhaps we can transcend our past folly; with the right mind, the right effort."

"They are more sanguine than our Greeks, then, who would have every man's fate written in the stars, immutable, twist and turn to avoid it as he will."

"Yes."

"And what do you believe, Mr. Cambourne?"

"I don't know," he said.

She smiled. "You are honest."

"It is not much to show for the years I spent."

She gave a snort. "I am surrounded by gentlemen who are very certain of all that they know. You are refreshing. Tell me more of what you learned from these *guuruus*. Can they work magic and charm snakes, as we hear?"

"Yes," he said.

She laughed. "Ah, now you cozen me."

"You may call them parlor tricks, if you like."

She nodded skeptically. "It is not real magic?"

"My lady, that is another thing I cannot say for certain. I have seen things—and learned things—that are not to be explained by any reasonable means."

"No, I will not have it. Come back some other day and bamboozle me with parlor tricks. And bring the ferret lady with you. Dear Mrs. Hamilton." She turned, the black plume on her cap bobbing as she beckoned to another visitor.

Robert bowed at his dismissal. He walked to the door of the drawing room, still turning his blinding new idea over and over in his mind.

It could not be true. Too crazy, to suppose that there was some likeness between his own mental state and the Prince Regent's. The old king was insane, had suffered spells of dementia for decades—what would be more reasonable than that his son should have inherited the same natural affliction? What more absurd than to suppose it could be—might be—induced by the same means Robert's mind had been deranged?

The only rational defense he could summon for such a suspicion was that there were far more people with obvious motivation to wish the Prince to appear insane than there were to make Robert seem so. Hardly a convincing justification.

He shook his head, standing on the pedestrian pavement outside Melbourne House. Robert's frustration with his inability to do or learn anything was affecting his common sense. He could see plots and enemies everywhere—even in that young rebellious gentleman from Lady Melbourne's drawing room who still lingered, leaning upon a lamppost across the street.

As Robert turned to walk along the pavement, the young man pushed upright and began to walk the same way. Robert took the length of the street at an easy pace. When he paused at the busy crossing, sweeping boys crowded up to him. He tossed a coin to one of them. Glancing up, he saw the young man pause. They looked directly at one another between the passing carriages and pedestrians.

The other man turned in the opposite direction and disappeared into the passing flow. And Robert thought he was either still insane or in grave danger of his life. He was not quite certain which he fancied.

Thirteen

FOLIE PULLED THE blue kashmir shawl about her, huddling over a steaming tisane in the drawing room at Cambourne House. Toot curled in her lap, tucked into a sapphire fold. She had dug the shawl out from the bottom of a trunk—on the few occasions when she felt a little ill, it was the only one she could bear to have about her—soft as goosedown; light and warm round her aching shoulders.

She was not concerned that her ailment would last more than a disagreeable evening. She was never sick or feverish. When all about her were lowered by the influenza, Folie had never succumbed to more than a few hours of the headache and shivers. Still, she would be glad to have it behind her.

There was at least one benefit—she was not obliged to attend the opera with Colonel Cox's party. She had sent Melinda and the girls off with Lady Dingley, attended by a rather recalcitrant Lander, who seemed lately to take his duty as a guard dog as something more irrationally holy than ever. Faced with a division of his territory, he had been most disturbed, going so far as to suggest to Folie that the whole household should remain home. But Folie had dismissed that, dreading the prospect of Melinda's attentive endeavors to nurse her. She liked to keep to herself when she felt indisposed; Melinda was well-meaning but unable to comprehend any disposition but her own, which fancied tender petting and constant care.

Sitting with her hot drink and Lord Byron's scandalous new poem, Folie was happy enough. The tisane—or the poem—did her so much good that she was startled out of a nap by the knock at the drawing room door.

"Sir Howard Dingley has arrived, ma'am," one of the footmen said apologetically. "He means to see Lady Dingley, he said. Shall I have him wait downstairs?"

"Oh!" Folie sat up, trying to gather her thoughts, dizzy from a dream of Childe Harold weeping while trying to find Toot amid the confusion of an Indian bazaar. "No. No, of course not. Ask him if he will come up and sit by the fire. I do not think he need worry about contagion."

"Yes, ma'am."

Folie straightened herself, tucking her hair back under her cap. Sir Howard entered, still in his hat and coat. He bowed, his cheeks very pink beneath the leathery skin. He took an extra step as he straightened—Folie realized that he was a little affected by strong drink.

She was not accustomed to dealing with gentlemen in their cups, but she invited him to sit down across the room, warning him with a smile that he would not wish to venture too close to her.

"I should not suppose any female would wish me to venture too close," he said, sitting down heavily and tossing his hat to the floor.

Folie did not know quite what to make of that—her mind was none too sharp at the moment. She wished now that she had not bid him join her, but she had not been thinking clearly. "I am sorry that Lady Dingley and the girls are not at home. We had no idea to expect you tonight, I'm afraid."

"No," he said with a glum look. "Of course not."

They sat for a long moment.

"Have you come direct from Dingley Court?" she asked. "Have you had supper?"

"No, I—" He stopped abruptly.

''Shall I ring for something? I'm sure there is a cold chicken.''

He shook his head. ''Mrs. Hamilton—''

A thought swam into her dulled mind. Sir Howard standing in the street with a weeping girl. Folie pulled the shawl about her and sat up very straight.

''Mrs. Hamilton, I must confess something—''

''Please do not!'' she said. ''I'm sure you must be famished.'' She stood up. Toot made a wild leap, disappearing underneath the sofa.

''No, no. I need nothing to eat.'' He reached over and poured himself a glass from a decanter of brandy on the side table. Folie realized for the first time that the tray and single glass was set out there every night, though no one ever drank from it. She resumed her seat, folding her hands under the shawl.

He sat there staring into the crystal glass, half slumped in the chair, looking worn and sad.

''I hope all is well at home,'' she said.

''Oh, aye, well enough.'' He turned the glass in his hands. The firelight winked off the crystal. ''Do you go out every night?''

''Oh, yes,'' Folie said. ''We are gay to dissipation, as Miss Jane puts it.''

He took a drink and stood up. ''I suppose she is all in raptures, being here in London!'' he said bitterly.

''Jane? Well, I suppose—''

''My wife!'' He swung across the room, taking a stance before the fire. ''My dear wife.''

''Oh. Yes, I . . . I would say that she enjoys it very much.''

He chuckled, glaring into the coals. ''I would never bring her to town,'' he said thickly. ''How she has detested me for it.''

Folie was silent. If she had not seen him on the street corner, she might have felt some sympathy.

''She has no sense!'' he muttered, almost to himself. ''What, was I to bring her here and let her fall in love with some fine buck oozing polished manners? She is a fool for a fashionable dandy. She has no sense!''

''I beg your pardon,'' Folie said, nettled. ''But I do not think that is at all true!''

He leaned on the mantel, looking at her over his shoulder. ''No? Certainly she has told me often enough that I have no refinement. No elegance, no graces.'' He made a mocking lilt with his fingers.

''I do not think that signifies that she would fall in love with a man of fashion!''

''No? She warned me of it herself. That I could not trust her here.''

Folie shook her head, bewildered at this image of Lady Dingley, so at odds with what Folie knew of her. ''I think I had better ring for another tisane.''

''To my face!'' he said, as if Folie were arguing with him. ''Not to trust her!''

She eyed him dubiously as he poured another brandy. ''I cannot imagine that Lady Dingley said any such thing. I'm sure you misunderstood her. I have not had an opportunity to thank you for providing us with such excellent horses. We have ridden in the park several times.''

He shook his head with a dismissive gesture. ''It's nothing. My pleasure. Did she try the little long-tailed gray?''

''No . . . no, Lady Dingley does not ride with us.''

He made a disgruntled sound. ''Of course not.''

''But the younger girls have ridden the gray,'' she added. ''They seem to like him very much.''

With a dejected shrug, he sat down again. ''A beautiful animal,'' he said. ''I wish—I had meant—'' He thrust his hands into his pockets. ''But what the devil is the use?''

''Perhaps you might have stayed with us a day or two,'' Folie murmured. ''Lady Dingley seems to be a rather timid rider.''

''Ha.'' He lifted his eyes from the floor. ''She made it clear enough that I am not welcome.''

For an instant, their glances met and held, as they had in that moment of discovery on the street corner. He flushed deeply and looked away.

"You don't understand," he said in a harsh tone. "What is a man to do? You don't know what it's like."

Folie said nothing. She braided the fringe of the shawl between her fingers.

"I do love her," he said.

"Yes," Folie murmured.

"She wants no more children." He pushed himself out of the chair. "Who can blame her? But I—" He made an anguished sound. "Oh God, look what's happened. Look what has happened. I never meant it this way." Brandy sloshed out of the glass onto his fingers. He stared down at them.

Folie bit her lip. "Perhaps you have had a little too much to drink."

"Not enough." He closed his eyes with a pained laugh. "Not nearly enough."

"Please have something to eat. You would not wish Lady Dingley and the girls to come home and discover you in this state."

He looked intensely at Folie. "I believe she is dead," he whispered.

"Dead?" Folie was beginning to become a little frightened of him.

"The girl. The one you saw."

She gazed at him wordlessly.

"That was the first time I ever did it—I swear, the first time." He swallowed the whole glass of brandy. "God."

"You have not killed her!" Folie gasped.

"No! For God's sake—" He blew air between his teeth. "I am not that much a monster. No, she was the first—my first—the first time—" He shook his head violently. "My God, I regret it. It was nothing, a passing moment. But I did not want Isabelle to find out. I couldn't bear for her to know. And then the girl followed me to London—" He shut his eyes. "My God, I regret it, I regret it. When I looked up and saw you in that carriage!"

"Of course I have said nothing," Folie murmured stiffly.

He looked at her, a strange, long stare. A strand of his

graying hair fell across his forehead. "God forgive me," he muttered.

"I do not believe Lady Dingley saw you."

He rubbed his hand across his face. "I don't know what to do."

Folie's head was aching. She pulled the shawl tight about her. These visitations by irrational gentlemen were wearing. "I am afraid I cannot advise you," she said. "Beyond suggesting that some cold meat and coffee might make things seem brighter. A little snack will often do so."

"No." Suddenly he reached down and collected his hat. "I was a fool to come here. A great, stupid, criminal fool. I must go."

Before Folie could gather herself to rise, he had walked to the door. "Wait," she said. "Where are you staying? If Lady Dingley should wish to communicate with you?"

"I cannot imagine that she will," he said caustically. "But I am at Limmer's Hotel." He opened the door and was gone.

Folie's head was pounding when Lady Dingley tiptoed into her bedchamber.

"Mrs. Hamilton," she whispered. "Are you awake?"

Folie sat wearily up among the pillows. "Yes." She had been unable to sleep for the pain in her head and Sir Howard's strange visit going round and round in her mind. "How was the music?"

"Oh, it was delightful." Lady Dingley came and sat on the edge of the bed, shielding her candle. She was still dressed in her opera finery, a pale cream ostrich feather curling down beside her cheek and a single diamond glittering at her throat.

"You look very pretty," Folie said, sitting up a little.

"Thank you. How are you?"

"I will survive," Folie said.

"The servants tell me that Sir Howard was here." Lady Dingley's voice was low, but Folie thought there was a note of eagerness in it.

"Yes. But he was—very weary from his journey, and

decided not to wait. I'm sure he will be back in the morning.''

Lady Dingley sighed. ''Did you tell him that he might stay here?''

''Well,'' Folie said. ''To be quite honest—he did not seem to think he would be welcome.''

''Oh no, oh no,'' Lady Dingley moaned. ''How could he think so? I so wanted him to come!''

Folie lay back on her pillow. ''I need a cold compress.''

''Oh—'' Lady Dingley half rose. ''Let me ring.''

''No . . . no. I was only funning.'' Folie smiled a little. ''Dear me. I'm afraid that you and Sir Howard are not quite comprehending one another.''

Lady Dingley looked contritely down at her lap. ''I should not bother you; you do not feel well.''

''I'm in no case to be a very good go-between,'' Folie said. ''He is at Limmer's Hotel—perhaps you will write him a note in the morning and ask him to remove here.''

Her face flushed hot. ''I could not!''

''No?'' Folie echoed helplessly.

''I have never—it would seem as if—'' She put her hand to her cheek. ''As if I *wanted* him to stay!''

''I thought you did!''

''Yes, but—it would be so . . . immodest! To ask him!''

Folie made a faint groan. ''I suppose it would not be immodest if I were to do it for you.''

''Would you?'' Lady Dingley grasped her hand. ''Mrs. Hamilton, you are so good at these things. You can make him understand.''

''I don't know that I speak English any better than anyone else,'' Folie said, feeling like pulling the covers over her head.

''Mrs. Hamilton . . .'' It was just Melinda's tone of voice, that soft plea.

Folie sighed. ''Yes, yes, yes. In the morning. I will write a note.''

''Oh, you are a peach!'' She hopped up from the bed like one of her teenaged daughters. ''I hope you are feeling better very soon.''

No doubt, Folie thought, turning over and pulling the coverlet up to her throat. The light from Lady Dingley's candle vanished as she pulled the door shut softly. Toot kissed Folie's nose and curled up next to her pillow.

"Do you suppose you will be up to Vauxhall Gardens?" Melinda asked anxiously at breakfast.

Folie sipped her steaming chocolate. "Yes, I feel much better. And nothing would persuade me to miss the fireworks!"

"You must stay inside all day," Melinda said. "Just to make certain you are perfectly recovered."

"I vow I shall do nothing but coddle myself."

"Perhaps you will write letters," Lady Dingley said.

Folie smiled wryly. "Yes, certainly I shall. The Misses Nunney must be wondering what has become of us!"

"And—"

"I have not forgot!" Folie said. "Or perhaps you would prefer to dictate?"

"Oh, no!" Lady Dingley made flustered gestures with a slice of toast. "No, no, I have complete faith in you."

"Of course!" Miss Jane exclaimed. "She got us an introduction to Lord Morier."

"And she got us this house!" Cynth added.

"And a ferret!" one of the younger girls cried.

"Mama can do *anything,*" Melinda said proudly.

"Yes, I am serving the moon on a silver platter for supper tonight. What will you have for dessert?"

"Lord Morier!"

"Buckingham Palace!"

"An *elephant!*" the youngest shrieked, laughing.

"You must apply to Mr. Cambourne for an elephant," Folie said. "I believe he has several in his stables. As to the rest—" She made an elaborate bow in her chair. "Your wish is my command."

But later, as she sat at her desk overlooking the back garden, the blue shawl still pulled close about her shoulders, she found herself at a complete loss in delivering Sir Howard to Lady Dingley. She had tried several times to explain his wife's modesty to him, but it all appeared so ridiculous when she attempted to write it down, and she felt like such an inexcusable meddler, that she finally decided that such things could only be said in person—if at all.

At last, all she wrote was, *We have a box reserved this evening for the fireworks at Vauxhall. Number 23 in the Grove, at seven. If you can come there, we will speak in private to your advantage, I believe. F. H.*

She folded it, sealed it with a Cambourne House wafer, and went to summon a footman.

Robert looked up from the newspaper at a knock on his door. For the past several days, he had been poring over every periodical in London, looking for any mention of the Prince Regent's condition. There were several; he had marked and saved them.

The prince was certainly incapacitated—he had not appeared lately anywhere in public. The reasons given ranged from "the Prince is presently engaged with religion, and reads daily a chapter or two of the Bible with Lady Hertford," in the Tory papers, to a scathing description in the progressive *Examiner* that accused the regent of being a libertine, a despiser of domestic ties, a gambler, in debt, and—worse—corpulent. Everything *but* mad.

"Who is it?" he called through the door, running his finger down the columns.

"Boots, sir," a boy's voice piped. "Message for you."

Robert had taken care to recognize the hotel servants. He knew this one, and opened the door, digging for a shilling. The envelope was blank outside, gummed shut. "Who brought this?" he asked, handing the boy a shilling.

"Dunno, sir. Porter give it me."

Robert closed the door, sat down again and opened the packet. The letter inside was sealed; he instantly recognized his own crest on the wafer.

The handwriting sent an electric surge through his veins.

We have a box reserved this evening for the fireworks at Vauxhall. Number 23 in the Grove, at seven. If you can come there, we will speak in private to your advantage, I believe.

F. H.

He pulled his watch from his waistcoat. It was already quarter past six. How she had known where to find him, he had no notion, but the very idea that she had gone to the trouble to discover it made his heart lift in the most absurd way. He had not hidden his new whereabouts: one of the best suites at the elegant Clarendon. Perhaps she had asked Morier, or Lander had tracked Robert down for her.

He touched the familiar double period at the end of the second sentence, and held the note up to his face, taking a deep breath. Patchouli. He smiled fiercely.

She might have decided to believe him. She might.

Folie shivered, sitting in the supper box. They had taken a boat across the Thames to Vauxhall, joining a pretty procession of little vessels just at sunset, with a spring breeze rippling the water. But the breeze had turned chilly as the sun went down, and though she delighted in the festoons of lanterns and the music, she was glad she had brought the kashmir shawl. The gardens were much larger than she had expected, crowded with people strolling and admiring the lights, parties large and small. She hoped that Sir Howard would be able to locate them. She had written the note with no very clear idea of the nature of the place.

She also had no very clear idea of what she was going to say to him, or how she would arrange any privacy, either. She was not overly enraptured with her role as mediator. But Lady Dingley kept glancing at her expectantly, as if somehow Folie might produce Sir Howard out of thin air.

Melinda suggested that they take a turn around the Grove, the area enclosed by the long colonnades. Folie hesitated, but Lander gave her such a frown that she relented and joined Melinda and the girls under his protection. Lady Dingley said she would stay with their maid to hold the box. Folie brightened at that. She hoped that Sir Howard would just stroll up and speak to his wife, and they could settle it all between themselves.

Amid the brilliant lights and the promenading crowds, it was easy to lose track of her own party. Lander, she could see, was almost beside himself when any of them lingered or wandered out of the main path. She smiled encouragingly at him—as annoying as he could make himself with his mother-hen worries, it was rather charming of him. At least Folie did not have to do the shepherding. She could relax and enjoy the scene.

It was truly lovely, like nothing she had ever seen before. From the rotunda, outlined in lights, the lilting strains of Handel filled the air with joyful sound. Melinda's face lit with an ecstatic smile. She stopped. When Lander put a gentle hand on her elbow to urge her to keep up with the party, she turned to him, lifted her arms and twirled him about in a light dance step, smiling up with such an enchanting expression that Folie saw him dazzled for an instant, before his face turned to stone and he stepped back with a servant's stiff bow. Melinda just laughed at him and curtsied, drifting ahead, dancing alone. It was all so beautiful and dream-like that Folie did nothing to discourage her, only made a note that she ought to remind her stepdaughter not to be thoughtless with the servants, Lander in particular, who had stood as their good friend so often.

Robert walked down the long row of boxes under the colonnade, reading numbers. He was not certain how he could signal Folie privately in this crowd, so he held back, trying to locate her before any of the rest of the party saw him. But when he finally came upon Box 23, only Lady Dingley and a maid sat inside it.

Robert paused, moving back until he became part of the throng gathered before the orchestra. He was partly concealed by the trees and the curved and ornamented flank of the orchestra's rotunda, but from there the sparkle of lights and harsh shadows beneath the colonnade made detail difficult to see.

He drifted toward the darker part of the garden, reckoning that he might observe better from outside the central colonnades. Once, he thought he caught a glimpse of Melinda, but if he had, she was swallowed up in the slow stirring crowd before he could be sure.

The place was certainly not a good choice for a private meeting—at least for anyone but clandestine lovers, who could take full advantage of the maze of dark garden walks beyond the blaze of illumination. Robert took up a post beneath an unlit tree, where he could just see the box through the entrance to the colonnade. But the people passing in and out blocked his line of sight except for momentary views. He crossed his arms and sighed.

Folie looked at Lady Dingley when they returned to the box, but there was no sign of particular pleasure on her face, or any evidence of Sir Howard. Their supper was laid out. The crowd began to settle into their places for the fireworks.

She had hoped that he would make an appearance early, so that she might get the thing over with and enjoy herself. But perhaps he would not come at all. Perhaps he was too cowardly after all even to speak to Folie.

The walk had warmed her a little, but her fingers were stiff and chilly as she ate. Almost before they had finished the delicate pies and puddings, the music was reaching a crescendo.

A crack of sound made them all jump in their chairs. With a great sigh of awe from the audience, a rocket flew upward from the trees, trailing gold and bursting in the air, scattering a shower of blue sparks. It was followed by a cloud of squibs and corkscrew serpents, crackling glitter across the sky over their heads. Folie forgot all about her cold hands and Sir Howard, sitting back with her mouth open while the garden and the heavens turned to colored lightning and fire.

Robert watched them in the box, debating whether he should wait until the fireworks were over or try to approach her under cover of all the sound and brilliance. He could see her entranced face, lit by the blaze of a spinning and fizzing Catherine wheel. The crowd moaned its approval as another pyrotechnic lit the sky with red and blue and green. Robert pushed away from the tree.

Something icy cold touched the back of his neck. He froze, feeling hands grab his arms from behind.

"Come or die here," someone hissed close to his ear. "A gunshot will never be heard."

The truth of it was already burning in his brain. Robert stared for an instant at the box, at Folie and Melinda and Lander, illuminated and shadowed by the bursts of fireworks. The gun pressed hard into his neck.

Robert nodded silently. He let his unseen captor pull him backward into the black garden.

"Well, that was quite stirring!" Folie exclaimed in satisfaction. The gardens smelled of acrid powder, multicolored smoke drifting through the trees. "I've never seen anything like!"

The music had resumed, sounding peculiarly muted after the noise and fury of the fireworks. People in the boxes began to gather their belongings.

"Oh, I wish it had never ended!" Melinda said. "That was better than a ball!"

The girls gushed and giggled while they collected shawls and reticules. When everything had been accounted for, they stepped out of the box, joining the flow of people headed for the river landing.

"I hope we can obtain a boat!" Lady Dingley said fretfully.

"Oh, Lander will see to it," Melinda said. "Mama, do you want my shawl, too? The water breeze is quite cool!"

Folie denied that she needed anything more than her blue kashmir. As they stood waiting with the growing knot of people on the landing, Lander made his way to the front to negotiate a passage. Folie turned back for one last look up at the gleaming garden lights.

Silhouetted figures moved against them, most walking toward the quay, others seeming to dart this way and that in the tricky light. She squinted, then looked closer at a man striding across the path.

Sir Howard! She had completely forgotten him. And obviously he was searching for them; he had that determined hunting pace, looking about him as he went.

"I will be back in just a moment," she said, touching Melinda's arm. "Hold the boat for me!"

Tucking her shawl about her, Folie hurried up the slope, leaving Melinda's puzzled protest behind. She caught a glimpse of Sir Howard's hat, and then lost him. Annoying man! Folie was of half a mind to leave him to his own devices. Why hadn't he come sooner, to their box? At least shown himself to Folie, if he would not approach Lady Dingley.

Folie paused at the entrance to the colonnade. She thought that she had lost him, but then saw him walk briskly through the opposite entrance. She lifted her skirt and ran after, calling.

He disappeared beyond the light. Folie dodged people walking toward her, determined by now to drag him back to Lady Dingley by main force if necessary. It was completely nonsensical, she thought, that two people who appeared to love one another deeply should entangle themselves in such a debacle that they required an interpreter between them.

Just past the colonnade, she saw him walking up one of the shrub-lined garden alleys. Folie increased her pace. She started to call out again, but people were looking at her oddly as she hastened past, so she remained silent, her slippers patting the ground softly.

Folie had almost caught up when he turned onto a side path. She stopped abruptly, thinking that that was rather odd. Surely he could not expect to find them there, so far into the unlit garden. A cold doubt came over her—perhaps he was here for some furtive assignation with his housemaid.

She stepped into the shadowy path, leaning forward a little. If she saw him with a female, that would be sufficient—she washed her hands of the whole sordid intrigue.

As her eyes adjusted, she heard his voice, pitched low

and urgent, from just beyond the shrubbery. "What the devil do you mean by this?"

Another voice answered, a man's. "Damn your eyes, Dingley! Why'd you come back here?"

"Never mind that!" Sir Howard said strongly. "What have you done to him?"

Folie shivered, pulling the shawl close. *This* was surely nothing she wanted to be involved in. She started to back away.

"That's Cambourne!" Sir Howard exclaimed, his voice low but clearly audible. "Oh my God, my God—if you've murdered him—"

Folie stopped. Her heart seemed to congeal in her chest.

Suddenly Sir Howard came plunging onto the path from the shadows. He saw Folie, pulled up short, and then without a word grabbed her elbow and turned her. She felt him jerk her with him just as another firework exploded right inside her head—bright, violent pain and sparkling blackness.

Fourteen

ROBERT HELD HER head in his lap. Somewhere deep inside him was terror—that she was dying in his arms—but it seemed far away, overlaid by a strange calm. All over her hair and ear was blood; he left it, not attempting to use any of the filthy water and rags the guard had left.

His mind seemed uncannily clear, now that the thing he had feared was happening. He was on a ship, chained by one ankle and wrist to a bulkhead. One of the prison hulks moored in the Thames, he guessed. They appeared to be in a former dining cuddy of the dismantled ship—there was a table bolted to the deck. Beneath its scratched and warped surface he could see Sir Howard chained to the opposite wall. The man's eyes were red-rimmed; his hair straggling down over his forehead. He stared straight ahead, never looking toward Robert and Folie.

Robert had never seen who had brought them here. Only voices, the gun in his back, and a blindfold and gag so tight that he had kept losing consciousness. By the time he had regained his wits sometime in the night, the gag had been replaced by chains, and his coat and boots were gone. He had thought he was imprisoned alone. Only at dawn, when a dim green light leaked through the porthole, did he realize with horror that Folie was lying in an inert heap at his feet.

He had struggled up, leaning over her, breathing dread deep into his lungs. She was dead; he had been certain. Her skin was chalk white, the blood like a black mat across her temple and cheeks, scattered over her gown. The blue kashmir shawl she had worn at Vauxhall was missing.

But bending over, he could feel her breath. He felt an irregular pulse. As he had tried to ease her into a less twisted position, the door had opened and a red-coated guard ducked into the cabin.

''Raikes?'' he demanded, dropping the pail of water and the foul rags on the deck beside Robert. ''William Raikes? She dead yet?''

Robert looked up into his ugly face. ''She's not,'' he said.

The guard squatted down beside her. ''Pretty gal,'' he said, not unkindly. ''Tried to escape off the quay, I hear.''

He did not answer. When the guard moved to touch her, Robert put out his hand and blocked it fiercely.

''Well, it's too bad. It's too bad—but better for her if she passes on now,'' the guard said.

Robert made a sound deep in his throat. The man glanced at him. He shook his grizzled head. ''Nay, put your mind to it, man. Take my word. You don't want her to suffer what's coming.''

''What's coming?''

The guard shrugged and stood. ''Fortnight, maybe, or a year down in the belly of this hulk picking oakum and gathering ballast, only God can say. Depends on the wind. Ten months under decks to Botany Bay, if you make it that far. I always reckoned transport better'n hanging, until I sailed guard on board one of them convict ships. You think the stench bad here—open the hatch after six months out on one o' them things. For a man, it may do, but a woman—aye, and one like your poor wife here, scent of quality on her—you let 'er go now, or see her made a whore down there while you watch, and then die o' putrid fever.''

Robert stared at him. ''Who brought us here?''

''Newgate warden, I reckon. I weren't aboard when you

come. There's a chamberpot—you'll have a biscuit later, visit with the prison master 'fore you're sent below. Do you want to request the surgeon, Raikes?''

Robert could only look down at Folie's limp hands, benumbed.

''Oh, a good man, our surgeon.'' He chuckled. ''He'll kill her for certain.''

''Keep him out of here,'' Robert said.

She dreamed of drowning and pyrotechnics. And Robert Cambourne's voice. She could not be sure if it was the real Robert, her own Robert. She had no way to tell. She did not know his voice. Everything about him was fading, lost to her, lost forever, supplanted inexorably by this dark man who spoke to her in such a soft, bleak voice.

''Robert?'' she whispered, attempting to touch the throbbing pain in her head.

''I'm here,'' he said, but everything was black. She could hear water, smell sour river-smell and sewage, hear stranger's voices with a bizarre hollow echo about them.

''Where?'' Her voice squeaked. She reached toward the sound of his voice, but her wrists felt so heavy that she could not lift them.

There was a sound of metal. A firm hand gripped hers. ''Here. Right here.''

She felt him lean close, felt his breath on her face. She realized that she was lying on a hard floor. ''I can't see you,'' she whimpered.

''You can't?'' His voice was very gentle. ''Right here. It's rather dark. You'll see me in a moment.''

Folie waited, squinting hard. Her head hurt terribly. She tried to quell the panic rising in her. ''I can't see you. Can you see me?''

He did not answer. Folie dug her fingers into his hand. ''Can you see me?'' she repeated. ''Where are we?''

''Folly.'' He spoke in a serious voice. ''I do not want you to try to move. Just listen. We are in one of the prison hulks.''

''What?'' She started to sit up, but pain flashed in her

head and he put his hand against her shoulder. The metallic sound came again, and something heavy slid across her breast.

"Don't move. You've been badly hurt; hit in the head. Just listen." He touched her face and gently turned her head to one side. "Do you see the porthole there?"

"No."

He was silent.

"Should I see it?" she asked frantically. "Can you see it?"

"Be calm. My brave Folly. Yes, I can see it."

Folie began to pant. "What's happened? What's happening?"

"Close your eyes." She felt his fingers over her eyelids, a soft rhythmic stroke, first one side and then the other.

"What is it?" she whispered, holding tight to his hand in the blackness.

He said nothing in reply. Folie bit her lip and held his hand very tightly. She could hear men talking, but it was all muffled, as if they were isolated behind thick walls.

He touched her face. "We are a Mr. and Mrs. Raikes, it seems—convicts. We are sentenced to be held on this hulk ship until transported to Botany Bay."

"Dear God." She felt a strong wave of nausea rise in her throat. "Oh, I am going to be ill."

"Turn over—" He supported her as she leaned on her elbow, dry heaves racking her body. Spikes of lightning went through her head with each spasm.

She moaned, opening her eyes. Briefly, she saw moldy straw under her hand, the floor tilting like a nightmare, and then everything went black again.

Robert sat silently, watching Sir Howard. Still the man had not spoken, and Robert said nothing to him. When a boy brought a biscuit and small ale, Sir Howard flicked the dry bread contemptuously onto the floor.

He looked up, meeting Robert's eyes, and then away again.

"I don't know how you and she were entangled in this," Robert said.

Sir Howard did not appear inclined toward explanations. He merely stared straight ahead at the deck between his bare feet.

"I'm sorry for it," Robert said.

Sir Howard closed his eyes and leaned his head back against the wood. His face was set in an angry sneer. Robert sat still, trying to put together what had happened at Vauxhall. He did not think Folie had received that wound while sitting in her box in the middle of the brilliantly-lit colonnades. He could not fathom Dingley's presence.

"Why was she not with Lander?" he asked Sir Howard. "I sent him to guard her."

But the man just shot him a scathing glare. Another suspicion began to congeal in Robert's mind: the gardens of Vauxhall were notorious for lovers' assignations.

Folie stirred. He supported her head while she was racked with the dry retching again. She was trembling. Robert found a red-hot fury rising in him against Dingley, that somehow, some way, he had let this happen to her. She should have been with Lander.

A jailer came, different from the first guard, without a uniform. He shoved open the door, looked at Folie and Robert, and then bent over, unlocking Dingley's shackles. "Up," he said, though Sir Howard was already standing, brushing himself off. "Superintendent to interview ye."

In spite of the low ceiling and his shirtsleeves and bare feet, Dingley held his shoulders very straight and proud. "I will take care of this," he announced, speaking to the air, or perhaps the cabin in general. His cheeks were burning as the jailer snapped manacles on his wrists. "It is all a great mistake."

The door shut behind them. "I'm glad to hear it," Robert muttered. He could predict what was going to happen. Dingley thought this was some case of mistaken identity, that he could merely explain who he was and be released with profuse apologies. But if money, and plenty of it, had not changed hands to get them here under false names, stripped of any way to prove themselves, then Robert was the devil himself.

"Thirsty," Folie whimpered.

Robert helped her to sit up and held the mug of watered ale to her lips. She groped for it, sipped and choked and shivered.

"I can't see," she said plaintively. "I can't see."

He held her hand hard for a moment. "Everything will be all right," he said, having nothing else to say.

"I don't understand how—" She paused, breathing hard and fast, as if to hold back a gag. "—how we came to be here."

Robert gave a savage chuckle. "My suspicion that someone is determined to be rid of me appears to be something more than my disordered nerves." He rested his head back. "Damn you, Folly. I meant you to stay under Lander's protection. I told you to."

"I'm sorry," she whispered. "I'm so sorry. I didn't believe you."

"What did you mean by that note to meet you at Vauxhall?" he asked. "What did you want?"

"Note?" she said drowsily. Her head was slipping sideways. He jostled her, recalling that it was best to keep a person awake after a blow to the head.

"Yes, that note. Folly, don't sleep. Answer me."

"Do you mean—I wrote to Sir Howard—meet . . . me . . . there . . ."

"Dingley? But—"

She slid away into unconsciousness again, just as the heavy lock on the door clanked. The jailer had returned. "The two of ye now," he said.

Robert looked up in amazement. "I'll go. She is in no condition—"

"Both," the man said. "Carry her."

"Nay," Robert said angrily, "there is no reason. She's badly hurt; she shouldn't be moved."

The jailer kicked her. "Get up, ye lying bitch."

Robert lunged at him, and got a boot in the jaw. It

knocked him back, agony that crashed through his head and ears.

''Get up,'' the jailer said calmly. ''The lazy bitch, too.''

Robert took a deep breath, swallowing rage and pain. He stood up, waiting while the jailer unlocked him and replaced the wall shackles with hand manacles. In a black frenzy he thought of swinging the manacle chain and killing the man—thought beyond that: a guarded deck, the river, no hope of carrying Folie. Reason choked him.

He knelt down, sliding his arm around her shoulders. She woke a little as he lifted her to her feet. ''Robert,'' she mumbled.

The jailer chuckled. ''Don't even remember your bloody name, do she?''

Folie buried her face in his shoulder. Robert held her, allowing her to find her balance.

''Come on, come on,'' the jailer said.

''The devil take you,'' Robert muttered, thrusting off his hand. Folie wilted against him. With a rattle of chains, he lifted her in his arms and carried her.

In the main cabin, Dingley stood alone, locked to a steel bar that ran along the deck. The superintendent's desk was stacked with account books and correspondence. Robert moved through the low door, carrying Folie, careful to avoid the hard frame.

''Can she sit?'' he demanded of their warden.

Wordlessly, the man flipped down a seat that hung on leather straps from the bulkhead. Robert eased Folie into it. She clung to his arms, half-awake.

He stayed next to her, supporting her against him. The jailer stood beside the desk while they waited for the superintendent to appear. He made no pretense of hiding his interest in the open book that lay on the desk.

''Raikes, William and Fanny,'' he said, casting Robert an evil look. ''Forgery! Fourteen years transportation. Good riddance, eh?''

Robert watched the man's face contort in vile mirth.

Long ago, he had watched Srí Ramanu face a man like this, an Englishman determined on power and mischief.

Robert's entire spirit rose in resistance against the jailer. His jaw throbbed where he had been kicked. He saw the same fury locked into Sir Howard's red face; the intent to meet power with opposition.

But it was wrong.

His blood pulsed with the urge to fight. And like a bright, cool light, he saw that it was an impossible combat; he was nothing but another faceless enemy to be crushed under the twisted, tormented souls of the men who governed this place. He could not win.

Robert had learned things from Srí Ramanu. He had not used them. He had not even remembered how. It was as if they had all been locked up inside him. Waiting.

Folie was trembling, unable to contain the shivers that racked her. She could see nothing but shadows, as if everything were enveloped in a foggy dusk. But she could hear Robert's voice: she clung to it like a child clinging to any hope of safety. She was sitting up now, leaning heavily against his side, fighting the waves of darkness and nausea that tried to drown her.

There was a heavy wooden thumping, and then a door closing. A chair scraped. Folie smelled tobacco and perspiration. No one spoke for a moment. She heard papers shuffled.

"You are the superintendent here, sir?"

Somehow hearing Sir Howard's brisk voice, amid the phantoms and dizzy pain, shocked and confused her more deeply than anything yet. Folie held herself up a little straighter.

"Speak when you are spoken to," a man's voice growled.

"There has been a grave mistake," Sir Howard said vehemently. "We have been conveyed here under false and illegal pretenses!"

"Oh?" There was a trace of surly amusement in the reply. "I suppose you say you are not Nicholas Hurst?"

"Certainly I am not! I am Sir Howard Dingley. This is iniquitous. We have been kidnapped!"

"Ohhh! Kidnapped!" The superintendent chuckled.

"I demand immediate release from this place!" Sir Howard said furiously. Folie heard chains crash.

"Now wouldn't that be a fine thing! I'll just release any fellow who claims he don't belong here!"

"I warn you! I warn you, sir—there will be hell to pay when the Home Secretary hears of this."

"Rubbish," the superintendent barked, all the humor gone from his voice. "Hold your insolence, my fine rascal, or you'll find yourself bound up for a flogging."

"Insolence! Damn your eyes for insolence! Listen to me, you commoner, if you can't tell a gentleman by his bearing then go ask your betters who I am!"

Folie heard another scraping thump. She dug her fingernails into her palms.

"Thirty strokes with the cat in the afternoon exercise," the superintendent snapped. "Take him to solitary to think about it."

"The devil you will flog me! I'll not suffer it! Take your hands off—By *God,* you'll pay—"

The sounds of a struggle and the crack that silenced him made Folie press back against the wall in terror. The door slammed shut.

"I expect you are the Prince and Princess of Wales," the superintendent snarled.

"No, sir. I doubt you are in any mood for more nonsense this morning," Robert replied, in a voice as gentle as he had used with Folie. "You do not feel well."

The man gave a surprised grunt. "You are an attentive fellow."

"Your aura is disturbed while your liver troubles you," Robert said. "You took too much of the Madeira last night, as your sister said."

"Now what is this chicanery? How the devil do you know what my sister said?"

"It is a gift I have," Robert said mildly.

"Oh, aye! Irish, are you?"

Robert chuckled, though Folie could not imagine he could summon any amusement at the situation. "No, sir. I learned of it in India, from a holy man."

"My 'aura,' eh?"

"Yes, sir."

Paper rustled. Folie blinked, seeing more light and color, but the images were blurred and doubled.

"William Raikes, Fanny Raikes. Forgery. Maybe you learned that from your holy rogue?"

"No, sir." Robert's voice was sober, faintly reproachful. But he said no more than that, did not deny that they were criminals.

The superintendent made a coughing growl. "I'll put you on the upper deck. Together—since the woman is injured. She'll have a cot there, and some privacy."

"Thank you, sir."

Folie had never heard so much tame humility in Robert Cambourne's voice.

"I'll send the surgeon to her," the superintendent said.

"You need not, sir," Robert said. "I rely on my own ways of healing."

"Well." The man raised his voice, loud and sharp enough to make Folie winch. "Jones! Get in here! Take 'em to the second cabin."

"Sir?" Clearly the jailer was shocked.

"You heard me."

With Robert's help, she stood, precariously balanced, with no equilibrium of her own in the spinning universe. Double figures moved dizzily about her, rattling metal. Step by step, she shuffled in the direction she was led. From behind her, she heard the superintendent call, "Jones! Did you tell him I live with my sister?"

"No, sir," Jones said, in a puzzled tone. "I didn't know it to tell him, sir."

"How do you feel?" Robert asked, examining the porthole and the door, running his fingers over them, finding nothing loose.

She was sitting very still on the cot in the tiny cabin.

Robert wanted to ask her why she had sent a note to Dingley to meet her at Vauxhall, but he did not.

"I can see," she said. "But everything is blurred."

"I have hope that that will improve," he said. "I think it will."

"What happened to me?" she asked tremulously. "Why are we here?"

"You don't remember?"

"No."

Whatever her reason for writing to Dingley, Robert could reckon no way the note had come to him but by a deliberate misrouting. Perhaps it had been stolen—or perhaps, Robert speculated, Dingley was not the harmless neighbor he had supposed.

But the man was here, caught in the same net with Robert and Folie.

"Robert," she said, "how did you know that man had a sister?" She was looking at him, a vague gaze, squinting a little.

In spite of everything, he was unable to suppress a smile at her mole-like expression. "Now and then things come to me."

"Oh," she said.

"Not very often. And never when they are of any use," he said. "Or we wouldn't be here."

"You learned that from Mr. Srí Ramanu?"

"He was the one who noticed it, before I ever did myself." Robert sat down next to her on the cot. "He claims we can all do that sort of thing, but it takes years of reflection and study to produce it at will. And there are all sorts of false *guuruus* who appear to have *siddhis* powers—but it is trickery." He lifted up her hand, turned it over, and laid a key in her palm.

She looked down, feeling the shape. "What is this?" she exclaimed.

"The key to Dingley's cell," he said softly.

"Robert!"

"Hush." He took it from her hand. "Another hidden talent Srí Ramanu discovered in me," he said wryly. "I am a natural pickpocket. I can also make things materialize, and work a good number of other artifices common among the *jaduwallahs* who conjure on the streets. He taught me the false ways, so that I might not mistake them for true *siddhis.*''

Her lips pursed. He thought for a moment that it was disapproval. Then she whispered, ''Good heavens, then why didn't you get the key to *our* cell?''

''Too dangerous. They'll notice this is missing directly. I have a safer way in mind for us, I hope.'' He drew a breath. ''I hope. We'll keep this, at any rate. Perhaps it will save Dingley his thirty lashes while they wonder what became of it.'' Robert scowled. ''Though I'm not sure he doesn't deserve a flogging.''

''Why did you never tell me you could do these things?'' she asked in wonder.

''Ah, yes. Announce at the dinner table that I could make a good living as a cutpurse if I liked?'' Robert gave her sidelong look. ''I did not suppose it would persuade you to like me any better.''

''If you can find a way for us to escape this place, I shall like you exceedingly!''

FIFTEEN

IT WAS LATE, long after dark, when the supervisor came to their cell. He came alone, and let himself in quietly.

"Raikes," he muttered, glancing over his shielded candle to where Folie was sleeping. He turned away from her, looming over Robert, his heavy belly protruding from beneath his coat.

Robert stood up from the deck. He was not chained in this cell, only wore the light manacles on his wrists, but there was no place to sleep except the cot.

"Yes, sir," Robert said in a low voice.

"Look at my aura now," the supervisor whispered. "Can you see it?"

"Put out the candle," Robert said. "It glares in my eyes."

The man hesitated. "Nay." He turned back toward the door. "This is foolishness." He thrust the key into the lock.

Robert let him go. In the faint light from the porthole, after his eyes had adjusted again, he could see Folie watching him.

The supervisor came again before dawn, looking as if he had not slept at all, his curled wig askew. Folie felt much the same, although the dizziness and blurred vision had disappeared. She had leisure now to be utterly miserable, hungry and weak, her clothing foul. What jewelry she had been wearing was gone. She thought briefly of Melinda, of how she must be beside herself with terror, but the thought was so upsetting that Folie put it quickly out of her mind.

The supervising officer of the hulk let himself into their cell with a furtive air that was hardly consistent with his position. "All right, Raikes!" he whispered, holding up a lamp. "I'll close the lantern door for just long enough."

Robert did not rise from the floor. "You need not," he said quietly. "Just hold it there."

"I don't have much time for this," the man said.

"No," Robert murmured, "you've more to do than a reasonable man could. And you are bone weary, I know that."

"Aye, that's God's truth."

In the shadowy light of the lantern, Robert smiled. "Last night, the night before—no sleep, bad dreams. Remember?"

"I had no dreams. I never dream."

"You were dreaming, but you thought you were awake." There was an intangible sweetness in Robert's voice, a strange compassion. "Sometimes this place seems like a nightmare that you can't escape."

The man stared at him. His face twitched, as if he was trying to remember something. "How do you know these things?"

"I can see them," Robert said simply.

"But am I sick?" the superintendent asked apprehensively. "My liver—my aura—can you see that?"

Robert looked at him for a long moment. "Your body is ill because your mind is betrayed. You are persecuted from above and below; your superiors and your inferiors."

"Yes!" the man said, and then, "Nonsense, nonsense. Gibble-gabble." But he did not turn to leave.

"I can't tell you merely what you wish to hear. You know something is wrong. You hope I will say there is not."

The superintendent began to look frightened. ''Something *is* wrong, then.''

''Your physical body is failing. Because your mind is deceived. If you let this deception command you, I think you will certainly die here.''

''What? What is this? How am I deceived?''

''You must see it for yourself.''

''I don't understand you.''

''Go, then,'' Robert said, with a sudden shift from tenderness to a sharper tone. He gave an impatient wave. ''I can do nothing for you.''

''No . . . no!'' The superintendent said. ''I will think. I will try. Help me.''

Robert stood up, the chains clinking. ''I want to help you,'' he said, more kindly. ''It's disturbing to me to see you in this painful state.''

''I'm in misery. I'm in misery.''

''When did it begin? Can you remember?''

The man shook his head. ''No. It seems I've been in pain forever.''

''That is an illusion. When this sort of pain comes, it seems to have no beginning and no end. The Hindus call it *avidya*—ignorance and mirage. But that is what you must overcome, that illusion, and begin to understand how you are deceived.'' He gave the superintendent another long and searching gaze. ''It began . . . I think it began not long ago. A week? A fortnight?''

The officer chewed his lips. ''I am not sure. I think . . .'' He nodded. ''A week, perhaps. It seems so much longer.''

''I know,'' Robert said softly. ''I know. Someone came to you.''

The superintendent blinked. He started to shake his head, and then paused.

''Yes,'' Robert said. ''Someone came.''

With a faint nod, the man leaned heavily back against the wall.

Robert held out his hand, palm downward, his fingers outstretched. He closed his fist and turned it upright. ''Here is what he brought.''

A golden guinea lay in his hand. Both Folie and the superintendent drew breath in sharply.

"This is what will kill you," Robert said. "This is how you are deceived."

"What do you mean?" the man exclaimed, staring at the coin. Even Folie could not conceive of how Robert had produced it.

"You know what I mean," Robert said. "You, better than any. The money will murder you."

"Nonsense!" the superintendent cried. "This is trickery."

"Here, then." Robert held out the coin. "Take it."

The man thrust out his hand. He grabbed the guinea, as if in defiance. Robert looked down at the man's closed hand with a smile that seemed demonic.

"Hold it tight," he said pleasantly. "Hold it as long as you can!"

The superintendent shook his head. He stared at his fist. Then he began to breathe faster.

"Hold it hard," Robert said. "Don't let go."

The man whimpered. His hand trembled. While Folie watched, he hissed air through his teeth.

"It is your money. Don't let it get away," Robert said.

The superintendent gave a choked cry and flung the coin from him. It hit the floor, flashing gold in the lantern light. He examined his palm, holding it up to his face, blowing on it as if he had burned his skin.

"Now do you understand?" Robert asked.

"I'm dying," he whispered in a horrified voice. "I'm dying—because I took their money to imprison you."

"I want to help you," Robert said softly. "Let me help you save yourself."

"What must I do?"

"Tell me the names of the ones who did this to you."

The superintendent swallowed. "I don't know their names! I swear I do not!"

"Who brought you the money? Who did this to you?"

"He gave no name. I never ask."

"Of course you do not. But they mean to snare you. This

time it is an entrapment. The men above you—they have never understood you or esteemed you. They mean to catch you out in corruption, with your hands red, and the gallows for you.''

The man's eyes widened. ''By God!'' he whispered. ''By God!''

Robert said no more. Folie waited, hardly daring to breathe. The river lapped gently against the hull, the only sound in the depth of the night.

''I want you gone from here!'' the superintendent exclaimed in a low voice. ''Tonight.''

Robert shook his head. ''I don't know how it is to be done.''

''Ha. I'll do it. Good God, those blackguarding bastards! Catch *me* out, will they? As if they ain't the prettiest bribemongers on earth themselves!''

''It is always so, is it not?'' Robert said.

''By God, I swear that it is. You wait quietly now. Be ready—I'll return directly.''

Robert rested back against the door of the cell, his head turned to hear through the barred window. He said nothing to Folie. But she could not seem to look away from him. In the first faint light, his unshaven face was menacing, his eyes half-shut in a still concentration, as if he listened to the heartbeat of the ship itself.

She might have been seeing him for the first time. Through the light-headed ache in her head, he seemed extraordinary.

''I think you are a bit more than a natural pickpocket!'' she whispered.

He shook his head slightly, without opening his eyes. Folie understood that she was not to disturb him. She eased her head back, allowing herself to sink into the bewildered weakness that spun in her brain. Robert was there, awake. She felt a mysterious faith in him, a trust that seemed perfectly familiar, as if it had been in her all along, hidden beneath the confusion and doubt.

• • •

He had confounded himself. Though he had seen Srí Ramanu lead many a skeptic on a merry dance, Robert had never supposed that he could do the same. But he had found easy game in the superintendent, he thought. Some people were primed and ready to believe, even though they would deny it vigorously to themselves and others. Robert had made a fortunate hit in his first attempt.

But at any moment, the man might reconsider. Away from Robert's voice and persuasive questions, from the subtle means of influence Srí Ramanu had taught him—the superintendent was liable to wake to a different notion. A true yogi like the Hindu priest might have real powers beyond the physical; Robert had never been quite certain of that, but he was utterly sure that he himself had nothing of the kind.

Still, he could not afford to allow misgiving to beset him. The delicate communication; the posture; the open gaze, sweet and forceful at once; all the elusive aspects of this deceit—they required a pure and perfect conviction.

Strangely, Robert had no real doubt that he could influence the man. His incredulous thoughts seemed to exist on some plane outside the present, ideas to be considered later perhaps, irrelevant to the moment. He had triggered deep fears in the superintendent, ancient fears of conspiracy and death and illness, of persecution from above. Powerful forces. He had only to wait for them to do their work.

So he hoped.

Folie jerked awake out of a half-dazed dream. Robert's hand was on her arm. She looked up into his eyes, those gray wolf eyes, light and haunting, and waited mutely for him to tell her what to do.

He thrust a pile of clothing into her lap—a heavy red coat, a shirt, and breeches. The early morning light was stronger now, the creaking of the hulk punctuated by the cries of shore birds. He had shaved, or at least scraped his beard down to a dusky shade, and his manacles were off, heaped in a corner. She could smell something cooking, but even in her famished state she could not call it appetizing.

Robert turned away, leaning down to buckle a pair of black gaiters over the same sort of pale breeches Folie held in her lap. She stood up and reached behind herself, attempting to find her buttons. The pretty yellow dress she had worn to Vauxhall was ruined beyond repair, but the laces and buttons, sewn so carefully by Folie and Melinda through a long winter of anticipation, did not give way easily. She had never expected to be undressing without Sally's help. Merely lifting her arms so high made her head pound.

She made an involuntary sound of distress. Robert turned around. Without hesitation, he moved to assist her, opening the buttons and pulling the laces on her stays free. She felt cold air on her back. Modesty seemed a foolish aside at the moment, and yet she grew flustered, making ineffectual attempts to help. All she did was manage to tangle her fingers with his.

He pushed them aside impatiently. The next thing she knew, he was tugging her gown upwards, pulling it over her head. Her loosened corset fell to the floor. Folie stood in her shift, shivering from cold and nerves and embarrassment. But if Robert noticed her nakedness, he made no indication; he swept up the shirt and put it over her head as if she were a toddling child. Folie had the presence of mind to pull the straps of the shift down beneath it before she put her hands through the sleeves.

The shirt came down to her knees. She sat down on the cot, wriggling into the breeches. They felt strange and rough against her bare legs, but she tucked the shirt tails inside and buttoned up the front panel. Robert was waiting with the red coat. It weighed her down, the heavy material and facings far thicker than anything she was accustomed to. He picked up a pair of white leather straps and criss-crossed them over her shoulders and breasts. A silver plate clipped them together in the center. Feeling like a harnessed pony, Folie waited while he knelt and buckled on her sword and gaiters, which wanted to fall down around her calves.

He held a pair of black shoes next to her foot, shook his head, and left her with her evening slippers.

He rose. They both had black hats, oddly fashionable, with deep curly brims and huge plumes. Folie pulled her hair up, tucking it high as well as she could, and settled the military hat gingerly on her head. Her hair filled it out, but it balanced precariously, top-heavy. When she was done, she turned to Robert.

His mouth twisted with amusement. Folie squared her shoulders and lifted her chin in what she imagined must be a more military air. The hat fell off backwards.

Robert shook his head. As Folie stuffed her hair back under the hat, wincing, someone tapped at the door. She froze. After a breathless moment, she heard a faint scrape. A key slid quietly beneath the door.

Robert picked it up. He cast a sidelong look at Folie, his eyes traveling up her breech-clad legs, his face sinister in the shadowy light. Then he winked, blew her a kiss, and put the key in the lock. Folie's heart was thumping. All her skin felt pink.

He supposed that the superintendent, convinced that Robert knew his thoughts, reckoned it unnecessary to communicate the plan in actual words. The uniforms had been pushed through the window in the cell door and the key provided with no further instructions.

Robert wasted no time in idle speculation. It was getting toward full light; the denizens of the hulk were stirring—a thump of feet on the decks, the occasional shrill sound of women arguing. Folie made a ridiculous excuse for a soldier, but at least the blood on the side of her face and her blackened eyes distracted from her feminine countenance. He thought she might just pass for an adolescent who had recently experienced the worst brawl of his young life.

She kept trying to hold her head up under the hat, fingering the sword and scowling with her chin thrust out. He suddenly realized that she was attempting to appear manly.

Robert felt a rush of love and fear for her. He wanted to

pull her into his arms and hold her safe; to kill dragons; to sprout wings; to vanish from this place in a magical puff of smoke.

But he faced instead a narrow passage and a monumental bluff. He pushed open the door and stepped out, closing and locking it behind Folie. She put her hand on his arm and leaned close to his ear.

"Sir Howard!" she whispered.

Robert groaned inwardly. He had meant to make straight for the upper deck, in hopes that the superintendent expected that. Dingley could hang, for all Robert cared. But her fingers pressed into his arm, and their urgency sent a spike of envy through him.

He nodded, pushing off her hand. He had no idea where Dingley was being held. At the end of this passage was a companionway that led upward—to what, Robert did not know. The other way was a dead end.

There was nothing for it but to go. He motioned Folie to come behind, and headed for the stairs.

At the foot of them, he looked up. They led onto the open deck, a thickly befogged morning, where ghostly figures moved back and forth in purposeful activity. Robert assumed an equally decisive demeanor, climbing the stairs without wavering.

At the top, he reached out and stopped the first figure that passed, an aproned scullion carrying an empty tub. "Where the devil is the solitary confinement?"

The boy looked startled. "Sir?"

"I'm to transfer a prisoner from solitary—" Robert flicked his key up between his thumb and forefinger. "Can't find the bloody solitary cell in this hellhole! It's not down there where they told me."

The boy gave him a queer look. "I'm sorry, sir. Wait here and I'll show ye."

Robert nodded. He had no choice now but to stand still, in the open, while the boy vanished in the soupy fog. He could see the cookhouse, dripping dew from the eaves, and a dark bulk in front of him that he guessed was the poop and the official quarters.

A great thudding of feet and drag of chains came through the mist, and then a line of men loomed into view, marching sullenly. There was a guard at their head, and another at the end of the line, swinging bludgeons casually from their hands. They stared at Robert as they passed, the same distrustful look that the scullion had given him, as if he were an unwelcome conundrum that had appeared out of the fog. He could feel Folie edge behind him.

Robert merely looked back at them soberly. He lifted his hand in a casual salute.

After a pause, the rear guard saluted back. The line of prisoners trudged ahead, lining up outside the cookhouse, each one holding his tin mug. The same scullion reappeared, moving down the line with his tub, ladling some ugly-looking liquid into the mugs. The men downed it eagerly.

Robert and Folie were near the head of the line. After finishing his breakfast, an unshaven prisoner grinned at them. ''Belted in some rough 'n tumble, eh, boy?''

The head guard cuffed him lightly. ''Respect your betters!''

''Betters!'' The prisoner chuckled unrepentantly, showing yellow teeth. ''What, that little shaver?''

Robert heard a faint growl. He turned to see Folie lift her lip and snarl. She sounded about as ferocious as an angry kitten.

The whole line of prisoners began to laugh. Robert judged it wise to join in with a smirk, though he could see that Folie was turning red as fire under the bruising. She held herself stiffly, glaring at her tormentors.

The guard put his truncheon hard against the prisoner's chest. ''Any honest man is your better, Norris. Better make your amends.''

''Oh, sar!'' Norris said in a high-pitched voice, as he feigned a curtsy. ''Oh, sar, I do be so sorry to offend ye! But you look pretty as a girl, can I help it?''

Robert saw her eyes widen. Before she could speak or do anything more foolish, he raised his voice. ''Come, I've not got all day to be amused by a lot of jailbirds—where's this fellow Hurst kept?''

''Hurst?'' the head guard asked.

''He's lookin' for the solitary cell,'' the scullion muttered. ''I was going to show him.''

''Well, show 'im, for the love of God,'' the guard said. ''The man's got a duty.''

''Lemme finish. Do you want me to do me own job or not?'' the boy asked nastily, pitching the dregs from his tub into a cask on the deck.

''Make some haste then, saucebox,'' the guard said. He poked the first prisoner in line. ''Off with you, too. Look alive!''

As the convicts shuffled and clattered past them, the scullion wiped his hands on his apron. ''Come on, this a'way.''

Robert followed him, not a difficult task, as the boy's idea of haste was a listless saunter, plucking at the hanging rings of steel on the bulkheads and swiping his hand along the wet railing as he went. Robert thought his nose had grown accustomed to the smell, but as they descended into a stairwell, and then went down to another, deeper deck, the stench of closely confined humanity grew appalling.

The solitary cells were in the very bilge itself, it seemed. On a dark open deck, full of convicts chained in long rows to the floor, the scullion stopped at last, leaning down to grab a hatch door. Robert leaned over and helped him heave it open. The mixed odor of sewage, putrid water, and rotting wood that drifted up was overpowering. The scullion grinned and motioned for Robert to go ahead.

He felt Folie's hand tug at the back of his coat. When he looked back, she was holding her hand over her mouth and nose, shaking her head.

He was afraid she would swoon. ''Stay here with the boy,'' he said with a grimace. Though it was she who wanted to save Dingley's hide, he thought cynically.

Robert took a breath of fetid air and climbed down into the hole. Rats scurried away from the dim square of light that illuminated the ribbed floor of the bilge. He had to stand for a moment to let his eyes adjust. Gradually he could make out planks laid across the hulk's ancient ribs, over the dank water pooling in the bilge, and three wooden boxes the size of shipping crates.

He felt a sick amazement as he realized that these were the solitary cells. Solitary rat traps, more like. A man could not stand straight in them; he would have to sit on the floor. It was difficult to take a breath in the thick atmosphere.

For an instant, the light failed. Robert looked up. To his horror, the hatch door was closing. He started to shout, but the deck above his head erupted in thumping and yells. There was a quick shriek, and the hatch fell open again with a thundering crash.

Robert stared upward, his heart in his throat. But to his vast relief, Folie's face peered down at him. She waved, urging him on. He had no idea what had happened, but he wanted out of here fast.

''Dingley!'' he hissed, knocking on the first box.

Thankfully, Sir Howard's voice answered, a querulous, wary echo from inside the cell.

''It's Robert Cambourne.'' He slid the key in the lock.

''Get me out,'' the voice moaned. ''Get me out, get me out.''

''Hurry.'' Robert opened the door. It was too dark to see much of the figure that crawled from the box, which Robert considered a blessing. ''Keep your wits about you, and do what I tell you.''

Dingley leaned heavily on the box. He pushed away, looking toward Robert, the whites of his eyes uncanny in the dark hold.

''We're walking out,'' Robert said, very low. ''Say nothing. Don't speak, no matter what.''

Sir Howard made a coughing assent, nodding vigorously. Robert moved back and looked up the hatch. No one appeared to be there.

''On guard,'' Robert shouted. ''I'm sending him up.''

He hoped Folie would have the presence of mind to unsheathe her sword, although he didn't suppose she would look very threatening if she did. Dingley started up before him, climbing the ladder so quickly in his chains that his feet slipped, but he caught himself and hauled upward through the hatch. Robert followed.

When he reached the convicts' deck, Folie was standing with her sword point in the scullion's apron. Every prisoner on the deck was staring at them, silent.

''He tried to shut you in there!'' she whispered hoarsely.

''T'were only a joke!'' the boy cried, holding his bleeding arm. ''He cut me!''

Robert nodded to Folie. ''Excellent judgment. Move on, Hurst! March! Shut that hatch yourself, boy, if you're so anxious to do it.''

''I'll report you for this!'' The boy skittered past them. ''I'll see that you—''

Robert grabbed his shoulder and hauled him backwards, holding him over the open hatch by his hair. ''Shut up,'' he growled, ''or you'll find yourself down there in the dark.''

The boy whimpered, his eyes rolling wildly.

''You won't make trouble?'' Robert demanded.

''No, sir. No, sir.''

Robert let him go. He should have kicked the little weasel down the stairs, he knew, but it was not in him. ''Watch out for him,'' he said to Folie.

She nodded, her face pale and set, absurdly delicate. With her sword, she motioned the scullion to go in front of her. Robert silently swore to himself that if they made it out of here, he would kiss every bruise from her skin.

When they made it out. He had a deep uneasiness in the pit of his stomach, for how easy it had been so far.

The journey back up onto the open deck was nerve-wrackingly uneventful. Dingley smelled like the Fleet Ditch, and looked worse. He stumbled into the foggy daylight, squinting, his hands and legs still chained together.

The superintendent was waiting, a heavy figure looming in the mist. Robert felt a surge of dread, that the man had changed his mind. But he only gave Sir Howard a sharp look, and then jerked his head toward the rail. ''Get him in the boat, then.'' He turned and walked back into his office.

The three-decker hulk had an ugly notch cut in her railing, set with a spiked iron gate. A guard unlocked it, wrinkling his nose at Sir Howard's stench.

Steep stairs ran all the way down the side of the three-decker hull to the water. Robert judged it nearly thirty feet down to the rowboat tied at the foot of the steps. The scullion stood by the gate, tugging at his forelock with a toady's bow. "I'll steady the boat for ye, sir."

"No need," Robert said briskly. "Stand aside." He nodded to Folie to go first, but she was watching the scullion fiercely, as if she expected him to make a pounce. Robert caught up Dingley's manacles, affecting to prevent any escape, and nudged with his sheathed sword.

Sir Howard moved out onto the landing. It was broad and sturdy, with head-high railings and another spiked gate opening off the outer edge, rigged with a heavy pulley and line for loading freight. Robert ducked to follow him.

"Hold there!" A booming voice made him freeze. "Stop!"

Robert's heart turned to ice. He looked back. Striding through the mist came a scowling man, tall and menacing, his fist clenched around a sword handle.

"What's going forward here?" he demanded, glaring at Robert. "I wasn't told any prisoners were to be taken off this morning!"

"You may apply to the superintendent, sir!" Robert snapped back. "Nor was I informed that I had to notify every man aboard while I go about my orders!"

"This is entirely irregular! I'll not have it!" He stepped forward, his face red with outrage, and caught Dingley's manacles, dragging him back onto the ship. Robert had a wild and fleeting thought of making a mad break for freedom, but Folie was too far away to reach, and they would never survive it.

"Take your hands off my prisoner!" he said vehemently.

"Nor will I! You won't leave this ship if I have anything to say to it!"

"Apply to the superintendent," Robert said, trying to prevent desperation from entering his voice. "I have my orders! Already I'm cursed late, but I'll wait five minutes while you speak to him.''

''To the devil with the super,'' the man bellowed. ''*I'll* manage this, by God! I know your sort! I've had enough of these deceits and dodges to get away!'' He dragged Dingley close, bending over, running his fingers down the chain links. Robert could see Folie standing rigid, looking toward him with terrified eyes.

''Deceit!'' Robert exclaimed savagely. ''Who do you suppose you are, sir, to accuse me of deceit?''

''I, sir, am the purser.'' He held up the lock triumphantly. ''There! Do you see the number engraved? These are *our* irons! Remove them this instant!''

Robert hesitated, confounded. ''Remove them?''

''Aye! You are to bring your own restraints—have you never escorted a prisoner off before, you red-coated lobcock? Why, what do you suppose would happen if I let every man take his chains away with him? We should have none left aboard!''

''I beg your pardon, sir,'' Robert said. He kept his lower lip determinedly stiff. ''I was not informed of this.''

''Well, that is your misfortune,'' the purser said balefully. ''I cannot allow you to take these irons. They must be removed before you leave the ship. Here.'' He pulled a vast set of keys from under his waistcoat. ''This is one of the Westport locks. That master should work.'' He twisted a key from the ring and handed it to Robert with distaste. ''My God, what a stink. You do it.''

Silently Robert released Dingley from his bonds. He rose from unlocking the ankle iron and leaned close. ''Don't give me any trouble now,'' he growled. ''Or I'll run you through.''

Dingley nodded, his eyes trained straight ahead.

''There you are, sir.'' Robert tossed the key to the purser. ''Come, boy,'' he said to Folie. ''Make haste, we're already an hour behind time. Close up here—keep your sword point at this man's back.''

He ducked under the iron gate again, pulling Dingley with him by the elbow, checking to see that Folie was right behind, then moving as fast as he could without actually running down the stairs. They were going to make it.

Five steps down, he heard her shriek—a sound that curdled his blood. Dingley ran into him as he turned on the stairs. Something splashed heavily below. Folie was nowhere—the cargo gate was swinging wide open over the water. Robert had a glimpse of the scullion's aproned figure fleeing back onto the misted deck.

Before he could react, Dingley tore free of his hold, pounding up the stairs. The purser and guard were crowding in, but Sir Howard barreled into them, flinging them both back with the strength of a desperate man. He grabbed the rail and launched himself overboard off the open gate.

Robert turned, racing down into the thickening fog at the waterline. He leapt into the rowboat tied at the foot of the stairs. It tilted and yawed under his weight as he frantically threw off the painter. He could hear them splashing, though he could only see a yard or two ahead in the mist. The men above had come after him, their shouts echoing off the water and the hull so badly that he could not tell which voice was which or the true direction of any sound. By the time they reached the foot of the steps, Robert was rowing out.

"Launch another boat!" someone yelled. "We'll get him back!"

"Quiet! *Quiet!*" Robert roared. He pulled at the oars, straining to hear as his own voice died away.

There was sudden silence. Faintly, he heard water splash. He sent the boat in that direction with a strong pull, then let it ride its own momentum. But the river's current was taking him; he began to spin and drift at some speed he could not discern.

"Folly!" he shouted. "Can you hear?"

The answer came indistinctly, a cry for help. Robert rowed quickly toward it. He saw something dark floating—skimmed close, found it was her red coat adrift and empty.

"*Folly!*" he bellowed.

"Help!" It was Dingley's voice that answered, hoarse and breathless. He made a vigorous splashing. "Help us! Here!"

Robert had to pull strongly against the current, but he could hear the splash clearly now. He cursed the fog. He was afraid the river was carrying his boat faster downstream than it was carrying them.

"Where?" he yelled, and got Dingley's weakening reply.

But suddenly they were on the opposite side from what he had thought—his boat was riding right down on them. Robert shouted, yanking on an oar to turn and hold long enough to reach out to Dingley.

Sir Howard was swimming strongly, his arm about Folie's chest, holding her before him. They both went under as he held out his free arm, but Robert dragged him up. Folie was sputtering, reaching for the boat. It spun around, the oars thumping in their locks. Robert was afraid she would panic and drag the boat over, but she only grabbed the gunwale with both hands and held on, her chin lifted above the water.

"At the stern, the stern," Sir Howard gasped.

Folie edged toward the back of the boat while Robert pulled on the oars to keep it steady. He could not aid her—if he moved too near, the rowboat would capsize from both their weights, so he had to sit helplessly and watch as Dingley pushed at Folie, helping her. She struggled and gasped and floundered one leg over, then with a great push from Dingley, came rolling in with a flood of cold water.

"Move forward," Sir Howard ordered her, working hand over hand toward the stern. Folie shifted, holding out her trembling hands as if to pull him in. But Dingley ignored her, heaving himself up on both arms, climbing aboard with one swift, balanced move. The boat barely tipped.

"Come," he said to Folie, drawing her shivering body back against him as he settled in the stern. "Give her your coat, Cambourne."

Robert pulled it off. Dingley took it, spreading it over her, diving his hands underneath it and pulling her to his chest. She was shivering, her teeth chattering audibly, her wet hair straggling down her face.

A great boom carried through the fog, cracking and echoing off the unseen horizon. Folie started up, her eyes wide and terrified. ''What is that?''

''A ship's gun,'' Robert said. ''They're signalling an escape. Or a drowning.''

''Get us to dry land,'' Dingley ordered. ''Be quick about it.''

SIXTEEN

ROBERT ROWED. BUT his sense of direction, never strong, was utterly perplexed by the featureless fog. Even the direction of the current was no help—he knew the tide could make the river flow upstream at certain times of the day, and he had no idea if this was one of them.

He could sense Dingley's exasperation. Things seemed to loom upon them out of the mist—larger boats and fishing weirs, cattails and mudflat islands—everything but somewhere they might land and walk ashore without sinking to their waists in marsh. And the entire time Robert had to watch Sir Howard hug Folie to him, her face pressed tenderly into the curve of his throat. He hauled doggedly on the oars, glancing behind himself now and then to check the channel ahead.

"For the love of God," Dingley said at last, "we must be going in circles!"

"You may row if you like," Robert said shortly.

Dingley wiped a dribble of water from his forehead and looked off into the fog. Folie seemed beyond hearing. She clutched the red coat and Dingley's wet sleeve, her eyes shut.

Robert rowed.

The river traffic seemed to be increasing as the mist

lifted, but he was not sure. No vessel came close enough to hail. Their dark shapes appeared and vanished like silent specters. The mist gathered in chill dew on Robert's face and hands.

"Watch out!" Dingley yelled, just as the rowboat struck hard.

Robert nearly lost the oars as the boat sheered. He grabbed them back, pushing off the black timber that thrust above the river. Folie sat up, the coat clutched around her.

Robert squinted up at the thing they had hit. With a crosspiece nailed to it akimbo, it jutted up alone as if it were a watery gallows, but through the fog he caught a glimpse of a derelict pier.

Robert shoved them off the piling and worked the boat along the old structure. Slowly, a dim shape through the mist resolved into a fisherman hauling in his net. He looked up at the rowboat as if it were some malevolent phantasm that had materialized before him. Rapidly he began to drag at his net, backing up in retreat.

Robert hailed him. "We need help!" He shipped the oars, putting out his hand to grab the weed-encrusted pier.

The fisherman hesitated, peering at them. "Soldiers?" he demanded querulously.

"Aye, the King's own." Robert gestured toward the river. "Did you hear the great gun? We're on a chase after that convict. Almost had him, but the boat went over with us. Couldn't find our way back to the prison ship in this soup!"

"Oh aye," the fisherman said, letting go his net. "Best wait'll it lifts. Another hour."

"Nay, I need to get my men ashore. This boy's half-drowned, and like to take a mortal ague."

"Now then!" their languid savior said, peering down. "He looks a bad way, right enough. Well, if you go along of the dock here—can't see 'em now, but there's some stone steps—take 'em up on top, and ye can find the way along the dike into the village. Mind you don't stray off the dike, or you'll be the wetter for it."

Robert thanked him, poling further along the pier with

his oar. They found the steps, looming up out of the water onto a low bank, going from nowhere to nowhere, it seemed, but once Robert climbed them, he could discern a line of stepping stones among the coarse rushes.

''Come on.'' Robert turned back, reaching to help Folie out of the boat, but Dingley was already handing her onto the steps. She clung to him, taking the stairs slowly, not looking up at Robert as Dingley led her past.

They caught a ride, perched among turnips, for the price of Folie's cheap army sword. The farmer would take them all the way to Westminster Bridge, six miles on, but Robert thought Folie would be dead of pneumonia by then. She was already fading, leaning hard against Dingley's side, making small, watery coughs. The fog had lifted, but the day was yet cold and clouded when the oxcart rolled into a village.

Robert did not know what might await them in London. To walk into Cambourne House alive was impossibly dangerous as long as he did not know who wanted him silenced. And Folie had become irrevocably involved. He could no longer hope they might ignore her or leave her safe. Even Dingley was entangled in it now—if he had not been embroiled up to his arrogant chin anyway.

But for the moment, Robert knew he must find shelter and dry warmth for her. He scanned the village. There appeared to be little to it, beyond a vague familiarity. The road was muddy, the houses small and warped with age. Chickens strutted in the ditch. Inside one garden gate, yellow daffodils nodded their gay heads, defying the dismal day.

He stared at the flowers. And then Robert recognized the place with a start.

He called to the driver to stop. The cart creaked to a halt right under the sign of The Highflyer. Robert said a short, silent prayer of thanks for one small blessing.

''We'll stop here,'' he said, sliding down to the muddy road.

"Are you mad?" Dingley exclaimed. "We must get her to town and a doctor!"

"Come down. We stop here."

"No." Sir Howard turned to the farmer. "Drive on!"

"Folie," Robert said.

She lifted her head weakly, looking at him. Her hair clung to her bruised face, dark limp strands. Her eyes seemed huge and tormented.

"Folly," he said in a quiet voice. "It's best to stop here."

She nodded, holding out her hands. Robert reached up and helped her down. Her whole body was quivering.

"This is madness," Dingley said. "You are responsible for this, Cambourne!"

"Dingley," Robert said. "Shut yourself up."

He led Folie into The Highflyer, past the little garden where the yellow daffodils brightened the gray day. To his relief, the same landlady looked up from her knitting with the same placid, cheerful smile that he recalled.

"Ma'am," he said.

She stood up hastily from her chair. "The Calcutta gentleman!"

"Ma'am," he said, "do you remember the lady of the letters? The lady I love?"

She stood, nodding in wonderment, just as Folie's trembling figure went limp, collapsing into him. Robert startled, barely catching her as she fainted. He lifted her in his arms, the red coat trailing.

"This is she," he said wryly.

"Good God!" The landlady hurried forward. "Whatever have you done to her? God bless us, sir—it's no wonder the poor girl won't have ye!"

Folie had no idea how long she had slept, but she woke in a warm, soft bed, so comfortable that it seemed dream-like. She did not know where she was, but gradually realized that the dark images rising and vanishing in her dazed mind were no nightmare. The prison hulk had been real, the river and the smell—she could still taste it in the back of her mouth.

But there was a bright stream of sunlight through the leaded glass windowpane, casting a sparkle of prismatic colors across the white quilt, and next to the bed a gay bouquet of daffodils gave out the sweet scent of spring.

She sat up, finding herself in a voluminous gown that was not her own. Beneath an unfamiliar nightcap, she seemed to have a head bandage wrapped firmly about her skull. Gingerly she felt the lump on her head, wincing. Beneath the cap and bandage, her hair was in such wild disarray that she did not suppose she would ever get a comb through it again.

Melinda! she thought suddenly, and threw off the counterpane. As she stood up, a wave of dizziness struck her, but she leaned on the bedpost until it passed and then shuffled out of the room into a low-ceilinged passage.

Immediately she could hear voices raised in contention. The short passage opened into a common room, where a fire crackled and a great number of bottles and mugs and a pair of kegs adorned the walls. Robert and Sir Howard sat at one of the tables in the center, arguing.

She did not discern the subject, since they both fell silent instantly upon looking up at her. Robert rose. A black and white shepherd dog trotted over to nose at her hem, wagging its plumed tail.

"You should not be out of bed!" he said, and turned to call, "Mrs. Moloney!"

"We must tell Melinda we are safe!" Folie exclaimed.

Sir Howard rose, coming to take Folie's hand and turn her back. "We are just preparing to do so, my dear. But you must lie down."

A stout woman trotted briskly up from the cellar stairs. "Ah, she is awake. And walkin' about barefooted in her night rail, the child! Turn about, me dearest; it's back to bed with you! You don't want your gentlemen to see you so immodest, now!"

Before she could protest, Folie was bustled back into the

bedchamber. Mrs. Moloney threw back the covers. "Are you ready to take a little broth?"

"I am famished," Folie said, sitting down on the bed. Her brain felt giddy. "I believe I could eat a roast!"

Mrs. Moloney laughed. "That is good news. Haps you ain't to expire of pneumonia after all."

"Not I," Folie said. "I am never ill."

"I'll gladly acquaint your gentlemen with that news. I told 'em ye looked pretty stout to me, after ye got warmed through, but they've been in agonies, a'worritin' on ye. One would have the doctor, and the other would not hear of it, havin' a mortal horror of leeches, which I commiserate with that! I'll tell you, me love, they have not let up on each another for one living moment."

"Oh dear," Folie said. "I thought I heard them disputing."

"Ach, just a little," Mrs. Moloney said dryly.

"We have had a terrible adventure." Folie found that settling back into the soft bed was rather necessary after all. "Do you think I might have a bath?"

The landlady chuckled again. "Aye, that's the fit end to a terrible adventure. I'll have my girl bring up the tub as soon as she gets the sheets in. You rest now. And we'll start you with some broth—haps your stomach's not so bold as your mind, missy!"

Folie nodded, already drifting back to sleep.

It was several naps later before Folie could find the vigor to bathe, but the faint fetid scent lingering on her skin finally drove her to insist that Mrs. Moloney allow her to attempt it. Clean at last, Folie dressed in one of Mrs. Moloney's Sunday gowns, tucked up behind and tied with crossed apron strings, with a crisp lace cap over her carefully washed and tenderly braided hair.

"Well, ye look the veriest ragamuffin in that getup," Mrs. Moloney said, "but better than the King's red coat, at any rate! Come sit down to the commons—since you took that broth well enough, you may have some bread and meat. We've no private parlor here, so ye must meet your gentlemen in the taproom, I'm afraid.''

Folie followed her into the public room. Robert and Sir Howard stood up simultaneously from an isolated cubicle tucked into the corner by the fire. They both bowed, incongruously elegant in the borrowed, shapeless dark coats of farmers. Sir Howard's graying hair was tied neatly back, but Robert's shorter mane fell black and shaggy on his neck, giving him a more feral wolfishness than ever.

''We have been beside ourselves, my dear,'' Sir Howard said gently, offering his hand. ''Sit down here, sit down. You must not overexert yourself.''

''I'm really quite all right,'' Folie said, sinking onto the bench. ''Aside from a little dizziness. I believe we can go home now. Have you heard yet from Melinda?''

Sir Howard sat back, crossing his arms. He gave Robert a scowling look. ''We have not. Mr. Cambourne insists that we remain here.''

His tone of voice was faintly sneering, as if this were an example of flagrant cowardice. Folie looked toward Robert questioningly. He sat deep in the back of the booth, returning Sir Howard's insinuation with a cold glance.

''Perhaps we'd not be so lucky as to end in the hulks next time,'' he said, very low. ''I believe it would be the bottom of the river.''

Folie gazed at him. After a long moment, she nodded slowly. She remembered the river, cold and choking.

Mrs. Moloney hustled up to the table, setting down a steaming pie with a flourish. ''There you are, my pretty girl. Just hot out of the oven, as fine a pork pie as you'll ever see. I left out the curry,'' she said, aside to Robert, ''as she might not be up to it.''

''Very wise,'' Robert said. ''We are in your debt.''

''La! You've paid me a gold guinea—I'm still owing you change. Ring if you need anything, child. I've got my eye on some chickens roasting for you gentlemen.''

As the landlady retired to her kitchen, Sir Howard leaned over the table. ''A guinea! Where the dickens did you get any money?''

''I stole it,'' Robert said coolly.

''Oh, of course.'' Sir Howard sat back. ''I dare swear you'll end up back in the hulks.''

''No doubt one of us will,'' Robert replied.

Folie pursed her lips and cut into the pie. ''This smells delectable!'' she said brightly. ''How is the food here?''

''Excellent,'' Robert said, at the same time that Sir Howard muttered, ''Adequate.''

She took a bite. ''It tastes marvelous,'' she said, and then added, ''Though I'm sure I'd think anything edible quite marvelous at this point.''

Robert smiled slightly. ''Fence-sitting?''

''Yes, I am devoted to peaceable pursuits. I've had enough of adventure lately.'' She felt odd and frivolous, almost blithe. As if in the release of tension, the terrors of the night dissolved in this flighty, light-spirited relief. ''But when can we send word to Melinda? And Lady Dingley? Please. They'll be frightened out of their wits.''

''Folly—'' He fingered a flat-bladed knife that lay on the table, looking up at her. ''Tell me what you remember of the note that you wrote.''

She paused with a bite poised. ''Note?''

''The note about Vauxhall.'' He glanced toward Sir Howard, and back at her. ''The one that came to me.''

Folie ate more of the pie. She shook her head, frowning. ''It's all a blur. Vauxhall—I remember the fireworks. But . . . did I write a note to you?''

''You told me—on the ship. Do you remember that? You said that you had written it to him.'' He nodded toward Sir Howard.

Folie looked doubtfully at Sir Howard. He said nothing, giving her no aid. ''Did I?'' She frowned down at the steaming gravy on her plate. ''I suppose . . .'' She chewed her lip. When she tried to concentrate on the recent past, her memory seemed a confusion of vivid, distinct pictures, like frozen scenes lit by the bursting rockets at Vauxhall. ''I don't remember a note. Are you sure that I wrote it?''

''Utterly,'' Robert said.

''How so?'' Sir Howard demanded. ''Perhaps it was a

forgery. It makes no sense whatsoever, that she wrote a note to me, only to have it delivered to you!''

''It was not a forgery,'' Robert said with certainty.

''Oh, are you so very familiar with Mrs. Hamilton's handwriting?'' he asked mockingly.

''Yes, Dingley,'' Robert said with some exasperation, ''I am.''

''Still—handwriting may be imitated.''

''She wrote it.''

''What makes you so sure—''

''Because it smelled like her letters, for God's sake!'' Robert snapped. ''Trust me, Dingley. I know she wrote it.''

Folie bit her lip, lowering her face and applying herself to her dinner. Then she looked up. ''*Robert!*'' she gasped. ''My shawl! I wore it to Vauxhall!''

He nodded. ''I know.''

''You do not have it? It wasn't with me?''

Robert shook his head. ''No. Nor your jewelry. I'm afraid they are all gone for good.''

''Oh!'' Folie cried, her heart sinking, ''I have lost my blue shawl!'' She hunched in the booth, trying to absorb the belief that her beautiful kashmir shawl was really gone. Now that they were safe, her emotions seemed to ride up and down on ungovernable waves. Somehow it seemed a greater disaster than anything else, all out of proportion to reason. She felt tears burn the back of her throat, and a wild urge to go back to the hulk to retrieve her loss.

''No doubt Cambourne *stole* it,'' Sir Howard said.

Folie turned on him. ''What a disagreeable thing to say! Of course he didn't steal it! He gave it to me.''

Sir Howard looked nonplused. ''Cambourne?'' He glanced between the two of them. ''I beg your pardon. Perhaps I am unaware of the true circumstances here. Is she your—''

''And you need not make odious, vulgar intimations,'' Folie exclaimed. ''He sent it to me years ago, from India.'' Her posture sagged again. She picked at her plate with her fork. ''It was my very favorite shawl—I always wore it whenever I felt low." She glanced shyly at Robert. "I always loved the scent of it."

"My, my, what a pair of noses the two of you have!" Sir Howard said.

"To our misfortune," Robert retorted, "considering your stench after we rescued you from the bilge."

Folie's humor rose irrationally. She smiled in spite of herself, touching Sir Howard's shoulder. "Oh dear! You really were awful."

"Thank you! I shall not pull you from the Thames next time!"

Folie put her hand over her mouth. *"Yes!"* She stared at him in dismay. "And I had forgot! Truly I had—I am so worried about Melinda—and my mind has been so bewildered! Oh, Sir Howard, I have not even given you a word of thanks! Forgive me! You must forgive me! You saved my life!"

"It was nothing," he said gruffly.

"Indeed it was! You saved me! All I remember is that wicked boy pushing me against the gate, and the water like ice, and that coat dragging me down, and then you were there. God bless you, Sir Howard. I owe you my life. How you held us both up I shall never know."

He shrugged off her effusions of gratitude modestly. "I am a strong swimmer. We were used to bathe all summer in the lake at Dingley when I was a boy. I taught all my girls to swim before they could walk."

"I have never been in anything larger than a copper tub!" Folie said. "I cannot swim at all. Thank God you were there."

"You must learn, for your own safety's sake," Sir Howard said. "I'll teach you. This summer, if you like. We could all go down to Brighton—"

"Let us return for a moment to our predicament, before you make plans for the summer," Robert said dryly.

"Yes—oh, yes—" Folie turned anxiously to him. "We must get word to Melinda directly. I cannot be easy until she knows we're safe."

Robert nodded, but before he could speak, Mrs. Moloney

returned with the roasted chickens. After setting out a generous table of vegetables and meat along with the fowl, inspecting Folie's plate and announcing that she ought to eat another portion of pie, or take a slice of roast chicken, she went away again.

"I believe I can send word safely to Cambourne House," Robert said low, "but if Folie cannot account for that note, then we have no lead at all as to who did this to us." He looked at her. "Until I'm certain we won't be attacked again, I can't allow you to go back. None of us should appear there alive."

Sir Howard made a dissenting sound, but offered no alternative.

"But Robert—" Folie said in a whisper. "Have you no idea what it all means? None whatsoever?"

He rubbed his fingers over his eyes, and then leaned on his hand. "You will think me mad again if I tell you what I suspect."

"Nay—we'll only think you criminally careless to allow Mrs. Hamilton to be involved," Sir Howard said.

Robert lifted his head. "Dingley," he said, "if I don't kill you before we're through this, remind me that I mean to do it."

"With pleasure," Sir Howard said.

"Oh, what a pair of—of—*lobcocks!*" Folie exclaimed, using a word she had overheard aboard the hulk.

They both looked at her as if she had just dropped her garter in Lady Melbourne's drawing room. "What?" Robert said.

"A pair of lobcocks," she repeated gamely. "Why, is it a very bad word?"

"Oh, perfectly applicable to him," Robert said graciously. "But do not trot it out to describe him in polite company."

"Robert Cambourne," she exclaimed. "Here we are, in danger of our very lives, and the two of you must act a pair of eight-year-olds. You are *both* lobcocks, whatever that may mean, but I hope it signifies that you have straw in your silly heads."

He looked a little abashed. "I did not mean that as it sounded."

"Yes, that is what you always say," Folie admonished.

"I do?"

"Whenever I remark that you have been particularly spiteful."

"Spiteful!" he said in surprise.

"Spiteful," Folie said firmly. "I don't know where you learned to say such mean, clever things. It is not like you."

He looked into the corner with a reflective expression, as if he were staring at some far horizon. Then he glanced back at her. "How do you know it isn't like me?"

Folie gave a small shrug. "I just know."

Sir Howard grunted irritably. "So let him cut at me with his sour tongue—we'll meet over a pair of good pistols and discover who is the cleverest."

"That you will not," Folie said, rolling her eyes. "Now—kindly tell us what you suspect, Robert. However mad it may seem. We are clearly in no case for common sense."

Robert sat back in the corner. "I believe this is a plot to make the Prince Regent appear insane," he said simply.

After a pregnant pause, Sir Howard threw back his head and began to howl with laughter. He gasped and chortled, then put his face down on his crossed arms, his shoulders shaking.

Robert watched him cynically. "I expected this."

Folie poked Sir Howard hard with her elbow. "Sit up and be still. Be still!"

Sir Howard choked with muffled laughter. After several jabs from Folie, he finally sat up, his face red and splotchy. "Oh, God give me strength," he snorted. "A plot to make Prinnie insane! A plot to make *Pr-prinnie* insane!"

"I apprehend that it seems unlikely," Robert said.

"Downright demented!" Sir Howard went off into sputters again, gasping for air. "What does the—what does the Pr-prince have to do with anything? More like it's a plot to make y-*you* insane, Cambourne. And it seems to have succeeded."

Robert looked at Folie, ignoring Sir Howard. ''Well, that is what I think, frankly. That I was drugged, to make me appear mad, and the same thing is being done to the Prince.''

''Come, come, you ninny, where's your proof of this?'' Sir Howard asked.

''I have no proof as to the Regent. As to myself—I have the word of a girl named Kathy, or perhaps Mattie, that she added something to my food at Solinger. After she told me, she vanished. I believe she was murdered.''

Sir Howard's chuckling ceased. He picked up his knife and fork and began to carve his chicken as if he were attacking it. His cheeks were flushed bright red.

''I think that somewhere in my Indian journals, I made some record of this—drug, or poison—whatever it might be.'' Robert still did not look at Sir Howard, but spoke directly to Folie. ''I can summon no specific memory, but I wrote hundreds of pages, on a number of *guuruus* and peculiar rites. Some of them used potions to induce eccentric mental states.''

''And this stuff was added to your food, you say?'' Sir Howard asked in a tone of disbelief. ''How, pray, do you propose one of these *guuruus* managed to get it from India into your plate in Buckinghamshire?''

''I think someone went to the devil of a lot of trouble to get it there,'' Robert said. ''And therefore had a damned good reason.''

''But what, Robert?'' Folie asked. ''I can't see any purpose to it.'' She frowned. ''Not that my mind seems very sharp today,'' she admitted. ''I'm all about in my head.''

He smiled at her. ''Sweet Folly. You have been a remarkable heroine. I can only conjecture that someone believes me to know much more than I do, and wished to render me incapacitated—and make sure that if I did speak, no one would take me seriously.''

Folie blushed. It was the second time he had called her that, sweet Folly. It seemed to make her heart dance about in her chest, and invoke the most airy fancies. She smiled back at him bashfully. She ought to tell him not to address her so, she knew—particularly before Sir Howard. But she did not.

"Still, I cannot see it," Sir Howard said. "You say that Mattie confessed?"

Robert looked up at him swiftly. "You know her? Mattie?"

"I—certainly, yes, I know her. Mattie Davis. She is a Dingley village girl, you know. I know the Dingley people. I keep up with them. In fact I recommended her father take the gardener's position at Solinger when you returned. I suppose she went to serve up at the house? A good church-going family. Salt of the earth. I can't believe the girl would knowingly poison a puppy!"

Robert looked at him for a long moment. "She gave me reason enough that she might."

"What reason?" Sir Howard asked, his voice strident and curious.

"She had a babe in her, and no husband."

Beneath his queue, the back of Sir Howard's neck turned beet-red. He took a large bite of chicken and shook his head. "You gaby—will you say such things before a lady?"

"The girl is dead, Dingley," Robert said, still looking directly across the table. "Is propriety all that concerns you?"

Sir Howard chewed sullenly. He took a long swig of ale. "God rest her soul, if that is true. Which I take full leave to doubt, sir."

Something tugged at Folie's erratic memory, slipping away even as she thought of it. She frowned a little. She lifted her hand—then lowered it, uncertain.

"I hope you may be right," Robert said. "I devoutly hope you may be right."

"Then you don't know for certain," Sir Howard said quickly. "What makes you suppose she is murdered?"

"I found her apron. Bloodstained." Robert glanced at Folie as if he did not wish for her to hear. "Gruesome," he said briefly. "I need not go into it. But I think she's dead."

There was a short silence. Folie bit her lower lip.

''Well. I cannot sit here twiddling my thumbs any longer,'' Sir Howard said, pushing himself to his feet. ''I'm going to take a walk.''

''Don't go to London,'' Robert said.

''I am not yours to command, sir,'' he said coldly. ''I beg your pardon, Mrs. Hamilton. You must excuse me.'' Sir Howard bowed.

Folie nodded, but he had already turned away, shoving open the taproom door and ducking through. Robert made a small flick with his hand, as if to say, ''Good riddance.'' He picked up his fork and ate a few bites, then looked at Folie.

''Do you still suppose I'm mad?''

''No,'' she said quietly. ''The world seems mad, perhaps.''

''I didn't want you in this. Folly, I didn't know what to do. I was so . . .'' His intense voice trailed off. He looked down at his plate. ''Well. Never mind.''

''If I had listened to you, I would not be here.'' She wrapped her hands in the borrowed apron. ''But . . . then—what if you had been all alone? They might have kept you; you might have vanished and I would never have known what happened to you.'' As she spoke, her voice began to rise with emotion. ''Oh, Robert.''

They sat silent, the table between them. His face was strangely severe.

''Be careful of Dingley,'' he said. ''I swear he's up to his ears in this.''

''Sir Howard?'' she said incredulously. ''No, I can't believe—''

''Listen to me for once!'' He stood up, leaning on his hands. ''Folly. Just once.''

Folie bowed her head. His vehemence had an odd effect; instead of stiffening her resistance, which nearly anyone else's sharp command would have done, it warmed her inside. Even if she could not really believe in his suspicions—it had been a long, long time since anyone had worried about her enough to give her overbearing orders.

"Yes, Robert," she said submissively, hiding a small smile.

He gave a caustic grunt. "Very convincing," he said. "I'm going to try to get word to Cambourne House now. Stay here in the house."

"Yes, Robert," she repeated.

He reached over and lifted her chin with his fingers. "Little scamp. Look me in the face and say that."

Folie lifted her lashes. She stared into his ice-gray eyes. "Yes, Robert." She was piqued to discover that she could not prevent the smile from playing at the corners of her mouth.

He stared back. The tips of his fingers were warm on her skin. His look drifted over her face, touching her cheeks and chin and forehead. Suddenly he drew a deep breath and stood straight. "I'm going," he said firmly, as if she might not believe him. He turned away, buttoning his coat.

SEVENTEEN

IT WAS AFTER midnight when Lander arrived at The Highflyer. Robert felt strong relief when he saw the butler's square, familiar face—sending a thin beggar boy to the back door of Cambourne House had not been the most certain of ways to convey an obscure message—but Lander had his wits about him, Robert could say that without reserve.

Folie and Sir Howard were in bed. The only light was from the fire, where Skipper lay curled by the hearth, casting a long shadow over the flagstone floor. Lander looked about the small public house curiously as he sat down with Robert, but as usual, he made no comment. Mrs. Moloney—who had flatly refused to discuss the party removing elsewhere when Robert had warned that they might draw something dangerous to The Highflyer—served out a pair of her creamy ales and left them discreetly alone.

"How is it at home?" Robert asked directly.

"I believe you saved Miss Melinda's life," Lander said. "I do not think she could have survived another day of terror."

"What did you tell her?"

"Only what you said, that Mrs. Hamilton is alive and well with you." He gave Robert a crooked smile. "She was not overly reassured, but just to know her mother is unhurt has revived her spirits greatly.''

''Have you notified anyone of her abduction?''

Lander paused. He took a deep draw on his mug, then set it down carefully. ''I must admit something to you, sir.''

Robert raised his eyebrows, waiting.

''You hired me out of Bow Street, as a servant and guardian. I told you I had experience with both—with the thief-takers and with being in service. That is not quite perfectly true.''

Robert sat back. He looked at his butler expectantly.

''I am well acquainted with thieves and ruffians. But my experience with service has more to do with receiving than giving it.''

''This is shocking news,'' Robert said mildly.

''My father is the Marquess of Hursley.''

Robert lifted his eyebrows.

''I am not the heir, I assure you,'' Lander said, as if Robert would wish to be confident on that point. ''I have four older brothers.''

''Ah. So you took up with thieves instead?''

Lander smiled sheepishly. ''My interests would not gratify my family, so I keep them to myself. But when I was a boy, I once visited Mr. John Fielding's courtroom in Bow Street. You mayn't have heard of him out in India—the Blind Beak, they called him—and they say he could recognize three thousand thieves by voice alone. Which is no doubt an exaggerated number, but I can tell you true that he could distinguish at least five, for I saw him do it that day. And I have been fascinated by the law officers and criminals ever since.''

''Have you indeed.''

''My father would not let me go into the army—he wishes me to become an MP. I'm awaiting a seat in his influence.'' He shrugged. ''But a tranquil life does not charm me. So when I was at loose ends for amusement, I volunteered my assistance at Bow Street, and because I am a little—unusual—in that métier, I am allotted some of the more unusual matters.''

"That I can well imagine. And am I one of these matters?"

"Yes, sir. You are."

Robert leaned forward. "Tell me what you know."

"Little enough. My mentor—you will forgive me if I do not identify him—is highly placed in the government. You came to his attention upon your arrival in England, and I was instructed to take the position with you—"

As Skipper lifted his head, Lander stopped speaking abruptly. The dog stared toward the passage to the best chamber, then laid his head down again, eyes open, tail sweeping the floor in a friendly beat. Folie peeked around the corner. She saw Lander and hurried forward, pulling an oversized robe about her. Her face was white and anxious in the firelight.

"Have you seen Melinda?"

Robert raised his hand, signaling her to keep her voice low. She nodded and slid into the nook next to him. Her hip touched his. Robert was instantly, vividly aware of her lithe body beneath the draping folds.

"Did you tell Melinda we are safe?" she demanded in hushed tones.

"Yes, ma'am. She is vastly relieved, as you may suppose."

Folie released a long sigh. "She must have been beside herself."

"She has been most concerned," Lander said.

"Only concerned?" Folie seemed taken aback. "I feared she would be having hysterics."

"I attempted to moderate her alarm, ma'am. I did not think it good for her nerves to become overly emotional."

She looked at him in wonder. "And you were successful?"

He smiled. "Tolerably."

"Well, you are to be congratulated, then. I'm not sure I wouldn't rather face that horrid scullion again than Melinda in a panic terror."

"She endured it admirably," Lander said with sincerity. "Indeed, I esteem her—"

Folie started, grabbing Robert's elbow as she looked abruptly round behind her. "Oh, I—" She frowned, holding tight. "What was that?"

"Stay still." Robert listened, but he heard nothing. The dog lay sleeping peacefully. After listening a few moments, Robert stood up, handing her out of the cubbyhole. He made a deliberate check of the room, the doors, and the windows. It was a simple house—there was little to inspect. Skipper got up and came with him as Robert looked down the passage that led to Folie's room. He carried a candle down the kitchen stairs and up to the attic door where he shared a bed with Dingley. It was closed. He could hear Dingley snoring even through the heavy wood. The staircase creaked badly—he did not think anyone could have walked up or down it without being heard by the dog.

"Nothing there," he said, returning to sit down beside her, this time on the outside.

"I suppose I saw a shadow." She gave a breathless laugh. "I am the one with unsettled nerves!"

"You have not yet told me what happened," Lander said.

Robert kept his voice quiet. "I'm still trying to sort it out. I received a note in Mrs. Hamilton's handwriting—there is no question in my mind that it was genuinely written by her, but she's received a bad blow on her head, and doesn't recall writing it now. It asked me to meet her privately at Vauxhall." He ignored Lander's slight blink at this. "I don't know how the note came into my hands. At one point, just after she regained consciousness, she told me that she wrote it to Sir Howard Dingley." He glanced at Folie. "You still don't remember that?"

She cast her eyes upward, then all about the room, looking rather like a student stumped for the correct answer. "No," she said finally, giving him an apologetic shrug.

"At any rate," Robert said, "it would appear that it was meant to cozen me into walking into a trap." He explained how he had been waylaid, and woken to find himself, Folie, and Sir Howard in the prison hulk.

"Sir Howard Dingley!" Lander exclaimed softly. "How did he come there?"

Robert shook his head. "He claimed to me that he saw Folie dart off into the darkness, and followed to give her a safe escort. That the next he knew he awoke aboard the hulk with us. But I'll tell you, Lander—I never saw him in the supper party at Vauxhall."

"He was not in it," Lander said. "Though Lady Dingley seemed to me to be rather unsettled, looking about her as if she might expect someone. She would not leave the box at all. Perhaps he had meant to join them there."

They both looked at Folie. She shrugged helplessly. "I remember the fireworks. And that's all."

"But you, ma'am?" Lander asked. "I never knew what happened to you. I turned my back to find our boatman, and Miss Melinda said the same—that you just suddenly walked away from us. And we could not find you. For two days I searched that park from tree to tree."

"I remember the fireworks," she said plaintively.

"We found nothing but your shawl."

Folie's face lit like one of her starry fireworks. "You found my shawl!"

"Yes, ma'am. Nothing else. Not a trace." Lander shook his head. "*That* was when Miss Melinda had the hysterics."

"Oh, Melinda, Melinda," Folie said, pressing her hands together. "What she must have endured."

"The whole house has been in turmoil. Lady Dingley was disabled by the vapors. If not for Miss Jane, I think the youngest ladies would have been terrified out of their wits by Lady Dingley and Miss Melinda, but shc managed to calm and distract them." He smiled wryly. "Lord Morier paid a call that next morning, and found himself telling pirate stories in the nursery."

"Morier?" Robert said in astonishment. "In the nursery?"

"*What* an admirable gentleman!" Folie said. "Who would have thought he had it in him!"

"Miss Jane gave him little choice," Lander said.

"So it is public now—Mrs. Hamilton's and Dingley's disappearance?"

Lander shook his head negatively. "We knew nothing of Dingley's being involved. Only that Mrs. Hamilton had been abducted. Or worse. I informed my own people in Bow Street, but otherwise we have put it about that she is taken very ill. The circumstances were too strange—I did not wish to let any details out."

"It was no ordinary robbery, certainly," Robert said. "They meant to be rid of me—perhaps to be rid of Folly and Dingley too, or perhaps they were accidentally snared."

"Folly?" Lander asked, in a puzzled tone.

"That is me, you see," she said modestly. "My Christian name—Folie Elizabeth."

Robert realized that he had not been quite circumspect, but somehow in the tangle of events he could not maintain a proper formal distance. He felt ferociously proprietary of her, in fact, as if he ought to be able to call her by any endearment that he pleased, and decorum—and Dingley—be hanged.

"It is very pretty, ma'am," Lander said politely.

"Thank you, Lander," she said. "You are a most gallant butler."

Lander glanced at Robert with a slight frown, as if to silence him before he could say anything of his "butler's" true background. Robert was willing to keep that private, but he intended to hear anything Lander might know of his adversaries.

"You were telling me why you came to Solinger," he prompted. "Go on."

Lander hesitated, glancing at Folie.

"I think it is only wise to inform her too," Robert said. "The more she understands, the safer I believe she will be."

Lander frowned down into his empty mug as if he might find some guidance there. Finally, he looked up. "Yes, you may be right. What little I can tell. I am with Bow Street, Mrs. Hamilton," he explained to a wide-eyed Folie. "I came into Mr. Cambourne's service advised that there might be some danger about him—in the nature of a radical political intrigue. The purpose of this intrigue was not known, but because of the identity of a gentleman who had shown a considerable interest in shipping lists and the date of Mr. Cambourne's arrival in England, we became concerned.''

''What gentleman?'' Robert asked sharply.

''One Erasmus Inman.'' Lander looked intently at Robert.

He shook his head. ''I've never heard the name.''

''He is an extremist—the hireling of radical Whigs, but we are not yet certain whom. Mr. Inman himself is not so much a political creature as a very clever terrorist. He has learned his trade at the foot of the Jacobins, and he has learned it well, I assure you. We were at first concerned that you might be a confederate, but I soon suspected that you were to be his victim. I did my best, sir, to prevent him from reaching you.''

''Why didn't you tell me this?''

''I wish that I had. But I could not be sure at the time if you were feigning your madness, or if it were a true lunacy, or—once, in a dark moment, you told me that you feared poison. It was then that I began to believe strongly that somehow it must be Inman's work.''

''You cannot arrest him?'' Folie asked.

''We can, ma'am, but we do not. Inman is vicious, but no more useful to us than the butcher's dog, if we wish to catch the butcher out red-handed.''

''What do you mean?'' Folie exclaimed. ''You have not taken this man up on purpose? When he was poisoning Robert's food? When he was murdering housemaids and selling people onto prison ships?''

''Hush,'' Robert said, touching Folie's hand. ''I understand you,'' he said to Lander. ''Go on.''

''We wish to flush out his master, ma'am,'' Lander explained apologetically. ''For that we must give him a bit of leash.''

"Humpf," Folie said. Then she gripped Robert's hand. "Melinda! Will he go after Melinda now?"

Lander frowned. "I will keep Miss Melinda safe. I swear to you, ma'am; I swear on my life—I will make certain she is safe."

The intensity in his voice made Robert study him with a new attention. But Folie was already talking anxiously of taking Melinda away from London, back to Toot, where she would be unharmed.

"Ma'am—" Lander said. "If you and Mr. Cambourne will put your trust in me—I believe I know a place where you may go with Miss Melinda that will be secure. Indeed, safer than Toot-above-the-Batch or anywhere else you might take her."

"Where?" Robert slid his fingers between hers, closing his hand against her palm.

"A few hours from town, in the direction of Norwich—it is a sheltered property where a proper guard may be placed. I am quite familiar with it. The ladies would be comfortable there, with a walled garden close by to the village, and every amenity."

Folie looked up at Robert. He nodded. "I agree that they must leave London. Solinger is too large, and already penetrated. Herefordshire is too far away. I know nothing of it."

"But Toot is—" Folie began.

"I don't want you so far away as that." He found that his hold was tightening on her hand. "Lander's notion is better."

As she teased her lower lip in thought, Robert had to look away, distracted by a precipitous rise of desire. He drew his fingers from hers and picked up his mug, taking a deep, quick swallow.

"I suppose you are right," she said reluctantly. "But—what will you do?"

"We must flush out the ringleader," Robert said. "I don't think we can breathe easy until we have him. Just how highly-placed do you suppose this fellow might be?"

"I will not mislead you," Lander said soberly. "Very high."

"I'll hunt down the prime minister himself to put a stop to this nonsense," Robert said, scowling.

Folie watched him silently. He did not say it, but he vowed to himself to take a black revenge on whoever had put those bruises on her face. First he would make sure they swallowed plenty of the same maddening drug they had given him, and when they were out of their minds with the fearsome apparitions, he would practice on them a few of those clever tortures favored by the Indian princes. He toyed pleasurably with a vision of it in his mind, staring into the shadows of the taproom.

"You frighten me when you look so," Folie said. "Robert—you will not be foolish!"

He came back to reality. With a distorted smile, he said, "Merely daydreaming."

"Unless you can see into the master's head, sir, I do not know how you are to pursue him," Lander said. "I have cudgeled my brain for some plan, but we do not know who he is, nor what he intends. 'Tis certain he has collected a fine pack of revolutionaries and rogues to do his bidding. There are disaffected Whigs aplenty, after the prince refused them office in his regency."

"With colleagues in India," Robert said. "This began in Delhi."

"Might it concern the East India Company?"

"The charter is to be renewed next year—or not," Robert said. "The Company always has enemies among the Whigs."

"Robert thinks someone means to make the regent appear to be mad like his father," Folie said.

"Well, it is merely one possible theory—" Robert began.

But Lander looked up at her abruptly. He had such an arrested expression that Robert's voice trailed away.

"My God," he breathed. He put his hand over his chin, rubbing his thumb, visibly reckoning. A long moment later, he exclaimed, "This poison that they gave you! It could be done. It could be done, and reason enough. They hate the Prince Regent with a passion, the Whigs. If they supposed they could put him out of his head like his father . . . force a change in the regency and the cabinet . . . Good God, that is altogether ingenious. It's a brilliant notion, sir."

"Robert is amazing," Folie said smugly. "He can tell what is in people's minds."

Robert snorted. "Of course I cannot. Not in truth."

"Srí Ramanu said that you had a gift for it."

"Why do you remember me saying that sort of rubbish, and can't recall if you wrote a note about Vauxhall?"

"But you did it! With the superintendent of the prison ship." She looked at Lander. "It was extraordinary. Robert knew precisely what the man was thinking."

"Several fortunate guesses," Robert said, "and a little observation. He had a tarot deck in his bookcase. A man such as that wants to believe."

"But it was more than that," Folie said. "I was there."

Lander was watching them with interest. "You are gifted for that sort of deception, sir?"

"No. No, not really. I learned a few tricks in India, pickpockets' and charlatans' work. Nothing very helpful in this case, I assure you."

"I wonder," Lander said thoughtfully. "I wonder."

At four in the afternoon the next day, Folie and Robert waited on the east side of the ancient Bow bridge, overlooking the River Lea. She sat on a bench beside the parapets, watching ducks pick along the river's edge beneath the pretty bow shaped arch of the bridge.

It was not quite a teeming spot, well outside the city bustle, but the traffic of hay carts, farm horses, and country squires driving their ladies to London in the dogcart created a steady ring of steel against stone as they crossed the bridge. Folie inspected every vehicle coming from the direction of London anxiously, watching for Lander and Melinda.

"It will be growing dark soon," she said. "Do you suppose they will arrive before dark?"

Robert crumbled the crust of his supper loaf and tossed a few bits to the ducks, who rushed to do quacking battle for it. "We'll wait inside the inn if they don't."

"In these clothes?" Folie asked, casting a glance at the elegant building of white stucco that graced the street beside the bridge. It appeared very genteel, and they looked like a farm couple, Robert in his baggy coat and a low-crowned hat belonging to Tucker Moloney; Folie in an apron, a scarf knotted under her chin, and the leftovers from Mrs. Moloney's pork pie tied in a bundle on her lap.

"Must you have a private parlor, madam?" he asked in amusement. "We'll sit in the back of the tap room like Mr. and Mrs. John Bull."

"But have we any money left?"

"Lander brought me plenty," he said. "We have no worries there."

Folie turned again to watch the bridge. It was very strange to be with him, alone and on the road, far from any whiff of a respectable female companion. As long as they had been at the Highflyer, she had not thought of it, for Mrs. Moloney had added an air of honest country propriety—and in the hulk, modesty and decorum had been the last thing on her mind. But now it struck her that she was quite alone in the company of a gentleman, looking naturally to him for direction, something that had not occurred to her since her marriage. Although when she considered it, she was not sure she had ever really looked even to Charles for guidance; he had hardly paid her enough mind to offer it.

But since the prison ship, it seemed that she had placed her whole dependence on Robert. It felt odd and yet perfectly natural, as if she had been used to do it forever, instead of heading her own independent household for six years. There had been moments in the past few days when she felt as uncertain as Lady Dingley, and she had simply turned to Robert to make the decision. She supposed it was a woman's customary inclination, to lean upon a man, until she tried to imagine placing her unquestioning reliance on

Colonel Cox. Abruptly, she thought perhaps it was not such a strong female instinct after all.

"I wish I knew where Dingley has got to," Robert murmured darkly.

Sir Howard had been gone from the Highflyer before the sun came up, without leaving any note. Once again, something seemed to flit through Folie's mind, but she could not catch it before it disappeared. She blinked at the late sun sparkles as a breeze rippled the water.

"You do not think he went to his family?"

"I hope he has the common sense to stay away from them, but I fear not. The faster Lander packs them all up to go home to Dingley, the better."

Folie sighed. "What a dismal end to our season," she said sadly. "It was to be so lovely."

He sat down on the brick beside her. "I'm sorry, Folly. To ruin all your pleasure."

"Oh, well." She shrugged. "To be perfectly truthful, I have found Society to be rather dull. Nothing so diverting as breaking prison and swimming the Thames."

"No doubt," Robert said ironically. "I am a guardian of surpassing excellence."

She gave him a sidelong smile. "But at least you are *interesting.*" She took a crust from his hands and cast it to the ducks. "I am obliged to say that, if you had not written to Charles, I do not think I would have had a modicum of excitement in my whole humdrum existence!" She looked into the distance down the river. "For all that I hid in the greenhouse and wept my eyes out afterward."

A small herd of sheep trotted briskly onto the bridge, their hooves on the stone like a cascade of pebbles. Folie watched a fat old ewe pause to grab a few bites of the new grass peeking up beside the stone bridge. The shepherd trilled and goaded his shaggy flock forward with a crook.

"Did you weep, my sweet Folly?" Robert asked softly.

"Oh yes," she said, folding her hands. The shadows of the town's buildings were beginning to creep down the riverbanks. The ducks paddled in and out of the bright arc of water beneath the bridge. She lifted her chin proudly.

''Well, you would not understand. I suppose gentlemen never weep over their foolishness.''

''Perhaps not,'' he said.

Folie bit her lower lip. She reached down and pulled a dry reed that had found its way up through the bricking.

''I think we walk ourselves to exhaustion, and if that does not suffice, then we drink ourselves into a stupor, and if that does not serve—then we take a pistol and put it to our heads,'' he said.

Folie looked at him aside. He was staring across the river, but his bleak gaze saw a thousand miles beyond. She bent her head over her lap, splitting the reed carefully with her thumbnail.

''There are things locked so deep that tears cannot reach them, Folly,'' he said quietly.

She pressed her lips hard together, working the reed until it bent into a circle in her fingers. She tied a bow in it.

''I am glad that I did not lose my shawl,'' she said.

''So am I,'' he said. He caught one end of her reed between his thumb and forefinger and tugged at it. Folie allowed him to draw the reed and her hand into his lap. He stroked his fingertips lightly over the back of her palm. ''Folly—''

Iron-shod hooves clattered on the bridge. The heavy wheels of a laden carriage thundered onto the stone. Folie looked up as a fresh team of four galloped across, drawing a coach with window blinds drawn to conceal the occupants. But even before the vehicle turned off toward the inn yard, she knew who it must be.

''Melinda,'' she whispered, and stood up.

''Not too fast,'' Robert said, without rising. ''Sit down. Let us make sure no one is following them.''

Folie sat down. She twisted the reed around and around her finger. But though they waited for what seemed an eternity, no one but a milkmaid swinging her empty pail crossed over the bridge after the carriage.

''Should I go now?'' she asked in an undertone.

He took her arm and stood. ''Folly—''

She was turning, but at the tone in his voice, she looked

directly up at him. Suddenly it came into her mind that he would be parting from them here, returning to London to take up residence at Cambourne House and execute the plan they had concocted. It had seemed bizarre and clever when she and Lander and Robert had sat safely at the Highflyer and contrived the scheme, just daft enough to work, but now the strategy seemed wildly dangerous. He would be living openly at Cambourne House, going into Society on purpose, trying to draw the attention of his enemies to him in the most flamboyant way. They might betray themselves, as the plan enticed them to do, or they might as easily find a way to murder him, or destroy his mind. Lander was taking Folie and Melinda to safety—Robert was not coming with them.

He was scowling down at her as if she angered him. But his hand was on her arm, holding tight.

Suddenly she reached up, put both palms on his shoulders, and in the midst of the street and the bridge and the river and the sinking sun, pressed her body against his.

He pulled her to him, his arms going urgently about her waist. Like a pair of countrified lovers, they hugged hard in full view of anyone who might be watching, but Folie did not care. She was trying to memorize him, trying to imprint the feel of his shoulders and his height and his chest and his very breath, to drink in the whole knowledge of his real living existence.

"Mrs. Godwin?" A voice called across from the innyard, the prearranged alias they had agreed upon for her. Folie pushed away from Robert. Golden angled sunlight glittered in her hazy eyes.

"Take care," she whispered fiercely.

With a brief nod, he brushed his fist against her cheek. Folie let go of him and walked away. A few steps beyond, she heard him murmur something imperatively, but the words were not clear. She looked over her shoulder, pausing.

He opened his fist, turning his palm toward her as if he let her go like a small bird from his hand. "Deferred kiss," he said between his teeth.

She nodded, wordless, and went quickly across the street.

Eighteen

THE GARDEN WAS in bloom, lilac-scented. Her blue shawl pulled about her, Folie walked there with Melinda as they had done every morning for two weeks. Pink and white tulips nodded over carpets of tiny violets.

One side of the garden enclosure ran along the high street of the village, though the wall was too tall and the geography too flat to allow any view of the street. A red brick church tower loomed over them, and farther away, a windmill's white sails turned endlessly—the only points of viewing interest beyond the wall, unless she happened to catch sight of passengers on the roof of a stagecoach as it swept through. Sometimes just before dawn, as Folie lay waking, staring up into the blackness, she could hear the royal mail make its regular halt at the Spread Eagle for a change of horses.

Melinda had been amazingly docile about the ruin of her season. After her initial transports of relief and rapture upon Folie's safe return, Melinda in fact had seemed so subdued that Folie had been worried about her health. And yet, she did not seem to mope. She had not wept once for London, or complained of boredom. But she was quieter, more thoughtful, than Folie had ever known her to be.

As they had driven in the closed coach to this house of

safety, Lander had undertaken to explain their situation to Melinda. Folie was glad to let him do so. Ever since the hulk, she could not seem to gather her scattered thoughts for more than a moment at a time. She had no concentration, and forgot the most everyday things. Only this morning, on the garden step, she had discovered the withered blooms she had picked yesterday lying next to the pail of water she had never put them in.

The servants here were more the ordinary sort, the standard of service serene and efficient, really quite polished for a country village. Lander did not even maintain the illusion of being their butler—the staff deferred to him, but more as if he were the master of the house than the head steward. After their arrival, he had gone back to London by stagecoach, leaving early in the morning.

Folie sat down on a garden bench, pulling the shawl close. Melinda sat down with her.

"It does not seem real," Melinda said. "Everything is so peaceful here. It's so hard to imagine danger."

Folie shook her head. "Sometimes I can smell the river and the prison," she said. "At night, it comes to me. And I can't sleep. As if I have that water in my mouth and lungs still."

Melinda locked her arm through Folie's, squeezing, saying nothing.

"To think there are those poor people there now," Folie said. "Perhaps when this is concluded, and we can go home, I shall form a Prisoners' Relief Committee."

"I don't know if the ladies will join you, Mama," Melinda said gently. "Perhaps they will not understand that criminals might need relief."

"Then it will be a committee of one." She smiled wryly, watching a flock of robins hunting through a patch of overturned soil. "I don't think I can go on embroidering handkerchiefs for a church steeple that will undoubtedly fall down long before we ever collect enough money to repair it."

"A committee of two. I'll be on it with you," Melinda said loyally. "I don't ever want to leave you, Mama."

Folie laughed, hugging her. "I don't think you need resign yourself to a life of spinsterhood and good works yet, my love."

Melinda bowed her head. She smoothed her gown over her lap. In a small, shy voice, she said, "But perhaps you will marry Mr. Cambourne?"

Folie could feel the blood rush to her face. "Wherever did you conceive of that notion?"

Melinda's lips puckered gaily. "Oh—perhaps it was when I peeked out of the carriage and saw you kissing him in the street!"

"I did not kiss him!" Folie said, flustered. "It was merely—an affectionate embrace. If not for him, I would not be alive."

"Oh," Melinda said. "I see."

"It was a perfectly natural thing. You should not weave such a great flight of fancy from such a small circumstance."

"Oh, no," Melinda said, nodding. "Certainly not."

"Melinda!" Folie lamented. "Do not tease me on this point."

"You do not like him?"

Folie turned her face away, watching a robin capture some hapless insect. She thought if she said one word about how much she was in love with Robert Cambourne, still in love with him, in love with him again, frightened for him, puzzled and scared and aching—if she said one word, she would burst into silly tears.

"I will be sorry for him if you don't," Melinda said, "because he seems to like you very much."

"There is a great deal you do not know of life, Miss Melinda," Folie said sternly. "Mr. Cambourne and I like one another, certainly. But marriage is another matter."

"Of course that is true," Melinda said, in her most adult tone. "We must take into account his prospects. His income. His family." She reached down and picked a tulip from beside the bench. "He is single." She plucked a petal. "He is wealthy." She pulled another. "His family is perfectly respectable." She pulled a third. "Now tell me what liabilities you see in this match.'' She handed Folie the flower.

''Well—'' Folie said, plucking all the rest of the petals at once, tossing them to the wind, ''he has not asked me!''

''He will,'' Melinda said smugly. ''You do not know the way he looked after you as you walked away from him!''

''You are a nonsensical, romantic, naïve child,'' Folie said irritably, standing up. ''I'm sorry that I ever pulled you from that gutter and gave you a home!''

Melinda looked up at her with a smile so loving that it made Folie feel quite wobbly inside. ''Perhaps I shall marry him myself,'' she said, ''as a reward for restoring you to me.''

''And puffed-up beyond measure!'' Folie exclaimed. ''A reward? I wash my hands of you. You may return to the workhouse.'' She swept away with a brisk step, wondering when this rampant tendency to weeping would leave her.

Robert began his first foray at the Malmsbury ball by modestly bowing out of a game of cards, where he had won a single hand for tuppence, apologizing that he could not take advantage of his opponents. Naturally this had led to some curious inquiry into his skill as a player, since his opponents, several aristocratic matrons, considered themselves no mean amateurs at a hand of piquet.

He deprecated his expertise, upon which they began to be a little suspicious, accusing him teasingly of being a Captain Sharp who wanted to lull them into complacency and then fleece them. But as Robert firmly refused to play, for money or not, they let him go--with some mystification.

He parlayed that carefully, taking his time, watching the play at another table, speaking to no one. He took note of one of the ladies at the first table watching him idly. Suddenly he turned full face to her, staring hard into her startled eyes, frowning.

Of course she averted her look, glancing down at her cards. Robert crossed the room and leaned down over her shoulder. ''Ma'am,'' he said urgently. ''I beg your pardon,

I—'' He stopped speaking and stood back. He shook his head with a faint laugh. ''I beg your pardon. It is nothing.''

He withdrew, leaving her whole party looking after him curiously. But he made certain to cast her a few looks while he conversed with other guests. She was quite plump and elderly, so that he could not be accused of flirtation—at least of the usual kind. But this was a darker sort of seduction; Phillippa had once told him, with a nervous laugh, that he had the most dreadfully wicked eyes when he looked at her just so.

He imagined Phillippa sitting where the matron did, and watched the lady grow more and more uneasy as her game went on. Finally, at the end of a rubber, she laid down her cards. As soon as Robert saw it, he added a comment to the avid conversation about boxing that was going forward among the gentlemen he observed. So their attention was upon him when his pigeon arrived.

He turned to her. ''I am glad you came to me,'' he said intensely.

''Why, sir!'' she said, putting her hand over her bosom. ''You've been near to giving me the evil eye this quarter hour past!''

He laughed, shaking his head. ''Have I? I beg your pardon. Lately I cannot seem to discipline myself. What did you dream last night?''

She blinked at him, fanning herself. ''Dream? I'm sure I don't remember.''

He silently thanked God for small blessings. ''Ah. Well then.'' He gave a slight shrug and turned back to the card game.

''Why do you ask?''

Robert did not face her directly; he kept his attention on the table, but spoke to her, smiling. ''I'm only sorry that you don't remember.''

He waited, containing any hint of expectation. It was important to let her go if she was not truly hooked.

''But why, sir?''

He glanced aside at her. ''You don't recall your mother?''

She frowned a little, tilting her head curiously, making her blue hat plume sway. "In my dream, do you mean?"

Robert nodded. He let his eyes follow the card play, but kept his face a little turned to her, visibly dividing his attention.

"Are you saying that I dreamed of my mother?" the lady asked, her voice pitching higher.

Robert looked at her then, and smiled. "The scent of flowers," he said. He shook his head slightly. "But you do not remember."

"No . . ." She moved her fan quickly, frowning at him. "No, I . . . but wait. I . . ." Her voice trailed off.

"What sort of flowers?" he asked. "Violets? Or lilacs, perhaps. Think of that. It will help you."

"Lilacs," she said instantly. And then, in a moment that startled even Robert, a look of brilliant pleasure came over her face. "Yes! I do remember! My mother's boudoir! I dreamed of her last night in her boudoir! Oh my! Her lilac water!" She put her fingers over her mouth in a girlish gesture, looking suddenly several decades younger.

Robert was glad that he had not said more—he would have begun suggesting a garden next. He grinned, gave her a conspiratorial wink, and moved away.

For the next hour, he avoided her entirely. He left the card room, and if he saw her come into the ballroom, he went to the supper room. If she followed him to the supper room, he slipped back to the ballroom and solicited the hand of a wallflower to dance.

He remained with his dance partner after the quadrille, a long-nosed girl with pretty chestnut hair and an air of haughty condescension that Robert suspected hid truly painful shyness. Miss Davenport had little to say, and barely looked at him, keeping her eyebrows lifted while she scanned the room as if some greater personage might appeal to her. But when he offered to bring her some refreshment, she allowed that she would like a cup of tea.

Robert returned to the supper table, allowing his matronly target to catch his eye. She followed him out as if there were an invisible cord between them, bringing her partner along, a tall, blustery sort of man who made Robert's original target appear as soft as a well-used down counterpane. Robert braced himself for a more difficult time.

They were well-acquainted with Miss Davenport, greeting her and then disregarding her as if she were a part of the potted palm she stood beneath. She stood sipping her tea and examining the far horizon.

"Mr. Cambourne." His matron, a Mrs. Witham-Stanley, assailed him with barely suppressed eagerness. "I have brought Mr. Bellamy to you."

"Thank you!" Robert said, as if this were something he had hoped for. Mr. Bellamy had a pinched, angry look, but he nodded politely in answer to Robert's bow.

"Mr. Cambourne," Mrs. Witham-Stanley said plaintively. "Did you not, a bit ago, tell me that I dreamed of my dear mother, God bless her soul, last night?"

"Lilacs," Robert said, smiling at her affectionately. "Of course."

"There, you see!" she said triumphantly to her friend. "My dearest mama used lilac water every day of her life. I knew there was a reason why I put it on tonight! I dreamed of her. Oh, in her own boudoir, I stood at her knee and watched her comb out her beautiful hair. But I had forgotten it, until Mr. Cambourne told me!"

Mr. Bellamy put his forefinger to the bridge of his nose, rubbing. "Indeed," he said incredulously.

Robert tilted his head, watching Mr. Bellamy. He said nothing.

"I wish that I could recall more of it!" Mrs. Witham-Stanley said. "It was so lovely."

"If you contemplate it, you will recall more."

"But however did you know, Mr. Cambourne? That is what we cannot fathom! Mr. Bellamy says I must be mistaken, and yet you *did*—"

He shook his head, touching her arm as if he were distracted. "I believe that Mr. Bellamy does not feel well," he said quietly.

Mr. Bellamy's dark eyebrows came together to a sharp fold. Robert lifted his hand, almost touching the man's cheek, and then dropped it away.

"A scrap of the headache, that's all. When Mrs. W-S tried to tell me that you—"

"Don't worry over that just now. Give it a color," Robert said. "Your pain. Does it have a color?"

Mr. Bellamy pursed his lips. "I cannot fathom your meaning." His whole face seemed to wrinkle into disapproval.

Robert looked steadily at him. "A deep reddish-black," he murmured. "Heavy and pulsing. Gather it up here. Between your eyes." He touched his own forehead at the place Bellamy had rubbed his finger against the bridge of his nose.

Bellamy's cheeks puffed. He moved his lips, as if he meant to speak, but instead he only frowned more deeply.

"Do you feel it there?" Robert asked. "All gathered there?"

Bellamy scowled at him.

"What color is it?" Robert asked.

Bellamy shook his head, frowning so hard that Robert thought he must give himself the headache with that alone.

"Dark," Robert offered. "Very dark. The color of darkened blood. It's constricted there, hurting you. Don't speak. Do you understand me?"

Bellamy had begun to look as if he were holding his breath under water. He blinked, and then after a hesitation, nodded once.

"Good. Now let me have it," Robert said. "Don't let it slip away. Keep the darkness between your eyes. Trap it there for me. You must help." Though Bellamy did nothing in response but stand still, stifling his breath, Robert smiled. "Good man. Keep it there. I know it is difficult."

Bellamy made a faint sound, his eyes squeezed shut. His eyebrows were drawn together agonizingly tightly. Robert reached up and touched him between the eyes with two fingers.

"Give it to me now," he said, increasing the pressure of

his fingertips. "Push it out to me." He bore hard against the man's forehead, intensifying his opposition until Bellamy would have fallen a step forward if Robert had taken his hand away. "It comes," he said commandingly. "Keep pushing, until I have it all. Push it to me." He watched Bellamy's eyebrows strain together, strain and strain, until at last they lost the strength to maintain it. "Now!" He lightened his pressure a little. "I have it in my hand. Tell me where to put it."

The man's mouth worked. He opened his eyes.

"Somewhere that it will hurt no one else," Robert said quietly.

"Into the pot," Bellamy said, his eyes darting aside.

Robert bent, without ceremony, and thrust his fist into the center of the fronds, near the soil. He opened his hand. "There. Look. Can you see it?"

Bellamy stared into the pot, along with the ladies. He shook his head, touching his temple. But the scowl had vanished from his face.

"Still, it is there," Robert said simply. "You must help me keep it there. I can't do it alone. Your anger will draw it back to you. Mistrust. Spleen. Leave it there. Leave it all there."

Bellamy nodded faintly.

"I hope you feel better," Robert said.

"Yes," he said in wonder. "I—yes—undoubtedly I do."

"Mr. Cambourne," Mrs. Witham-Stanley said in an awed voice, "what are you?"

Robert hesitated. Then he shrugged. "It pleases me to help."

"Yes, but—" Mrs. Witham-Stanley's blue plume bobbed in agitation. "You knew what I dreamed! In my own head!"

"You must tell no one," Robert said. "It was only a fortunate guess. Now and then they come to me. Now if you will accept my excuses—Miss Davenport, Mr. Bellamy. I'm afraid I must depart."

• • •

Outside the door of the Malmsbury house, Lander stepped from the shadows, joining Robert as he strode quickly down the steps. This was a dangerous moment, leaving the house. They were both exposed; there was no way to know if Robert's enemies had yet discovered his escape from the hulk. They might lie in wait, determined to dispatch him now without mercy.

As they turned the corner, walking fast, taking a roundabout return to a waiting hackney, Lander whispered, "Any success, sir?"

Robert grinned. After the long evening of tension, the tonic of excitement ran high in his blood. He made a sign of triumph with his thumb. "It may work," he said under his breath.

He hiked himself into the cab. Lander followed. Robert lay back on the seat with a great sigh, resting his head.

"God only knows, Lander, but it just may work," he said. Suddenly his pulse was pounding painfully in his head and chest, as if he had taken Bellamy's headache into his own body. "Provided my heart can stand the strain."

Folie and Melinda were not allowed to be at home to any callers from the village. Folie supposed that they must be the topic of a deal of speculation, though Lander had assured them that the staff would suffer no dangerous intelligence to leak abroad. Folie could only too well imagine the effect such a circumstance would have on Toot—the occupation of the largest dwelling in the village, obviously built for a pretty sort of parsonage or dower house, by strangers who neither showed their faces nor let their servants talk!

The result seemed to be an unspoken understanding among the villagers that the new occupants must be nursing a grave illness, one requiring absolute peace and quiet. For Folie had noticed from her upstairs window that not long after their arrival, the noise of the traffic in the high street had been muted by a thick layer of straw put down on the cobbles, and once, walking in the garden, she had clearly heard a woman's voice over the wall, silencing a little boy's shouts with a fierce, "Hush now! There's sad affliction here!"

Their hall table was often laden with a pie, or a clutch of tiny, speckled quail eggs, or an offering of tender asparagus shoots left to "tease the appetite of the invalid." These gifts came with no caller or card, no way to identify the donors—just a simple village kindness that made Folie feel homesick for Toot-above-the-Batch.

She tried to read the improving novels and sermons from the well-stocked bookcase in the parlor, and every day there were newspapers from London and Norwich, but the sense of anxiety that sat at the center of her chest only seemed to grow. After supper they sat in the parlor, Melinda writing her never-ending letters—though she could not even mail them now—and Folie stroking the ferret in her lap, reading the papers. She began, out of pure tedium, to become an avid follower of Norwich city politics, annoying Melinda with informative tidbits about the guilds and the progress of the new paving on streets they had never heard of.

Just before bedtime, she put a tiny harness on Toot and took him for a stroll in the garden. At first, Melinda had objected to this as a perilous and unnecessary exposure to danger, but after joining the stroll for several nights, she admitted that the quiet garden was not quite so hazardous as the unlit, rogue-haunted paths of Vauxhall, and went back to her letters.

To Folie, it was the most bearable part of the long, somber days—she took no lamp, but learned her way along the simple garden path in the dark, Toot gamboling and sniffing, turning somersaults between the budding rose bushes. She had a daft notion that at these times, with the blue shawl close about her in the soft humid darkness, she could somehow feel Robert more clearly, know that he was safe and alive.

It had an old familiarity to it, this idea that she was connected to him over vast distances. She labeled herself a silly noodle, and then went unrepentantly on with her absurdity. There seemed to be no other choice. Whatever invisible tie bound her to Robert Cambourne, it seemed to grow stronger with distance.

''What's that?'' a young voice whispered from somewhere ahead, making her heart leap with alarm.

Folie stared into the darkness. She gripped Toot's leash and opened her mouth to scream or demand identification, she hardly knew what—but then another childish voice hissed, ''Shush! Shush! You looby! Someone's here!''

A quick thud of feet, a scramble on short legs, and Folie could just make out two small figures racing toward the wall, clambering up onto the garden bench. She hurried down the path, just in time to catch the pantaloons of the trailing culprit, who was hiking himself up off the bench, trying to drag himself over the top. She hauled him down.

He fell backwards at her feet and rolled over, coming face to face with an excited, inquisitive Toot. The little boy froze. ''What's that?'' he yelped.

''It is a vicious guard-ferret,'' Folie said calmly. ''If you move one inch, it will tear your nose to ribbons. And don't suppose you can get away, for once they bite down, they never let go.''

The small figure lay obediently limp, panting.

''Now, who are you?'' she asked.

''Neddie, mum,'' he squeaked, while Toot patted his hair and cheek, nuzzling him in a friendly way. ''We was on a dare! Don't let it bite me!''

''What sort of dare?''

''To touch—to touch that rainbarrel, mum, on the back stoop. That's all!''

''That's all?'' Folie asked. ''What a piffling dare! How can you prove you did it?''

''*Yolke!*'' Toot was crawling over his throat. ''Don't let it bite my neck!''

''I have him under control,'' she said. ''Barely.''

''Wer 'n to bring out a cup to drink! To prove it.'' He held up a tin cup timidly. ''That's all mum, that's all.''

Folie had her doubts as to whether that was quite *all* that had been intended, but the child seemed harmless enough. Still, it was disturbing that their fortress could be breached so easily by such small boys. ''Where did you get in over the wall?'' she demanded, reaching down to retrieve Toot from the child's heaving chest. ''Show me.''

The boy scrambled to his feet. She could not see him very clearly, but thought he could be no more than six years old. She caught his collar before he sprinted away.

''Show me,'' she commanded. ''Or I shall put this ferret down your back.''

''Yes, mum!'' he said, pulling her along. He led her to a section of the wall that divided it from the old churchyard. ''Here, mum!''

''You could not climb that!''

''Me n' Nic—hmmmmnh—'' He loyally mumbled over his cohort's name. ''We got a ladder over t'other side.''

''Well,'' Folie said, ''You should know that I am a frightfully genteel widow—indeed, trampled flowerbeds give me an alarming case of the vapors—''

''Oh no, mum! We didn't touch 'em! Not one bloom!''

''But what I cannot *bear*—what gives me hysterics of no mean order, is ladders leaning up against my walls. You cannot conceive of how I should screech if I were to come across one in the daylight.''

''I'll move it, mum! I'll remove it directly!''

She shook her head ominously. ''I must confiscate it, I fear. Otherwise, how will I know that some other boy—who doesn't know about the ferret, or how it patrols the grounds at night—will not lean that very same ladder up against my wall?''

''I'll push it over to you, mum! That I will.''

''Excellent. Come, I'll help you over.''

They returned to the bench. She lifted him by one arm as he jumped up, and then with an excess of pointless pushing got him to the top of the wall. As he tottered there, she held him back by his wrist and said ruthlessly, ''Of course you know that the ferret has your scent now. If you don't do as you promised, put the ladder over to this side, this animal can find you in any room in any house, and sneak through the walls and cracks, and crawl into bed with you as you sleep, and—''

"I'll do it!" He yelped as he slid off the wall, landing with an audible thump. Folie stood back. She could see little, but she heard him, following his panting and his scrabbling progress along the outside. At one point he stopped, right over the primrose bed. With a great deal of huffing and chuntering and scraping, the top rungs of the ladder appeared over the wall. It teetered, the wall much too tall for the boy to heave the ladder completely over. Folie tied Toot to the wire staked for climbing vines, reached up and grabbed the top rung, dragging it toward her. It fell to the ground, doing she knew not what damage to the primroses.

She heard the child scoot away. Folie sighed. She almost wished she could slip away with him, freed from this comfortable prison.

The lights in the parlor had been extinguished. She could break the news about the primroses to the housekeeper tomorrow. With a little cluck to Toot, she turned and went inside.

It was as she was pouring water from the pitcher into the bowl to wash her face that the memory struck her. The recollection came from nowhere, simply appeared in her mind as she looked at herself in the mirror, the candlelight gleaming on her loose hair.

She remembered talking to Sir Howard.

Folie stared into the mirror, turning it over in her mind, her heart beating swiftly. She *had* written him a note to meet her at Vauxhall, on Lady Dingley's behalf. And she had sent it to him at Limmer's Hotel by one of their own footmen.

Folie tilted her head, frowning at herself. But Robert had said that he had come to Vauxhall because *he* had received the note.

That made no sense.

She pressed her hands over her eyes. The house was silent around her. Still, she could recall no more of Vauxhall itself than the bursting fireworks, the bright pinwheels like the colors and patterns behind her eyelids. But she had sent the note to Sir Howard, not to Robert. Of that she was absolutely certain.

She picked up her washcloth, drawing it across her cheeks. And another strange recollection came into her mind—seeing Sir Howard in a London street with a girl, her eyes puffy and red from weeping.

Folie sucked in her breath. Her washcloth fell from her limp fingers, splashing gently into the basin.

She *had* seen that girl at Solinger Abbey. Slipping the warming pan under the sheets in Folie's bedchamber at Solinger. They had caught one another's eye in the mirror as Folie washed her face, just as she was doing now.

The same girl. And Robert thought she was horribly murdered.

Mattie.

A chill coursed through her. It was as if a ghost had materialized in the mirror. Folie turned about, her flesh rising.

There was nothing there. But the idea of Sir Howard with that girl seized her mind. Folie liked Sir Howard; she loved his daughters and even felt an odd affection for Lady Dingley. She could not imagine that he was in league with the men who had abducted her, who had put them aboard the prison ship, who had murdered a country maid.

And yet—she had sent that note to him, and Robert had received it.

Slowly, Folie sank into her chair. Robert must be told what she remembered. Perhaps it meant nothing. But perhaps it meant everything. He had been suspicious of Sir Howard. She picked up her hairbrush and then sat with it in her lap, staring blindly.

She could wait until Lander returned, and send him back with a message. Doubtless that was what Melinda would insist upon. And yet—when would that be? They had no notion what was passing in London. What if Folie knew even more than she thought? What if she had memories that seemed insignificant to her, but carried important clues? What if more recollections came as her mind grew sharper . . . what if she should remember how she came to be with Sir Howard at Vauxhall? She could not depend on anyone else to convey everything.

And what if—any night, even this very night, in the midst of their absurdly shaky scheme—Robert was in grave danger, because Folie had not recognized the menacing signs in Sir Howard's behavior?

She lay down, pulling the bedclothes over her. But she could not sleep. She squeezed her pillow up under her head and buried her face in it. She must go to London; she could not wait for Lander to return. And yet she knew that if she announced that she was leaving, Melinda and Lander's household staff would try to prevent her. Not that they could. If she wished to go, she could go. But then, like as not, Melinda would insist on accompanying her. Which was out of the question. Folie would not allow Melinda to place herself in the remotest danger. There would be a great scene. Folie hated scenes.

Her thoughts went round and round in her head. She did not close her eyes all night—she heard the pendulum clock at the foot of the staircase mark every hour. And when it struck 3 A.M., she rose and lit the candle. By its wavering light, she packed a small valise, dressed as warmly as a runaway child, and sat down to write a note.

My love,

I must go back to town to warn Mr. Cambourne of something very significant that has come into my mind. I know you will disapprove, but I must do this directly, and depart as soon as I can. I will send you word the moment I arrive—if the Royal Mail will take me up as a passenger this morning, I shall be in London by ten A.M.

All my love,
Your affectionate Mama

P.S. I am sorry about the primrose beds. The ladder is the property of a nefarious character discovered lurking in the garden last night. He is a desperate fellow, by the name of "Neddie," but you will find that a mention of the ferret, in a suitably ominous tone, should suffice to keep him strictly within bounds. Take care, do not worry, I promise I shall return to you soon.

She slipped into Melinda's room and left the note propped on her washbasin, leaning over her stepdaughter to blow a butterfly kiss. Melinda would be quite wild, but Folie saw no help for it. As she let herself out of the house, the deep, thick scent of predawn, laden with damp soil and spring foliage, filled her lungs like a new perfume. The night was still fully dark, starlight and a late half-moon the only natural illumination.

Folie felt excitement rise in her heart. She placed the ladder firmly against the wall, hiking her skirt to climb over, tossing her valise down into the churchyard. Before she jumped down, she pushed the ladder over into the ravaged primrose bed, silently promising a particular present to the gardener when she returned. She sprang down, landing and stumbling in the dewy grass.

Folie wiped her wet gloves against her cloak, picked up her valise, and found her way out of the churchyard gate. She walked down the center of the village street and sat down on the windowsill of a greengrocer across the street from the Spread Eagle, which even at this hour had a lantern lit in the far back of the yard.

She had left the house at a quarter to four, by the ring of the clock. And precisely on time, at half past the hour, the rumbling sound of horses and wheels became something more than her imagination. There was a quick warning blare from a coaching horn. The Royal Mail swept into town, drawing to a jingling halt outside the Spread Eagle Inn.

Amid a bustle of hostlers, strangely silent in the night, Folie hurried up to the guard in his scarlet livery. He held up his lantern as she approached. "Can you take a passenger into London, sir? I must get there as soon as I can."

He looked a little surprised, but hardly astonished. "Aye, ma'am, there's room up on the box, if you'll ride outside."

"Yes, certainly."

"Settle with the coachman after you're up, then," he said, reaching for her valise. "Make haste, we'll be off in three minutes."

By the dim light of the coach lamps, Folie saw that the new team was already halfway in harness. She climbed up onto the box, the coachman reaching down a hand to help her. With a handsome three-shilling tip, he seemed quite satisfied that she had unexpectedly joined his passenger list.

A soft, expert cluck, a swish of the whip, and Folie grabbed the seat for balance as the team picked up their trot, rolling gentle thunder through the village. She could see nothing but the vague outline of the leaders, and the rumps of the gray wheelers lit by the lamps. The air passed swiftly against her cheeks. She took in a deep breath, feeling something near to happiness surge inside her as they gathered momentum, galloping through the night—carrying the mail, carrying the news—carrying her to Robert.

Robert sat with Lander in the small breakfast room at the back of Cambourne House. Their caller, his neckcloth beautifully folded and impeccably white, his slender hand lifting a coffee cup with well-bred grace, would be more well-known on the inside of one of the prison hulks than the inside of any French palace, but Monsieur Belmaine had an undeniably blue-blooded air. Unless he happened to transform himself to a Scottish chemist, frowning until his eyebrows bristled as he discoursed in a fierce brogue upon the properties of base metals.

Robert had no notion of what the man's true name might be. But he had developed a profound respect for his chameleon tutor's talents. When, after the morning lesson, Monsieur Belmaine transformed himself into Mr. McCann, his very cheeks seemed to grow rosy with northern winds, and it was hopeless to refer back to the French imposture—Mr. McCann would simply snort and fix Robert or Lander with an incredulous eye. "The French be damned to the De'il Himself!" he cried. "Say na' more! Say na' more! M'bonny wife, ach!"

"Your wife?" Lander inquired. Mr. McCann always

spun an amusing yarn if he had a little encouragement.

"T'were a French mahound, the bloody churl, wooed her yonder-away, so fair away!" he moaned.

"She left you?" Lander asked, looking oddly distressed at this farrago.

"Gone away. The world away," Mr. McCann announced in a voice of doom. "Ye'll not ken where to."

"Where?"

"Japan." Mr. McCann pulled out his handkerchief and blew his nose.

"Japan!" Lander said, shocked. "Good God."

"It sounds an excellent place for a wife," Robert commented. "Send 'em all after her, that's what I propose."

Mr. McCann chuckled. "There. 'Tis a canny lad."

"Oh, come," Lander said, with a little irritation. "A man must marry. They are not all so bad."

"Ah. The word of experience!" Robert said.

"Well, I have not been married, of course," Lander admitted.

"If you don't need a successor—spare yourself," Robert said pointedly.

"Aye, take a bonny lass to keep yer bed warm," Mr. McCann suggested, nodding. "But stay off the church porch!"

Robert watched Lander's reaction to this advice. The younger man smiled, but his face was a subtle study in disapproval. Robert had been practicing his lessons in observation and inference wherever he could. A man who could not take a joke about marriage was like enough to be a man deep in love.

Robert had his opinions on who the fortunate lady might be, but he did not speak of it before Mr. McCann. The rogue might well have drawn his own conclusions in any case—there was not a thing that escaped his attention. Observation, intuition, self-control: Robert had been training in the realms of the human mind as intensely as in sleight of hand.

If he thought he had made any progress, Mr. McCann set him back in that instant by putting his finger to his lips.

"Careful, my lads—we're like to offend the lady herself."

"The lady?" Lander asked curiously.

But Robert had caught McCann's faint sign toward the door. It stood closed, but Robert obeyed his teacher's warning signal. He stood up, drawing the pistol underneath his coat, and opened the door swiftly.

To his utter astonishment, Folie stood there, her hand poised over the knob. She stared wide-eyed down the barrel of his gun.

NINETEEN

"FOLLY!" ROBERT SAID blankly.

She made a small curtsy. "I'm sorry," she said, feeling suddenly and intensely stupid for coming. "I know I am not expected."

In the face of his disbelief and the words she had just overheard, Folie rather wished that she might be transported to Japan with all the unwanted wives. She stood hesitantly in the doorway, hoping that at least Robert might lower the gun.

"Mrs. Hamilton!" Lander stood up, the first to react sensibly. "Is something wrong? Why are you here?"

"I'm sorry," she said again. "No—nothing is wrong—nothing at the village—at least—I came at once because—" She glanced at the stranger. "Robert," she said helplessly, "may I speak to you privately?"

"Of course." He slid the pistol under his coat as naturally as if he were a thoroughgoing highwayman. "Come."

Folie stood back, then followed him to the stairs. She paused at the bottom, biting her lower lip. "Robert—I did not have a full fare for the cab from the Post Office," she said. "Someone must pay him."

He stopped, one foot on the lowest stair. "My dear," he

said severely, "you should never have come here. I thought you understood that."

Her cheeks flamed with windburn and mortification. "I must tell you something," she said. "Something that I remembered about Vauxhall."

His scowl relaxed a little. "I see. Go on up, then. I'll have Lander see to it."

Folie mounted the stairs slowly, feeling rather like a chastised puppy. The big drawing room was dark, the curtains still drawn. Folie went about pulling them open, letting the bright sunshine of a spring morning through. From the dust motes that sparkled down the beams, she thought the drapes had not been drawn open for the entire two weeks she had been gone.

"Don't!" Robert's abrupt command startled her. "Come away from the windows," he said sharply. "Folie, for the love of God, have you no sense at all?"

She scooted away from the tall panes. "Is someone watching?" she asked anxiously.

"Come here." He moved to a position near the white marble mantelpiece, pressing his back to the wall in an odd stance. As Folie came closer, he reached out, turned her about by the shoulders and held her back against his chest. "There," he said. "Do you see him?"

From the strange position, she could see an angle of the street that was not visible from most of the windows. "I see a . . . oh, come, surely you don't mean that child bowling his hoop? That's only Christopher. He lives across the street."

"No, the donkey with the cart beside him, of course!" Robert said, squeezing her shoulders. "My dear." She could feel him shake his head.

"But I see no one else."

"In the house on the corner. That left-hand window on the first floor."

Folie squinted. "I can't—" But then, as she looked, she saw that something moved in the opening—she realized that she could see right through it to the window on the farther side of the house. The light silhouetted a shape inside whenever it moved. ''Goodness. What excellent eyesight you must have.''

''Lander has a bit more resource than ordinary eyesight,'' he said. His hands still rested on her shoulders. ''But yes, we are watched.''

She could feel the pistol under his coat. ''Who is it?''

''Only a succession of petty rogues so far, unfortunately—some known to Bow Street and some not. One of the higher class—'' He dropped his hands from her shoulders, clearing his throat. ''I beg your pardon, a lady of light virtue—holds the lease. Lander is having her patronage investigated.''

''Oh,'' Folie said. She moved away from him immediately, so that he should not suppose that she liked his hands upon her shoulders. ''What jolly diversions you have been having here!''

''You said that you had recalled something?''

''Yes!'' Folie turned to him. ''Robert—I remembered about that note. I *did* write it to Sir Howard!''

Instead of the incredulity she had expected, he watched her without expression, as if he were still waiting for her to tell him what she had discovered.

''Robert, he must have arranged to have it delivered to you! Don't you suppose? How else could it have gone from Limmer's Hotel to wherever you were? I don't even *know* where you were.''

''Yes. I've assumed that must be the case. Did you remember any more?''

''Well—'' Folie was feeling rather flattened. ''Perhaps this means nothing. But just after we arrived in London, Lady Dingley and I were returning from some calls, or shopping, I don't remember clearly, but I believe that from the carriage, I saw Sir Howard standing on a street corner!''

''Yes?'' Robert did not seem overawed by this information.

''But he should not have been here. In London! He had returned to Dingley Hall directly, you see! Or at least, that was what we all understood. And there he was in Bond Street, standing on the corner with a girl. I saw him. And he saw me, I believe, though I said nothing of it to Lady Dingley, of course.''

Robert gave her a narrow glance. ''A girl? Do you mean a streetwalker?''

''No, no—'' Folie looked back at him, shocked. ''I'm sure he would do nothing of that sort!''

His mouth curved mockingly. ''Perhaps not.''

''She was dressed like a maid from the country. Her eyes were red, as if she had been weeping. I think . . . I believe I saw her once at Solinger, though I did not realize it at the time.''

''Good God—you just remembered this?'' He took a step toward her. ''At Solinger? In the house? Are you certain?''

She wet her lips. That stunning moment of recollection in the night, staring into her mirror, seemed distant now. ''I—believe it was the same girl. I think she was a maid.''

''You are not sure.''

''I am—certain. Almost certain.''

''Did Melinda see her?''

''Well, I did not ask Melinda. I suppose—I should have. But she was asleep, and I wanted to warn you, in case you should be in danger.''

He gazed at her. ''Folly—you came on the morning mail? When did you leave the house?''

''At half past three,'' she said, lowering her face.

''Melinda was asleep?'' He seemed to home to her guilt instantly.

''Well—I did not wish to wake her. I left a note.''

His dark lashes widened. ''Damn you, Folly! Damn you, do you tell me you left there without telling anyone?'' He locked his arm behind his back and took a pace. ''Of course you did! You would not have arrived here alone in a cab, if anyone with a grain of sense could have prevented you!''

She sank into a chair. ''I'm sorry. It came upon me so suddenly—I was worried for your safety—I did not think.''

''You had better begin to think!'' He stood still, facing away from her. She could see his fist working. ''You might have sent a message, or waited for Lander—instead you put yourself in the most flagrant, unprotected situation, riding here on the bloody Royal Mail, marching up the front steps where anyone might see you! And what the devil are we to do with you now? You can't go back.''

She lifted her head. ''I can't go back?''

''Certainly not! How am I to smuggle you out of here with any assurance that you won't be followed? Lander and I are dogged wherever we go. And you cannot remain here, with no companion, in the same house with me.''

''No. No, of course not.'' With a faint horror, Folie saw instantly that he was right. She could not remain in Cambourne House unaccompanied—without Melinda or Lady Dingley, not while Robert was here. It would be impossibly unseemly.

''I suppose none of that occurred to you in this mad rush to save my life from Dingley,'' he said sarcastically.

''I had intended that I would go back on tonight's mail,'' she offered, to prove that she had at least planned that far ahead.

''A happy notion.'' His lip curled derisively. ''Doubtless we could expect to find you deported to Tasmania this time!''

''I apologize if I did not act in an ideal manner.'' She gave a stiff shrug, goaded. ''But why worry? Marry me for the sake of propriety, and then banish me to Japan!''

''You may believe me, it's just this sort of half-witted female behavior that makes Japan sound an excellent notion!''

''Oh, the farther the better!'' she retorted. ''Why not the Arctic? Or the moon? We wives are perfectly at home with cold indifference.''

He narrowed his eyes at her. ''Jest about it if you will,'' he said with a sneer. ''I'm not sure that I have much choice in the matter now, damn it.''

''I beg your pardon.'' She leapt to her feet. ''Pray do not feel obligated to offer yourself merely on this account, Mr. Cambourne!''

A belated look of consternation crossed his face, as if he had just heard his own words. He lifted his hand to arrest her progress toward the door. Folie knew before he spoke precisely what he was going to say.

"And pray do not declare that you did not intend *that* as it sounded!" she exclaimed, rounding on him. "I am well aware that you do not wish for a wife. Nor do I care for a husband, certainly not one forced to make his offer over a stupid idea of decorum. I am far too old to care for that! I had supposed that we were fast friends—that was why I came here so precipitously. It was a great misjudgment, clearly. But I am sure that the situation may be retrieved in some manner which will not inconvenience you *quite* so far as saddling us with one another for life."

She turned her back on him—remembering just at the last moment, as she went out the door, to shut it as softly as possible so as to maintain her full dignity. Then she mounted the stairs to her bedchamber, closed that door very gently too, sat down on the bed, and stared at the drawn curtains.

She did not cry. She stared harder and harder at the pink velvet. Her whole body trembled.

But she did not cry. Her lip curled downward with disdain. She spread her fingers over the coverlet and crushed it into her fists. Still she did not cry. She was finished forever with weeping over Robert Cambourne.

Robert glared at the back of the closed door, and then turned away. He braced his arms against the mantel and pressed as if he could shove it over.

Why the devil had Folly come? How did she do this to him, touch that fuse so easily? It was half-fear that had made him speak to her that way, like a badly frightened parent abusing a child for its carelessness, driven by a crystalline vision of how exposed she had allowed herself to be—half-fear and half-something else.

It was as if Phillippa still possessed him, he thought wildly. He looked up and stared at himself in the mirror over the mantel. His eyes were dark, clear gray; focused—there was no madness in them. And yet it was if she were here inside his brain, in command of his throat, spurring him on to say the sort of acid things that had burned through every hope of love, or respect, or even truce between them.

In truth, the very idea that Folly had put herself in danger—that she had even thought of bestirring herself at all—because she was worried for him—because they were fast friends—Robert swallowed hard against a block of something in his throat. He snarled at himself in the mirror like a silent tiger. Stupid little ninny, she was. Maddening little half-wit. How was it possible to love her with every fiber of his body and soul and want to tear her to shreds for overhearing a senseless joke never meant for her ears?

Well, he had sunk himself, now. He had begun to entertain some hope that she might trust him again after the prison hulk—in fact, he had to stop himself frequently from beginning so many musings with, ''After this business is finished . . .'' But it all remained in fleeting fantasy—moments before he fell asleep, thoughts that passed as he ate or dressed. By main force, he had prevented himself from thinking about her further, focusing his mind completely upon the precarious task at hand—another reason he could wish she had not flung herself back into his consciousness with such exuberance. The last thing he needed was a mortally offended female—and one that he adored at that—to complicate his life at just this moment.

He shoved himself away from the fireplace and left the room. Just as he reached the top of the stairs, one of Lander's ''footmen'' opened the door. Robert heard a child's voice.

''Please, did Mrs. Hamilton bring the ferret home with her?'' the boy piped eagerly.

Robert cursed silently. He went quickly down the steps, about to tell the footman to send the child packing, when a woman spoke.

''Hush, Christopher! The ferret indeed! We've come to inquire after Mrs. Hamilton. Chris thinks that he saw her just now return!''

The servant cast Robert an inquiring look. He shook his head. Lander had come out into the hall. ''I'm sorry, Mrs.

Paine,'' he said briskly. ''Mrs. Hamilton is not at home.''

''Yes, she is!'' Christopher cried. He managed to insinuate his towhead into the door, in spite of the unseen lady's hand on his collar. ''I saw her come in a cab!''

''Christopher William! Come here! It was your imagination, my dear. Come—'' The hand jerked him back out of view. ''We are all so concerned about Mrs. Hamilton, Lander. Have you had any word of her health?''

''I believe she is expected to recover fully, ma'am,'' Lander said, while Christopher leaned against his mother's hold like a straining dog on a leash, peering around the door. He looked at Robert, and then upward to the stair landing.

''There she is!'' he cried. ''I *knew* she had come home!'' He broke free of his restraint. The front door flung wide as he burst into the hall. ''Mrs. Hamilton! Good day!'' he exclaimed, with childhood's happy certainty of welcome. ''It's Christopher! Where is Toot?''

They all turned. Folie stood at the stair landing, the picture of good health. Robert stepped forward. ''Come in, please!'' he commanded, so that at least the door might be shut.

Mrs. Paine entered with nearly as much cheerful aplomb as her son, though she apologized profusely for his outrageous behavior. She held out her hands as Folie came down the stairs. ''My dear Mrs. Hamilton! How good to see you well! Gracious, we have been beside ourselves to hear you had taken ill so sudden! And Christopher has pined to play with the girls. But the country has done you a world of good—your cheeks are like pretty apples!''

Folie greeted her, casting a guilty look toward Robert. But before he could even speak, another authoritative rapping from the door knocker reverberated in the hall. The footman received a pair of visiting cards, stood back with a proper formality, and announced, ''Mrs. Witham-Stanley. Miss Davenport.''

Robert and Lander exchanged looks as the new callers entered the house. Mrs. Witham-Stanley sought Robert with an eager smile, holding out her hand. He saw no help for it now.

''Lander,'' he said, ''conduct the ladies up to the drawing room.'' He gave a brief bow to Mrs. Witham-Stanley and the unexpected assemblage in the hall. ''I am Robert Cambourne, by the way.''

Mrs. Paine gave a small gasp. ''Oh! I beg your pardon, sir! I did not realize.''

''No matter, madam. Pray excuse me—I shall join you in a moment.''

His nameless teacher waited in the breakfast room, calmly sipping coffee. Robert closed the door of the breakfast room behind him. ''The ladies who just arrived—'' he said. ''I believe we have an opportunity.''

The other man lifted his eyebrows in question.

''Can you play a doctor?'' Robert asked.

''My good man, I am an F.R.C.P.!''

Robert grimaced. ''Whatever that may be.''

''A Fellow of the Royal College of Physicians.'' He rose and brushed back his hair, becoming prim and spruce—and a good two inches shorter with no visible stooping, Robert could have sworn. ''Dr. Ignacious Joyce. Magdalene College, Cambridge, offices in Jermyn Street.''

''All right. You treated Mrs. Hamilton, the lady who just arrived, a fortnight ago.''

''Ah! And perhaps I saw no hope for her, in spite of my most extreme exertions on her behalf.''

Robert nodded. ''She was at death's door.''

''Beyond the help of any medicine, even the most modern and efficacious treatment. I called in several colleagues, but to no avail.''

''And now she is in perfect health.''

Dr. Joyce smiled. ''Indeed. I understand you, sir.''

Folie sat perched on the edge of a chair, trying to say the right things. She knew something of the story that had been spread to cover her abduction—Folie had succumbed to a sudden illness and was removed to the country to recover under Melinda's tender care, while the Dingleys, who naturally could not impose themselves by remaining at Cambourne House, packed themselves off home, cutting short their season.

All that was simple enough. But she found that the details were deceptively easy to botch. Naturally Mrs. Paine, one of their more inquisitive neighbors on Curzon Street, would want to know all about what had happened, what physician had attended her, how she had borne the trip, why she had returned, and had Miss Melinda not come back also? Folie had never met Mrs. Witham-Stanley or Miss Davenport; she recognized their faces only distantly, from some party or other; she had no notion why they might have called at Cambourne House. She managed to look confused, ignored the greater number of the inquiries and appealed to Robert as he entered the drawing room for the name of the physician.

"He is right here, my dear," Robert said solicitously. "Dr. Joyce."

On his heels was the man Folie had glimpsed sitting with Lander and Robert in the breakfast room. He looked more genteel now, sleeked down like a very modern professional man. He came at once to Folie and sat down next to her, lifting her wrist. "I'm not surprised that you don't remember me," he said. "You were insensible at the time!"

Mrs. Paine clucked sympathetically, shaking her head. Folie blinked at Dr. Joyce. He smiled at her absently as he felt her pulse.

The room fell quiet. Folie could not imagine that they would be so prying; she had thought perhaps that this "doctor's" appearance was some attempt by Robert to shame them all into excusing themselves and departing. However, if that was his intention, it miscarried completely. Mrs. Paine was affectionate, honest, kind—and one of the busiest gossips in Mayfair. Perhaps Robert was too innocent to recognize it, but Folie was well acquainted with the breed. Rivalry was paramount, and the earliest report secured the highest prize. Accurate particulars might be secondary to speed, but they were still significant. To have both, in the original firsthand account of such interesting news as Folie's illness, would be a coup of no small measure.

Everyone hung upon the physician's pronouncement. Even young Christopher was silent, gripping his mother's hand and staring with all the repelled wonder of a six-year-old boy who had stumbled upon a brain surgery.

Dr. Joyce nodded to himself. He let go of her wrist and patted Folie's hand as if she were a good student. ''Perfect.'' He turned to Robert. ''I am not a man given to hyperbole, sir—but I believe this must be accounted one of the most astonishing recoveries I have ever had the good fortune to witness. Not a fortnight ago, when I was called in, I did not suppose this patient could survive the night.''

''You are an excellent practitioner, sir,'' Robert said, with a slight bow.

The doctor hesitated, then shook his head. ''Nay, sir. I do not take credit for this.''

''Indeed, you must not be so modest. Your attendance was invaluable,'' Robert said. He smiled at the other ladies. ''I think I could recommend Dr. Joyce to your service without reservation.''

The doctor rose, clearing his throat gruffly. ''Too generous.'' He bowed to the room, and once, deeply, to Folie. ''I shall not disturb you further. I had merely wished to verify Mr. Cambourne's happy report with my own observation.''

''I thank you,'' Folie said.

''Ha. Do not thank me, ma'am. I am an honest man—I will take no credit when it is not due me. I even called in two colleagues of mine, as Mr. Cambourne can tell you. I shall not mention their names, but in that association, I think I may say without undue prejudice, you had in attendance the highest learning and experience that modern medicine can provide. And we were helpless. We could do nothing for you.''

Folie saw that Mrs. Paine and the other women were listening raptly. She nodded, somber. ''I must thank God to be alive.''

"Aye!" The doctor cleared his throat. "Aye, God be thanked. And perhaps this gentleman here." He nodded toward Robert, who shook his head negatively. "Well, sir, deny it if you will. But I am a physician. I am trained in scientific observation. I know what I saw."

"What did he do?" Mrs. Witham-Stanley asked, leaning forward in her chair. "Did he lay hands upon her?"

"Madam, it was astonish—"

"We thank you, Dr. Joyce," Robert said, interrupting him. "I am sure you are a busy man—we will take no more of your time. Lander will see you out."

The doctor bowed and went to the door. Lander was holding it open for him when abruptly he stopped and turned. "I wonder—" He lifted his finger. "You would not—but no . . ." He shook his head.

"Sir?" Robert prompted.

Dr. Joyce kept shaking his head. "I made considerable notes upon Mrs. Cambourne's condition. I wonder—if I might be so entirely and unforgivably presumptuous—I wonder if I might ask her to condescend to appear at lecture I am to give upon—"

"No," Robert said firmly. "That will not be possible."

"Of course not." The doctor's cheeks grew ruddy. "You must accept my excuses for such audacity. But knowing what I saw—what you have done here, sir—"

"Good day," Robert said brusquely, nodding. "Lander will see you out."

"Of course. Of course." The chastened doctor scuttled out of the drawing room. Robert closed the door behind him.

"What could he mean?" Mrs. Paine was looking at Folie with barely suppressed excitement. "Whatever did he mean? Dear me, one would think the man had witnessed a miracle!"

"I have no doubt that he did," the older lady said wisely. "I saw him cure Mr. Bellamy myself."

"Who cured Mr. Bellamy?" Mrs. Paine demanded.

"Why, Mr. Cambourne, of course!" She nodded at

Folie. ''You are blessed indeed, Mrs. Cambourne, in your husband.''

Folie shook her head quickly, groping for some reasonable reply. But she was afraid to make any mistakes—she knew that Dr. Joyce must be part of the grand scheme, and she did not want to create any more glaring public contradictions than she already had by her very presence. She looked in dismay toward Robert, hoping that he could pass it off lightly.

Instead, he looked back at her with an unreadable expression. The moment seemed to spin out to an agony of mortification. ''I beg your pardon, ma'am,'' she mumbled at last. ''Mr. Cambourne and I are not married. I am Mrs. Hamilton.''

''Oh.'' Folie could see Mrs. Witham-Stanley's face change even as she said it. ''Forgive me.'' Their visitors all looked from Folie to Robert; the other ladies seemed—at least to Folie's apprehensive vision—to grow stiff with affront.

''Miss Melinda is with you?'' Mrs. Paine asked kindly. She turned to the callers. ''Have you met Miss Melinda Hamilton? No? She is a darling girl—so unfortunate that her season was interrupted, but now that Mrs. Hamilton has recovered so beautifully, all can go on gaily! Will the Dingleys be returning?''

''No, no,'' Folie said. ''I am only here because I had to consult Mr. Cambourne upon—urgent business.'' She waved her hand vaguely. ''It was all so quick—Miss Melinda could not come.''

''Oh! You have come alone?'' Mrs. Paine asked. Folie could see her storing that scandalous tidbit away like a diligent squirrel.

''Melinda could not come,'' Folie said. ''It was really impossible.''

''How vexing. But you will remain at least a few days? Where are you staying?''

''I—'' Folie looked at Robert. She was sinking fast. ''I really have not thought of that. This was a very hasty trip—I could not make arrangements ahead—I really must attend to that, but I haven't yet had a moment to think of it.''

''My poor dear! Do not trouble yourself over that trifle, then! Of course you know our home is open to you. You must stay with us.''

Folie began to trip over her tongue, completely at a loss. She made helpless noises, wringing her hands in her lap.

''No,'' Robert said, in the same brusque tone he had used to dismiss the doctor. ''That will not be possible, I am afraid.''

''Nonsense, sir,'' Mrs. Paine said. ''She cannot stay here alone with you, and I will not hear of her going to a horrid hotel! Even if you are to move out of your own home, Mr. Cambourne—to have her stay in this great huge place by herself? No, no—it is out of the question. I know that you haven't any relatives in town, Mrs. Hamilton, but consider us your family for the nonce.''

''Thank you,'' Folie said meekly. She glanced at Robert. ''It might be for the best—''

''No,'' he said. ''It will not do.''

''Well!'' Mrs. Paine ruffled a little. ''I cannot see any objection!''

''Truly, I believe Mrs. Paine's kindness could be the solution.'' Folie was thinking of Melinda's prospects. If she insisted upon staying here now, with Robert, the knowledge would be all over Mayfair by evening. Bad enough, that she had already been discovered here in town without a decent companion—she desperately did not want Melinda's reputation and future to be tarnished by any hints of improper behavior by her stepmother.

''No.'' His answer was adamant. He scowled at her. ''What are you thinking of? Mrs. Paine, we are much obliged to you, but it is impossible.''

''But, sir—'' Mrs. Paine was sitting stiffly at the edge of her chair. ''Why ever should it be impossible?''

''Circumstances,'' Robert said. ''Private circumstances.''

Their neighbor looked at him, her eyebrows lifting. ''Allow me to be frank, Mr. Cambourne. I have every sympathy for your desire for privacy, but perhaps, as you are not very well acquainted with our London ways, you should listen to those who are more experienced. I do not know how it may be in India, but in London, it does not look well for Mrs. Hamilton to be here.''

''I am perfectly aware of that, madam. I thank you for your advice and interest.''

''As a gentleman,'' Mrs. Paine persisted, ''I apprehend that you do not quite understand how delicate a lady's reputation can be, and how easily damaged. A pretty young widow's in particular.''

His face had begun to change. Folie had seen that look; hunted and yet hostile. She gripped her hands uneasily together.

''Yes, I do,'' he said. ''However, there are other circumstances in this case—''

''I know you would not wish to compromise Mrs. Hamilton or her stepdaughter in the slightest manner!''

''Mrs. Paine—''

She grabbed Christopher, clapping her hands over his ears. ''Mr. Cambourne!'' she hissed in agitation. ''Do you not understand me? People will suppose she is—''

''Thank you, Mrs. Paine!'' he snapped, cutting her off. ''You need not sully anyone's ears with your insinuations, madam. In fact, you may tell the entire city that we are engaged. Now that she is recovered, Mrs. Hamilton and I are to be married in a private ceremony this afternoon.''

Folie felt as if the floor had sunk into the basement under her feet. The room fell silent. She just managed to keep herself from exclaiming, *What?*

She gathered her senses and shook her head vigorously. ''But—Robert . . .''

''Everything is arranged, my sweetest,'' he said, giving her a pointed glare. ''I'm sorry that we could not keep our secret. Pray do not exercise yourself over it.''

Folie took the hint. She said nothing more. He had landed them in the soup now. Of course he was inventing anything that might throw Mrs. Paine off her dogged notion. Folie would have staked her whole jointure that he hoped his announcement would shame them all into going away with their tails between their legs. And then this ''engagement'' could be forgotten.

It was a grandly foolish attempt, hastily conceived and hopeless. But let him extricate himself. It served him quite well, she thought, for the mean, low things he had said of marriage and wives.

''Oh!'' Mrs. Paine cried, recovering from her stunned silence. ''But how splendid!'' She hurried over and clasped Folie's hands. ''Oh, what a shock! Forgive me! Do forgive me.''

''No, no,'' Folie murmured. ''It's quite all right. You could not know.''

''Do tell me what I can do! Have you a proper bouquet?'' She looked over her shoulder at Robert. ''Are the flowers ordered?''

''Yes, everything has been taken care of.''

''What nurseryman did you use? Not that paltry fellow in Shepherd's Market, I hope! Have they been delivered yet?''

''Indeed,'' Mrs. Witham-Stanley said, ''I used him myself just last month—I was wholly disappointed. His lilies were perfectly atrocious. I cannot endorse him.''

''Cancel it!'' Mrs. Paine straightened up militantly. ''You may leave the flowers to me. Depend upon it, I shall see that you have the loveliest bouquet you can conceive!''

''And pray let me send over a plum cake!'' Mrs. Witham-Stanley exclaimed. ''But what sort of bride cake have you planned, Mr. Cambourne?''

''We have a plum cake,'' he said swiftly.

''But is it to be iced? My cook creates the most splendid marchpane icing for a decoration. You have not seen the like. I should consider it an honor, my dear Mr. Cambourne. I have recalled so much of that dream of my sweet mother—you don't know what pleasure it has given me! If you had not brought it into my mind, what would I have done?''

''And I have a recipe for a French kickshaw,'' Miss Davenport offered shyly. ''I should be happy to have one made up for the occasion.''

Folie bit both her lips together. Robert looked as if a calamity had overtaken him.

"You are all very kind—" he said. He glanced at Folie. She sat still, wickedly innocent.

"Come, Christopher! We have much to do! I vow I shall pick out the most perfect blooms myself." Mrs. Price took her son's hand. "Oh—I have just had the most charming notion! Would you like for Christopher to stand up with you, and hand Mr. Cambourne the wedding ring? I have just bought a new lace collar for his blue velvet coat—he is such a darling in it!"

"I shall allow Mr. Cambourne to answer that," Folie said.

Mr. Cambourne gave her a baleful look. She smiled back virtuously.

"What a delightful idea," he said dryly.

"Oh, you will not regret it!" the boy's fond mother promised, growing a little teary. "It will be so sweet—you will want to weep."

Mrs. Witham-Stanley sighed. "How I wish I could see it!"

"Why, you must come!" Robert's voice was loaded with mockery, though no one else but Folie appeared to hear it.

"What fun!" Mrs. Paine cried. "We can help Mrs. Hamilton to dress!"

"May I bring Mr. Bellamy? He would be so crushed if he should hear that I attended without him. He can talk of nothing but Mr. Cambourne this and Mr. Cambourne that since you cured him of the headache!"

"Everyone come!" Robert said, with the expansive tone of a man who has partaken of too much strong drink. "Why not?"

TWENTY

"I CAN ONLY suppose that you have taken leave of your senses," Folie said, after the drawing room had been cleared of their callers, all ushered off by Lander to their various projects and plans.

"Yes, you have driven me perfectly mad," Robert said savagely. "From your first letter, now that I think of it."

"What ever are we to do now?" she demanded. "We cannot actually marry!"

"Do not look at me as if it is my doing! As of this morning, I was perfectly content to spend yet another night as a wretched bachelor."

She gasped. "*You* are the one who claimed we were engaged!"

"What else was I to say, for Heaven's sake? That I mean to keep you here as my dolly-mop?"

"I could have gone to Mrs. Paine's," she said. "I would be happy to!"

"Nonsense!" His voice rose. "How can you be so heedless as to suppose you could be safe there? Or put *her* family in danger? And come away from that window!"

Folie stood where she was, lifting her arms like a bird's wings. "Oh, yes, what terrible peril I must be in, here in a

Mayfair drawing room! Perhaps they will fly in at the windows and abduct me!''

He strode forward, grabbing her arm and hauling her bodily away. ''You make me want to strangle you.'' His voice had gone cold and quiet. He let her go instantly, but somehow the transformation from hot wrath to icy control was more alarming than any threat. He stood staring at her with the chilling stillness of a cobra that might strike at any moment. ''Do not cross me in this, Folie.''

She could not hold his eyes. It was true that it was her fault. If she had not come to London in such a silly, happy rush . . . she turned her face aside, her eyes suddenly burning with shame and consciousness.

''I'm sorry,'' she said. ''I did not intend for this to happen.''

''No, I cannot suppose that.''

''I'm sure that if we put our minds to it, we can concoct something. Perhaps—the way the gentleman pretended to be a doctor. Perhaps we could only have a mock wedding.''

''Hmm,'' he said, in a tone she could not interpret.

''Perhaps that is what you have meant all along?'' She looked at him tentatively under her lashes. ''A mock wedding?''

''The notion occurred to me,'' he said.

''Well, then,'' she said, turning. She looked at their distorted reflections in a pier mirror hung on the wall. ''That is what we will do.''

There was a long silence. Folie was trying to focus her mind on what excuse might extricate them after a counterfeit ceremony performed before the greatest gossip on Curzon Street, but all she could think was that Melinda would be ruined by this. Irreparably ruined. Folie knew of a Tetham girl who had lost her chance at becoming engaged because her mother, still youthful enough to be charming, had been seen conversing with the mayor while he was in his shirtsleeves. For all Folie's defiant claim to Robert that she was too old to care for such things, she was well aware that to be only thirty and a widow was to be judged on a razor's edge of decorum, just as Mrs. Paine had said.

"I do not think it will suffice, Folie," he said.

She wet her lips. "What shall we do?"

"Marry," he said harshly. "There appears to be nothing else for it."

No, she thought. You will wish me to Japan, and I cannot bear that.

"I know!" she said. "We can have a terrible argument just before the ceremony, and break the engagement!"

"And what does that accomplish, pray? Even more talk, and still nowhere for you to stay with any safety."

"I cannot believe we are in such a spot over such a stupid thing," she said miserably. "I cannot believe it. But—if I should ruin Melinda's chances by my behavior—oh, I don't know what I should do!"

"Come, you make it sound worse than the prison ship." He reached out and pushed her chin up with a rough touch. "Show some spunk."

Folie pulled her face away. "Do not mock me, if you please." He had that derisive edge in his voice, and she was afraid that he would say something even more cutting if she did not prevent him. "I must have a moment to compose myself," she said, moving toward the door. "I will be upstairs."

Lander was waiting with "Dr. Joyce" in the breakfast room. When Robert returned, both of them hit him instantly with the same comment Folie had given.

"Are you mad, sir?" Lander demanded, standing beside the table. "This is not at all what we had planned."

"No," Robert said shortly. "Of course it is not. Of course I am mad." He sat down in a chair, his hands in his pockets, his legs sprawled before him.

"We've been talking it over," Lander said. "We don't see how the thing can be counterfeited, not to any purpose. For one thing, I refuse to participate in a fraudulent marriage ceremony—it's illegal as murder—and for another—"

"It isn't going to be fraudulent." Robert flung himself out of the chair. "Isn't there something—a special license—how do I get it? Where do I go?"

Lander stared. "Sir! You don't mean you're going to marry her?"

Robert paced to the small window that overlooked the back garden. "I said I was mad, did I not?"

"I do not think Mrs. Hamilton deserves that sort of disrespect," Lander said angrily.

The fact that Robert agreed did not improve his temper. He shrugged as if he did not care. "She'll have a whole lifetime to punish me for it, won't she? A woman's supreme object!"

"You surprise me, sir," Lander said in a lower voice.

Robert did not answer. He rubbed his thumbnail over a speck of white paint on the window glass, peeling it off and flicking it away.

"I don't suppose that Mrs. Hamilton's object can ever have been to punish anyone," Lander said.

"You don't know much of women," Robert said. "Now tell me where I must go for the documents."

"Doctor's Commons," his rapscallion mentor offered obligingly. "Just to the south of St. Paul's. It will cost you a pile of guineas to have a special license of the archbishop, but simple enough, you've no residency to prove, and you may be married right here at home—even at midnight if you please. I'll see to a parson for you."

"A real one," Robert said firmly.

"Of course. I'll fetch a local, so that Lander may vet him if you do not trust me."

"I would be a fool to trust you," Robert said without rancor.

The man grinned. "I take it as a compliment. But I can be honorable when it suits me. You shall have an honest parson to preside, on that you may count."

"All right," Robert said, turning toward the door.

"I had better be the one to go to the law court," Lander said. "After all the commotion here this morning, their nerves will be hung on a hair-trigger."

No one needed an explanation of who "they"; might be. Robert checked an argument—Lander was right, he could leave the house with greater ease and safety. It was only

Robert's inner agitation that made the idea of standing here waiting for everything to happen seem intolerable.

''Fine,'' Robert said. ''Go.'' He went to the sideboard, poured himself a cup of coffee from a silver pot, and sat down. He felt as if a heavy weight was slowly pressing down on him, crushing his lungs.

With an effort, he swallowed the black, sharp liquid. Lander went to the door. He paused there, with his hand on the knob.

''Sir,'' he said, ''I must ask you, before I do this—have you any warmth of affection at all for Mrs. Hamilton?''

''Oh, Christ, Lander,'' Robert said, laying his head back.

''You feel nothing for her?'' Lander's voice rose mistrustfully.

''Do I feel anything for her,'' Robert repeated, his eyes fixed on the intricate plaster crown molding that adorned the ceiling. ''Do I? Only I have had her in my heart every day of my life for ten years.''

''You do little enough to show it,'' Lander said. ''To be frank.''

''The devil with you.''

''I feel a great deal of attachment to Mrs. Hamilton. I would not wish to see her made unhappy. I believe she deserves to marry a gentlemen who truly loves her, and not just—''

''Just what?'' Robert sat up, eyeing him.

Lander's mouth set mulishly. ''Someone who will not appreciate her properly.''

''I love her.''

Lander appeared unconvinced, lingering at the door.

''All right. I am vastly, desperately, deeply in love with her,'' Robert said in elaborate assurance, mocking Lander's serious tone. ''How mawkishly must I say so to satisfy you?''

''I don't—it is not—sir. It is just that you seem so—bitter about it.''

Robert lifted his lip in disdain. ''How young you are.''

''I must hope I never grow older in that sense.''

''Then make sure that you never lay your life in a woman's hands,'' Robert said. ''So that she may cut you with a look, or run you through the heart with her judicious opinion of your character, or mention the men she might have had if fate had been kinder to her.'' The venom in his own voice was startling to him. It was as if some other man spoke through him, and yet he knew every word was true. ''Fall in love all you like, my friend,'' he said harshly. ''And the more you love her, the farther you had better run.''

Lander gazed at him. Slowly he shook his head. ''I won't believe that. I can't believe that.''

''Take yourself off,'' Robert said sullenly. ''This is a waste of time.''

Lander left the room without another word. Robert closed his eyes, sipping the coffee, attempting to calm himself while plain, primitive fear was strangling him. He heard the other man's chair scrape.

''I had better be off for the parson,'' Dr. Joyce said.

Robert opened his eyes. He looked up.

''Still certain you want a real one?'' the man asked, with a faint ironical smirk.

Robert held his coffee between his two hands. The liquid trembled in the cup. He took a deep, sharp breath, half-choked, like a hidden sob. ''Yes!'' he snarled. ''Cease asking me that.''

His mentor nodded. He gave Robert a wordless cuff on the shoulder as he passed toward the door.

Folie had thought of several more ways to avoid a wedding, but each of them had been systematically ridiculed as hopelessly unavailing when she suggested them to Robert. After her third trip downstairs to offer her suggestions, she had to sit on her bed, stuff her knuckles into her mouth like a child, and bite down until she whimpered in order to prevent herself from weeping.

As much as he seemed to insist on this wedding, he became colder and angrier at any mention of it, even any idea to prevent it or afterwards annul it. Lander was gone to obtain a license, she knew. Folie was beginning to feel frantic, like a bird trapped into a cage with some unpredictable beast waking in a dark corner. No matter how amiable or careful she tried to be with this creature, she had the sensation that she was somehow doomed to be mauled and broken.

Her brief fantasies, nurtured by Melinda during those moments near the sunlit bridge, seemed far away and foolish now. Even the idea that she and Robert could be real friends receded, when he was so baffling and ominous; when she could never seem to understand or foresee what would move him, only feel the shadow moving beyond sight or touch.

When Mrs. Paine returned, everything seemed to become completely dream-like. Like a good fairy bent on happiness at any odds, she bustled about the bedchamber—Folie had brought no wedding dress? Well, she must wear one of the gowns Melinda had not packed in her rush. A seam attacked to enlarge the bodice, a biscuit-colored ribbon substituted for the pink, some blonde lace added, and it would be as elegant as you please. Miss Davenport was given the task of adding lace, and when Mrs. Witham-Stanley arrived, bearing some pretty marchpane candies to regale the bride's attendants, she declared that no bodice seam had ever defeated her yet, and began snipping expertly at the gown.

Miss Davenport, becoming uncharacteristically enthusiastic, began to fashion a little headdress from a matching length of lace and arrange it in Folie's hair. When Folie was dressed and curled, the ladies sat back, giggling over a tray of tea and marchpane while she stood before the mirror, gazing at herself in bemusement. There was general agreement among her lighthearted attendants that the gown looked very well, but something was missing from the bodice.

"A flower," Mrs. Witham-Stanley suggested.

"Do you have a necklace, my dear?" Mrs. Paine asked.

"Melinda took our jewelry home," Folie said.

The ladies began to search their minds and persons for an alternative. Mrs. Witham-Stanley bemoaned the fact that she had not thought to bring her mother's single diamond drop from home.

''Even a small pin,'' Miss Davenport advised. ''Not gold, that would be too extravagant. Something rich and pale.''

''Oh!'' Folie said, remembering. She turned suddenly, and stooped to look beneath the bed. It was there. With a little effort, she reached under and retrieved a hat box. Inside was a small ivory casket. Folie lifted it out, set it on the dressing table, and opened the box.

Robert's letters were there, bound in a yellow ribbon. She laid them carefully on the table—she had not taken them out in years, though she still could recite every line.

''Oh,'' Mrs. Paine breathed, her eyes glistening. ''My dear. Are those your love letters?''

''Yes,'' Folie said. It was the first time she had ever allowed anyone, even Melinda, to know that they existed.

At the bottom of the box lay the pearl stickpin. She held it up to view.

''He sent me this from India. For my twentieth birthday. It came from a pirate ship in the China Sea.'' Folie smiled a little. ''And I had never been past Tetham in my life.''

Mrs. Witham-Stanley sniffed. She pulled out her handkerchief and dabbed at her eyes. ''It is lovely.''

''Yes,'' Folie said, almost defiantly. ''It is. It is—and he gave it to me, and I am going to wear it.''

''Of course you are!'' All the ladies were wiping tears. Mrs. Paine stood up. ''Let me pin it for you. And then I must go down and see that Christopher has not managed to wriggle out of his coat. He looks so sweet, I vow you will just want to eat him up!''

Robert was truly afraid that the sudden prospect of marriage had sent him plunging back down through the gauzy net of reason to insanity. He could not seem to get any command of his words or actions. Though Phillippa did not appear to him with the maddening reality of his worst visions, the memories of her seized him close. What she would say, what she would do. And he answered in hostile kind—but the person he was answering was not Phillippa. It was Folie, something he seemed to realize only after he saw the flicker in her expression with each injury that he did. Which did not seem to check him from wreaking another after that.

It was all very different from his first wedding. Mercifully. He at least remembered to send out a footman for yellow roses. That was nearly all he remembered; he forgot that Mrs. Paine was providing flowers for the bride.

After the ladies arrived, he did not see Folie again, though there were auguries, signs, and tokens from time to time from the upper floor—Lander had to be applied to for sewing supplies; the kitchen was required to send up tea; Robert's bouquet mixed at the last moment with Mrs. Paine's, ribbons changed and colors mingled to suit a proper sense of taste and refinement. Robert, dressed in a dark blue coat, was immured with Christopher in the breakfast room. They stared glumly at one another across the table, prisoners in common in their wedding-clothes.

''I hate this,'' Christopher said. ''Why do I have to do this?''

''The Lord only knows,'' Robert said, drinking another of the uncounted cups of black coffee he had consumed this day. It was beginning to have an inebriating effect: his heart skipped and raced as if he could not get enough air to breathe.

Christopher wrung up his face disconsolately. ''But why can't you hold the ring?''

''Damn!'' Robert thrust himself out of his chair. ''The ring!''

He opened the door, starting out to search for Lander. But a lady—they seemed to be multiplying themselves—posted on the staircase chased him back, hissing and spreading her gown like an angry swan pursuing him away from a riverbank.

''Ring!'' Robert managed to exclaim, seeing Lander walking through in the hall beyond.

The younger man paused, fished in his vest pocket, and held up something. Robert could not really see it beyond the irate matron who cried, ''Get back! Get back! We are not ready for you!'' but he presumed it was a gold band. He lifted his hands, retreating backwards into the breakfast room, pulling the door closed with relief.

''I only wanted to play with the ferret,'' Christopher said accusingly.

''It bites,'' Robert said.

''No, it doesn't! It never bit *me!''*

''Just you wait,'' Robert muttered. ''It will.''

At dawn, Folie had been riding into the outskirts of London, shielding her eyes against the rising sun and thinking of nothing but reaching Robert Cambourne. At 3 P.M. she was married to him.

She knew the time because the room was so silent as he slipped the gold band onto her wedding finger that she could hear a single parish bell tolling the hour. Even the closed curtains of the drawing room did not muffle the clear echoing sound.

Fifty candles lit the chandelier. Along with the thin beams of sunlight from between the curtains and candle sconces on every table, the scent of flowers gave the room a strange funereal atmosphere, as if there should be a body lying in state instead of a wedding in progress.

Christopher broke the moment with a snicker. Having handed up the ring, he appeared to believe he had done his duty manfully, and deserted his position, turning to run back to his mama. Folie heard her sniffing proudly.

Robert held Folie's wrist with the lightest possible contact, as if he did not wish to touch her. Out of pure pride, she had spoken her own lines steadfastly, but her heart felt like a kite quivering and careening in a high wind, tossed between sudden ascents and raking plunges. There were yellow roses in the bouquet—*he remembered*—but his voice paused, hesitating to speak every line—*he abhorred her*—she listened to his halting words after the priest: ''With this ring—I thee wed—with my body I thee worship—with all my worldly goods I thee endow.''

Never once did he lift his eyes from their hands.

They knelt. Folie squeezed her eyes shut during the

prayer. She did not even open them when the priest lifted her right hand and placed it in Robert's.

"Those whom God hath joined together, let no man put asunder."

Self-protective defiance and the bizarre surroundings erased any sense of reverence in her for the solemn moment. *Well,* she thought impudently, in the very midst of the prayer, *what a pair of silly fools. He did not have to marry me, and I did not have to marry him. More hair than wit, they would say of us in Toot!*

The impertinent thought made her smile. She glanced aside at Robert, her head bowed, the curve lingering mischievously on her lips.

He was looking at her. One of his black-Satan looks, fit for the local executioner, as if he would as soon chop off her head as marry her. Folie deliberately held her smirk in the face of it. They locked glances, Robert scowling, Folie smiling—like a pair of fencers clashed and poised in balance, faces close enough to feel the warmth of one another's breath.

The priest intoned his prayer of holy matrimony over their clasped hands. "I pronounce that they be man and wife together, in the name of the Father, and of the Son, and of the Holy Ghost. Amen."

Oddly, the corner of Robert's mouth turned up. He closed his eyes and turned his face away. As the priest went on with the blessing, Robert lifted his free hand to his face, like a man covering it in prayerful intensity, but Folie thought she could see him fighting a smile.

She listened to the clergyman's exhortations to love and obey. She had not been obliged to obey anyone or anything but her own inclinations for a long time. She began to feel apprehensive again. Easy enough to think of it as a silly muddle, to recite the ancient words by rote, as if they had no personal meaning, no intent beyond this moment. The priest seemed to repeat, "Wives, submit yourselves unto your own husbands," with a dreadful regularity.

If Robert had squeezed her hand or done any patronizing thing, made any effort to reassure her at that moment, she would have felt as if a trap closed on her. But he did not. When Folie sneaked a look, his expression had changed again—she could have vowed that he appeared more alarmed at the thought than she did.

She relaxed a little. She even closed her fingers and gave his hand a slight, comforting pressure.

Really, she would do her best. Her very best. She closed her eyes and said her own particular prayer, asking for God to help her love and honor and obey this man, even though he baffled her. Even though he frightened her. Even though he seemed to have a devil inside to oppose every angel that touched him.

Mrs. Paine bustled about the dining room where the cake and kickshaw had been set out, placing chairs and arranging Folie and Robert and the guests to her satisfaction.

"Now, Mrs. Ha—Lord bless us—Mrs. Cambourne, I mean to say! You must cut the first piece of the bride cake for your husband." She took them both by the hand and led them to the table, where Mrs. Witham-Stanley's cook had indeed outdone herself in the few hours available. A beautifully iced cake, garlanded and flowered in white marchpane and cream, graced the head of the table. Mrs. Paine handed Folie the knife and stepped aside.

But before Folie could raise her hand, Mrs. Paine gasped. She struck her hand to her bosom as if a silent gunshot had just hit her. "Good God! Someone has cut it!"

Indeed, when Folie leaned over, she could see that a slice had been taken from the back of the cake, the icing repaired clumsily, sagging and cracking over the theft.

"Christopher!" Mrs. Paine exclaimed in a voice of doom.

"I didn't!" the boy cried. "I didn't do it! I didn't!"

"Christopher William Paine!" his mother cried, reaching for him.

Christopher dived for safety behind Lander. "I *didn't!*" he howled. *"He* did it!" He yanked at Lander's coattail.

"Nonsense! Do not add prevarication to your crime!"

Mrs. Paine descended on Lander and her son with a determined stride.

"Ma'am," Lander said, standing forward while Christopher clung to him. Considering the expression of rage on Mrs. Paine's face, Folie thought it was a very brave thing to do. "Mrs. Paine, I apologize. The boy is correct. I cut it."

"You?" She stopped still.

Lander looked toward Robert. He cleared his throat. "It was thought prudent."

"Prudent!" Mrs. Paine cried. "Why, it is a wicked trick! You had no right! You've ruined it!"

"What did you do with the piece, Lander?" Robert asked. His voice had a strange crack in it.

The butler maintained a grave expression. "Cat, sir."

"Cat?" Mrs. Paine repeated. "And who might Cat be?"

"Gave it to a cat," he clarified. "Stray cat."

"You gave it to a cat?" Mrs. Paine screeched. "You cut the first slice of Mrs. Witham-Stanley's beautiful marchpane bride cake and gave it to an *alley cat?*"

Robert was making the most peculiar sound—rather like a cat himself that could not quite swallow a fishtail. Folie did not dare look at him.

"Mrs. Witham-Stanley—" Lander said soberly, turning from Mrs. Paine and bowing to the older lady. "You must understand that a gentleman of Mr. Cambourne's—uncommon nature—must be very careful of his diet. In the absence of the ferret, we have found a cat to be a useful barometer of his digestive tolerance."

Robert cleared his throat again in that singular manner. Folie was really afraid that he would burst into hysterical laughter at any moment.

She looked brightly at their guests. "I hope you will not be offended, dear ma'am," she said to Mrs. Witham-Stanley. "I deeply apologize that a stray was resorted to—I have not yet had time to choose the particular cat that we will use on a daily basis. Lander," she added sternly, "you will present me with a selection of suitable cats directly. Also I shall need to interview housekeepers. But that is for tomorrow. First—'' She turned to Robert, smiling up at him as if he were her whole dependence. ''I shall like to celebrate my wedding with a slice of this exquisite cake.''

He had a vicious frown. But Folie was beginning to realize that it was his method of containing himself—the more fierce he appeared, the harder he was laboring at it. He made it through the cutting of the cake and a rather inexplicable speech by a Mr. Bellamy—Folie had not a notion who Mr. Bellamy might be, but he had no headache, by his own admission—and he seemed to be a great admirer of Robert's.

''How kind of you, sir,'' Folie said, giving the man a small curtsy when the toast had been drunk. ''How kind of you all to come!'' She could hear Robert breathing in a way that she feared would bring on a dead faint if he did not regulate it. She looked up at him. Sure enough, his face was pale, and he was scowling like a demon.

''I daresay I feel a little dizzy with all the stimulation!'' She put her hand on his arm. ''Please take me into the air for a moment, my dear Mr. Cambourne. Lander, you will see that everyone is served their cake!''

Robert nodded, walking toward the door. The guests stood aside. ''The shoes, toss the shoes!'' Mrs. Paine cried gaily—and a small rain of slippers and wedding favors followed Folie and Robert into the hall, as if they were leaving a normal wedding breakfast for a normal honeymoon.

Just outside the door, he took a stronger grip of her arm. He drew her quickly toward the breakfast room, pulled her inside, and closed the door. The sounds in his throat were of a man who had just run twenty miles.

He fell into a chair, dragging her down before him onto her knees. Folie looked up, terrified that he was going to have a seizure or a swoon. He put his palms on her cheeks, gasping.

''A . . . selection . . . of . . .'' he wheezed. ''Cats.'' He gulped for air. ''Suitable—cats!''

Folie relaxed. She sat on her knees on the braided rug, looking up at him. ''Lander started it,'' she said.

He was laughing so hard that he did not even make a

sound. His whole body trembled as he leaned over her, pressing his mouth against her temple, gulping air against her skin. Folie shook her head, softly chuckling, leaning against him.

As she moved closer, she could feel the nature of his touch change—his hands pressed her face, and then skimmed over her hair. He buried his face hard into her throat. To her confusion she felt wetness on her skin.

"Robert?" she murmured, lifting her hand to his hair.

He shook his head violently. He began to kiss her ear, to score her throat with his teeth. He slid from the chair onto his knees. His hold on her grew rough, imploring. "Folly," he whispered. "My Folly."

She turned her face to his. He sought her mouth, kissing her, a hot sugared taste of almonds. His fingers pressed painfully into her arms.

"It will be all right," he said into her hair, soft and slurred, as if to reassure himself as much as her. "It will be all right." Then as suddenly as he had begun to kiss her, he pulled back.

He stood up, walking away. While Folie still knelt on the rug, he went to the window and leaned his forehead against the pane.

"Put yourself to rights," he said. "I suppose we must go back."

Her cheeks flamed with agitation and chagrin. How quickly he could toss her into a maelstrom! She rose, smoothing down her skirt. To gloss over the moment, she said, "I hope they do not suppose we have been—" She stopped, caught in the middle of an imbecilic sentence. Of course, everyone would suppose they had been doing precisely what they had been doing.

"Never mind," he said. "We have only to say that you fainted in my arms, and I revived you from certain death with handsome compliments on your coiffure."

"Oh, they will be perfectly ready to believe that!"

"My dear, I am learning that the world is full of gulls. They seem to wish to believe all sorts of rubbish."

"Such as Mr. Bellamy and his headache?" she inquired.

''Ah, well,'' he said, slanting an appreciative glance down her figure. ''Bellamy may not believe I revived you with compliments, I admit. He might be a simpleton, but he's not a fool.''

Twenty-One

WHEN THE GUESTS had gone away, and Robert had vanished like a genie into some magic bottle, Folie and Lander were left to see the house put to rights again. By the time she had reached her bedchamber, Folie was exhausted. She went to bed without the help of a maid—no small task after the ladies had dressed her—unpinning the lace headress and brushing out her hair, scattering flower petals on the floor. She popped one of the buttons on Melinda's gown while trying to slide out of it, and writhed arduously to loosen her corset strings. But that was better than having Mrs. Paine attend to her, as that lady had merrily threatened to do. Folie put on the worn and comfortable nightgown she had stuffed into her bag in the middle of the night—a thousand years ago, it seemed—and climbed into bed.

Nervous and excited, she sat up against the pillows in the middle of the bed. He might not come soon. He might not come at all. She thought of him in the breakfast room—and left the candle lit.

After a while, she climbed out of bed, trimmed the candle, and got in again. She thought of reading, but her eyes were so tired that she could only look without ambition toward the bookcase. She really did not think that he would come. Charles had not. Not the first night. He had given them time to become better acquainted with one another.

Folie was not certain about Robert's delicacy of feeling in that regard. She was by no means averse to his love-making. She had a trick in her mind when she thought of it—when those strange, enflamed moments at Dingley Hall came to her—she did not examine them in detail, though she knew perfectly well that she could if she wished—but rather hastily transferred her attention to some other topic, leaving herself a little breathless, as if she had a cryptic incantation for pleasure that she never quite dared to use.

What she did know was that Charles had never been that way with her. Probably he had with the first Mrs. Hamilton, but his ardor had died with his first wife. In an odd way, Folie felt very much a virgin, sitting in the big bed with her hair down around her shoulders. She had been a wife. But she had never been a bride.

She hoped that Robert would come to her. She did not want delicacy of feeling, or consideration, or respect, not from Robert. Somehow it was crucial that he come tonight, this first night—if he did not, she would never be certain how to approach him or act with him. If he did not, she would not know if she was a real wife or not.

And she would have to bury her veiled and secret hope forever. He had spoken of trust. She had spoken of friendship. She supposed that they liked one another reasonably well. But she had kept a flame that burned beyond all of those things in her heart. It had flickered and waned, half-forgotten—but it had never wholly died. She might be plain Mrs. Charles Hamilton, of Toot-above-the-Batch, Herefordshire, a genteel widow in the eyes of the world—but someone, once, had seen her for a princess. And since then, she had never in all her life known passion for any man but Robert Cambourne.

If he did not return it, Folie thought, she could not bear for him to know that it still endured in her heart. If he wanted her as she wanted him, then he would come tonight; he must come tonight, because any delicacy of feeling would be like the wings of a moth beating against a fire—burned away in a moment.

But he did not come. Folie sat watching the door until the candle burned so low that her eyes hurt.

At last she ceased attempting to keep them open. She could not quite give up. She had never been one to give up. She tried to stay awake even with her eyes shut . . . but finally dejection sank her deep into the bed and distant dreams.

Robert lay on his back, wide awake. Since moving into Cambourne House, he had avoided sleeping in the bedchamber Folie had used—he had not needed to ask anyone which one it was; he simply knew it, emptied of her belongings or not.

She had taken possession of it again now, of course. She was sleeping directly below him. He wanted to get up and pace, but he thought that the floor would creak and give him away.

He turned over, punching his pillow. God damn him, that he had drunk a hundred cups of coffee and then let himself kiss her—if he ever got to sleep again in his lifetime he would be lucky.

It was his wedding night. Not that it signified anything. The one thing he would not do was put himself again in the position of beggar. The last thing he would do was let her know that she held any power over him.

He sat up suddenly, hearing Phillippa somewhere, laughing at him. But there was only silence in the room when he listened. The sound was a carriage or a wagon rolling past, the resonant turn of the axle echoing in the street like a low chuckle.

Robert lay back on the pillow, his arms behind his head. No— it would be the other way around this time. This time he would be the one who enticed and withheld, who promised and never gave, who kept the secret cards.

He hoped she was lying awake. Tossing and turning. Bewildered and hurt. Robert turned over, throwing his pillow onto the floor. Why the devil had he kissed her?

But then he thought, of course that was the way to seduce her. Kiss her and caress her and make everything a promise.

She had seemed to like it well enough. He had a confused memory of lying with her at Solinger—or was it at Dingley's? Memory or reality—everything from that time was jumbled in his mind, so that he could not know if her heated response was truth or mere fancy. But that kiss on the floor in the breakfast room today—that he remembered. She had reached up her hand and touched his hair.

Well, he would make her want him.

Phillippa had wanted him at first. At least—looking back, he was not certain that she ever had in truth. But first she had given him a deep drink of her, enough to make him want to drown. He'd had a consummate teacher when it came to arousing and then frustrating desire. If he had learned his lessons well, then he would go to Folie now and begin to weave her bondage, using her own will against her.

Robert sat up on the edge of the bed. He lay down again. From where he was, he could see the black shape of his closed door.

With an irritated grunt, he reached down and retrieved the pillow, dropping it over his face. He counted as far as forty-seven before he threw it off again.

He stood up at last. He had nothing on—in the heat of Delhi, living among natives at the palace at Shajahanabad, he had grown accustomed to sleeping without nightclothes or a cap, and now they seemed to choke him. He found his shirt, a shapeless pile of white linen tossed over a chair, and pulled it over him.

Quietly he let himself out of the room, on a cold mission to seduce his wife.

Folie had a pleasing dream. She walked through the Indian bazaars in her blue shawl, among incense burners and elephants adorned with pearls and gold, but she was not alone this time. One elephant moved its great, slow ears and turned to lead her. "This way," someone murmured. "This is the way home."

"Who are you?" she asked.

"Sweetheart," the elephant said, and smiled like a child.

It turned into a little boy in blue velvet. He took her hand, pulling her through the gauzy, narrow streets. A man reached out to catch her as she ran—for an instant she was afraid, but then he drew her into his arms, and she knew that it was Robert.

"I'm home," she said to him. "The elephant brought me home."

"Sweetheart," he murmured, holding her back against him, leaning over her, kissing her neck. As she rolled toward him, he bent and kissed her breast. She felt a surge of desire, a wash of shyness, but this was a dream, and she gave herself up to it. His hand slipped downward, lining her hips and legs as he kissed and sucked at her nipple.

Folie gave a sharp sigh. She did not know what woke her; she hardly knew when—only that the dream turned into warm darkness, the warmth into a solid touch, the pleasure into a hot, mounting urge. She did not question it, but gave herself to the reality as easily as the dream. She felt his teeth close on her nipple and the soft cotton of her gown; she caught her breath and panted. She did not need respect and polite kisses—she needed this, she wanted *this*.

He knew all about her. Each nip and pull of his mouth on her breast made her whimper. "Robert," she moaned, biting her lip and pressing her legs together, moving her body like a mermaid swimming.

He answered with a low wolfish sound, his hand on her hip, pulling her back to him. He pushed his hard man's part against her, as if he would invade between her legs from behind, straining the gown tight to her bottom. She had left all modesty in the dream—he had only to touch her to transform shame to something delicious between them. When she arched her back, he ran his hand up the curve and made it beautiful. He cupped her breast and gathered her body against him, biting her throat and squeezing her nipple, creating pain and sharp pleasure at once.

"Let me see you," he whispered through his teeth. "Let me see you."

Suddenly he rose above her on his knees. Folie lay looking up at him, lost in dreamy amazement. He was a dim outline of light and shadow looming over her—his white linen shirt gaping open; his chest dark, and his throat and his face—a column of darkness; his shoulders shaped in white.

"Take off your gown," he said.

Folie swallowed against a wave of heat that washed up her body; heat from his words alone, spoken with a low demand. She had not thought she could be so wanton—and yet without hesitation, she sat up, knowing the light was enough for him to see her as she could see him. She drew up her legs and her gown, sitting straight and proud before him as she crossed her arms and lifted the gown over her head.

He caught it away from her and tossed it off the bed. As Folie's hair fell down her back, he ran his hands along her arms and lifted her hands. He spread them out, gazing at her naked breasts. Then he put his palms at her waist and slid them upward, marking the shape of her body and breasts. He made a faint moan, as if it hurt him to look.

"My God, you are beautiful," he said.

"So are you," she said simply.

He gave a soft laugh. "Folly. I want to touch you all over. I want to touch every inch of you."

"Yes," she said. "Yes."

He leaned forward, kissing her gently at the corner of her mouth. The very tenderness of it made her want to be crushed against him. Their breath mingled. She felt the light roughness of his cheek, smelled the scent of him, the familiar beloved scent of him, only this time warmed with reality, with flesh and blood.

"Lie down," he said, and when she obeyed him, he leaned over and began to caress her feet. He stroked her ankle, drawing his finger slowly under the arch of her foot and up the back of her heel. Her skin prickled with a luscious sensation all over her body. He bent and kissed her knee, cupping his hands about her thigh and sliding them up to the place between her legs, just touching it with his finger, stroking and then leaving it. Folie whimpered.

"Mmmm?" he murmured wickedly. "What is it?"

She lifted her knee, hoping he would stroke her again there. He drew his thumb up the inside of her thigh and rolled it across the place, sending fire through her body to her fingertips. She made a faint urgent sound.

"Tell me," he said.

"Robert—" she said plaintively.

"Say it."

"Oh, Robert," she whispered, arching anxiously.

"Say it," he repeated, moving his fingers up close to the place and then away—not quite there, and then away.

She slid her legs apart. "Please. Please."

"Tell me what you want."

Folie could feel all her skin turning hot with desire and embarrassment. "I don't know."

He made a low growl. "Oh, yes you do." He leaned over and kissed her belly, drawing his tongue downward.

"What?" she said, frantically kneading his hair. "What?"

She felt his mouth moving softly on her curly hair, teasing and tickling, then a touch into the depth, to the wet place that made her gasp with pleasure. She lifted her breasts, pushing them outward, pushing her body up to his mouth.

He lifted his head. "Tell me what you want."

"Kiss me," she panted.

"Where?"

"There, there."

He slid his hand under her buttock and gave her a light squeeze. "You have to say it for me, sweet Folly. I'll make you say it."

"Say what? I don't know. I don't know."

He kissed the inside of her thigh, chuckling. "Ah." He slid his thumb about on a moistness that was new and strange to her. "Here, where you're all wet for me. You don't know what this is?"

She made a wordless small sound, shaking her head.

"What a naive widow!" he said, his voice amused.

"Well, I have only been married once, Robert!" she exclaimed in agitation. "And he never did this to me!"

"Good," he said strongly. He leaned over her on both hands and kissed her hard on the mouth. "Good."

He licked her upper lip with his tongue, then ran it along the outside of her mouth. He pushed his fingers inside her body as he kissed her. The sensation made her open, spreading her legs as he rolled his thumb in a deep searching circle, a pressure that brought soft moans from her throat. "Did he do this to you?"

"No," she whispered.

She could see his teeth when he smiled down at her in the darkness. "You like it?"

"Oh, yes," she whimpered.

"This is your sweet pussy," he said, "this pretty dark hair, this soft pink skin, the place I go inside you."

Folie nodded.

He put his mouth next to her ear. "Say it," he whispered.

Her eyes widened. It was an ordinary word, but suddenly it seemed the most impossible sound in the universe to repeat. Her body burned. "I can't," she said helplessly.

"Oh, Folly," he said low in his throat. "Then I'll have to leave."

"No," she said. "Don't go."

"Say my name."

"Robert," she whispered.

He caressed the corner of her mouth with his tongue. "Say, 'Robert, please.' "

"Robert . . . Robert . . . please."

He made that deep delicious circle inside her with his thumb. Her body arched in ecstasy. "Say, 'Robert, please kiss my pussy.' "

"Robert!" she wailed softly.

He drew away a little, as if he might leave her. She knew it was a deliberate torment, to make her do what he said, but she could not even make her tongue shape the words.

"Ah, Folly, what a wicked disobedient wife you are already," he murmured. "Say it."

"Robert," she said breathlessly. "Robert . . . kiss . . . my pussy."

" 'Please.' "

"Robert," she moaned, "you are horrid!"

"I have not even begun being horrid," he said, biting her earlobe. "Say it all, like a good girl."

"Robert please . . ." she gasped. "Please . . . kiss-my-pussy." She hurried so quickly over the worst part that the words slurred together.

"Mmmmm." He kissed the skin at the base of her throat. While Folie clutched the bed sheets, he shaped her hips between his hands and trailed kisses down her breasts and her belly. He licked the place he had made her give a name to, kissed and ran his tongue over it until she was shuddering.

A great urge came upon her to arch up beneath him, wildfire running through her body. She took in gulps of air and could not seem to let them out of her lungs—his hands held her still but she wanted to move and move, and every tiny thrust of her hips to his tongue made the sensation intensify. She was shivering in hysterical delight, with no control over her own limbs, when he suddenly sat back.

"Tell me what you want," he ordered.

"Please kiss my—" Her voice cracked. "Robert, please kiss my pussy, please, please."

He was silent. For a long moment he did not move, and then he put his arm about her bent knee and pressed his cheek against her leg very hard. He let her go.

"No," he said. "Later. Later, perhaps."

His words were so unexpected, so at odds with everything, that she hardly even understood what he meant. But then he stood up. He found her gown on the floor and laid it beside her on the bed.

"Put on your gown and go to sleep," he said. Without another word, he left her.

Robert walked into his room. He went to the window that overlooked the back garden, opened the curtains, and raised the sash. He stood with the chill air flowing under his shirt and over his skin.

His body was raging. He put his hands to his hair and sank to his knees, his head tilted back, his mouth open in a silent howl of need.

Twenty-Two

IF THERE HAD been a housekeeper, Folie would have rung for breakfast in her room. If she could have arranged it, she would not have left her bedchamber for at least a decade or two. She remembered every single moment of the night before, clearly and with hot mortification.

But there was no answer to her tug on the bell pull. She was not surprised—Lander could not run a household properly if it consisted of one room and a sty, she thought bitterly. All very well to have a Bow Street Runner on hand, but a decent servant would be more welcome at the moment.

She dressed, perforce in her country clothes that did not require a maid's assistance, and took a deep breath at the top of the stairs. She descended with a queenly tread, as if she always went downstairs like royalty. It was the only thing to do in these moments of pure agony, act as if all were quite well, or perhaps even superb.

Voices emanated from the breakfast room, along with the scent of coffee and ham. She found Robert and Lander seated at the table, chortling more like boyhood chums than acting like a gentleman and his butler, while ''Dr. Joyce'' performed some apparently comical act with his plate at the sideboard. Folie assumed it was meant to be a comedy by the audience reaction—the moment she appeared, everyone fell silent, so she could not know for sure.

The men stood up hastily. She had the distinct impression of schoolboys caught out in some silly mischief, which naturally placed her by default into the role of repressive mistress. She had no intention of accepting it. Instead of making any stuffy comment on their guilty looks—though several occurred to her—she took the opposite tack, falling into a deep curtsy.

"I am very sorry to be late," she said contritely. "Please forgive me, I had so little sleep last night!"

To her consternation, both Lander and the doctor looked toward Robert at this. If they had looked puckish a moment before, they appeared downright abominable now, smirking like demons. Folie realized her error. Worse, she remembered what Robert had done to keep her awake, with vivid and agitating clarity. She blushed to her eyebrows.

"There was no hurry," Robert said lazily. His complacent tone made her want to strangle him. "You should sleep as late as you like."

"Well, one must eat eventually," she said with a small shrug, turning to the sideboard, where a breakfast suitable to six farmers and a few blacksmith's boys was laid out. "I see that you are not going hungry, in spite of no suitable cats."

"Madam," said the doctor, sweeping a bow, "I have been informed that your performance in regard to the subject of cats was inspired. My compliments."

She made a slight curtsy to him.

"I believe that we can make excellent use of your talent for a quick rejoinder. I propose, gentlemen, that Mrs. Cambourne be made a central figure in our little scheme."

Robert frowned. "I don't think so. It's too dangerous to have her going in and out of the house. We'll stay with the plans we've already made."

Folie lifted her eyebrows. But she said nothing, only took a small sausage and a piece of cold toast, and sat down. Lander poured her tea from the pot.

"As you prefer, of course," the doctor said. "But allow

me to mention that flexibility is a virtue in these matters, as we saw demonstrated nicely yesterday. I believe that in a day or two we will find that, through the medium of those lovely ladies who attended your wedding, much progress has been made in bringing your person and talents to the attention of society. There is nothing like a bizarre marriage to attract gossip—far from bewailing it, we must thank Mrs. Cambourne for precipitating the episode. I daresay she has saved us a good fortnight's work."

"I am so glad to be of use," Folie said.

He remained solemn, but in the momentary glance that he gave her, she could have sworn that she detected a wink. Folie softened a little toward Dr. Joyce.

"So we ought to go ahead at Lord Morier's dinner tonight?" Lander asked.

"With certainty," the doctor said. "Belle Packard will put me in the way of an invitation to that—Morier owes her a little favor, but she's the sort of lady who don't like to take it in cash or jewels. This will be just the ticket. I shall be a French emigré, I think, fresh from exile in Italy. L'Comte de . . . somewhere." He gave a vague wave of his hand. "I'll have a look at the atlas. I am a philosophical scientist, a severe skeptic, an investigator of animal magnetism. A student of the great Dr. Mesmer himself, who does not like to see pettifoggers and pretenders imposing themselves on a credulous public."

"Will Bellamy be there?" Robert asked.

"Unless he has the headache," Lander said, grinning. "I took the liberty of mentioning you would attend, and he said that he never missed Morier's race-dinners if he could help it."

"I hope he comes because he *has* the headache," Robert said. "He was fatally easy to dupe."

"You should stop thinking of it as deceit," the doctor said reprovingly. "That will begin to show in your presentation."

"Sorry," Robert said. He frowned a little, looking down at his thumbnail, flicking it past his fingers.

Folie had been reaching for the teapot. She startled and

squeaked as it moved away from her hand, sliding a few inches across the table.

"Study on that trick—" The doctor nodded. "You are not sufficiently easy with it yet. When you can do it so well that it is no longer a trick, but a belief in the powers of your own mind to affect actuality, then you are ready."

"How am I going to believe it's some sort of mental power, when I know how I'm doing it?"

The doctor shrugged. "You are concentrating on the wrong thing," he said obscurely. "Reality is a much broader element than you suppose."

"It is a trick?" Folie asked in astonishment. "Do it again!"

Robert made the flicking motion with his fingers again. The teapot obediently migrated another inch across the glossy wood.

"How are you doing it?" she demanded.

He gave her a wide stare. "With my occult powers," he said ominously.

"There is a string," she said.

"See if you can find it, Mrs. Cambourne," the doctor said.

Folie put her hands over the teapot, feeling for any attachment. She lifted it, passing her hand underneath. She set it down.

"Do it again." She held her hand between Robert and the teapot, waving it up and down, but discovered no thread or obstacle. "Now do it again," she ordered, staring closely at his fingers as she kept her hand in place on the table.

Robert made his magic gesture, and the pot moved—a little less this time.

"How are you doing that?" she cried.

"Indeed, you are very close, Mrs. Cambourne," the doctor said. "In a moment you will find it."

Folie felt all around. She left her chair and swept her arms all about the table. She even took Robert's hand, pushing her fingers between his. She felt nothing but the warmth of his bare skin. She glanced up—he was smiling down at her with an affectionate look. As she took her hand away he caught her fingers in a quick squeeze. ''You wouldn't like to explore me further?'' he asked, in mock disappointment.

''Hmmpf,'' she said, with an arch look. She straightened, leaning on the table with one hand on her hip. ''Do it again.''

The doctor chuckled. ''I believe she has you now!''

Robert frowned ferociously at his hand. He did not move his fingers, but shook his head. ''Never mind. I'm not in the mood for this nonsense anyway.'' He looked up at her, still scowling. ''Come, finish your breakfast, ma'am,'' he said, with a sharp impatience, ''so that we may get on with matters of some importance.''

Folie's smile faded at his petulance. She resumed her seat, her back stiff. ''Yes, Robert,'' she said, in her best imitation of a royal princess.

She reached for the teapot. It ran wildly away from her, nearly to the edge of the table.

''Well done!'' the doctor cried. ''An excellent diversion.''

Lander began laughing. ''You'll end up with a teapot in your lap, sir!''

''Serve him right,'' Folie said darkly. ''He'll end up with it over his head if he doesn't take care!''

But Robert only smiled at her, a tender look that sent a shaft of pleasure through her, as sharp as the cutting barb of a moment before. She could not fathom his trick, though clearly he could not accomplish it until she had sat down again, but it was not the teapot legerdemain that disturbed her. It was the trickery he seemed to practice with such ease on her heart.

''Here, ma'am,'' the conjurer said, producing a paper scrawled with strange symbols. ''He must practice these hand signals—you'll oblige me by seeing that he's mastered them by tonight.''

''Yes, sir,'' Folie said.

The lighthearted spirit among the men at breakfast had diverted Folie's mind from danger, but Robert had soon disabused her of any naïve hope that things were normal. He vetoed any suggestion that might take her out of doors, even into the back garden, and she was to be at home to no callers whatsoever. She had spent the greater part of the day with a candle in the darkened drawing room, trying to write an announcement and explanatory letter to Melinda that did not sound entirely deranged.

Now, waiting for them to return from Lord Morier's annual race-dinner held in honor of the horse he would be running in the Derby, Folie could not keep her attention on anything, not book or letter or London paper. She could only think of watching Robert and Lander leaving, slipping out of the back of the house under cover of darkness, and a loud altercation between the porter and a footman, created by intention at the front door.

They had not said when they would return. Folie sat on the edge of the chair, chiding herself. Over time she had forgotten some of the key habits of being a wife—one must be sure to inquire after the most mundane information. She promised herself that she would not begin to worry until after midnight, but in fact she began to worry as soon as they left the house. She could not shed the image of Robert pulling a gun from beneath his coat. She knew that he must have it with him now.

The clock struck half past twelve. Folie peeked between the curtains. The traffic in the street below had lessened through the evening hours—now it had picked up again, guests beginning to return to their homes from the theater or progress to the next ball or late supper.

Lord Morier's dinner would become a bachelor party, she told herself. They might not be home until 2 A.M. at the earliest—the gentlemen would sit about and drink and smoke and talk of horses until very late. They might play cards. Lord Morier was a notorious gambler, though he was wealthy enough to afford his losses.

Folie tried to focus her mind on something innocuous. The Dingley girls. It was certainly an interesting piece of information that Lander had dropped about Lord Morier calling at Cambourne House and finding himself in the nursery. Folie and Melinda had mulled it over at length, although Melinda said she had been so much beside herself that she did not even know His Lordship had called.

Unfortunately, thinking of the Dingley girls brought her directly to thinking about Sir Howard. Robert had not seemed to take her worries very seriously. Folie remembered how Sir Howard had come here to Cambourne House late one night. She frowned, looking about the room, trying to recollect the details of what he had said, how he had acted. She had not felt well; she only recalled being annoyed that he would not go away. But had he not seemed guilty and distracted? He must have been planning even then to betray Robert to his enemies.

Yet, he could not have known Folie would write to him. She had not even known she would herself, until she had done it. He must simply have taken advantage of the chance when it came.

She pulled a piece of paper from the secretary, intending to try to transcribe what she could recall of their conversation. But the more she thought of it, the more it seemed Sir Howard had mostly been mooning about his wife and imagining a flock a gentlemen admirers ready to elope with Lady Dingley.

How absurd it all was. The man was clearly in love with his wife; his wife was in love with him. And yet, given half a chance, they hardly seemed to keep to the same house—instead dragooning poor innocent bystanders like Folie into conducting their affairs for them. And where did she end up for her trouble? In a prison hulk.

No matter how hard she tried, she could not quite imagine Sir Howard as a hardened villain, lying to her and fabricating deliberately on that late-night visit. For one thing, she had never known a gentleman to lie about love. Of course, she had not known many gentlemen all that well. Only her elderly uncles and Charles, none of whom had been in any state of visible ardor in all the time she had known them.

She supposed, when she thought of it, that there was nothing to prevent a man from lying on the topic. Ladies certainly fibbed about love with relish. Out of self-defense, really. Would Folie, for instance, declare her true feelings about Robert to his face?

Of course she would not.

Sitting in the stillness of the empty room, Folie came to a slow realization. It was not something so astonishing, and yet she had not ever directly considered it before. Robert's strange behavior—his kisses and sudden irritations and faltering, his cutting sarcasm and impulsive tenderness—and last night . . . last night . . .

Folie bit her lip. Why *did* a lady lie about love? To protect herself. To bluff. To make sure that she did not overplay her hand and end up with nothing. Folie herself had lied—had been lying, to him and to herself, since the day she had received his last letter, declaring to herself that she had no interest in love, that she would never fall in love again, but only cared for practical things. When all along she had kept that secret passion in her heart.

It seemed an imminently feminine tactic. Everyone knew about it; almost expected it—in fact Folie was not sure, when she thought back, that she had not had a lesson in "a lady's natural modesty" from her governess that had strongly encouraged her, for her own good, to deliberately obscure her sentiments. And yet somehow gentlemen were supposed to be perfectly straightforward and honorable about their devotion.

But why should such an expedient be confined to ladies? Why, after all, could Robert not lie quite as well—or as badly—as she?

She was deep in fascinated speculation on the point when the doorbell gave a muffled ring. Folie jumped up. But she had hardly opened the drawing room door when she saw Robert already coming up the back stairs. He paused, seeing her, and smiled—holding up his hand in a gesture to wait. She heard the front door close, wafting a breath of cool air through the hall. He leaned over the stair rail and beckoned.

Lander came bounding lightly up the front stairs. They were both grinning like idiots, walking about the passage, opening doors, looking inside each room and closing it again.

"Up here, *mes amis*."

Folie jerked her head up. She saw a man standing at the head of the next flight of stairs. He wore a sky-blue coat and froths of lace, skintight primrose pantaloons that matched his gloves, and a huge diamond at his throat. His hair was curled and oiled under a prim little tricorne hat. Rouge pinkened his cheeks.

Folie could smell eau de jasmine from where she stood. His sideburns were so extravagant that they nearly met under his chin. She apprehended, logically, that this was the doctor, but if she had not known he was to be transformed to a French dandy, she would not have recognized him at all.

Robert shook his head. "I'll find out where you're breaking and entering, you old rogue," he said. "I swear. Come down to the drawing room."

The man tripped lightly down the stairs. He swept an extravagant bow before Folie. "Eugene, L'Comte d'Aulaye, madame," he said, kissing her hand and adding a compliment in French.

Folie's French—never very useful in Toot—had grown extremely rusty. "*Merci,*" she said, with a curtsy. "There, you have exhausted my vocabulary."

"That is fortunate, madam," he said, "for I just told you that you have married a man born for the gallows."

"How gratifying!" she said, as they entered the drawing room. "I presume that he made teapots fly across St. James Street in both directions?"

"Port decanters," Robert said with a smug grin.

"Oh, good. Perhaps you can coax a tray of sweet biscuits to walk itself up from the kitchen."

"I'll fetch some refreshment," Lander said, belatedly recalling that he was a butler.

Folie trimmed a candle for brightness and sat down. "Tell me all about it. I've been sitting here clutching my bosom and supposing you were in peril of your life, while you have been commanding brooms to dance the polonaise.''

''I wish you could have been there!'' Robert said. He did not sit down, but walked about the room. He had a buoyancy about him, as if he glowed with a dark, jubilant light.

Folie could not help smiling. ''It went very well, I see.''

''The great comte could not catch me out, not for all his science,'' Robert said. He cast a glance at Aulaye. ''Though I had a bad moment when I saw that tablecloth at dinner.''

The comte shrugged. ''They would have taken it away before the port, but I thought it well to spill my claret, just to make sure.''

Folie had an enlightenment. ''Why, did you use the wood to slide things upon?'' She drew a breath and sat up straight. ''Yes! You tilted the table to make the teapot slide! You could not do it while I was leaning on it!''

''God save us from witty women,'' the comte said in amusement.

''But—but . . . why did the other things not move, then? And I could not see you lift it—your hands were free.''

''We must retain some secrets, my love,'' Robert said.

She narrowed her eyes. ''Did you do it with your knee?''

''Really, it was the least part of the evening,'' Robert said, glancing at his confederate. ''I thought my debate with you upon Indian philosophy was more effective.''

''Ah, yes,'' the comte mused, sitting back and steepling his hands.

''Only by looking on the world as *maya*,'' Robert intoned solemnly, ''as illusion, vanity, deceptive appearance, can we approach the face of the Divine.''

''Whatever that may mean,'' the comte said with disgust. ''Give me a rousing demonstration of animal magnetism, if you please.''

''Animal magnetism—it's only another word for what the mystics know as *kundalini,* the power of the serpent that coils at the base of the spine. But what use is to be made of it? Your scientific investigations, your skepticism, your discoveries—that's quite well, but all this has been known for ten thousand years to the East. It is the use of this power that must concern us—the human potential for evil, the political consequences—most certainly if untaught Europeans are to discover how to wield it before they understand the cost. I shudder to imagine the consequences.''

Aulaye inclined his head. ''A nice detour, sir—away from the skeptical question to the consequences of misusing a power. To suggest political implications . . . that may make them concentrate a little.''

Robert chuckled. ''My finest moment.''

''Did anyone seem to show a particular interest?'' Lander asked, coming in with a tray of tea and three wineglasses. ''Who was there? I saw Effingham and Tom Pethering go in, and the Duke of Kent's carriage was waiting outside all evening.''

''There must have been forty at the table,'' Robert said. ''Morier at the head, Kent on his right, Alvanley on his left—''

''Write them down,'' the comte said. ''We'll go down each side—I think we can recover them all.''

''I'll write.'' Folie took a seat at the secretary where her pen and ink was still set out. ''The Duke of Kent,'' she said. ''One of the Prince Regent's brothers? There are so many, I never got them straight.''

''Number four of seven,'' Lander said. ''He and the prince are like cats and dogs. Whatever the regent may do or think, Kent will go his length the opposite direction. Does Prinnie show himself a Tory, then Kent goes to the Whigs. Or worse.''

Robert gave him a long look. ''That is interesting.''

''Aye, sir.''

''What is worse than the Whigs?'' Robert mused.

''The radicals,'' Lander and the comte both said at once.

''Perhaps you should make a note of that, sweet Folly,'' Robert said. ''Who was seated next to Kent?''

As Robert and the comte went down the list, Lander added comments and asked questions about the reaction of each man. Folie took a memorandum, nibbling on sesame seed cakes and sipping tea. Late into the night they worked, until she had ten pages of closely written lines, and the clock chimed half past three.

"Mrs. Cambourne must be wearied to the bone," the false count declared, draining his wineglass and standing up. "When do you wish me to return?"

"Tomorrow afternoon will do," Robert said. "Lander and I will go over this list and single out the most interesting targets."

The comte bowed. "Until tomorrow, then. Mrs. Cambourne, I bid you good night."

Folie and Robert walked upstairs in companionable conversation. His mind seemed still intent on the evening's success—he easily answered her question about the next stage of their strategy. To Folie's surprise, he did not leave her on the landing, but followed her into her bedchamber in the midst of a sentence about the nuisance of gaining an invitation to the regent's upcoming levee.

They both paused inside. Folie saw him realize where he was; he hesitated for an instant and then walked forward, sitting down on her dressing table bench. "Have you been to one of the drawing rooms?" he asked casually.

Folie closed the door. She did not really know what else to do, as he appeared to intend to remain, at least for the moment. "Yes, it was the first charge upon us. So that Melinda would be 'out' in Society, you know."

"Ah. Of course." He picked up a small hair comb from her dressing table and made it vanish, opening his empty palm.

Folie smiled. "You are worse than a child."

He closed his fist again, and opened it magically on the comb. "Come here. Give me your hand."

She went to him and held out her palm. He placed his fist over it. Something fell into her hand—not the comb—but a tiny carved elephant of ivory.

"That is for you," he said.

Folie touched it. She turned the small piece over and bit her lip. "Thank you."

He shrugged. "I have trunk loads of that rubbish."

She held it in her lap, sitting against the edge of the high bed. "Perhaps it's an enchanted talisman."

"No, don't say that. It's too easy to lose the boundary between conjuring and enchantment." He shook his head. "I cannot believe everything has gone so well. It's as if nothing can go wrong."

"Are you worried?"

"No. Only about you. For me—I don't know, it's all rather . . ." He hesitated. "Lander and the magician—I don't even know his real name. They're good men. We work well together. It's as if . . ." He seemed to search for words, then opened his hands apologetically. "You know, I have never before had anything like this."

Folie tilted her head. "Like this?"

"*L'esprit de corps,* I suppose," he said. "That's what the army calls it."

"All this French! My head is spinning."

"Comradeship. Pulling together. Good fellows; they depend on you, you depend on them." He shook his head, as if it bewildered him. "It's dangerous enough, what we're up to—but my God, I had not realized . . . it is fun." He lifted his face. "In truth, I enjoy it!"

"You like the danger?"

"No. Not the danger itself, so much. That is just—spice. The thing that makes it happen. What pulls us together. Tonight, when we all stayed while you wrote out the notes—" He shrugged, turning to look into the cold fireplace. "I liked that."

Folie watched him, saying nothing. It was like watching a wild fox come out of the woods—she did not wish to startle him away by her response. He made a coin appear between his fingers, staring absently into space.

"I suppose I've been rather a solitary fellow in my life," he said.

"Yes," she said. "I know."

He looked up at her, as if that surprised him. Then he grimaced. "I wrote you about it."

"Knight errants must be solitary on their journeys."

''Ah, Folly.'' He sighed deeply. ''When do they end, these journeys?''

Their eyes met and glanced away. Folie felt that they had tread onto quaking ground, that in a moment she would betray her own little secret by blurting out the words to him.

''They end when you come to a halt, I suppose!'' she said brightly. She turned to the bed and slid her hand beneath the cushions. ''I'll keep the elephant under my pillow. Perhaps it is not enchanted, but one can never be too prudent.'' She faced him again, backed against the bed. ''Good night, my dear friend.''

''Yes.'' He stood up, looking at the floor and the bed and the dressing table, everywhere but at her. ''Good night, Folly. Sleep well.''

Twenty-Three

ROBERT FELT AS if he had caught himself in his own snare. He spent his days in mastering tricks and sleight of hand, his evenings in illusion, and his nights burning. Twice he had gone to Folie's bed, waking her and kissing her—gone that far, and known that if he went any further he would not be able to stop short of completion. So he had left.

It was supposed to be enticing her. Instead, it seemed to be merely driving him out of his mind. She welcomed his advances and calmly accepted his retreats. She did not complain, she did not grow irritable as he remembered he had done with Phillippa when she had teased him beyond endurance.

In the daytime, he could put it from his mind, in the same manner he had always put Phillippa away, forgot her while he was free to wander outside the sucking marshes of her will. Folie he did not have to forget in quite that way—in fact he liked having her about him; sitting at the secretary or the breakfast table scribbling down notes, asking questions, and making her whimsical remarks. In the midst of their most serious speculations, she would mutter some odd and entertaining thing, and he and Lander and the conjurer would smile covertly at one another over her bent head.

But at night—he fought his demons the same way he'd fought Phillippa. It was fruitless to pretend that he was cold, that he could practice the same sort of gull upon himself that he was attempting to lay upon the world at large. He had no mystical abilities, and he was growing more desperate for Folie each night. But he could not fail at either deception. He dared not. If society learned that he was a fraud; if Folie realized the power she could wield over him, how he could lose himself to her . . .

His mind always stopped at that precipice. *Don't think about it,* he commanded, and then stared into the black night as if it were a hole into Hades.

Still, things were going uncannily well. Every evening appearance he had made had been successful. Their notes now concentrated on who showed the greatest interest in him—who appeared regularly and watched him closely. Robert had begun to drop hints that his ''powers'' had been gained through a terrible transforming experience—something mysterious and formidable, nearly fatal. He had survived the ordeal, but it had changed him to the core.

He intended that whoever had drugged him should begin to fear that their potion had altered him in a way far beyond what they had intended.

How they would catch their quarry was yet a riddle. Just to identify him beyond doubt was the first step. They took each performance as it came, trying to winnow and interpret the subtlest of clues. Usually Robert was on his own, at social events that Lander and the conjurer must necessarily be excluded from, but after each affair they met together and went over every detail, with Folie writing it all down.

''The Duke of Kent is quite my favorite suspect,'' she said, perusing her notes in the breakfast room after Robert's appearance at the regent's levee. ''He appears to be perfectly sinister! Murdered his valet!''

''Beg pardon, ma'am,'' Lander said. He passed her the butter dish for her toast. ''But you mean the Duke of Cumberland. He's the one whose valet was found with his throat cut.''

Folie shook her head, crossing something out. ''I vow I cannot keep them apart. But Kent is the radical?''

''Indeed, yes. He has been corresponding with certain persons who advocate revolution as the only method of reform.''

''Lander,'' Folie said severely, ''however do you know what is in the poor man's correspondence?''

Lander pursed his lips and shrugged.

''I suppose it is no use to try to carry on any clandestine love affairs while you are about,'' she said with a sigh. ''Now, is it the last brother, Cambridge, who has been spreading talk of the regent's inheriting his father's madness?''

''Aye, that's Cambridge,'' Robert confirmed. He took a sip of coffee, looking over the top page of his newspaper. ''You were considering a clandestine love affair, my dear?''

''Yes,'' she said, scribbling, ''I intend to elope with the collier, the next time he delivers the coal. It is the only way I can see to get out of this house for some fresh air.''

''My favorite suspect would be Brougham,'' Lander said thoughtfully. ''If we could corner him.''

''Brougham!'' Robert said, startled. ''Lord Brougham? The lawyer?''

''He's a far-fringe Whig—though they don't sleep easy with him, I hear. He's brilliant. Ambitious. Leads the radical opposition. And he hates the regent.''

''Circumstantial evidence.''

''Still, I should like to see his reaction to you.''

''I don't know him,'' Robert said. ''He's not been in attendance anywhere I've yet gone.''

''I know. I heartily wish we could discover some way to arrange for a meeting.''

''How do you spell 'Brougham'?'' Folie asked, writing.

Lander spelled it for her.

''Would a party at Lady Melbourne's house be useful?'' she asked idly.

"Useful for what purpose?" Robert asked.

"It would be excellent, ma'am!" Lander said. "A grand Whig hostess—her soiree would be just the place we could hope to find Brougham."

"Ah." Robert nodded. "But how are we to persuade her to toss this soiree and invite me?"

Folie looked up. Humming a dramatic air, she held out one closed fist, running her other hand all about it, as if she were a stage magician proving there was no invisible trick. Then she turned her fist over and opened it.

It was empty. Hastily, she reached under her paper, pulled out a card and slapped into her open palm.

"There!" She held out the card, fluttering her eyelashes. "*Voila tout!*"

Robert took the card. " 'Lady Melbourne proposes to hold a select evening party in honor of the nuptials of Mr. and Mrs. Robert Cambourne . . . ' " he read. "Craves our indulgence, suggests time and date, wishes to know if we have any particular guests we should like to have invited."

"Now tell me that I am not a magician," Folie said smugly.

"Conjuring and French, too!" Robert said. "You make progress."

"Lady Melbourne sent it this morning. I was just about to write back with our excuses and refusal, being such an *obedient* wife." She made a face at him. He had not allowed her to accept any of the invitations that had begun to arrive with her name included on them. "However, in this case, I am afraid that if you are to have your party, you must have me, too."

"Why?" Robert asked casually, hiding a smile.

"Because!" she said, sitting up with a militant air. "It is in honor of *both* of us!"

"Just because you are Mrs. Cambourne! I doubt anyone wants to see you. It's the bridegroom they come to ogle at these affairs."

"Ha. Wait until the coal is delivered."

Robert stood up, folding the newspaper. He put his

thumb under her chin and tilted it up. "I would hunt you to Japan if you escaped," he said.

"Your hopeless sense of direction! We'll be running away to Newcastle, of course."

"Oh, yes. Somewhere off that way." He made a vague gesture.

Lander chuckled and shook his head. "That's west, sir. Newcastle is to the north."

Folie smiled sweetly. "I'd better leave you a map."

There had been no attempt yet to interfere with their comings and goings, but still Robert insisted on extreme care on the rainy night that they attended Lady Melbourne's evening party. In fact, he had Folie leave the house early in the day, with all of her paraphernalia, and go to a hotel. Since she could dress there with the help of a maid, she had no objection to it. She was ready precisely at half past seven, dressed in Melinda's made-over gown, when Lander arrived to escort her across the windswept pavement to a plain black carriage.

Robert waited inside it, looking quite handsome, Folie thought, in a snowy cravat and the dark blue coat he had worn at their wedding. He handed her a posy of yellow rosebuds.

"Thank you!" Folie said, pushing back her bedewed camlet hood. "How pretty they are." Then she did something daring, because things had been going so well between them in the past ten days since Lady Melbourne's card had arrived. She put her gloved hand on Robert's and leaned her cheek against his shoulder. The carriage took a turn just then, balancing her the other way, and she straightened and put her hands in her lap with the bouquet. Just that brief touch; he did not say anything, or return the contact—but she thought, in the dimness of the closed carriage, that his mouth curved a little in a half-smile.

Once they arrived at Melbourne House, the precautions did not have to be so severe. It seemed unlikely that even the most audacious of villains would attempt an abduction of the guests of honor in the midst of a party. Sheltered by the umbrella of a footman, Folie walked openly inside, received warmly by Lady Melbourne in her throne-like chair. They had arrived early, invited to a dinner before the assembly.

''I have a surprise for you!'' Lady Melbourne said with her throaty, pleasant laugh. ''Come out, Belle!''

From behind the Chinese screen, Lady Dingley stepped out, blushing and protesting like a shy girl. She held out her hands to Folie. ''Mrs. Hamilton!''

Folie gasped in pleasure, completely surprised. They clasped hands—Folie was amazed to find Lady Dingley, normally so reserved, pulling her into an impulsive hug.

''Oh, dear! I meant to say Mrs. Cambourne!'' she said, giving Folie a hard squeeze. ''I am so glad to see you! You cannot know—we were so worried! But—'' She pressed her lips. ''I shall say no more of that. When we received Godmama's letter, we could not possibly refuse to come!'' She gave Folie a significant look.

''Sir Howard is here, too?'' Folie asked.

Lady Dingley nodded, her eyes wide, as if it were a miracle. ''He's here! Waiting in the other room.''

''Then this is an honor indeed!'' Folie said. She turned to Lady Melbourne with a curtsy, forcing any unease about Sir Howard out of her mind, at least while she spoke to her hostess. ''I must thank you from my heart, ma'am! How good it is to see my friend!''

''Oh, that is not all,'' Lady Melbourne said, as mischievous as a gypsy. ''Perhaps Mr. Cambourne will meet some old friends too, in due time!''

Robert bowed and smiled politely. He did not appear to be overly gratified by this prospect, but Folie thought it would be quite interesting to meet old friends of his. But she wished that she might know what he was thinking of the Dingleys' appearance. It was entirely unexpected, and yet—what more natural than for Lady Melbourne to invite them?

It was not a large group—no more than ten sat down in the dining room, but Lady Melbourne's table could never be dull—she was too clever and experienced a hostess to allow apathy to enter the conversation. The other dinner guests were soon deep in a discourse upon Napoleon Bonaparte. It seemed odd to hear a gentleman like Lord Byron arguing that the tyrant was in fact an admirable character. Folie could not quite comprehend how a liberal-minded man could appreciate a despot, but she supposed that she must not be deeply shocked at anything bandied about in a dedicated Whig household.

Poor Sir Howard, she thought, took the disaffection and displeasure with the Tory government much harder. Though he said nothing, he was so red in the face with emotion that Folie almost felt sorry for him. His wife cast him frequent, dubious glances—Folie knew she must be terrified that he would lose command of himself, but he did not.

When Folie asked after all the girls, Lady Dingley went on at nervous length about her daughters. "And Sir Howard insisted that we bring Fanny and Virginia to town with us," she exclaimed, as if it were a great mystification to her that her husband would consent to travel with his two youngest daughters. "He says that they ought to learn to drive a gig in Hyde Park! Can you imagine? And Ginny is only just turned five!"

Robert and Sir Howard studiously ignored one another during this family gossip. Try as she might, Folie could not be afraid of him. In truth, Robert himself seemed far more sinister, with his black panther countenance and the way he kept a watchful silence, his gray eyes observant but impenetrable.

It had a strange effect on the table, his stillness. Gradually, Folie became aware that the other guests kept casting glances in his direction—as if they could not help themselves, the way one might cross a field with a bull on the far side—boldly enough, but keeping an eye out for any sign of movement.

"And what is your opinion of the matter, Mr. Cambourne?" Lord Byron demanded at last. "I understand that you are a diviner of the future. What will become of old Boney?"

"I am nothing of the sort," Robert said calmly. He looked straight at the poet, lifting his eyebrow.

"How unfortunate!" Lord Byron smiled. "Has Lady Melbourne brought us here under false pretenses?"

"I cannot say, as I do not know what those pretenses may be." Robert rested his fingers against his wineglass. "I thought the assembly was in honor of my bride." He lifted his glass toward Folie, smiling affectionately. "To my lovely Mrs. Cambourne . . . she walks in beauty, like the dusk."

As everyone hastily lifted glasses, joining in the toast to her, Lord Byron choked on his wine. He began to cough so hard that he had to push away from the table and rise. "Excuse me," he wheezed. "M' 'cuses!"

He walked quickly out. Folie thought that Lord Byron, supposed to be quite dark and dashing, looked rather foolish limping from the room. She thought Robert would make a far better Gothic hero in any case. He had certainly done a masterful job of putting to use the lines of unfinished poetry that Lander's emissaries had scavenged from a search of Lord Byron's rooms while he had been dining out the previous night.

Folie carefully did not look toward Robert, for fear that she would burst into exultant snickers. Instead, she turned to Lady Melbourne and assured her that Toot the ferret sent his regards and regrets that he could not attend.

Robert was aware of Byron's attention returning again and again to him as the rooms began to fill with guests. Folie stood beside him at the head of the stairs, accepting compliments and congratulations. He was trying to watch both Byron and Dingley; at the same time nod and smile to the line of arrivals filing past to shake his hand. He did not know a third of the names bawled by the servant at the foot of the stairs—all he was listening for was the announcement of Brougham's arrival. So when a vigorous voice hailed him, at first all Robert recognized was the accent of an old Qui Hai of Calcutta. He looked at the man who had just climbed the stairs and seized his hand—saw a handsome brutal face and the uniform of the 10th Bengal Infantry.

"Sly fox! Ran away back home, did you?"

Balfour. Robert's whole body reacted. Automatic shame fountained up through him. A numbness enveloped his brain. He stared insensate at the man who had cuckolded him with Phillippa.

"John Balfour!" the man said heartily. "Has it been so long you don't know me?"

Folie turned toward them. "Ah!" she said warmly. "Is this an old friend?"

As she dropped into a deep curtsy, Robert tried to fight his way from the nightmare deadness that held his tongue. "Mrs. Cambourne," he said—meaning Folie, of course, meaning only to introduce Folie, but in the instant that he spoke that name, Balfour looked into his eyes. Phillippa's image was like a burning ghost between them.

Robert could not speak. He shook his head.

"Major John Balfour, ma'am. We was garrisoned together for ten years and more! Marched all over India with this gentleman." Balfour seemed to be having no problem with his voice. But then, he never had.

Before Robert could marshal any hope of composure, he recognized the next guest laboring up the staircase, a white-haired old lion in a resplendent dress uniform. St. Clair. Robert was suddenly an ensign again, called up the hill for a thundering upbraid.

"Sir," he said. He lifted his hand, aborted the salute midway, and said stupidly, "General St. Clair."

"Shabby as ever," the general said with a great barking laugh. "This fellow was never meant for a military character, ma'am, I am sorry to tell you. Cambourne, you are a civilian to the bone."

He said it as if it were a joke. Folie smiled in appreciative innocence, not knowing that the general had just delivered a scathing insult to an army man. He gave Robert a fatherly slap on the shoulder, made an apologetic grunt, and bowed to Folie.

"Have you come recently from India, sir?" she asked.

''Ten days off the boat!'' he said. ''Retired! Can you believe it? I don't know what to do with myself.''

''You must come and visit us at Solinger Abbey,'' she said, to Robert's horror. She nodded toward Balfour. ''And you, Major Balfour. I long to hear more of India.''

''Thank you, my girl!'' St. Clair gave a crooked smile. ''Good of you.''

Robert was relieved that his old nemesis said nothing more positive in reply. Neither did St. Clair offer Folie any congratulations before he and Balfour passed on into the house. Robert fervently hoped he would never have to lay eyes on either of them again in his lifetime.

He had lost track of Dingley. Byron still lingered within view, the obvious target, ready to be plucked further. But even after Balfour and St. Clair had moved away, Robert felt shaken. He resolved to pass on any displays of his ''power'' tonight, then changed his mind and determined that he would not let unpleasant apparitions from his past deter him. The powdered servant at the foot of the stairs bawled, ''Lord Brougham!''

Robert drew a breath. He had to go on; there was no missing this opportunity, not for any mere failure of nerve.

Lord Brougham was tall and energetic, the sort of man who moved in jerky pauses like a live marionette. As he stared at Folie with an eye that was bright and wild, he reminded her of Toot, restive and eager to sink his teeth into something interesting.

She and Robert seemed to be the plaything he had targeted tonight. After they had greeted the guests and returned to Lady Melbourne's throne in the drawing room, he wasted no time in cornering them.

''The famous Mr. Cambourne!'' he exclaimed, booming in an orator's voice that seemed to catch the attention of the entire room. Folie could easily believe that he riveted a courtroom with his style. ''I've been intending to see to you for some time now!''

Folie took Robert's arm. She did not like this man.

''See to me?'' Robert said calmly.

"Look into this stuff and nonsense about divining thoughts and moving articles about the room. Come, prove it to me if you can."

Folie saw guests gathering closer. She noticed Lord Byron and Mrs. Witham-Stanley—and Lady Dingley, looking as white-faced and nervous as a rabbit.

"Sir," Robert said, hardening his jaw. "I have nothing to prove to you."

That was not what Folie had expected him to say. She had thought he would be anxious for a chance to perform before Lord Brougham.

"What?" Brougham asked. "You will not press these claims before a man of reason and intelligence?"

"I make no claims," Robert said.

"He never was worth a dog's damn," someone muttered among the guests. Folie saw General St. Clair shaking his head. "Stand up, man."

"Pshaw! Shame upon you!" Mrs. Witham-Stanley pressed forward. "Mr. Cambourne is not some quacksalver, who must trumpet his accomplishments up and down the street!"

"Ah! An advocate!" Lord Brougham bowed. "My dear lady, come and testify."

"With pleasure," she said. "I have myself seen Mr. Cambourne work several cures and discover dreams and thoughts."

"Aye." It was Lord Byron who spoke up. "He plucked a line right out of my mind," he said dryly. "I should like to know how you did that, sir! I swear I should!"

"It comes to me," Robert said. "It comes to me sometimes."

"What comes to you?" Lord Brougham demanded.

Robert ignored him. He stared at the poet. "Your work," he murmured. "It burns in your soul. It is—you have a strong light about you."

"I say." Lord Byron cleared his throat.

"Starry nights . . ." Robert said. "Midnight climes." He seemed to look very far away. "Beautiful and dark-eyed."

He smiled at the poet. ''Very beautiful. But you are not done with it.''

The celebrated Lord Byron shook his head rapidly. ''Good God. You make my spine tingle.''

''Oh, come now. Come,'' Brougham exclaimed. ''What are you talking about?''

Lord Byron drifted backward. ''If you want to have your hair stand on end, then let him look into *your* brain!''

''Nonsense. Stuff and nonsense.''

''My dear Brougham,'' Lord Byron said sharply. ''I am no more gullible than the next man. He has just related lines I've shown to no man alive!''

''Nay, I don't believe it.''

Byron gave him a cold look. ''Do you give me the lie, sir?''

Lord Brougham snorted. '' 'Tis Mr. Cambourne I might give the lie, eh?''

''Have a care, my dear,'' Lady Melbourne said. ''Mr. and Mrs. Cambourne are my honored guests.''

''Why, I thought you invited me for the prosecution, my lady.'' Brougham bowed deeply. ''I cannot see why else I should have received a card to this delightful affair.''

''I asked Lady Melbourne to invite you,'' Folie said. ''I hoped to have the opportunity to meet you.''

''Oh?'' Brougham turned his bright glance upon her.

Folie gave him a pert smile. ''Lord Byron should not have *all* the ladies at his feet.''

''I cannot but agree,'' he said. ''But do you say you have chosen me instead? May I expect impassioned epistles, madam?''

She curtsied. ''I shall write you pages of fervid admiration for your brilliant defense of Free Speech,'' she said demurely.

''A bold female you have here, Cambourne.''

''Cambourne adores brazen women,'' Major Balfour said, raking a bow toward Folie. ''Beautiful, brazen ladies.''

She felt Robert's arm tense under her fingers, but Lord Brougham was smiling like a mad cat. ''Now there is an interesting topic. Tell me, Mr. Cambourne, if you can discover my thoughts—do I like or dislike impudence in a woman?''

A silence fell. Folie was not quite certain if they were being deliberately insulted or if this was only meant as the sort of bloodthirsty flirtation that some London dandies favored. Robert's face was stone.

''Give me a few of your cards,'' he said. ''I'll write it down.''

''You've only to tell me. Look into my mind!''

''Nay, what is to be proved by that? I'll write your answer, and then you write it yourself, and we shall compare.''

Lord Brougham smiled. He put two fingers inside his waistcoat pocket and drew forth a card case, flipping it open and holding it out. ''Take all you like.''

Robert took several visiting cards. He turned them over and wrote on one of them inside his palm. He turned and handed the card to Lady Melbourne. ''If you will hold this, madam, without looking at it, so that no one may say that you aided me somehow. Now, write your own answer, sir.''

Lord Brougham chuckled. ''Is this a yes or no question?''

''Write what you think, sir—do you like impudent women?''

The lawyer shook his head, writing, carefully concealing his pencil behind his hand. But Folie noticed now what she would not have before—that Robert stood just a little in front of Lady Melbourne, so that it was perfectly natural for him to take the card from Lord Brougham and pass it to her between two fingers, keeping the card face down, so that he could not see what was on it.

The guests pressed closer, craning to see. His friends from India were part of the audience, looking even more absorbed than Robert himself, who seemed to Folie to be in an unsettled mood, as if Lord Brougham's aggression angered him.

''Let us get it all over with at once,'' Robert said, ''because you will say this is only luck. Your mind is hot with challenge—so give me another. Something that may be written down in a word or two, so that there is 'proof.' " He sounded slightly disdainful. "It is solid evidence that you prefer, is it not?"

"All right. Tell me then, in what year did I begin school?"

Robert looked at him, then at Mrs. Witham-Stanley, who was standing anxiously beside Lord Brougham. He smiled, more amiable with her. "Are you thinking of a year too, ma'am?"

"Oh!" she said. "Oh, yes, I am—the year I married! I am so sorry! Does it interfere?"

Robert grinned and handed her a card. "Write it down." He waited until she did, then took the pencil back. He wrote on two cards, looking first at Mrs. Witham-Stanley, then in turn at Brougham as he did it. He waited for Brougham to write his answer, and collected all the cards to pass to Lady Melbourne.

"There, ma'am. You may turn them over and show them to us."

Lady Melbourne turned up the cards. On the first pair, "1788," in Robert's handwriting matched "1788," in Mrs. Witham-Stanley's. The lady gasped, and several of the guests standing about murmured appreciatively. "Amazing! How close!"

But Folie saw that Robert frowned slightly at the cards. He glanced up, patently uneasy to Folie's eyes, as if he expected that the audience must see through this. "The next pair, please ma'am," he said in a stiff voice.

On this pair, Lady Melbourne displayed, "1784" in Lord Brougham's strong hand, and "1788" in Robert's. Folie saw him look warily toward Brougham.

"Humpf," Lord Brougham said. "I cannot call that a match."

The spectators began to dispute among themselves whether 1784 and 1788 could be called a very close approximation.

"Why, Mrs. Witham-Stanley, you are as strong as government interference!" Folie said gaily.

This brought a shout of laughter, but she could see that Robert was disturbed. He did not take his eyes off of the last two cards in Lady Melbourne's hand as she turned them over.

No was writ large on Lord Brougham's card.

And on Robert's, the word *Perhaps.*

The guests groaned.

"A clear miss," Lord Brougham said. "Two out of three missed—I do not think I can call this very impressive."

"It is true, then, Lord Brougham?" Folie asked, turning down her lips in a saucy pout. She put her fingertips on his arm. "You really dislike impudent women?"

"Oh, perhaps," he said, smirking back.

A look of self-surprise crossed his face. His brows snapped together.

The spectators were silent for an instant, as if absorbing his reply. Then they burst into hoots. "A match! A match! A clear match!"

But Robert looked far from happy. He ignored the congratulations, shaking his head, disengaging himself from the guests who squeezed around him entreating to have their thoughts divined.

Twenty-Four

''YOU WROTE 'PERHAPS'?'' The conjurer shook his head with a baffled look. ''Whatever did you write 'perhaps' for? With yes or no, you'd have at least an even chance of a hit.''

''I don't know why,'' Robert said. He sat in a half-lit corner of the drawing room, working a deck of cards on the table, cutting and shuffling aimlessly. ''I lost my concentration. Besides, it made no difference at that point.''

''You'll always hit two out of three with that trick, if it's done properly. And you have even odds for that third hit if you confine the answers to yes or no.''

''I didn't even make the first two marks,'' Robert said sullenly. ''Ask Folie.''

''I thought it was quite successful,'' she said.

He cast her a skeptical glance, riffling cards past his thumb.

''You hit Mrs. Witham-Stanley's anniversary perfectly, and even if the school year was a bit off—you certainly caught him out with 'perhaps'!'' She made a disdainful snort. ''He was obviously lying when he wrote his answer down—but you snared him anyway.''

''Snared him!'' Robert bowed the cards between his fingers until they burst into a chaotic pile. ''My dear girl, I started into that trick and realized halfway through that I had it entirely backwards.'' He ran his hand through his hair. ''My God, what a bungle. In front of Brougham, too.''

''It was not a bungle,'' Folie said. ''I don't know why you insist that it was.''

He gathered up the cards and went back to shuffling.

''It was not a bungle,'' she said to Lander and the conjurer.

Robert blew air through his teeth. ''Don't patronize me,'' he said in an ugly tone.

''I am not—'' Her voice choked. ''Well, never mind. I don't know what is wrong with you.'' She went to mending her pen with clumsy strokes, her head bent over the desk.

Well, so he had upset her, Robert thought brutally. Best that she discover the truth now. He was not the clever, brave and heroic fellow that she—and Robert himself—had begun to suppose he might be.

Never was worth a dog's damn. If Robert had not supposed he was beneath the brigadier's scorn, he would think St. Clair had intentionally made that mumbled insult loud enough for Folie to hear.

But it was for the best, no doubt, that his old commander had casually set the record straight. Everything had gone so perfectly—so terrifyingly well. It was a fantasy that he could not sustain. And yet Folie's disillusionment was more than he thought he could bear.

I don't know what is wrong with you. How many times had Phillippa said that to him?

''We shall have another go at Brougham,'' Lander said. ''From what you describe, Mrs. Cambourne, he was more than ordinarily belligerent. We'll goad him into a misstep if we can.''

''A challenging adversary,'' Robert's tutor said soberly. ''You'll have to keep your wits more about you the next time.''

''I do not propose that there will be a next time,'' Robert said.

He began to play solitaire. Silence reigned.

''Sir?'' Lander asked uncertainly. ''You are not serious.''

''Deadly serious. I am putting a halt to this. Tonight.''

''I do not understand you. A halt?''

''No more of these tricks and exhibitions of sham powers. I'm done with it.''

''Why, because you botched one trick?'' the conjurer exclaimed. ''Grow up, my boy—you'll botch ten thousand more before you're through.''

''No doubt I would,'' Robert said coolly. ''But I am through now.''

''But we're making amazing headway—'' Lander protested. ''And from the way Mrs. Cambourne says you saved that trick with Brougham—they must be frothing at the mouth to discover the truth of things.''

''If it's your courage that fails you, my friend,'' the conjurer said, ''you needn't worry that they'll try to rid themselves of you again. Just consider—if their drug has given *you* the second sight, they'll be terrified that it could do the same to the Prince Regent. They'll have to know for certain—and your life is secure until they do.''

''I'm not in fear of my life,'' Robert snapped. ''The whole thing is a stack of cards, that's all. It will never work.''

''It has been working. Everyone but the poor mad king himself knows of you now,'' Lander said. ''We're closing in on our quarry.''

''No we aren't,'' Robert said. ''We've nothing but mist and smoke to show for our efforts. Tell me one concrete fact that we have discovered.''

''Brougham wants you discredited. Badly.''

''So?'' Robert snorted. ''He appears to be the sort of man who lives to discredit everyone but himself.''

''Sir Howard Dingley—why was he there?''

''Yes, I thought something great of that myself,'' Robert said dryly, ''until Folie informed me that his wife is Lady Melbourne's goddaughter, not to mention the person who introduced her at Melbourne House. What more natural than that the Dingleys are invited guests to a party in Folie's honor? It would be strange if they weren't."

"Did Dingley say anything to you, ma'am?" Lander asked Folie.

She shook her head. "Nothing out of the way. He acted as if nothing had ever happened." She wrinkled her nose. "Though I would vow I could still smell the river on him."

"In truth, sir," Lander said. "I do not think we ought to change our strategy now. We would lose all that we've gained."

"*What* have we gained, Lander?" Robert demanded. "I am now a trained bear for the hostesses to exhibit. If there is a plot against the regent, we know nothing specific of it, not who or what or where or why." He slapped a card down. "Like as not the whole idea was no more than a demented illusion. You saw me—you and Folie did. Can you say I was in possession of my reason? It was dementia. A natural dementia, no doubt, and I'll be fortunate if I don't end up bound in a strait waistcoat like the old king."

"The prison ship was no dementia," Folie said.

"A coincidence," Robert said. "We were robbed in the park. They could not let us go, so they dumped their victims aboard that ship, rather than murder us outright."

"How kind of them!" Folie said. "What of the note that I wrote to Sir Howard?"

He gave an ironic laugh. "I cannot say I trust your memory of that incident any more than I trust my own reason. We have no clear idea of how that note came about."

"The apron," Lander said. "The maidservant's apron."

"A hallucination."

"Sir—" Lander said.

"Better to stop now, before we create a real debacle." Robert stood up. He tossed the cards left in his hand onto the table.

"Just stop?" Lander demanded. "Just throw away what we've accomplished?"

"We've accomplished nothing!" Robert's voice rose.

"We are on the very brink," Lander exclaimed, jumping up from his chair. "I know we are. I'm no greenhorn in these matters. I can feel it."

"Nonsense," Robert said.

"Nay—it is not. There are clues enough, outside of what we've been doing. Something is afoot among the worst of the radicals."

"I can't go on—I'll make these mistakes." Robert shook his head. "You have to understand that. I'll blunder it."

Lander gave him an incredulous look. "Are you afraid?"

"I am not afraid," Robert said savagely.

"It seems to me that is what you are saying."

"Then let us meet at dawn, and I'll show you that you're wrong!"

"Robert," Folie exclaimed. "Listen to yourself!"

Her appalled voice made him pause. He realized that he was standing with his hands clenched, his whole body ready for combat. Lander had squared his shoulders, as if in unconscious response.

Robert made a dismissive gesture. "I beg your pardon," he said coldly. "I misspoke myself."

Lander relaxed his hands. He pulled at his waistcoat, as if he did not quite know what to do with them. "Myself also," he said. "It is just that I am—surprised. Sir."

Disappointed, sir, Robert heard unspoken.

"Very well," he said stiffly. "You are surprised. I bid you all good night."

He left them in the drawing room and mounted the stairs. Inside his bedroom door, he tried to light a candle and burned himself on the brimstone match. Caught between shame and anger, mortified by his own excuses, he fiercely wished himself in some remote wasteland, where any mismanagement of his own could touch nothing and no one. Some cold mountain pass where there was only wind and ice. Someplace where the best companions he had known in his life could not be disappointed when he failed them—and Folie would not be there to see it.

Rain pattered on the window. Robert stood in the dark. He felt Phillippa in this room. Phillippa and Balfour. It was imagination and madness, he knew that. But he did not try to light the candle again—it was as if he might illuminate the bed and find them entwined there.

The walls of the house seemed to press in upon him. He had to get away. He had to be gone.

"By Jove," the sharper said, "it appears as if our cock won't fight!"

"This is unexpected." Lander looked troubled, glancing toward the door where Robert had left them. "I think I must make a call on someone. Immediately. Ma'am—I'll leave Martin in charge. If you need anything, you may apply to him. I should return in a few hours." He nodded to his companion. "Come, I'll drop you on my way."

Folie lingered in the drawing room long after everyone else had left. She listened to the rain fall gently.

If she ever understood Robert Cambourne, she thought, she would be fit to go touring as an all-seeing magician herself. He was without a doubt the most bewildering, perverse, and distressing man on three continents. He came to her with a man's desire and left her burning. He teased her like a sister in the day and kissed her at night as a lover—demanded that she plead for more, and then withdrew. It was as if he wanted to strip her of her every defense, as if he could not be content to leave her alone, but kept himself barricred within his own castle walls.

Or as if he were wandering in some impenetrable forest. She thought of that moment in her bedroom, when she had held her breath, keeping silence so that she would not startle a wild creature as it cautiously showed itself. Something chary and magical, like a unicorn—a fleeting glimpse of a white shadow half hidden in the depths. Something that was not quite entirely feral, something that yearned to come forward and eat from her offered hand. And yet with every step forward, the distrust grew, until the creature came so close and feared so much that no desire could hold it beside her—it shied and bolted, lost in the darkness.

That was what his letters had been, she realized now. Letters from her unicorn man, dreams and love at a safe distance for them both.

A part of her wished to flee him. He might be beautiful and lost, but he was dangerous, too—wielding his cutting words, as sharp as that mythical twisted horn, each one a well-placed laceration. He knew exactly how to wound.

She thought that if she stayed with him, she would bleed to death from a thousand tiny cuts, delivered over years of holding out her hand for those brief moments of enchantment.

And yet . . .

She remembered Melinda, an unhappy, angry, grieving child. How hard it had been, how hard, to accept the unfair indictments and complaints, to meet a deliberate stab with a gentle reply. How hard to cherish her difficult stepdaughter, and how much worth it in the end.

To be loved, you must love. Folie did not know where she had heard that. It came into her head; a simple truth, an arduous lesson—something that it seemed she had always known.

She could not shout or scream or burn down the woods and expect her unicorn to draw near. As long as they were both afraid, he would not—could not—leave the wild, dark woods. As long as she did not trust him, he would hide himself.

She could leave him there. Or she could offer her love—openly and without defense—hold out her hand and be still, and trust that he would come.

Robert stood under the dripping eaves, leaning against the house. The tiny back garden smelled of stable and wet bricks. He thought of walking out the gate into the mews, of vanishing into the night.

It was an old and tempting invitation. He knew alleyways and corners. He knew strangers and the sound of street music. He knew what it was like to have no destination and no time he must return.

No reason to return.

He could go now. Robert Cambourne could disappear. He did not know where or how far he might go. America, perhaps. China. Study the natives, take notes, sit down at a desk and suppose that he would begin his book very soon.

He could leave Lander and the Prince Regent and

Brougham and the radicals to their own devices. He could leave Folie to live in splendor at Solinger Abbey and spend all of his money that she pleased. She was welcome to it. She would be safe enough once he was no longer near her.

Perhaps he would send things to her now and then. Something pretty and exotic, to please her. He would write her letters as he used to do, and tell her of everything he saw.

But he must get away. He must go. It was as if Balfour and St. Clair had come to him as messengers, demons pricking him with reminders of what he had begun to forget. Flushed with success, he had begun to believe in this new mask of his, but it was a charade. She would find him out.

He heard the back door open. Lander, no doubt. Robert did not turn his head to look, but only shoved his hands deeper into his pockets and stared into the dark. He could not defend himself further—if the man called him a coward now, Robert could only nod and depart.

"Robert," she said. Folie's soft voice made him turn toward her in consternation. She paused on the step, coming no nearer to him. "I want to tell you something." Her voice sounded ghostly, echoing in the walled space. She wore a dark cape, her figure a graceful sweep against the silver slips of rain.

"Yes?" he asked gruffly.

"I have been thinking of what you said tonight. That you believe you should stop this—intrigue."

He squinted into the dank shadows. "So?" he said.

"I just wished to tell you that—whatever you may decide— that—" Her voice seemed to get lost in the soft chime of a gutter that spilled water onto the bricks between them. "I cannot seem to put this quite as I mean it, but . . ." She cleared her throat. "You know—whatever you decide is best—you will not lose me as a comrade."

They stood three feet apart. Robert listened to the water as it ran. He could not seem to bring any words to his throat.

He heard her take a deep breath. ''I love you, Robert,'' she whispered. ''Very much.''

His chest began to hurt. No one had ever said that to him, but he could not tell her that. In one sentence she could reduce him to beggary. Make him think that he could not even breathe without her.

''Sweet knight,'' she said. ''Your armor will rust if you stand in the rain.''

There was a tiny quiver in her voice. The pain in his lungs grew deeper. He swallowed and scowled. ''Well, it is my armor, is it not?'' he said roughly. ''You needn't concern yourself.''

The water gurgled in the rain gutter. From the corner of his eye, he saw her pull the cloak closer about her. ''I suppose not,'' she said in a quiet voice.

He waited for her to go away, driven off by his rebuff. She would. It was necessary and inevitable, and he could bear it better now than later. The accusation and tears; a woman's contempt—or worse, this soft, slow whisper of disappointment that scored his heart into ribbons.

''I think you are all frozen up in rust already, sweet knight,'' she said, with an odd, unexpected note of affection. ''You stand here stupefied because none of your joints will move.''

Robert gave an ironic laugh. It struck him as one of those things an Indian saint could say—so utterly true that it laid his whole life before him in a single picture.

''I'm going for a walk,'' he said abruptly.

''A walk? Now?''

''Yes. Go inside.'' He didn't wait to see if she obeyed him, but pushed away from the bricks and strode out into the rain. He thrust his key into the lock of the garden gate, pushed out, and heard it clang shut behind him.

The narrow alley lay ahead, overhung by the black bulk of houses and garden walls. At the end, a street lamp threw light onto the pavement, rain-slicked and puddled, like a shining path that led into mist and darkness.

• • •

It had been midnight when he had left—at one in the morning Folie was still sitting up in her full party dress, waiting to hear that he was safely back, and cursing every chance she'd had to stop him somehow.

Lander had not returned, either. Martin, the rather ponderous footman left in authority, had all the helpful instincts of a willing dog, but unfortunately not much greater intellect. He did not know where Lander had gone, and could not think of a way to contact him, but he would be happy to bring ma'am all the trays of tea and cakes that she could hold.

Folie started up in her chair at the sound of a carriage drawing to a halt outside. *Robert,* she thought. He might have hired a cab to bring him back. When the doorbell rang, she rushed to the top of the stairs.

But it was neither Robert nor Lander. To Folie's shock, when Martin demanded identification of the nocturnal caller, it was Lady Dingley's shrill voice that answered through the door.

While Martin stood looking nonplused at the sound of a woman pleading entry in the middle of the night, Folly ran down the steps. The note in Lady Dingley's muffled voice was frantic; Folie could not leave her stranded on the doorstep in the rain. She opened the front door carefully, peeping out. The carriage was pulling away. Her friend stood alone on the steps, a forlorn and trembling figure.

''Come in!'' Folie urged. ''Quickly! What is it? Are the girls all right?''

''He has turned me out!'' she wailed, stepping into the hall in soaking wet slippers. ''Oh, my God, what am I to do?''

''Out? What—''

''Oh, I hate him, I hate him! He—he—has—another—'' Her words fragmented into choking sobs. ''Cannot bear—sight of . . . me!''

''Come upstairs.'' Folie took her dripping cloak and held it out to Martin. She put her arm around Lady Dingley's heaving shoulders. ''Bring us some brandy,'' she said to the footman as she guided her friend to the staircase. "And some handkerchiefs."

In the drawing room, Folie pulled two chairs close to the fire. Martin floundered in with a decanter and glass, clearly enervated by the sight of a hysterical female. Lady Dingley kept attempting to speak, but each time her face would crumple into misery and she sobbed so deep in her chest that no sound emerged, like a child weeping with such force that it could hardly draw breath. Her face was red and white.

"There," Folie said, patting her hand and pressing the brandy and a handkerchief into it. "Take this. Be careful now—not too much at once."

Lady Dingley gulped the brandy, wincing heartily and gasping. "Oh, dear!" But it seemed to break the hold of the sobs upon her. She sat with her head down, breathing jerkily, and then took another large sip. "I hope I drink myself to death!"

Folie bit her lip. She knelt beside the chair. "I'm sure it is not so bad as that."

"It is. It is."

Folie did not press her, but only stroked her hand and waited.

Lady Dingley lifted her tearstained face. "I am sorry to disrupt everything this way." Her voice squeaked upward. "In the middle of the night!"

"It's quite all right," Folie said. "I was not in bed, as you can see."

"I h-had nowhere else to g-go." She swallowed convulsively. "He said . . . he said—oh, terrible things . . . I said I would *leave* if that was how he—I said *you* would take me in—and h-he said . . . I'll *drive* you there!"

"The beast," Folie said gently.

"Yes!" she cried. "He is a beast! Oh, you don't know. You can't know. Don't get married, Mrs. Hamilton, it is an awful thing."

Folie did not remind her that the dreadful deed had already been accomplished. "He has not hurt you, has he?"

she asked. "He has not . . ." She left the sentence unfinished.

"No, he does not beat me," Lady Dingley said, sitting up a little. "I—no—but . . ." She sniffed. "That is not the only sort of hurt a man can do to his wife."

Folie said nothing. She squeezed Lady Dingley's hand.

"What did I do wrong?" Lady Dingley moaned. "I don't know what I did wrong."

"It is not your fault."

"I loved him so much! That was what did it. I loved him too much. It's not a good thing, for a woman to be in love with her husband. Oh, but we used to be . . . it was so . . ." She made a whimpering sigh that turned into a sob. "And now he has . . . some horrid . . . some awful—g-g-girl!"

Folie handed her a fresh handkerchief. She wished that she had Sir Howard at the point of a sword.

"I don't know what to do," Lady Dingley cried. "I don't know what to do."

"You can stay here as long as you like," Folie said soothingly. It was only after she said it that she realized that it might not be such an excellent idea—still, at least for tonight, it must do.

"But the girls." Lady Dingley blew her nose. "When they wake up, they'll want me."

"Where are you staying?"

"At that h-hideous Limmer's Hotel. I hate it! And he said the girls must have their own room—probably because he *knew* he was going to shout at me until I could not endure it! It was as if he meant to do it! As if he would not be satisfied until I s-said I would leave him!"

Folie remembered that Limmer's was where Sir Howard always stayed. She sat back on her heels, wishing desperately that Robert or Lander would come back. The later it grew, the more her nerves tightened. She should never have let Robert walk out that gate, never. It seemed insane now.

The doorbell rang again. Lady Dingley drew in a sharp breath, but Folie was already on her feet and running to the stairs. ''Robert?'' she called, halfway down, before Martin even made it to the front door.

A heavy fist pounded on the door. It rang again.

''Hurry!'' Folie cried, thinking it must be Robert in danger. ''Open it!''

Martin flung wide the door. Sir Howard stood in the rain, his hat brim dripping. ''Please,'' he said, without stepping inside. He looked up to where Folie stood on the stairs. ''I wish to speak to Lady Dingley.''

Folie stood rigid. She was not at all inclined to let him in—but the door stood open, and suddenly he took off his hat.

''Oh, God. Let me see her.'' His voice was strained, hardly even audible.

''All right,'' Folie said coldly. ''You may stay a few moments.''

''But, ma'am—'' Martin said.

Folie knew she should not allow Sir Howard inside. But the look upon his face was nothing calculating—it held as much unhappy desperation as his wife's.

''Close the door,'' she ordered. ''Be quick. And keep close watch for Mr. Cambourne's return. I'm frightened that he's been gone for so long.''

''Yes, ma'am,'' Martin said unhappily. ''I've sent to Mr. Lander to tell him Mr. Cambourne's gone missing, ma'am, but nothing comes back.''

''They are not here?'' Sir Howard asked, pausing with his hand on the newel post.

''Not at present,'' Folie said briefly. ''But you may see Lady Dingley in the drawing room. And I will just mention, sir, that she is welcome here at Cambourne House as long as she likes to remain.''

He put his head down and mounted the stairs. Folie went ahead of him, and made him wait in the passage while she went in to warn his wife.

Lady Dingley met her news with wide terrified eyes. ''Stay with me!'' she whispered. ''Don't leave me.''

''Yes—all right.'' Folie opened the door and beckoned to Sir Howard. He came inside, holding his hat between his hands. As Folie closed the door behind him, he turned quickly.

"Cambourne is not here?" he asked.

Folie kept her hand on the door knob. A new note had entered his voice—something in it made the base of her spine tingle.

"No," she said. "You did not wish to see him, I presume?"

He stood facing her, not even looking at his wife. His mouth was pale; quivering. Folie's heart began to pound in her throat. She could see his hand behind his hat—hidden.

"H-howard?" Lady Dingley said unsteadily.

He turned his head. But still he did not move, or take his eyes from Folie. She wondered if she could pull open the door and race out fast enough to escape him.

"Are the g-girls still asleep?" Lady Dingley asked in a small, shaky voice.

His face worked, his mouth tight and his eyes wide. He began to look as wild as a silent madman. He stepped forward, seizing Folie's arm just as she yanked at the door. His hat rolled away on the floor, leaving him holding a gun openly, but he did not aim it. Instead he squeezed her arm until she squealed, the pistol clutched in his white fist. He was panting like a dog. "You're hiding him!" he exclaimed. "Tell me where he is!"

"I don't know!" Folie cried. "He left the house! He is gone!"

Sir Howard stared at her. As Folie watched, a disintegration seemed to overtake him. His menacing stiffness failed; he let go of her. His limbs seemed to give way—he fell to his knees on the floor.

"Oh, my God," he whispered. "God save me."

"Howard?" Lady Dingley whispered. "What is it?"

He shook his head, lifting the pistol in his hand, covering his face.

"What is it?" Lady Dingley cried. "What is that? Put it down! Put it down!"

Folie held her breath. Sir Howard knelt on the floor, the

gun at his head. She saw his hand tighten on the handle, aiming the muzzle toward himself.

''Howard,'' Lady Dingley said, in a voice that had suddenly gone icy and clear. It was as if someone else in the room had spoken. Some voice like a cold angel, a ruthless guardian. ''You cannot do that. Your daughters need you.''

Sir Howard began to shake all over.

''We need you,'' his wife whispered, her own quavering self again.

Sir Howard make a choked sound. He closed his eyes and laid the gun down on the carpet. Silent tears ran down his face.

''Please,'' he mumbled. He opened his eyes and looked up at Folie. ''Please help me. I can't do this. My little girls—'' His eyes widened again and his jaw grew rigid in that maddened look. ''I need help!''

''The girls?'' Lady Dingley asked, her voice peaking to a panic.

He never took his eyes from Folie. ''They have my little girls,'' he said, barely audible. ''I have to bring Cambourne back.''

''Who has them?'' Lady Dingley cried. She grabbed her husband's arm, dragging at him. ''Who has them?''

Folie stared back at him as a clear, terrible understanding dawned. ''You came for Robert,'' she whispered. ''You staged this all to get in.''

''What?'' Lady Dingley tugged at him frantically. ''What is it? Who has my girls?''

''Quiet!'' Folie said, dismay adding a biting command to her voice. ''Get up. Get up and tell me everything.''

Sir Howard rose, ignoring his frenzied wife. ''I must have Cambourne by dawn,'' he said. ''They are holding the girls until dawn.''

Lady Dingley turned to Folie, gone mute now, holding her husband's arm with a grip like death.

''I tried to refuse,'' he said. ''I told them I'd have nothing to do with it. I never from the beginning wanted anything to do with it!''

Folie gazed at him, her body as still as the silent street outside.

''Please help me,'' he said. His voice broke. ''I have tried to handle it; I thought I could handle it. I never wanted Belle to find out. I could handle it alone. But they just—whatever I do, they want more.'' He looked down at the gun at his feet. ''I could not do this. I told them I would not do this. But my girls. My girls.'' He made a deep sob and closed his eyes. ''Pray God, please help me.''

''Yes,'' Folie said. Her mind was racing wildly. ''Let me think.''

Twenty-Five

THE SALE HORSES at Tattersall's Repository dozed and nibbled hay and snorted softly. Even deep in the night, the trading stable was alive with gentle rustling; now and then the deep thud of a hoof sounded against a stall partition. Robert sat on a stool tilted up against the wall, watching the night grooms roll dice and clean leather tackle.

He was not the only gentleman who had wandered in out of the rain. In the far corner, two drunken young lords leaned against one another, having fallen fast asleep in the midst of an argument over what horse had come in fifth last season in the Hundred Guineas at Ascot. A veterinarian came in and out, checking every hour on a horse that seemed like to colic, shooting dice in the intervals to keep himself awake. The grooms addressed a nod and a civil word to whoever rambled in, and scrupulously avoided any illicit monetary bets on their devil's bones.

Robert had spent a thousand nights this way, sheltered among tolerant strangers. He had not gone far away from Cambourne House—his retreat had taken him only as far as Hyde Park Corner, a few streets off, before rain and hard reflection drove him to take cover in the auctioneer's stable.

He sat there a long time, locked in his rusted armor. The image she had evoked was so vivid that he felt almost physically frozen, benumbed and unable to move.

He had fallen in love with his sweet Folly so long ago that it hardly mattered when it had happened. Fallen in love with her stories of wayward geese and pigs, with her dreams of knights and her embroidered "R. C." on a handkerchief—with the way the stitches were not quite even toward the right-hand side, as if she had grown impatient to finish and send it off. He had fallen in love with her fears and her sorrows, her life that had come to him through her letters—in love with a grown woman who called in a solicitor's office with an evil-tempered ferret wrapped in a shawl.

There was so little in all of that to fear, and yet he was terrified. It was as if his heart skidded down an endless drop and he could not see the bottom.

Are you afraid? Lander demanded, with such an unbelieving look.

Of course I'm not afraid, Robert thought hotly.

But he was. Afraid of failing. Afraid of falling back into madness. Afraid of losing Folly.

So what did he do? He failed his task. He claimed the madness for reality—there was no plot, no enemy; only his irrational mind. He walked away and left her. Point by point, he insisted that what he feared must be the truth, even if he had to make it true.

But still he sat frozen, caught between going away and going back.

A gray tabby cat slipped into the stable and moved among the shadows, keeping close to the wall. The animal was missing an ear and walked with the stiff hind legs of advanced age. Its fur was drenched, its white paws muddied.

The horse doctor murmured, "Kitty, kitty," but the cat only glanced at him warily and sat down at the edge of the light. It began to groom itself carefully, starting with its remaining ear.

"Kitty, kitty," the doctor said again, gently. The cat gave him an aloof look and moved farther away, into a half-lit corner.

''Cool old campaigner,'' one of the grooms said. ''Won't have no truck with a kind word.''

Sitting alone, the cat worked its fur. When it had cleaned and dried itself, it looked out from its safe corner, slowly waving the tip of its kinked tail.

When the veterinarian had gotten up again to examine his horse, and the grooms were absorbed in their game, Robert felt something rub against his leg. The old tabby leaned against him. It began to purr.

Robert pushed it away with his knee. In response, the cat lifted a white paw and tentatively touched his leg. Then with a graceful spring it came into his lap. It curled up and lay down, purring so loudly that he could feel the vibrations in his belly.

He picked it up and deposited it on the floor. The cat, undaunted, rubbed its leg and rose on its haunches, placing both front paws on its thigh.

''No,'' he said irritably. ''I can't keep you.''

The animal ignored him, leaping up into his lap again in sublime confidence. He thought of Skipper, lost—he thought of Phillippa; he thought of Folie.

I love you, Robert.

I can't keep you.

I can't keep you; I can't bear to lose you. It's because I'll lose you that I can't . . . I can't . . .

Rusted. Rusted solid in his armor.

Robert looked down at the old cat settling in his lap. Lander was wrong; his magician-tutor was wrong. It was not his life Robert feared to lose. It was his life that he feared to live.

Folie's stomach had that quivery, light, sick feeling of too little sleep and too much tumult. But her mind was abnormally clear. She sat in the carriage, blinded by a scarf about her eyes, her hands bound in her lap.

The rain had stopped. As the vehicle drew to a halt, she heard a distant watchman call two o'clock. Sir Howard laid his hand over hers and gave a hard squeeze. ''Are you ready?''

Folie nodded in return. He held the muzzle of the unloaded pistol against her ear. She could feel it trembling. Once they had embarked upon their program, Lady Dingley, with the difficult role of staying behind to await Robert or Lander, had undertaken her task with a rigid determination. She was a mother intent on saving her children, and Folie did not fear for an instant that she would crack. Sir Howard was another matter. He was gone beyond logic or judgment, like a man half-drowned, allowing himself to sink the last time without even attempting to struggle. But Folie's plan of action and Lady Dingley's determined self-possession had seemed to rally him. Folie could only hope that he could hold up to play his part.

A wash of chilly, damp air rushed into the carriage as the door opened. The vehicle rocked a little. Strong hands grasped her arms and pulled her forward. Someone clapped a palm over her mouth. Folie took a deep breath and did not resist. She was half-urged and half-dragged down onto the pavement. In utter silence, her unseen captors hustled her up the stairs.

Inside, the building smelled of dust and linseed oil. They did not take her far—turning her into one of the rooms on the ground floor. The sound of footsteps echoed on a wooden floor. Folie stumbled against a table and gave a little sob. A hand on each arm steadied her. They pressed her forward.

"Stairs," Sir Howard said. "Down."

One by one, she descended three steps, feeling forward with her foot like a blind person. In fact, she could see quite well once there was sufficient light—her blindfold was a trick that she had learned from Robert's conjurer, a scarf rolled and tied just so about her head. The bindings on her wrists were not impossible to escape, either.

She was led up another set of steps and seated by her captors on an odd sort of pedestal. A strong, bright light shone down from above, though she could not see its source through the slit in her blindfold. Before her rose several tiers of seats and tables—a studio classroom for artists, lined by rows and rows of plaster busts mounted on the walls. The windows were shuttered and sealed. Scattered about the room, half-finished canvases leaned against easels, casting long, rectangular shadows over the drapery of Greek statuary.

The Royal Academy. Folie felt a small flicker of relief—Sir Howard had told the truth of that much. But still, her shakiness was not completely feigned. She might have walked into this voluntarily, but she was frightened beyond her wits. There was no predicting what would happen—her plan ended with giving Sir Howard a captive to trade for his daughters. And hoping that Robert or Lander would find some way to rescue her.

''What the devil have you done, Dingley?'' a man demanded in a low voice. It was vaguely familiar, but Folie did not recognize it. With her field of vision limited, she had yet to see who else was in the room. ''Where's Cambourne?''

''I had no choice,'' Sir Howard hissed. ''But we have him. Mark my words. This is—''

''I can see who it is, damn you!''

''I had no choice,'' Sir Howard repeated, more agitated. ''He wasn't at the house.''

''You've hashed it, Dingley.''

''No. When he returns and finds her gone . . .'' Sir Howard let his voice trail off suggestively. ''I left him a note. That he'd hear from us.''

A silence met this information. Folie turned her head, lifting her chin slightly to give herself a clear view.

Her eyes widened behind the bandage. It was one of the Indian officers she had just met at Melbourne House—the younger of those two old friends of Robert's. She could not remember his name . . . something Norman or French.

''My daughters—'' Sir Howard said.

''We'll have to see what he says,'' the officer muttered. ''I've sent for him.''

Who? Folie wanted to cry. *Who would do this?*

''How long will it take?'' Sir Howard demanded. ''I want my daughters safe. I was told they would be safe.''

"You were supposed to bring Cambourne," the other man said.

"We can get to him easily through her. It worked before."

"Yes, true," the officer conceded. "But a bird in the hand, my friend, is worth two little girls in the bush, I should say."

"You blackguard," Sir Howard exclaimed. "I hope you burn."

"Well, I don't want anything to happen to 'em either. You should have done what you were told."

"For God's sake! I tried!" Sir Howard passed in and out of Folie's view, walking in jerky strides across the studio floor. She realized that she was seated on the model's pedestal in the center of the room. "You said to get into the house! I got in! He wasn't in the damned house!"

"Maybe he knew you were coming," another man said. Folie involuntarily turned toward the new voice. St. Clair. General St. Clair, she remembered that one's name. He was sitting in the second row of the student tiers, his white hair curled and gleaming, the harsh light casting shadows in the wrinkles on his face. He chuckled deep in his chest. "Maybe he divined your thoughts."

"Don't say that sort of thing, sir," the younger man said. "It's not wise."

"Fiddle of a rod, Balfour. Cambourne's a buffoon."

"Aye, that's so. But you don't know what that concoction might do to a man."

"It ain't going to turn a clown into a sharp," the general said dryly.

"*He* isn't so sure," Balfour replied.

"If Cambourne's transformed into such a clever fellow, then why'd he leave his wife alone, hmm? To own frankly, it'd be just like him to forget all about her and wander off to watch some *fakir* levitate goats. Swallowed so much of that mystical pap that he's begun to believe he can do it himself."

"Aye," the younger man said bitterly. "I hate him. The way he treated her."

''She were none too kind to him,'' the general said.

''She was an angel,'' Balfour said—and Folie realized they were speaking of Robert's late wife.

''I'll say she was an angel to look upon,'' St. Clair agreed. He nodded in Sir Howard's direction. ''Had all the young fools like Balfour here at her feet. But I never saw such a strange temper as that girl had.''

''Women,'' Sir Howard said hollowly.

''There be women and women,'' the general said. ''Phillippa Cambourne was a devil's daughter.''

''That's not true!'' Balfour exclaimed. ''You did not know her heart.''

''What about the fire?''

''She did not start that fire! That's a damned lie. Cambourne spread that lie.''

Folie could see the white-haired general shake his head. ''Nay, that's one thing he didn't do. I had my best *jemadar* investigate. Her own *dubashee* swore he saw her put that candle to the foot of Cambourne's bed—''

''A cursed native!'' Balfour's voice held a high note of fury. ''A sneaking servant! It's a lie. It's a lie!''

''Shut up,'' Sir Howard said. ''Keep your voices down.''

''Aye, he's right. You hold your wits about you, Balfour. I hope she went straight to Heaven, if it makes you and him happy, but that's all water under the bridge.''

Balfour muttered something Folie could not understand, but he said no more. She sat still, folding and unfolding her fingers in her lap. It was the first report she had ever heard of Robert's wife—the first time Folie had even learned her name. The strange conflict in their description of her seemed in keeping with the insanity of everything else.

A clock struck half past two. They waited in silence for whoever was to arrive.

Robert, Robert, she thought. She squeezed her fingers together and closed her eyes, praying that she and Sir Howard had done the right thing.

But what choice had there been?

• • •

In the shades and phantoms of the studio, the artworks seemed to have a frozen life of their own. Each time someone moved in the room, their long shadow flickered motion across a plaster hand or made a portrait seem to shift. The largest work was a great canvas or paper mural tilted against the wall, the life-size cartoon only partially sketched in pencil. It appeared as if it was to be a battle scene, with a horse and officer in the foreground, though Folie could not make out the drawing clearly enough to be sure.

The clock had chimed another hour when she heard a door open and close. A man with a white scarf tied over his mouth and nose came into her vision. He gave no greeting, only walked up to the mural and stood it upright, balancing it in some way she could not discern. He turned toward them, made a slight, ironical bow, showing nothing of his face for the scarf and his hat pulled low over his eyes.

The door opened again, and a slightly built figure walked into Folie's line of view, a man of some age—possibly older than General St. Clair. He carried a cane with an ornate silver head, but walked nimbly, disappearing so quickly behind the huge canvas that she did not get a clear view of him, but she thought she had never seen him before. Another man, taller, his face disguised by a scarf like their escort, followed him into seclusion behind the screen. Their guard stood attentively beside it.

"Mrs. Folie Elizabeth Cambourne." After a moment, the pleasant voice came from behind the canvas. It could have been the voice of any distinguished older gentleman she had met at any drawing room or soiree or Wednesday night ball at Almack's. "A most unusual name."

She looked straight ahead, without answering.

"Cambourne wasn't in the house," Sir Howard said quickly. "But we can use her to lure him."

"Mr. Cambourne is certainly a slippery fellow."

"But he'll come after her," Sir Howard said. "He'll come after her, when and where we tell him to come."

"I'm a little disturbed by his absence. Might it be one of these tricks of his?"

"How could it be?" Sir Howard's voice rose and cracked. "I took her out of the house at the point of my gun. The servants meant to stop me if they could."

"You were not followed?"

"Of course not. We drove around London five times before we came here. I'm no fool!" Sir Howard said. "I've done your dirty work. Now give me my daughters and let me out of this."

"Your daughters are quite safe," the man behind the canvas said.

"You told me that—"

"You ought to have brought Cambourne to us, my dear Dingley, and these points would not be at issue."

"I could not—damn you!" Sir Howard's voice quivered. Folie held her breath, but he managed to get control of himself. "I've brought you the bait. Set the trap for him yourself."

"We appear to have no choice now," the guard said, his voice harsh even through his mask, "thanks to your mismanagement."

"Mr. Inman," the man behind the canvas chided his guard gently. "Even you could not successfully breach the house. Do not throw stones at Sir Howard. I think the situation can be turned to good account."

Inman, Folie thought. It was the man Lander had called a terrorist. She thought of the smallest Dingley girls and felt as if she could readily hold a gun between his eyes and pull the trigger. It amazed her that Sir Howard did not do it.

She heard herself speak, a breathy, scared pitch. "It's my husband you want," she said. "If you let Sir Howard go away with the children, I'll do what is necessary."

No one answered her. It was as if one of the statues had come to life, they all seemed so startled by her words.

"Bravely spoken, madam," the gentleman behind the screen said. "Perhaps we can work with that."

"You must let him have the children. Or I shall do nothing. I shall lie to you about everything. You will not get what you want short of murdering me."

"Which is not at all what I desire to do," he said. "Give me a moment to consider what will be best for all concerned—"

A thunderous echo arrested his words, the crash of wood splintering, a door exploding open. Metal tinkled as it hit the floor. Folie jumped so hard at the smashing sound that she pulled one hand free of her bonds. Through her mask she saw Robert standing in the doorway, his pistol trained into the room.

Quickly she stuffed her wrist back within the rope, her breath harsh and frantic. Robert was here, Robert was here. She swallowed a gulp of air, trying to keep her sense and watch for what she ought to do.

But there was nothing she could do. While he stood in the door, before he even spoke, before Folie could cry out a warning, a man stepped into view behind him. His face was hidden like the others, wrapped in black. He held a gun to Robert's head.

In an instant, her hope of rescue turned to irretrievable calamity. Folie's throat closed with fear.

"Cambourne!" Improbably, General St. Clair began to laugh. "Good God, man, did I never teach you to watch your flank?"

Robert sent an agonized glance toward Folie. Gradually, reluctantly, he lowered his pistol and gave it up to the man behind him.

"Robert?" Folie asked uncertainly, as if she could not see him. She had no need to dramatize to make her voice sound fearful. She could barely force it from her throat.

"Come in!" said the elderly voice from the screen, ironically cordial. "Mr. Robert Cambourne, is it? Just the gentleman we wished to entertain."

Robert's captor prodded him with the gun. He walked forward, down the steps, stopping below her pedestal in the center of the room. Folie had been sure he would not come alone—that he would bring Lander or at least Martin—someone, anyone, to guard his back.

Surely he had not tried to come alone. Yet he stood under the bright studio lamps with his face lowered, as if he were ashamed, except for a sideways glance like a dagger toward the Indian officers.

''The honorable John Balfour,'' he said, his lip curling. ''I knew you would be here.'' He lifted his head and stared at Sir Howard. ''And Dingley, of course. I should have left you to rot in the bottom of that bilge.''

''Ah, but this is precisely what we must discuss with you,'' the man said from the screen. ''What you know—and what you don't know.''

Robert turned toward the screen. ''Ask me,'' he said shortly. ''If you suppose it will do you any good.''

''Then tell me,'' their unseen enemy said, ''how came you to find us in this place?''

Robert gave a dark chuckle. ''I looked.''

After a short silence, the man said, ''Lives are at stake—your charming wife's among them. How did you come here?''

Robert shook his head a little. ''I knew. I looked.''

''Dingley told you!'' Balfour exclaimed suddenly. ''How else?''

''I told him?'' Sir Howard said on a squeak. Then he snorted convincingly. ''Do you suppose I'm a fool?''

''I hope you are not,'' General St. Clair said. ''But perhaps you might take his gun away, Balfour. In case.''

''Oh, you're all quite safe from Dingley,'' Robert said, as Balfour reached for Sir Howard's gun. Robert made a quick motion with his hand, as if he caught a fly from the air. The masked guard behind him thrust the gun into his back, grunting a warning, but Robert only opened his palm. A white powder-wad and a leaden ball lay in it. ''I've unloaded his pistol for you.''

Sir Howard gave him a look of consternation. Robert held out his hand and let the ball and wad tumble from his palm onto a table next to him.

''You've unloaded it, eh?'' Balfour said, lifting his chin in challenge. He aimed the pistol at Robert. ''You'd better hope.''

''Hold your fire!'' the general snapped. ''You young jackass.''

"Nay, go ahead," Robert said, staring at Balfour down the pistol's muzzle. "I know what's in your mind." He smiled slightly. "So kill me. For Phillippa's sake."

"Balfour!" General St. Clair half-rose from his seat.

"I do not want him killed," the hidden man said loudly. "For the moment."

Balfour narrowed his eyes and shrugged. He lifted the gun, aiming just above Robert's head, and pulled the trigger. Folie's muscles contracted involuntarily.

The hammer fell with a dead click.

"*Johnnie,*" a woman's voice whispered.

It was so soft and unexpected that Folie was not certain that she had really heard it. But Balfour's head turned sharply. He looked up toward General St. Clair. "What was that?"

"What was what?" the general said, scowling.

"That voice!"

"Voice!" the general grumbled. "Don't let go your grips, my dear fellow."

"It's Phillippa," Folie said. "Robert! I heard her!"

"Inman! St. Clair." The man behind the screen spoke sharply. "Inspect the room. Be quick about it."

While Balfour stood staring up after them, the two men mounted the tiers into the shadows of the studio, their feet thumping heavily.

"It was Phillippa," Folie said, allowing her voice to rise, trembling. "I heard her, Robert. I heard her again."

He looked toward her. Folie lifted her hands, as if she were straining at the bonds, and made the brief, simple hand gesture that the conjurer had taught them, the one that signified, *I'm ready, go ahead.*

He showed his teeth and laughed, raising his voice on a strange wild note. "Phillippa, my darling wife! Of course she's come. Look who's here to greet her!"

The screen shook, as if someone took hold of it with an invisible hand.

"There's no one here," General St. Clair said in a loud voice from the dark heights of the room.

"*I want . . .*" The woman's ethereal whisper came again,

loud enough to be unmistakable this time. ''*I . . . want . . .*''

The yearning sound of it was ghastly. Folie felt the hair rise on her neck. She did not mean to let the illusion take her in too, but when Balfour made a strangled sound in his throat, she could hardly blame him.

''Cambourne!'' Balfour exclaimed savagely. ''Stop!''

''Do you think I can stop it?'' Robert asked. ''You gave me this genius. This is what it's done to me. I can't stop it now.''

''What genius, Cambourne?'' the man demanded from behind the screen. His voice was harsh and strained. ''Do you claim you can call the dead?''

Folie's heart was beating rapidly. She stared down at Robert and the man who held the gun on him, ransacking her brain for more hints to give out of what little she knew. As she looked, she noticed the guard's sandy-colored hair under the black scarf and hat—realized that a long queue was tucked down beneath his collar.

Lander.

Robert laughed, the sound echoing crazily. ''Call the dead? The dead call me. I can't get away from 'em now, or what they tell me.''

She swallowed, closed her jaw and lowered her face. Through her unmoving lips, she said Lander's name. He did not seem to hear her. Folie was afraid to raise her voice more. ''Lander,'' she whispered, barely enunciating each syllable under her breath. ''Say—you—smell—smoke.''

''What do they tell you?'' the hidden man asked, his voice strangled and loud, as if the words were choked from him.

''Nay, sir—'' Another voice spoke from behind the screen, authoritatively calm. ''This must be nonsense. I've never known any such thing to occur before with this drug. Never.''

''Examine him, examine him! That's why we're here!'' The elderly gentlemen seemed frenetic, almost as if he might weep. ''Lord! Oh, Lord.''

''Doctor,'' Robert said, as a tall man emerged from behind the canvas. The man paused, lifting his concealed face.

"The prince . . . the prince . . ." The woman's moan whispered through the shadows of the room. *"The prince . . . must go mad . . ."*

Nothing—no one—moved as the sound died away.

"Come and examine me," Robert said invitingly. "Come and discover what you've done."

"What I've done?" the tall man demanded.

"What you've made of me. You don't know what you toy with." Robert shook his head. "Who told you about that potion, little Englishman? It's not meant for an unknowing mind. It should have killed me."

"You tested it, Varley!" the elderly man quavered from his hiding place. "You said it worked on him! It was only to make him lose his wits."

"Aye, it made me lose my wits!" Robert said fiercely. "I see dreams. I hear voices. I'll never be what I was before. I can do things now—I open my empty hand and something is there. I look at a thing and it moves toward me. And I hear Phillippa when she comes. You should have given me enough to kill me, but it's too late now."

"Drawing room tricks," the doctor sneered. He swept away the bullet and wad from the table.

"Varley!" the man cried helplessly behind the screen. The canvas rocked. His hand appeared, gesturing excitedly with the cane. Silver light glanced off a pair of dragon heads on the handle. "Are you sure? What have you done? What if it does the same—"

"Quiet! I've not given the prince as much. Not nearly as much," the doctor said quickly.

Folie saw Lander stiffen. He butted the gun several times into Robert's back, a gesture so obvious and excited that she was amazed no one detected it.

Then Lander drew a deep, audible sniff. He turned his head, covering his face and pulling at his mask as if he drew it away from his nose. "Balfour," he said in a troubled tone. "Do you smell smoke?"

"No—" But Balfour's face changed.

Robert's face contorted. His breathing quickened. "She's

burning,'' he said through his teeth. ''She's always burning.''

''Lord, oh Lord,'' the old man moaned. ''What have we done?''

''Look!'' Lander exclaimed, staring toward the top of the room. Folie watched every man in the room succumb to a trick even a child knew. While they turned to the shadows, she saw Lander lean against Robert's back and whisper in his ear.

Robert's body went rigid. For a long moment, as the others searched the top of the room, he did not move. Even when Balfour said, ''I saw it—I saw it!'' Robert did not speak or react.

''What did you see? What?'' the man behind the screen shrieked.

''I've seen nothing, I smell nothing!'' General St. Clair exclaimed. He strode toward Folie. ''I think this woman's naught but a ventriloquist!'' The next she knew, St. Clair tore the blindfold up off her head. With a firm hand, he retied it about her mouth. ''Now let us see if dead women speak!''

Folie looked helplessly down at Robert and Lander. Robert slowly shook his head. ''Nay, sir,'' he said, almost as if he felt sorry for the general's ignorance. He seemed distracted now, lifting his hand in a dismissive gesture. ''She will speak to her papa. She'll tell the truth.''

''No!'' The canvas vibrated. ''Phillippa!''

''Papa!'' the woman's voice whispered through the room. *''I'm in Hell.''*

''Noooo, Phillippa.'' The gentleman gave a terrified sob. ''My little girl. My little girl.''

''I'm waiting for you, Papa. You will . . . come . . .''

The sounds from behind the canvas were wretched. Everyone listened, transfixed, as the man there snuffled and moaned. ''Don't, don't. I must not!''

''Come to me here . . . Papa! Come . . . burn with me!''

''It's unnatural, child; I must not, I mustn't,'' he muttered, a hideous gibbering to himself.

''The truth . . . Papa!''

"No, don't tell, don't tell, my sweetest, don't speak of it! You love me! You love me too much!"

"The truth . . ." the woman's voice whispered. *"The truth . . . only you and I . . . know . . ."*

"You must not tell!" the old man screamed.

"I'm dead, Papa . . . I'm burning. You must say it, Papa . . ."

"It's unnatural sin, I must not. Unnatural, unnatural—Phillippa darling, my darling girl, my sweet."

Inman backed away from the screen, staring at it. He came to halt against the desk near Sir Howard, never taking his eyes from the canvas frame.

"Tell it, Papa . . ." the voice whispered inexorably. *"Tell them what we know . . ."*

"You are a wicked temptress!" he shrieked. "I'll kill you if you tell!"

Folie was riveted, gazing at the screen like everyone. But when Robert made a wordless noise, she looked down and saw that he was moving his head back and forth, as if he were denying something.

"No," he said, taking a step back. "No. Stop. *Now.*" He turned to Lander with a wild look, as hunted as the hidden man seemed to be.

And to Folie's bewilderment, Lander nodded. Just at the moment she was sure the old man was about to confess everything, Lander turned. He aimed his firearm toward General St. Clair, who was standing next to him. In the same instant, Robert had a gun in his hand, pointing it toward the doctor and the canvas screen. Sir Howard glanced back at them as it all happened—instantly he seized his unloaded pistol from the desk and swung his arm in a wide arc, slamming the butt into the back of Inman's head, following with a vicious kick. Inman stumbled into the screen. It tilted and swayed as he dropped, hit the wall and bounced, falling back upon him in a smash of canvas and wood as it came down.

No one moved. A corner of the broken frame revealed a small gentleman who sat with his hands folded tight together over his cane, his head bent, rocking back and forth and mumbling to his dead daughter as if he did not even know the screen was gone.

Lander whistled a shrill signal. While Inman groaned, the door opened and the room filled with scarlet-uniformed guardsmen and tough-looking fellows in red waistcoats. It all happened so quickly and quietly that there was no sound but the thump of boots on the wooden floor and the old man's plaintive whispering.

"What's the meaning of this?" the doctor said loudly, but no one answered his bluster as a Bow Street Runner fastened handcuffs about his wrists. The two Indian officers did not say anything at all. The entire arrest proceeded in silence, as if everyone had been struck dumb.

"Is it done?" the whispery woman's voice asked.

"It's done, ma'am," Lander said firmly.

"Where are my girls?" Her voice rose to a dreadful chilling note, reverberating all around the room. *"Find my girls! Are they hurt?"*

"I'd never hurt you, darling," the old man said, lifting his face.

"Your daughters are safe, Lady Dingley." Lander looked up from conferring with one of the guardsmen. "They have been located upstairs. Sound asleep."

Sir Howard tilted his head back and released a long breath. He sank onto a chair, burying his face in his hands.

"Our thanks to you, m'lady," Lander addressed the air. "You were superb."

No one answered him. Folie pulled her hands free of their loose bonds and yanked off the stifling scarf. From the corner of her eye, she thought she saw Lady Dingley's figure hurry past in the dim passageway outside.

As two guardsmen took the old man's unresisting arms and escorted him toward the door, Robert stood still, watching. He said nothing. But his face was white and set. There was nothing of triumph or relief in his expression. He looked instead as if he were watching someone drown before his eyes.

Twenty-Six

"I DON'T QUITE understand," Folie said, as they waited in a carriage outside the Royal Academy's premises in Somerset House. The streets held the first hint of dawn, a rain-soaked gray, with wisps of smoke from a few chimneys rising somberly into the clouds. "I rather thought—Lander wished for a confession? It seemed as if he was near to confessing. That little man."

Robert and the conjurer sat opposite her. Robert gave her a stiff smile. "Lander will do whatever is required, I'm sure."

Folie looked in bewilderment at the conjurer. He nodded reassuringly. "Once the subject's will is broken, ma'am—it shouldn't be difficult to discover the details of his crimes. I'll wager that's what Lander and his men are about at this moment."

"Oh," Folie said.

There was something she was not being told—something in Robert's and the conjurer's manner that caused all the rest of her questions to die in her throat. She understood that the elderly gentleman was Phillippa's father—Robert's own father-in-law. She understood that Robert would be shocked and grieved to discover who his enemy had been.

It must be as if one's own family had turned traitor and foe.

"I really think that he is not quite sane, Robert," she said. "Whatever he has done to you—I think it must have come from a sort of sickness in his mind."

Robert gave her a look, a long, intent glance, as if he wished to see inside her head. Folie looked openly back at him, puzzled.

"To me?" he said. "What he did to me?"

"Well, yes," Folie said, tilting her head. "The drug. And the prison hulk. Sometimes, you know, when people grow old, their minds become feeble. In general, it is not a vicious change, but I think your father-in-law fell in with wicked men. Perhaps he became confused, and grew malevolent towards you."

He studied her face. Then he smiled faintly, shaking his head a little. "Folly," he said. He turned away to look out the window. "You do not know how much I need to know you are in this world."

The carriage rocked as Lander climbed inside. He pulled the door closed, sitting next to Folie, and yanked the check-strap to signal the driver. The horses began to move, pulling away from the curb into a street that had to come to life with early morning traffic.

"The duke is not able to speak rationally," he said without preamble, "but we've cobbled together quite a story from what we've got from the others." He nodded toward the conjurer. "You were brilliant, man. How you discerned so quickly that Lady Dingley ought to play that daughter role instead of Mattie's voice—" He shook his head. "It was a deep stroke. I could believe you are a mind reader in truth. We could not have planned it."

"The early play with that Balfour fellow," the magician said. "Mr. Cambourne fed us his first name—John. That was nicely done, sir—always deal out as much information as you can in passing. And the antagonism—" He shrugged. "Well, one may conjecture these things. I could see that there was considerable emotion about the name

Phillippa. And again, Mr. Cambourne let us know just who she was.''

''But where were you?'' Folie asked.

The conjurer smiled. ''In the service passage,'' he said. ''While Mr. Cambourne kicked down the door, I took the opportunity to remove the handle to the service door. If you were to look, you would find a very elegant brass knob fallen on the floor just behind the podium where you sat, ma'am. With a little private science worked on the other side, the lock case made a nice sepulchral voice box.'' He looked pleased with himself. ''Also, we were blessed with a fortunate acoustic. We could even hear you whisper about the smoke, ma'am. So I suggested to Lady Dingley that she talk a bit about burning.''

''So what of the plot?'' Robert asked abruptly. ''You've found it out? And how the devil did you discover who was behind that big canvas?''

''Ah!'' A slow grin broke across Lander's face. ''I'm not so slow at the small details myself. His cane!''

''Very sharp,'' the conjurer said in an approving tone. He nodded. ''Very sharp of you.''

Lander laughed. ''Sharp indeed! I first saw that double dragon's head when I was still in short coats. One of my brothers stole it for a lark, off a gentleman who was visiting at Hursley. Got a whaling for it, delivered by the very gentleman in person, with his dragon stick. I'll tell you, for a week after, my brother had a pair of dragons' heads tattooed on his—'' He glanced at Folie and paused. In the growing light of day, Folie could see him redden. ''Ah. Well. It was the Duke of Alcester, you see.''

''Your brother stole the Duke of Alcester's cane?'' she asked, her eyes widening. ''My gracious, Lander—no wonder you're so wretched at domestic service. You have not the family temperament for it.''

He looked at her as if she had spoken in some foreign language. To clarify her point, Folie added, ''Perhaps next time you ought to impersonate an army officer, or something more suited to a bold and enterprising nature.''

"Thank you, ma'am," he said solemnly. "I shall consider your advice."

"Shall I buy you an officer's commission, Lander?" Robert asked, grinning. "God knows I owe you that much."

"Perhaps I'll ask you for a different favor, sir," Lander said, "at a more salutary time."

"You'll have it." Robert sat back on the seat. "But you were about to tell us what you've learned."

"One plot," Lander said, "but several aims among the plotters, it would appear. This potion—or powder, rather—is some Indian brew used to induce religious visions, I gather. I'm not certain where the duke obtained his information about it—"

"He had a number of correspondents in India," Robert said. "He and my father were great cronies, and I know he had other friends high up in the Company. He used to put his money in some Indian and Chinese ventures, when my father advised him."

Lander nodded. "Yes, sir. Your father did well by him, it would seem. But after your father's death, he seems to have gotten into some very bad investments."

"He wrote me. Afterward. Kept commanding me to increase Phillippa's allowance." Robert frowned. "I just told the secretary to give her whatever she wanted without ruining me entirely. But I wonder . . ."

"Perhaps she sent funds to her father," Lander said.

"Yes . . ." Robert rubbed the shadow of beard beginning to show on his chin. "I did not pay it much mind—but . . . ten thousand a year. Even she could not have been spending so extravagantly on herself."

"Ten thousand a year?" The conjurer made an overly dramatic face of astonishment. "You did not pay it much mind, sir?"

"I did not spend a great deal of time at home," Robert said shortly.

"It makes sense," Lander said. "Perhaps, sir, after your wife passed away, he could no longer appeal for money from that source."

"Oh, he appealed," Robert said dryly.

"Just so," Lander said. "If you did not endear yourself to him by obliging with funds, he may not have felt much compunction toward you. He made some desperate financial moves—the details remain to be seen, but they must have been extreme, because his goal appeared to be the entire destruction of the East India Company."

Robert swore softly. He nodded. "The charter."

"The charter. Up for renewal before Parliament and Crown. By controlling the Prince Regent, he meant to see the monopoly broken. No renewed Company charter ever signed by the Crown—or, at least, delayed until the shareholders tore the Company apart."

"So he was drugging the Prince! Just as Robert said!" Folie exclaimed.

"Yes, they'd infiltrated this Dr. Varley into Carlton House, and begun to administer their potion, just enough to cause the headaches that the excellent doctor knew precisely how to cure. They felt sure they knew how to measure their dosage—having tested it thoroughly on you, sir, before the first drop of the stuff ever left India. They knew how to induce visions and how to decrease the measure to relieve the hallucinations without the—subject—regaining his full acumen."

Robert closed his eyes and laid his head back. "A test."

"Yes, sir. I'm sorry, sir."

He drew a deep breath. "I don't even remember. I remember her funeral. Time after that . . . a long time of just . . . everyday sorts of things." He opened his eyes and looked briefly at Folie. "Drifting, I suppose. As if I did not know what to do with myself. But I could not tell you when those visions began. Or how I ever got out of there."

"You simply vanished," Lander said. "General St. Clair believes you had friends among the natives, who discovered your plight and spirited you away."

"Mr. Ramanu," Folie murmured.

Robert nodded slowly. "Perhaps. Yes."

"By that time, the duke had gotten Mr. Inman as an accomplice," Lander said. "Which changed the color of things considerably. The duke's intentions ended with blocking the charter, but Inman claims he was not going to be satisfied with less than the whole ruin of the Government. He's talking all sorts of mayhem—I think that clip on the head has dissolved whatever prudence he ever had. He despises the duke. But he could not waive a chance to make the Prince Regent go mad as his father did—he's even hinted that there may be another plot, still in motion if we can't track it down, to assassinate the Prime Minister. Throw the Government into complete chaos."

No one spoke for a moment, absorbing this alarming news. A stray dog ran alongside the carriage, barking fiercely until they outpaced it.

"I would not have believed it," Robert said. "My God. There were times when I was certain I must be insane, that it could be nothing else."

Lander nodded solemnly. "Aye, sir. And they meant to keep it that way. After you got away from them in Calcutta, they were intent upon tracking you, since they couldn't be certain of what you knew, or might piece together. Once you made it to England, the duke insisted that you must be kept under the influence of the drug, to prevent anyone from taking you seriously if you did talk. You may thank General St. Clair for your life, because Mr. Inman thought that killing you would be much the simplest—they got into quite a dispute over it again just now. But at any rate, the general seems to have prevailed." Lander scowled, an unhappy expression darkening his square face. "I do not know quite how he became involved in this—he has a reputation as an excellent officer—but I suspect that he was in on some of the duke's more—questionable—investments."

"Blackmailed into it," Robert said.

"Most likely. The prison hulk was his notion . . . Inman says even now that all three of you ought to have been 'eliminated' at Vauxhall."

"Eliminated!" Folie said, sitting up and leaning forward. "And Sir Howard!" she said fiercely. "He did pass that note to Robert, to lure him there, but I cannot conceive—why did he help them, even a jot?"

Lander shook his head. "I can only conjecture at this point, ma'am. I think . . . perhaps . . . the maid, you know." He gave her an embarrassed look. "Mr. Inman went to Solinger searching for someone he could coerce. I think—uh—that Sir Howard did not wish for his wife to—um—discover his—mistake."

"Oh," Folie said. "Yes. I—yes." She blushed. "I see."

"How love will make a fool of a man," Robert remarked.

"I do not think he made that 'mistake' out of love!" Folie said indignantly.

"No," Robert said. "But perhaps if he'd been less in love with his wife, he'd not have been so beef-witted as to knuckle to the likes of Inman just to keep her from finding out."

"I suppose she'll forgive him," Folie said, with a small frown. "Even now."

"Well, of course," Robert said dryly. "Anyone but Dingley could see that. Which is why he's a beef-wit."

"And I suppose you would shout it to the whole town rather than submit to blackmail, if you made the same mistake."

He lifted one eyebrow. "I do not intend to make that particular blunder, my dear."

"Good," Folie said. She swept a regal glance about the carriage. "Perhaps you have all learned a salutary lesson from Sir Howard's distress."

"Distress!" the conjurer said. "I should call it torture, myself."

"Purest agony," Robert said.

"I cannot even imagine the pain, ma'am," Lander added humbly.

"Yes, and I happen to know that you are all three incorrigible, irredeemable frauds," she replied with a snort. "You need not suppose you can bamboozle *me*!"

• • •

Cambourne House seemed silent, almost unfamiliar, as if everything that had happened since she had left for Lady Melbourne's party had changed the house—and herself—in some irrevocable way. No one answered the door when they walked up the front steps. All of Lander's hefty footmen were gone. Entering in the marbled hall, with its white pilasters and elegant chandelier, Folie felt like a child in a bedraggled party dress, wandering in off the street.

She was not even certain, suddenly, if she was quite welcome here. Lander had not left the carriage with them, but gone on to make his report in Bow Street. Folie paused as Robert pulled the front door closed behind them.

"Gracious," she said, with a little laugh. And then felt exceedingly foolish.

They both stood awkwardly, as if someone ought to tell them what to do next.

He looked down at her from beneath his dark eyelashes. "You must be tired," he said.

"Oh, yes. Though I vow if I laid my head down I could not close my eyes. I must write a letter to Melinda. Or—or perhaps I should—I suppose—" She could not seem to reach the tail of the sentence. "Is it safe for me to return to her now?"

"You wish to?" he asked.

"I wish to see her as soon as I may."

"I'll take you there," he said. "If that is what you would like."

Folie looked about at the staircase and the hall as the echo of his voice died away. She ought to be exhausted—she was—and yet the sun was coming up.

"We are free, Robert," she said wonderingly. "How strange it seems!"

He had a fleeting way of smiling at her—she had always felt it, but just now recognized it as a particular smile, a strange tender amusement on his satanic features. The way a demon would look, she thought, if one ever caught it smiling with affection. "Yes," he said. "We're free."

"I do not know what we will do with ourselves."

"Take you to Melinda. Go and get your things."

"Now?" Folie felt consternation. "But—you are not too fatigued?"

"I'm no more ready to sleep than you. There is nothing to stop us. Besides, after ruining her season, the least I can do is present her with an excellent *partí* as a suitor."

"A suitor! Who might that be?"

"What do you think of Lander?"

"Lander?" Folie squeaked. "I beg your pardon! He will not do!"

"But I owe him a favor," he said.

"A favor! That is nothing to the point. I'm very sorry, but it is quite out of the question. I have never wished for her to marry a—an earl, or a marquess, or any such thing as that, but I cannot countenance her marriage to a man so far beneath her."

"He seems perfectly gentlemanly."

"Perhaps so, but what are his prospects? His connections? Why—where would he take her to live? In Bow Street? Has he spoken to you about it, or is this some absurd scheme of yours?"

"I am her guardian, you know. I think Lander might do very well."

"She will not have him!" Folie said.

"You do not think she ought to be the one to decide?"

"That is precisely what I mean. Melinda is far more of a stickler for her position than I am, I warn you! Why, she would not even consider him! It is very kind of you to think so much of Lander, and I'm sure he's done more than we can ever repay, but—"

"Would it help any if he were the youngest son of the Marquess of Hursley?"

She pursed her lips at him. "Robert Cambourne, you are a very odd man."

"Not half so peculiar as you, my dear."

"I am not at all peculiar. I am perfectly ordinary."

"Yes, you and your man-eating ferret. And since you see fit to pucker your lips in that provocative fashion, madam, I rescind my offer to convey you to Melinda. You may convey yourself upstairs directly into bed."

''Oh?'' Folie looked at him warily.

He smiled again, in that diabolical way.

''Robert,'' she said, taking a step backwards.

The hint of laughter in him vanished at her move. He pushed his hands into the pockets of his coat as the moody demon seemed to rise in a black scowl. ''No. Never mind. Get your things,'' he said in a flat tone. ''We'll go to Melinda.''

Folie hesitated, bewildered by him. It was as if he went away, retreated into some far place inside himself where she could never go. And suddenly she wished to do the same herself. He made her angry, this way in which he enticed and teased her and drew her to him with the promise of warmth, and then as suddenly, for no reason she could ever seem to fathom, pulled back into his bleak solitude.

She turned away. She meant to walk up the stairs, her back stiff—she could lock herself up, too; she could lock her bedroom door, if he supposed he had any access to it. She went as far as the foot of the stairs.

Then she turned, her hand resting on the newel post. ''Robert,'' she said, staring at a corner of the hall, ''we are married, but we need not live as man and wife. I find it very difficult to bear, this—way you have. Of making me—feel wanted—and then—leaving me.''

''Then don't go away from me,'' he said angrily, turning aside. ''Don't step back away from me.''

Folie watched him standing with his eyes fixed on the floor like a sullen schoolboy. ''I only did because—'' She made a sound of despair. ''I do not really understand it. Robert, I have not the nature to resist when I do not wish to do so. When you do that—when you go away just as . . .'' She took a deep breath. ''It is—humiliating.''

''I know,'' he muttered. ''Believe me.''

She sank down upon the step, resting her forehead in her hand. ''I suppose we will never understand one another. I suppose we will be like the Dingleys. You will find some consuming interest—keeping prize red hens, or translating Hindu texts into Greek tragedies—and I will play the pianoforte very badly and stare out of windows.'' She swallowed. ''Only . . . only there won't be any Robert far away for me to write to, and dream about—'' Her voice cracked. She swallowed hard again. ''Because you are the only man I've ever loved. Or ever will. Even if you are as beef-witted as Sir Howard. Perhaps even stupider.'' She sniffed. ''In my opinion.''

''Never worth a dog's damn,'' he said mockingly.

''Oh!'' she exclaimed, fumbling for a handkerchief she could not find. ''That made my blood boil, when he said that! But what verily makes me want to scream is that you listen to it.'' She snatched the linen that he held out to her and blew her nose.

With an effort, she recovered her composure. He said nothing, only stood there with that constrained, persecuted air of a gentleman with an unhappy female—as if she were impossible to comprehend and her presence was barely tolerable. It was maddening, Folie thought fiercely, when *he* was the one who had upset their friendly accord for the most inconsequential reason. She had stepped back away from him. Whatever did he make of that, the silly man? That she could not suffer him to touch her?

The thought struck her with a sudden perception. What had they said about Phillippa? That his wife had not treated him kindly. That she was a devil's daughter. Or an angel. Never once, in his letters, had he mentioned her name with affection—never mentioned her at all—or even hinted at her existence.

''I am not Phillippa, you know,'' Folie said, crumpling the handkerchief tightly in her fingers. ''Whatever she was—whatever happened—''

He looked around at her sharply. ''I know that you aren't,'' he said. As he looked at her, his tone softened a little. ''I know that.'' He turned away again, but she could see his face reflected in the big gilded mirror on the wall. ''Your letters—knowing you were there, just knowing you were there—'' His mouth twisted wryly. ''In Toot-above-the-Batch, with the geese and river and the white-faced cattle—'' He shrugged.

''It was a difficult marriage,'' she said, a faint question.

''It was hell.'' He took a deep breath. ''But perhaps I understand her a little better now.''

Their eyes met in the mirror. Folie waited.

He shook his head. ''You don't realize, do you? About her.''

''Realize what?''

He shook his head again. His jaw was tight, as if he were imprisoning the words. He looked about at the walls and ceiling like a man searching for a way out of a locked room. ''I don't want you to understand,'' he said at last, his voice breaking.

Folie rose. She went to him, reaching up to touch his cheek. She ran her fingers along the dark stubbled line of his jaw, felt the muscles set hard. ''Then do not tell me,'' she said quietly. ''Perhaps it is better so. Only remember—when you get lost in her dark places . . . remember that you have a way home.''

He closed his eyes. She could feel a tremor in his jaw. ''Folly,'' he said roughly. ''You love me, Folly?''

She took a step back. ''Oh,'' she said, nodding to herself, ''he really is a stupid man!'' She looked up at him over the handkerchief pressed to her nose. ''What I should like to know is whether you love *me!*'' she said flippantly, to prevent herself from breaking down into nonsensical tears. ''But do not put yourself out by saying so, Robert Cambourne. You warned me once that you could never fall in love by letter!'' She turned her back on him. As well as possible in a wrinkled and tattered ivory gown, with all the bows untied and most of the seed pearls missing, she flounced up the stairs.

She did not know what time it was when she woke, but it was certainly afternoon, for the sun shone in the windows she had forgotten to cover. Her eyes felt gritty. And she was cradled in a warm embrace.

It seemed to take a moment to sort that out. She was not accustomed to waking in a man's arms. In fact, she could not recall that it had ever happened before. For a time she lay there, hardly breathing, just feeling the long contour of heat pressed to her back. His bare arm lay over her shoulder. In his hand was a note, turned so that she could just read the words aslant.

Folie squinted as she scanned it. A slow smile grew on her lips. Carefully, so as not to wake him, she slipped out of bed and took a sheet of paper from the desk. She wrote her reply.

He turned on his back, still asleep, as she lay down with him again. She rested her forehead against his shoulder and put the paper on his chest, where each breath lifted it lightly. She began to place whispery kisses along the line of his jaw.

His eyes opened. He did not look at her, but stayed still, gazing upward at the canopy as she touched her mouth lightly to his skin, her lips soft as Toot's tickling nuzzles. After a moment, he made a faint dubious sound, his mouth curving up like a man who wanted to laugh but could not quite.

Folie guided his hand to the note she had written. He looked down, lifting his head slightly to read it.

"Well?" Folie said archly.

He gave a bark of laughter and dropped his head back on the pillow. "Kiss your what?"

"*You* know," she said, pushing out her lower lip.

He rolled over suddenly, on top of her, resting his elbows on either side of her shoulders, trapping her against the bed with a growl. "Say it."

Folie parted her lips, gazing up into his gray eyes, feeling the heat of his skin on hers. "I will say my line if you will say yours."

He buried his face in her throat and mumbled an unintelligible phrase.

"*What* a coward!" she said, pressing her cheek to his hair. "I love you, sweet Robert."

He mumbled the phrase again, impossible to decipher. Folie smoothed her hand down his bare shoulder and his back. He arched his body against her, groaning with pleasure. A tautness grew in his embrace, a purpose; he held her face between his palms and kissed her deeply. Folie kissed him back, more lightly. She did not move, she did not press up in answer, though her body was warm and urgent. She felt as if she were holding her breath, waiting.

"My Folly," he whispered. "My Folly."

"Robert," she said helplessly. "Please."

He closed his eyes with a low sound, a moan of surrender and desire. He pushed between her legs, spreading them apart. The hard shaft pressed and opened her; impatient thrusts, as if he could not wait to be gentle. Folie did not even move—every time he came to her, stretching her, invading deeper and deeper into her, it sent a wave of delight upward, closing her throat. She began to make small whimpers, the pleasure caught there, pulsing, spreading through her trembling limbs. The whimpers became sharp gasps, his hard breathing mingled with hers. He slid his arms under her waist, drawing her upward. Folie felt as if she could not command her own body; her head fell back and her breasts arched upward to him, a happy, shameless offering.

He sucked air between his teeth, gripping her against him. She felt his muscles contract, pumping into the depth of her, holding on a long, hard shudder. His eyes squeezed shut. Folie's own ecstasy burst as she watched him. She lay back with his arms under her, his thick pressure inside her, the hot joyous waves coursing through and consuming her.

They lay panting and relaxed, soft against one another, afterward. After a few moments, Robert turned his face into her shoulder and chuckled. "Kiss your what?" he mumbled against her skin.

She scrambled away as he began to tickle her. "I'll never say it again! Robert Cambourne!" She squealed as he tackled her and pressed her down into the pillows. "I won't! See if you can make me!"

"All right." He sat up suddenly, scowling, swinging his legs over the edge of the bed. Folie's heart fell as he stood up and left her so abruptly.

But he only went as far as the desk, leaning over to scratch a short note with the pen and half-dried ink. He came back to the bed, collected the other sheets of paper, and stacked them together in a businesslike manner. Then he slid in beside her and laid the whole sheaf over her nose, the words becoming great black blurs so close to her eyes. He wrapped his arms about her, drew in a long breath, and sighed deeply, settling in.

"Made it, sweet Folly," he murmured into her ear. "Made it home."

Epilogue

Dear Folly,

Of course I could never fall in love by letter. I had to know you to even learn what love could be. It is hard for me to say these things aloud, Folly. I love you. I love you. I love you. Is that unequivocal enough? My foolish, smiling, cherished princess, don't leave me, don't ever let me go. You can even keep the ferret if you must.

Your Knight,
Robert

P.S. Lander *is* the youngest son of the Marquess of Hursley.

Dear Knight,

Well, all right. I suppose Melinda may marry him, then. Of course I will never leave you, sweet Robert. I am your homing princess. Who else will show you the way back when you're lost?

Love,
Your Folly

P.S. Besides, who else would I ask to kiss my kitten?

Ah, my dear sweet Folly,

Who else could make me want so badly to kiss her?
Next time. You won't even have to beg.